Pulitzer's Prize Editor

John A. Cockerill -

PULITZER'S PRIZE EDITOR

A Biography of

JOHN A. COCKERILL

1845-1896

by

HOMER W. KING

Duke University Press

Durham, N. C.   1965

49807

PRINTED IN THE UNITED STATES OF AMERICA
BY THE SEEMAN PRINTERY, INC., DURHAM, N. C.

To

CHARLES A. KING

as much a friend as a father,

and always an inspiration

Acknowledgments

To Appleton-Century-Crofts, Inc., New York, N. Y., for permission to reprint excerpts of *Three Rousing Cheers*, by Elizabeth Jordan, *copyright* 1938 by D. Appleton-Century Company, Inc.

To Department of Special Collections, Butler Library, for permission to quote from letters and memoranda of John A. Cockerill, which are the property of Columbia University.

To Yale University Library for its permission to make use of letters from Colonel Cockerill to Thomas Davidson, which are part of the Thomas Davidson Papers.

Other Cockerill letters are from the Daniel S. Lamont Papers, the Grover Cleveland Papers, and the William C. Whitney Papers in the Library of Congress.

Preface

With their allusions to an editor of such extraordinary competence that he was never replaced, Joseph Pulitzer's biographers drew my first attention to John A. Cockerill. I was intrigued by a contemporary's characterization of Colonel Cockerill as debonair, audacious, caustic and with more personal courage than Pulitzer. Cockerill's defense of himself by gunfire heightened interest in the editor. The Colonel was controversial and he was colorful. Some observers of the era insisted that he was more responsible than Pulitzer for the "new journalism" usually attributed to Pulitzer, that it was Cockerill, not Pulitzer, who really made the New York *World*. These enticements plus the encouragement of Pulitzer biographer James W. Barrett and of a number of other persons set me sniffing the Colonel's trail, grown cold at every stretch and at some points dim beyond recognition.

Apparently neither Pulitzer nor Cockerill left an account of his professional associations. To bridge a few gaps in Cockerill's career it was necessary to reconstruct situations and events on the basis of incomplete data. If any assumptions are at odds with verifiable facts eluding my searches, they must be consigned regretfully to casualties inherent in this kind of undertaking.

Cockerill shunned personal publicity, an admirable trait but not helpful to a biographer. The editor's passion was to record the feats and follies of others, a function he performed on eleven newspapers. They ran the gamut of affluence from a village weekly to the world's most lucrative daily. Obviously newspapers are a major source of this book. Yet newspapers of the Colonel's era present the researcher a formidable problem. Bylines were far more sparse, masthead information skimpier than in modern newspapers. A journalist could take a reporting job without a single mention of his name in the newspaper concerned. This state of affairs complicated the exacting task of spotting the Colonel's writing and handling of news situations. The Colonel's distinctive style lessened the hazard of identifying his own stories and editorials. A number of byline articles in national magazines and hitherto unpublished letters written by the Colonel add insight to his philosophy and ideals.

I have no quarrel with those who see in this work a friendly accounting of the Colonel's career, yet I contend that it errs more in understatement than in adulation. For as dim as the editor's meandering trail has become at some points, it is clearly the path of a pioneer in newspaper techniques and responsibilities. In this story of the Colonel's career, of the times in which he edited and wrote and swore and laughed, and of a few of his most colorful colleagues, it is intended that a richly deserved niche in the history of American journalism shall be reserved for a name that might otherwise fade into obscurity.

My gratitude belongs to many persons who were helpful in this undertaking.

Mrs. Margaret McClure Stitt of Cincinnati read sections of the manuscript and contributed information that would be accessible only to a relative of the subject. Two of the Colonel's contemporaries, Louis Thorn Golding and the late Samuel Hopkins Adams, contributed recollections. Joseph Pulitzer, Jr., publisher of the St. Louis *Post-Dispatch*, was helpful to the author in compiling a bibliography. Lee Allen, a former Cincinnati *Enquirer* staff member, made available unpublished data on the life of Lafcadio Hearn.

For a wide assortment of suggestions, admonitions, assistance, and ideas, my warmest thanks also are due the following persons (situated as listed at the time of consultation): Dr. Frank Luther Mott, Dean Emeritus, University of Missouri School of Journalism; Frank F. White of the Maryland Historical Society; Beatrice Strauss of Cincinnati, granddaughter of Samuel Burwell, Cockerill's first editorial mentor; Mrs. Alene

Lowe White, librarian, Western Reserve Historical Society; James Newton, George Cummins, and Mason Cockerill of Hamilton, Ohio; Janet Haslett, librarian, *Editor and Publisher* magazine; Hillier Krieghbaum, chairman, Department of Journalism, New York University; Dr. Julian Rammelkamp of Albion College, Albion, Michigan; Thomas W. Eylar of West Union, Ohio; Alexander Cockerill Howard of St. Louis; Irving Dilliard and Rufus Terral, both of the St. Louis *Post-Dispatch*; M. Carl Andrews of the Roanoke, Virginia, *World-News*; Robin Turkell of the New York *World-Telegram and Sun*; Paul L. Berry of the Library of Congress; staff members of the Rochester, New York, Public Library and Historical Society; Arthur Louis of the Philadelphia *Inquirer*; Joseph Watkins, Ivan Conklin, Herbert Schaeffer, Gerald Maloney, Ike Shynook, and Shirley Hazel, all colleagues of the author at the Rochester *Democrat and Chronicle*; John W. Germond and Paul W. Ramsey of Gannett News Service. I cannot overlook the counsel of my wife, Pauline, and my son, David A. King. Finally, I am grateful to Ashbel G. Brice, director of the Duke University Press, for his unsparing patience and valued advice in guiding the manuscript into print.

HOMER W. KING

Rochester, New York

Contents

	Introduction	XV
I.	Distinguished Sire	3
II.	Cockerills at War	12
III.	Sam and the "Scion"	20
IV.	Hamilton, Dayton, and a Copperhead	33
V.	City of Serenity and Sin	51
VI.	Murder a Profitable Commodity	57
VII.	Fortune Made—Exit Editor	69
VIII.	Summons from St. Louis	89
IX.	Homicide with Honor	100
X.	Ordeal and Exoneration	109
XI.	The Colonel Bows Out	119
XII.	Park Row Invasion	125
XIII.	Gal Reporter	147
XIV.	Outfoxing a "Fox"	155
XV.	Conflict: Cockerill vs. Smith	164
XVI.	For the Good of the World, Mostly	171
XVII.	Leonora Barner	182

xii
Contents

XVIII. Press Club Prestige   188

XIX. Walkout on the "World"   194

XX. Pulitzer's Portrait   206

XXI. Cockerill and the "Advertisers"   219

XXII. Cockerill, Critic and Prophet   234

XXIII. Cockerill as Wit and Stylist   250

XXIV. John Cockerill, Foreign Correspondent   258

XXV. Accolade from an Emperor   266

XXVI. Murder of Queen Min   275

XXVII. Night Falls in Cairo   288

XXVIII. "Gathered to the Quiet West"   295

Notes   305

Bibliography   324

Index   330

Illustrations

frontispiece

John A. Cockerill

following page 172

General Joseph A. Cockerill

Ruth Cockerill

Clement L. Vallandigham

Joseph Pulitzer

Nellie Bly

Bill Nye

Park Row

James Gordon Bennett, Jr.

Introduction

Early in May, 1883, Joseph Pulitzer addressed a telegram to St. Louis. With the impatience characteristic of the sender it ordered the recipient to report at once to New York. In a few days an editor of frightening competence joined Pulitzer and the New York *World*. The awesome newcomer was Ohio-born John Albert Cockerill. The summons set the stage for the New York career of the editor who never won a prize in journalism in the usual sense of the term. (The first agreement with Columbia University establishing the Pulitzer Prizes was signed in 1903; the prizes were first awarded in 1917, twenty-one years after Cockerill's death.) But for Joseph Pulitzer, Colonel Cockerill performed as a prize editor in every sense. His dedication to the Pulitzer principles and policies, his resourcefulness, and his aggressive command of the newsroom thrust the *World* into triumphal orbit. With what seemed to be exaggerated credentials, Colonel Cockerill swooped into New York as a maker of newspaper publishing fortunes, a human dynamo of efficiency and a super idea-man. As the *World*'s counting-room could attest, the newcomer lived up to his billing. Rumors apprehensively circulated on Newspaper Row ahead of Cockerill's arrival portrayed him as a trigger-happy editor who would gun down a man at the slightest provocation. In his managing editor's office at Pulitzer's St. Louis *Post-Dispatch* the Colonel had shot to death a lawyer incensed by a Cockerill editorial jab.

A fast and sensitive judge of news, a fiercely energetic born executive, Colonel Cockerill seemed to function in perpetual fury. A contemporary saw him as a "versatile, incisive and epigrammatic editor whose censure bore a barb." Cockerill could usually spot a phony with the instinct of a terrier pouncing upon a rat. Despite an external brusqueness, the Colonel was widely known in his profession for his generosity to young or needy newspapermen. In business affairs affecting his personal interests he was astonishingly naïve. On formal occasions his erect, compact body and impeccable attire presented a distinguished figure. In his command post at the *World* a long cigar seemed as much a part of the Colonel as a black, frowzy mustache. He could handle a pistol and a sulfurous vocabulary with equal dexterity. Having lived under the pressure of haste, he was not a well-read man, yet his writing is strewn with allusions to the classics. Scholars would not call him profound, but he could quickly sift the essentials from the most complex situation.

Colonel Cockerill was destined to perform in the shadow of a celebrated publisher. Joseph Pulitzer, properly enough, took the bows. But the Cockerill story disputes the popular theory that the *World* was exclusively Pulitzer's inspiration and handiwork. For the nearly blind and often ailing publisher it was imperative to have an editor who understood Pulitzer's passion to expose fraud and incompetence in government, to thunder on behalf of the public interest. And, even more than Pulitzer, the Colonel appreciated the need to sharpen and brighten news-writing style and to capitalize on pictures as a reporting tool. Binding the pair was a strong tie of mutual respect. In the early period of their association they were "Joe" and "John" to each other. Their frankness of speech was electrifying, their editorial conferences were noisy affairs. While their association flourished, the *World*, with Colonel Cockerill at the editorial wheel and the roaming publisher calling shots from all over the globe, zoomed to its pre-Hearst heyday of political power and affluence. When the Colonel joined the *World* in 1883, the sheet was floundering in the bottom level of circulation among New York's five morning newspapers. On the day he terminated his eight-year stay on the paper, it was by far New York's most valuable newspaper property.[1]

Cockerill had left an editorial trail of distinguishing marks in West Union, Hamilton, Dayton, and Cincinnati, Ohio;

Washington, D. C., and Baltimore, Maryland. Upon the basis of his record in those cities plus an extraordinary confidence in his potential, Pulitzer early in 1880 had installed Cockerill as managing editor of the *Post-Dispatch*. Transplanted to New York, the Colonel injected new life into the weary *World*. He engineered news beats, exposés, and crusades that rocked the city, shook competitors, and enriched the *World*'s coffers. He encouraged new methods and techniques in handling news and pictures. Pulitzer, contrary to a commonly accepted image of the publisher, often had to be persuaded to try fresh ideas. The Colonel was often the persuader. Pulitzer chose to let others do the experimenting.[2] Cockerill's willingness to experiment earned for him the appellation "father of the new journalism."[3]

Cockerill was prepared by temperament and experience to meet the challenge of merciless competition among New York newspapers. He took delight in developing brilliant reporters out of applicants who had been turned away by other newspapers. Nellie Bly was a conspicuous example.

The Cockerill story unveils curious anomalies.

The Colonel was involved in the sensational brand of journalism that Pulitzer deemed necessary to build circulation. Cockerill wielded a skilled hand in the unsavory art, yet he later became one of its severest critics, and his wrath did not spare the *World*. The Colonel's soul-searching upon his exit from the *World* stamped him as one of the nation's most articulate exponents of the responsible and respectable press.

The editor could be accurately described in one breath as "rough in speech and picturesquely profane" and in the next as "sensitive, warm-hearted, and generous." The paradox is apparent in a colleague's impression: "Although Cockerill could be effectively repulsive, he had the faculty of holding the affection of his men."[4] In Pulitzer newsrooms the Colonel was a bearcat with a mighty wallop, but he could be gentle as a kitten. One of Cockerill's reporters, in Pulitzer's presence, categorized Cockerill as a tyrant. "You're a poor judge of men," Pulitzer, bristling, retorted. "He is really tender-hearted as a child."[5] Among Cockerill's attributes that attracted Pulitzer was the editor's readiness to admit errors. "When Cockerill would say, 'I've been a damn fool, wrong, damn wrong,' I always melted," Pulitzer recalled.[6]

Why did this superb publisher-editor team fall apart? A seasoned staff member of the *World* who knew both men well may have come close to the truth when he said that "a colossal success is never big enough to be shared." After Cockerill walked out of the *World* to take on a publishing venture of his own, Pulitzer's thoughts of his resigning managing editor, in the version of a Pulitzer biographer, "were always kind. . . ."[7] The kindness did not take a substantial form satisfying to the Colonel. Compared to the millions that streamed into the *World*'s business office, the Colonel's salary to him seemed pitifully inadequate.

The late Samuel Hopkins Adams, whom Pulitzer once hired, acknowledged Pulitzer's journalistic expertness but considered Pulitzer, in relations with his staff, to be "as much a tyrant as James Gordon Bennett of the *Herald*. He was notoriously ill-tempered and abusive. . . ."[8] A circumstance that had much to do with the splitup of the publisher-editor team was Pulitzer's progressive loss of eyesight and his continued absence from the *World* offices. He slowly dropped friendly ties with close associates as he wandered in quest of better health.

A *World* man asserted that Pulitzer would not have undertaken the New York enterprise without Colonel Cockerill. It is a conjecture to be sure, but it carries substance in the words of Don C. Seitz who, in the authorized Pulitzer biography, declared: "Colonel Cockerill was never replaced by the *World* . . . although many were called and some chosen."[9] Without the implementation of Pulitzer objectives in the Cockerill-directed newsroom, the Pulitzer star, in its formative years, might have fizzled before it could blaze new concepts in American journalism.

The periods of Colonel Cockerill's career before and after his tenure with Pulitzer's St. Louis *Post-Dispatch* and New York *World* are no less revealing than his tenure with Joseph Pulitzer. For four years he published and edited the New York *Advertisers* (*Commercial, Morning,* and *Sunday*) in what is most charitably described as an exciting effort journalistically but a disappointment financially.

After his break with Pulitzer he wrote the final and perhaps most fascinating chapter of his fast-moving career. As Far Eastern correspondent for the New York *Herald,* Colonel Cockerill was awarded his only "prize" for excellence in journalism. The Japanese government was so grateful for his interpretive articles on Japan that it bestowed upon him one of the nation's most cherished citations. In Korea Cockerill found himself in the midst of violent upheaval climaxed by the fiery death of Queen Min, on which the correspondent scored a news beat despite a clumsy effort to suppress his report.

Prior to his association with Pulitzer, Colonel Cockerill, at the Cincinnati *Enquirer*, established his right to wear the moniker of fortune maker. There a sensational murder sensationally played by the Cincinnati *Enquirer* under Managing Editor Cockerill's direction catapulted the *Enquirer's* circulation to a new high. The Colonel's adeptness in making sensationalism a highly salable commodity helped put Cockerill on the way to becoming the nation's top news editor.

Testifying to the respect and affection in which he was held by Park Row were his three years as chairman of the board and his five years as president of the rollicking but influential New York Press Club.

Colonel Cockerill's voice was heard in an era in which newspaper crusades against civic corruption and private iniquity sharpened the public's moral conscience; in which the sordid experiences of the poor and downtrodden increased the public's trust in newspapers; in which newspapers through greater circulation and advertising revenue achieved editorial independence from political pressures; in which the daily press as a powerful manipulator of public opinion made history while writing it. It may not have been wholly coincidental that in the three decades of 1870 to 1900, during which the Colonel edited half a dozen metropolitan journals, the number of American daily newspapers quadrupled, from 489 to 1,967, and their circulation soared from 2.6 million to 15.1 million.[10]

John A. Cockerill, with much of his potential unfulfilled, died at fifty-one.

Pulitzer's Prize Editor

I. Distinguished Sire

If one father is worth more than a hundred schoolmasters, Joseph Randolph Cockerill was qualified by natural endowment and experience to be a teacher in many fields. "He had a fund of anecdotes that was inexhaustible," wrote a contemporary. "A fact once acquired by him was always ready for use. He knew more of the history of Adams County, Ohio, than any man of his time. He was a man of independent, broad and liberal views. As a conversationalist he had few superiors. He was a born soldier."[1] A colonel in the Civil War, he was also, at various times, a school teacher, surveyor, clerk of the court, lawyer, state representative, Congressman, and politician. When John Albert Cockerill, Joseph's third child, was born December 5, 1845, at Locust Grove, Adams County, his father's sights were set on a career in public service. His choice was not unexpected. Joseph's father, Daniel Cockerill, a veteran of the War of 1812 and subsequently a major general of the Ohio Militia, possessed a passion for public service that he bequeathed to Joseph and three other sons.

The Cockerill line strengthened its foothold on American soil in 1713 when John Cockerill, a forebear of our subject, acquired 200 acres of Westmoreland County, Virginia, farm land in exchange for 6,500 pounds of tobacco. A son, Thomas Cockerill, of Loudon County, Virginia, sired several children, of whom one, Sanford Cockerill, was the father of General Daniel Cockerill.

Joseph Cockerill was nineteen when his carpenter-father and family pulled stakes in Loudon County, Virginia, where Joseph was born in 1818, and resettled in Youngsville, Adams County, Ohio. The Daniel Cockerill offspring consisted of five sons and two daughters. Daniel Cockerill, who found it easy to shift from carpentry to farming, called himself an old-

time Democrat until 1861. As such he had served in the lower
house of the Ohio Legislature in 1845-1846 and 1848-1849.
The moment he heard the news of the firing upon Fort Sumter,
General Cockerill switched to the Republican party, turning
his support to those who wanted the seceding Southern states
whipped into submission.

The Adams County to which the Cockerills entrusted their
future was carved from a wilderness challenged chiefly by
Virginia pioneers of Scotch-Irish and German descent. It was
nearing the 13,000 mark when the Cockerills arrived in 1837.
Almost everything fantastic and catastrophic that could happen to make news in a frontier community had happened in
Adams County: In 1808 hordes of migrating squirrels destroyed the corn crop. In 1832 the great flood inundated
thirty miles of the Ohio River lowlands. The county's only
duel in 1812 cost the loser, Thomas Marshall, a shattered
thigh. In the holdup of the stagecoach near West Union the
mailbag was seized but the culprit was never caught. Older
neighbors of John Cockerill's father could remember when
the whipping post was legal punishment (thirty-nine lashes
to the back laid bare) for major crimes. It was not unusual
to see Negroes, in response to posted notices of rewards for
their apprehension, being returned to their Southern slave
masters.

Shortly after the Cockerills settled in Scott Township,
Adams County, Joseph Cockerill was teaching in a one-room
log school. His interest in school affairs persisted. Later, at
West Union, he was named to the first board of directors of
the school system which authorized the construction of a
two-story brick school building for $2,500, a price considered
staggering at the time.

In 1840 Joseph Cockerill was appointed county surveyor
by the Court of Common Pleas, a post in which he served
three years. In the strenuous and exacting task of marking off
land in a raw frontier state, Cockerill met his neighbors in

all sections of the county, thus laying the groundwork for his political future.

The year was memorable for another reason. He courted and wed Ruth, the daughter of Judge Joseph Eylar of Winchester Township. Judge Eylar's father, Joseph, born in Germany, left home in 1777 to escape serving in the army and shipped to America. He eloped with Mary Ann Rosemiller, daughter of a Philadelphia Tory. After pursuing his trade for a few years at Bedford, Pennsylvania, Joseph Eylar, a wagoner, and his family came by way of a keelboat to Three Islands, an offshore segment of Adams County. Thereafter Eylar, whose three hundred pounds bulged over a five-foot, five-inch frame, built the first cabin in Tiffin Township and won acclaim as a model farmer. His son, Judge Joseph Eylar, was one of twelve children. Ruth Eylar was the fifth child of Judge Eylar and Elizabeth Fenton Eylar. Elizabeth sprang from a line of Fentons who could trace their ancestry to Lord Delaware.

Something of the affection in which Ruth Cockerill was held is indicated in the following eulogy published upon her death in 1878. Authorship has been attributed to her son, John Cockerill, who wrote it for a West Union newspaper upon his return to Adams County for his mother's funeral:

Perhaps you've never noticed it. We have. In every small community, one comes across a woman—a woman with magnetic influence, about whose lap the children love to clamber; a woman to whom maidens trust their secrets, and from whom they seek sympathy in their petty troubles; a woman before whom the gossip's tongue is silent; a woman whose cheery face lights up the sanctuary of the Lord, preaching the love of God in more enchanting words than tongues have ever told.

Such a woman was Mrs. Ruth Cockerill. Hers was a holy womanhood whose open treasury poured forth its wealth of love, and charity, and truths, and constancy, and sympathy and sincerity. A womanhood whose influence about the hearthstone, about the social circle, about the community, made men and women of triflers and the giddy, whose ambition seeks naught but the setting

of life's sun; a womanhood which opened up to view that higher
nobler life, whose floral-gemmed pathway leads to bliss eternal.

She's gone, this woman, wife and mother. Gone to her gallant
husband, whose name now glitters upon the entablature of a
nation's grateful memory. Gone to the raptures of the pronuncia-
tion of her Maker's approval. Through her whole life, so familiar
to us, we seek her blemish but fail. So insignificant, 'tis lost amid
the wealth of her virtues, which enthroned her in the affections
of her family, her church and community. They have laid bright
flowers upon her grave, but never a flower so fair as the phantom
of her holy life, which rose before our tear-dimmed eyes, as the
sod closed upon all which remained of Ruth Cockerill.[2]

Joseph and Ruth Cockerill built a log cabin as their first
home in Locust Grove, Franklin Township. From their union
came three sons and two daughters: Armstead Thompson
Mason Cockerill, born in 1841; Esther Elizabeth, born in
1843, wife of Dr. John Campbell, a captain in the 70th Ohio
Volunteer Infantry; John Albert Cockerill, our subject, born
1845; Sarah Mary, born in 1847, wife of Lieutenant W. R.
Stewart of the 70th Ohio Volunteer Infantry; and Oliver
Oscar, who died at three years of age, date of birth unknown.

John, in line with a popular custom of loading several
names upon defenseless infants, was christened Joseph Daniel
Albert Cockerill. The Daniel and Joseph were dropped, probably to avoid confusion with a grandfather and a father bearing those names, and, for reasons not clear, John was added.

After John's birth Joseph Cockerill's political career
picked up speed. The young father was appointed in 1846
to fill an unexpired term as clerk of the Court of Common
Pleas and was reappointed and served until 1851, the year
he was admitted to the bar. A contemporary, Emmons B.
Stivers, remembered Joseph Cockerill as an effective lawyer.
In a trial involving the theft of a watch, Stivers said he listened
first to the prosecutor and was convinced of the man's guilt.
But after hearing Cockerill, the defendant's attorney, he was
then sure the man was innocent.

In the year 1851 terror struck West Union. Having been

hit twice before by cholera in the past two decades, Adams
County looked upon the pestilence as a visitation of the devil.
Between July 24 and August 2, 1851, business was suspended
and all but a hardy few West Union residents fled town.
Joseph Cockerill took his family to the home of his father,
Daniel Cockerill, in Mt. Leigh. In fifteen days eleven deaths
in four families left the town limp with fear. Only one doctor,
David Coleman, remained to minister to victims of the epi-
demic, the only other doctor having skipped town. Barrels
of tar were burned in the streets to purify the air. Farmers
refused to trade in West Union lest they be stricken. The
people ate freely of mutton, which was thought to build resistance to the disease. For a long time the town was depressed;
the superstitious thought it was cursed; real estate prices fell
to absurdly low figures; grass grew in the streets, so effectively
had West Union been isolated. But as in all things time healed
the wounds. Life returned to normal and the Cockerills resumed life in their West Union home.

Democratic party leaders shrewdly sized up Joseph
Cockerill as a political comer. Running for a seat in the
50th General Assembly of Ohio, the first under the state's
new constitution, the young candidate confirmed their judgment. The thirty-year old lawmaker, serving in 1852-53,
quickly drew favorable notice as chairman of the committee
which accomplished the herculean task of revising all statutes
on corporations.

The assumption is that, prior to the Civil War, the family
of Joseph Cockerill were members of the West Union Methodist Episcopal Church. The probability is drawn from the
fact that Cockerill later helped to organize the Christian Union
Church as a result of dissensions over politics in the Methodist
Church.

In West Union son John, an energetic, inquisitive, undersized lad, made his presence felt. In school he showed an
avid interest in history and geography and he did well in
spelling and grammar. He was forever asking questions be-

yond the lessons taught in school. He was enchanted by his
father's comings and goings. John watched as his father very
early in the mornings mounted a horse and galloped away to
court or to visit a client, his saddle pockets stuffed with legal
papers and coattails flapping in the breeze.

As a curious lad who one day would become a gatherer
and disseminator of the news, John Cockerill very early became aware that his father was a news maker. John was
eleven when, for example, his father defeated Jonas R. Emrie,
a Highland County Republican, in the latter's campaign for
re-election to Congress. As a member of the 35th Congress
in 1857-1859 representing the sixth Ohio district of Adams,
Highland, Brown and Clermont counties, Cockerill, by the
terms of a Democratic party agreement, did not run for a
second term.[3]

Congressman Cockerill's career in Washington was in-
conspicuous, due presumably to the traditional reticence expected of freshmen legislators. A perusal of the record shows
that he made no stirring speeches. His name appears only in
routine matters such as when he paired his votes with other
representatives, explained his colleagues' absences from the
floor, and moved that the reading of the yeas and nays be
dispensed with. He introduced one bill, a minor one, calling
for continuation of the pension of Katherine M. Hamer, an
invalid constituent.[4] But Congressman Cockerill was held in
high respect by his colleagues. He knew how to get a laugh.
One day the Speaker's voice boomed forth: "Mr. Cockerill
of Ohio, you have been arrested . . . for absenting yourself
from the sittings of the House without its permission. What
excuse have you?" To which the Ohioan retorted: "Not being
willing to fast longer than eight hours, I went to dinner. I
have no other excuse. I am here now, ready for business."
As his colleagues chuckled Representative Cockerill paid his
fee for tardiness and the lawmakers resumed their business.[5]

Just as Joseph Cockerill's career was gaining further luster, it was threatened by disaster. The young lawyer told his

family the story upon his return from the state Democratic convention in Columbus. When the stagecoach carrying Cockerill and a friend to Columbus stopped to change horses, a foreigner who could not speak English boarded the vehicle. After mumbling to himself, the stranger quieted down, wrapped his cloak about himself, and indicated he wanted to be left alone. The two delegates ignored him as the coach rumbled into the night. Suddenly, they heard a choking sound. Seeking the cause, Cockerill felt blood as he opened the man's coat to give him air. The driver was notified and the coach rolled hurriedly to Chillicothe. There, as Cockerill reached to assist him, the man toppled onto the seat.

When the station attendant held a lantern inside the vehicle, a hideous sight greeted him: the stranger's throat had been cut from ear to ear. A German-speaking passerby exchanged words with the injured man just before he died. The translation was ominous: "He says he got on the coach at the last station, and during the ride these two men jumped upon him and slashed his throat."

Despite Joseph Cockerill's quick explanation that the two of them were on their way to the convention in Columbus and had nothing to do with the stranger's misfortune, the small gathering aimed angry looks at the pair. Providentially a bystander asked whether the travelers knew anyone who could identify either man. It was not until someone sent for an acquaintance of Cockerill, who assured the crowd there was no need to suspect the two West Union men, that the politicians were permitted to reboard the stage coach. They resumed their journey with a promise they would return after the convention for possible questioning in the unexplained death.

The two continued their journey. When the pair returned to Chillicothe after the convention, they learned that the stranger was a mental patient who had cut his own throat. Joseph Cockerill sighed with relief, reflecting how ruthlessly a web of circumstantial "evidence" can snare innocent men.[6]

The tradition of the Cockerills as a "dynasty" of doers was contagious. While his father was representing the Sixth Congressional District in Washington, young John Cockerill was promoting his own interests. In 1859, at fourteen, he persuaded Samuel Burwell, editor of the weekly *Scion,* to take him on as a helper. From this point John Cockerill's practical education progressed at phenomenal speed. He learned much from hearing his father talk about his experiences as a teacher, surveyer, lawyer and legislator. He may have learned even more from editor Burwell.

It is a matter of conjecture how much time the elder Cockerill could spend with his son. The busy father was always going somewhere as his political responsibilities mounted. In 1860, for example, he found himself in the middle of the historic National Democratic Convention, first in Charleston, South Carolina, next at Baltimore, Maryland. Temptation set a snare for Joseph Cockerill just as he was leaving West Union. Edward Patton Evans, an admirer of Horace Greeley, offered to pay Cockerill's expenses if the young delegate would let himself be seen carrying copies of Greeley's New York *Tribune.* Greeley, General John Fremont, and Thaddeus Stevens were leaders of that "radical" new party known as Republicans. In 1856 Evans had campaigned for Fremont when the latter, as Republican nominee for president, had lost to James Buchanan. Democrat Joseph Cockerill icily declined.[7]

The Democratic party was torn by dissension on whether slavery should be protected in the territories. Southern extremists wanted a plank declaring that neither Congress nor a territorial government could abolish slavery or impair the right to own slaves. Northern Democrats accepted the Supreme Court ruling on the Dred Scott case but were unwilling to support a guarantee of slavery. Delegates from eight Southern states walked out when the convention refused to endorse federal protection of slavery. Stephen A. Douglas, whom the Northern Democrats supported for the presidential nomination, failed to win the nomination. The Charleston convention adjourned. At Baltimore the Southern delegates again bolted and Douglas was nominated on a popular-sovereignty platform. The Southern wing convened later, choosing John C. Breckinridge of Kentucky as nominee for president. Delegate Cockerill as a member of the Northern wing in support of Douglas found himself opposing a tall and awkward political newcomer from Illinois by the name of Abraham Lincoln, the Republican nominee. Lincoln was elected, although his popular vote was a million less than a majority. The split of the Democratic party was costly. Douglas polled 12 electoral votes, Breckinridge 72, Lincoln 180.

Joseph Cockerill remained loyal to the Democratic party, despite blandishments of Edward Evans, who as a member of Lincoln's winning party picked up new prestige in Adams County. Evans liked to throw his political weight around.

Before the year ended the Union was in deep trouble. In South Carolina a state convention repealed an ordinance of 1788 ratifying the United States Constitution. Up to February, 1861, seven Southern states had seceded. War clouds were gathering. John Cockerill's father felt the rebellion should be crushed as quickly as possible and was prepared to back his conviction with his blood. When Fort Sumter fell to the Confederates, Lincoln called for volunteers. Ohio promptly responded, organizing thirteen regiments. The Cockerills' role in the war is reserved for the next chapter.

After the war Joseph Cockerill was twice returned to the state legislature, serving in 1868-1872 in the House of Representatives. While in the legislature he was the Democratic nominee for state auditor but lost the election. Nationally the Republican tide was powerful and might have engulfed a weaker man than Joseph Cockerill. Influential Republicans made overtures to Cockerill, recognizing that he would be an asset to their party. There were assertions that a switch could have won him the governor's chair. None of the approaches softened the Colonel, a Democrat to the core.

Joseph Cockerill bore a striking resemblance to William Jennings Bryan in the latter's earlier years. He was a persuasive and entertaining speaker. "He knew everyone in his county, their faults and foibles and all their good qualities," wrote historian Emmons B. Stivers. "He should have written the history of Adams County. By his death valuable information about citizens and events has been lost. . . ."[8]

When Colonel Cockerill died in 1875, his son John, as a Cincinnati editor, was making newspaper history in the dubious art of sensationalism.

II. Cockerills at War

When in the early summer of 1861 Armstead Cockerill, a newly commissioned first lieutenant, began raising volunteers for Company D of the 24th Ohio Volunteer Infantry, he did not have in mind his fifteen-and-a-half-year-old pint-sized brother John. But John had heard of the shelling of Fort Sumter on April 12, 1861, of the secession of seven Southern states, and of President Lincoln's call for a volunteer army. He shared the excitement of war talk among the Cockerills, a military family by tradition. John wanted in. He proved he was an effective persuader. In June, 1861, apparently with his parents' consent, he accompanied Armstead to Camp Chase to enlist in Company D. He was rejected on two counts: he was too young and too small.[1]

The lad's disappointment was brief. The Union cause had not seen the last of irrepressible John Cockerill. How he hit upon the idea of joining as a musician is not clear, but since he was well below the legal age for military service it is certain that his persistence played heavily in overcoming whatever barriers lay between his status as a civilian and as a member of the 24th Ohio Volunteer Infantry. A native resourcefulness that would function well in metropolitan news-rooms appears also to have helped "open the ranks" to his military career. Under the Ohio constitution a captain of the militia could appoint his own musicians, consisting of a fifer and a drummer. John may well have capitalized on this information, persuading his brother Armstead, as captain of Company B, to appoint him as drummer. Whatever were the circumstances, young John Cockerill, on July 18, 1861, was proudly mustered in as a drummer in Company D and a member of the regimental band of the 24th Ohio Volunteer Infantry.[2]

The drummer boy somehow circumvented the minimum age set by law for enrollment in the state militia. The legal age span for enlistment was eighteen to forty-five years, but with parental consent volunteers between sixteen and eighteen were accepted. John would not be sixteen until December 5, 1861. He could not have deceived his brother or his parents about his age. Presumably the Cockerills interposed no objection to his enlistment. Since young Cockerill had access to the West Union *Scion*'s type, he may have presented a "doctored" certificate of age. Such things were done. At any rate joining as an under-aged musician could not have been particularly difficult. Benjamin A. Gould, a Sanitary Commission actuary, in a study of 1,012,273 Union volunteers, found that of the more than 8,000 enlistees under eighteen years of age, 773 were fifteen years old, 330 were fourteen, and 127 were thirteen.[3] In the Northern states' desperate haste to mobilize the minimum total of 140,000 volunteers requested by President Lincoln, there was a widespread looseness in verifying age requirements.

The young musicians were regimental mascots held in high favor. Drummer boy Cockerill thus found himself in a select category of youngsters who, although receiving the protective attention of their older colleagues, were nevertheless a remarkably resilient group. Their buoyancy exercised a cheerful effect on the troops. Yet they could not always be shielded from danger, nor were they spared the hardships of war. In such circumstances those who survived bore the stamp of a maturity far beyond their years.

Company D, 24th O.V.I., was Adams County's first contribution of armed forces to the War between the States. The regiment itself was part of the Army of the Cumberland. It fought with distinction and its dead were left in such blood-soaked battle scenes as Cheat Mountain and Greenbriar, West Virginia; Chickamauga and Buzzard Roost, Georgia; and Shiloh, Lookout Mountain, and Mission Ridge, Tennessee. Lieutenant Armstead Cockerill served under Captain Moses Patterson until the latter's death on September 2, 1861, when he was promoted to the captaincy. On December 31, 1862, Captain Cockerill became Lieutenant Colonel Cockerill.[4]

A document dated October 2, 1861, and signed by Ohio Governor David Tod, was father Joseph Cockerill's call to action. It was a colonel's commission. With it came the order that Colonel Cockerill organize the 70th Ohio Infantry Regiment.[5] Recruits, rough, raw and willing, were assembled from Adams, Hamilton, and Brown counties and were trained at Camp Hamer near West Union. In November, 1862, Colonel Cockerill took command of the brigade formed by the 70th O.V.I., the 53rd Ohio, and the 97th and 99th of Indiana.

Like his father, Colonel Joseph Cockerill was totally dedicated to the Union cause. The wrong kind of "peace" talk could move the Colonel to forceful or dramatic action. Reuben Smith, an Oliver Township farmer, swaggered into West Union one day passing out "treasonable" remarks favorable to the secessionists. As the highest ranking military officer available in the village, Colonel Cockerill was notified. He responded in characteristic fashion. "You are under arrest in the name of the Union!" he curtly informed the talkative farmer. Under guard the offender was whisked to the probate court, where he was compelled to take an oath of allegiance, a method considered to be effective in dealing with "subversives."

The Colonel was irritated by Ohioans who urged compromising with the Confederacy. He happened to be home on furlough at the time of the Democratic party's county convention. Under fire was the government's war policy. Colonel Cockerill slipped in just in time to hear Squire Jacob Rose of Green Township declaiming, "I favor peace." He proffered his right arm, adding: "We must approach our southern brethren with the olive branch in the right hand." He extended his left hand. "We must also approach them with the olive branch in our left hand. . . ." This was too much for the angry Colonel. Joseph Cockerill, attired in full colonel's uniform, sprang to his feet and, shaking his fist, interrupted the speaker: "In case Jake hasn't heard, we are at war and we can't very well win it by waving olive branches. No, gentlemen, we must approach them with a sword in each hand."[6]

Colonel Joseph Cockerill's brigade left its blood in thirty struggles, including the Battle of Shiloh, the Siege of Vicksburg, and at Chattanooga, Missionary Ridge, Kenesaw Mountain, and Jackson. A total of 244 were killed in battle or died of disease.

Other Cockerills fought for the Union cause. Three were uncles of John Cockerill: Daniel T. Cockerill, a captain and major, First Ohio Light Artillery; Giles Jackson Cockerill, a first lieutenant and captain of the same regiment; and Oliver H. Eylar, brother of John's mother, captain of Company F, Seventh Regiment, Ohio Volunteer Cavalry. John's older sister, Esther, married Dr. John Campbell, a captain in the 70th O.V.I.; and Sallie, the younger sister, was the wife of lieutenant W. R. Stewart of the 70th O.V.I.[7]

Private John Cockerill's company served in West Virginia under Major General William S. Rosencrans and General Joseph J. Reynolds. In the spring of 1862 his regiment was transferred to Louisville to become a part of the Army of Ohio under General Don Carlos Buell.

Although identified in Adams County as the "Drummer Boy of Shiloh,"[8] Private John Cockerill was more than a musician. He was in the thick of the Battle of Shiloh, where,

General Grant recalled, the field was so covered with the dead "that it would have been possible to walk across the clearing . . . stepping on the dead bodies without a foot touching ground."[9] A memorial to Cockerill published by the Ohio Commandery, Military Order of the Loyal Legion, reports that as "a musician in the regimental band of the 24th Ohio Volunteer Infantry, and absent from duty on sick leave, he carried a musket in the ranks of the 70th Regiment, Ohio Volunteer Infantry, then under the command of his father, and as such was engaged in the Battle of Shiloh, April 6 and 7, 1862."[10] Could it be that Private Cockerill feigned illness in order to get into direct combat?

Thereafter the musician-musketeer's spirit proved more durable than his physical capacity. He contracted pneumonia. Until his recovery he remained at Paducah, Kentucky, where his father's regiment was bivouacked. Young Cockerill's regiment marched on to join General Ulysses S. Grant, a one-time Clerment County, Ohio, neighbor, at Fort Donelson. Their meeting at Paducah was the only time father and son met for a visit during the war. Joseph Cockerill abhorred any treatment of a son that smacked of favoritism. He made no effort to have John transferred to his own command. As a contemporary put it, "Joseph Cockerill was not cold or unfeeling but there was a good deal of the Spartan in his composition. He did not wish to make a mollycoddle of his boy by spoiling him with privileges. His son John had enlisted on his own hook, and he should stand or fall on his own merits."[11] Subsequently the young editor-to-be tramped and fought and sweat and cursed in the mud of battles in Mississippi, Alabama, Kentucky, and Ohio.

In the meantime Colonel Joseph Cockerill's brigade joined the troops with General William T. Sherman in his triumphant march to the sea. In General Sherman's words, "Colonel Joseph Cockerill behaved with great gallantry . . . and held together the largest regiment of any colonel in my division; and was with me from first to last."[12]

Yet neither his valor nor his skill as an officer appeared sufficient to earn for Colonel Cockerill the rank of brigadier-general at the time the promotion was normally due. Both Generals Grant and Sherman recommended the advancement that seemed always lost in the Washington shuffle. In April, 1864, Colonel Cockerill resigned from his position in the brigade. The Colonel's friends blamed Republican politicians in Washington for bypassing the Colonel, who, although an outspoken Democrat, was a supporter of the administration's war policies. Belatedly Joseph Cockerill, on March 13, 1865, was brevetted by Congress as a brigadier-general.[13]

The War Department's order of September 10, 1862, abolishing regimental bands[14] knocked Private John Cockerill out of the war, for a time at least. But again the Cockerill resourcefulness scored. Reasoning that as long as soldiers sleep they will need to be awakened, he re-enlisted as bugler in an Ohio battery of the Artillery. In one of the very few comments preserved on his war experience Cockerill recalled that he was in southern Ohio at the time of General John Hunt Morgan's raid, in which "we did all running and no fighting."[15]

Without the wily Morgan's penetration in June and July of 1863 into Northern territory, Ohio might have had no battlefields to commemorate. To the Confederacy the thirty-eight-year old Morgan was a figure of courage, resourcefulness and dignity; to the North, a victim of his hard-hitting cavalry raids, he was an unholy combination of freebooter-guerrilla-horse thief and Blackbeard with a bridle.

In what has been tagged as a "Fortnight of Fear," Morgan's raid was explained as a means of distracting General Ambrose Burnside at Cincinnati and of delaying his invasion of eastern Tennessee. But as Morgan's men sliced through Indiana and headed toward Ohio, rumors spread that his objectives were to incite an uprising of Copperheads and to seize the state treasury at Columbus. Both theories have since been discredited.[16] Whatever his motives, Adams County, which had sent so many of its sons to war, realized the war was charging toward it. The ordeal revealed the need for a well-trained militia and introduced Ohioans to the realities of war. The raid marked Salineville as the nothernmost point of penetration by Confederate forces.

In Adams County, Morgan's men, led by General Morgan and his brother, Colonel Ralph Morgan, swept through several villages happily plundering and pillaging stores, stalking through unlocked houses, and terrifying women and children. In Winchester the raiders forced a carrier to surrender his mail bags so that Morgan could read the Cincinnati newspapers. The news was not good. General Edward H. Hobson's army of seven thousand men, including Private John Cockerill, was in hot pursuit. Morgan's troops continued through Grace's Run, Harshaville, Wheat Ridge, and Dunkinsville to Locust Grove, where they encamped for the night. Hardly had the thudding hoofbeats of Morgan's cavalrymen been lost in the distance when the vanguard of Hobson's forces swarmed into Manchester. Every kitchen on or near his route became a beehive of activity; food supplies that could not be found by Morgan's men magically appeared to bolster the soldiers' spirits. John Cockerill had time for a hurried meeting with his mother and sisters in West Union.

Militarily the Morgan raid was a farce. Despite the panic it touched off, it produced no real gains for the Confederates. Its frustration cost two hundred Northern lives as against three hundred Morgan followers killed or wounded. Three hundred of Morgan's cavalrymen escaped across the Ohio. More than four thousand Ohioans submitted claims for nearly half a million dollars; interestingly enough, Union troops were charged with $141,168 worth of the damage. As one historian put it, "it is astonishing how insignificant was the injury done in Adams County. It is true many stores were pillaged, seemingly for diversion, certainly not, in most instances, for gain."[17]

Private Cockerill, upon his discharge, heard numerous stories portraying the lighter side of the raid. All sorts of ruses

were used, for example, to hide valuables from the foragers.
Mike Nessler, a thrifty old German hotel owner at Piketon, was
told a soldier with Morgan was about to pull up his cabbages
and throw them around for fun. "Oh, don't do that, Captain,"
pleaded Mike, knowing full well his visitor was a sergeant.
"We need them for winter." The soldier was persuaded with
a quarter not to disturb the cabbage under which the inn-
keeper had hidden all of his money.[18] Because the raiders were
hard pressed by General Hobson's cavalrymen, horses were
the prize booty. One terrified farmer's wife, in the absence of
her husband, resolved to protect the family carriage horse at
all costs. She succeeded by stabling it in the parlor.

Cockerill concluded his military career late in 1862.[19] He
was inclined to belittle his stay in the army. "My war record is
soon told," he said. "I saw all that I cared to of war and prefer
reading about it to being in it." The Colonel was over modest.
Nowhere can there be found the faintest hint that John
Cockerill was anything except a plucky teen-age soldier. He
had seen men die in action. He took part in hand-to-hand
combat. He added luster to the Cockerill military roll of honor.

After the war John Cockerill, who did not advance beyond
drummer-bugler-private, was dubbed "Colonel" John Cockerill
for life. "When it comes to military titles," the Colonel explained, "I'm out of it. My father was a colonel, and so I
presume my friends think the title is hereditary. When I was
in Cincinnati, I tried to break up the custom of conferring
military titles promiscuously. I wrote an article in which everyone referred to was a phony colonel. But it is hard to shake a
title once it is conferred upon you by acquaintances, whether
it be colonel or judge."[20] Cockerill signed himself "Colonel"
only once. The government insisted he do so in order to draw
interest on bonds on which his name so appeared. As he
matured he took on more flesh, added to his height and presented a figure that looked far more like a colonel than he did
as a skinny, energetic youth who may have connived a bit
to get into the army.

In the editorial and news departments of half a dozen metropolitan newspapers, Cockerill behaved like a colonel on the battlefield. In subsequent years a stranger invading a news conference would have instinctively picked him as the man in charge, as indeed he usually was. "Colonel," although unsolicited, seemed to belong to the editor.

III. Sam and the "Scion"

The mushrooming newspapers in the middle decades of the nineteenth century testified to a young, supple nation growing more articulate. They were springing up in villages, towns, and cities. The mortality rate was high, but there were always a dozen plus to take the place of every dozen sheets that expired. Many of them served a temporary cause, then disappeared for lack of any further reason to exist. In John Cockerill's neophyte years a newspaper could sprout on a modicum of capital and a healthy bundle of editorial zeal. It would stay alive at least long enough for the community to see what it was up to. If the publisher-editor-printer of a weekly newspaper could be satisfied with a used hand press, a few cases of type, some paper stock, and a willingness to work sixteen to eighteen hours a day, he was in business.

Osman Castle Hooper in a history of Ohio journalism eulogized these publisher-editors as the "pioneers and progressive spirit of their times." "Few attained wealth," he wrote. "All of them struggled under serious handicaps for the things in which they believed."[1] Some of them chose unusual, even bizarre, ways of showing it, but they all believed in the essential goodness of the new America. In the clash of political opinions the zeal to convince their readers led editors to be extravagantly laudatory of their political favorites and abusive of their political opponents.

Such extremities of partisanship pushed the editors into risky predicaments. Violence was an occupational hazard. Sharp-tongued editors expected it and were prepared, as best they might, to deal with it. The rough and tumble days of southern Ohio newspapers were more than a historian's phrase. Their annals are flecked with stories of pillages of newspaper shops and offices and bodily attacks upon publishers and editors. The fiery partisanship of most newspapers could be attributed to the large number of Ohio editors who had learned their trade in the East. They reflected the bitter rivalry between Alexander Hamilton's Federalists and Thomas Jefferson's Democrat-Republican party. The political alignments shifted with the rise of Andrew Jackson's Whig party and the birth of the Republican party in 1856.

The first newspaper of the Northwest Territory, the Ohio *Sentinel*, professed to be "open to all parties but influenced by none."[2] Such a pledge of non-partisanship was high-minded but, as the subsequently expiring *Sentinel* learned, economically unviable for the typically Western small-town editor. To make ends meet, editors, besides being their own printers and bookkeepers, found it expedient to be county officials, legislators, militiamen, postmasters, justices of the peace. Not to be overlooked was the public printing, a part of the political spoils rewarded to "deserving" editors. It was not unusual for some communities to find themselves served by half a dozen papers, all militantly partisan. The newspaper's most compelling concern was to help steer the party to victory or, failing that, to comfort it in defeat.

By the time the smell of printer's ink had captivated fourteen-year-old John Cockerill, a procession of weekly newspapers had marched through Adams County. In the vanguard was the *Political Censor* of 1815 published by James Finley. Next came the *Village Register* in 1823, succeeded by the *Advocate* of 1831. There followed a string of drum-beating papers: The anti-Masonic *Courier*, brainchild of a Yankee named Jacob Crapsey; the West Union *Register*, exponent of Jack-

sonian Democracy, whose editor, George Menary, brother of
the eminent Ohio statesman Samuel Menary, is tagged in
Adams County history as the "first live newspaperman," and
the *Free Press*, strongly Whig and belligerently anti-Masonic.
The Adams County *Democrat*, spawned as a Democratic
organ in 1844, survived its extreme partisanship until 1860.
In 1866 Joseph W. Eylar founded the *People's Defender*,
another Democratic voice. As this was written the *Defender*
was still serving Adams County readers under the editorship
of Thomas Eylar, a descendant.[3]

Among the few Ohio weekly newspapers that weathered
the fierce political rivalries and economic pitfalls was the
West Union *Scion of Temperance*. The ramshackle one-story,
one-room, frame structure that housed the journal when it was
born February 17, 1853,[4] became a citadel into which editor
and publisher Samuel Burwell put his life and soul. Burwell,
the son of Nicholas Burwell, a native Virginian and legendary
mender of George Washington's shoes, learned his trade on
the Adams County *Democrat,* the *Free Press* and the Hillsboro *News*. He was brought up in an atmosphere of rigid
discipline. He was occasionally the object lesson of Leonard
Cole, a teacher whose custom was to whip every boy in school
when one or more transgressed.[5] Yet Sam Burwell, perhaps
to counter boyhood inhibitions, was a tolerant, understanding,
affectionate and fallible man. The enemies of John Barleycorn
welcomed the *Scion of Temperance* as "their" paper. It seemed
to be just that until the day two years after its founding when
Burwell blundered. The young editor was no drunkard, but
he kept a bottle of brandy under cover. He happened to be
refreshing himself when a village teetotaler caught him red-
handed. The next issue bore the abbreviated name of *Scion*.[6]

The editor was "human" in other ways. A contemporary,
Nelson W. Evans, wrote that "Sam Burwell is a born exag-
gerator. Some uncharitable people have accused him of plain
lying, but as that charge has been laid to every editor from
King Solomon to the present, we shall not notice it. The most

remarkable thing is that Mr. Burwell is not conscious of this
fault. He will know it for the first time when he reads this
book. But understand, Sam Burwell never told a lie, either in
the *Scion* or out of it . . . . With him everything is the very
best or the very worst. The village statesmen whom he admires
are all Websters and Clays. Compared to his enemies the devil
is a saint."[7] The editor's unshakable faith in West Union and
Adams County and an addiction to hyperbole may have been
the strongest factors in the community's affection for the *Scion*.

It was vivid stories like that of the Terry lynching of 1856
and editor Burwell's acute sense of justice that made *Scion*
subscribers of the Cockerills and other West Union families.
Eleven-year-old John Cockerill saw the lynchers ride into
town to claim their victim. The hanging was unique in mob
justice. Not until the noose slid over the head of the accused
for a second time was his death accomplished. The *Scion* of
November 28, 1856, in keeping with its customary restraint,
played the story on page 3 under the caption "Horrible Outrage" just above a notice of an Adams County Bible Society
meeting.

On the preceding Saturday morning Mrs. Albert Morris
was at home with her three children in the Ohio River town
of Manchester. William Terry, apparently aware that her husband was away, forced his way into the home and raped Mrs.
Morris. Screams brought the neighbors. In a few hours the
Negro was captured by indignant citizens who took him to
Manchester Island offshore from the village. "A rope was
placed around his neck, the end of the rope put over a limb
and he would, doubtless, have met with a terrible death,"
reported the *Scion*, "had the limb not broken. Some interference taking place, he was brought to West Union and
imprisoned in the county jail."

Word of the raping and the frustrated hanging spread
over the county. On Tuesday morning a party of "about fifty
angry residents on horseback and in wagons" thundered into
West Union. "They were armed and prepared for any emer-

gency," said the *Scion*. Destination: the county jail; mission: summary justice. Sam Burwell was in the courtroom adjoining the county jail, covering a murder trial, when the self-appointed posse arrived. Court was hastily adjourned as snarling cries of "Let's get that black fiend" knifed through the judicial atmosphere. In fifteen minutes the mob, wielding axes and sledge hammers, had rammed into the jail and taken prisoner William Terry.

The Negro, told that he would be hanged, was unafraid, even contemptuous, replying that "this will save someone some trouble." The posse thundered out of town again with Terry bound to an extra horse. Arriving in Manchester the "better citizens" considerately let the prisoner have time to arrange his worldly affairs. "He kissed his wife and left laughing," wrote Burwell in the *Scion*. At the west end of Manchester Island near the water's edge the posse, with an assist from a stately sycamore tree, administered "summary justice." This time there was no broken limb.

Concluding his lynching story Sam Burwell wrote: "Thus far we have given the facts and nothing more." Then the *Scion* denounced the lynchers: "We have always been opposed to the spirit of mobocracy. It will be heralded forth that we are not a law-abiding people, that we are not willing to submit to that government which is characteristic of a civilized community, that we are barbarians and everything else which a law-abiding people are not."[8]

The event or circumstance that prompted John Cockerill's initial fascination with newspapers is buried in the past. Did his interest stem from being the son and grandson of men active in public life who made news? Was he intrigued by watching the lynchers ride away with their prisoner and reading the printed version? Did some member of the Cockerill family arouse his interest? It apparently was not his father, who hoped John, like Armstead, would study law.[9]

Whatever the motivation, it first took active form when John, in 1859, began idling in front of the *Scion* office.

Through the window he could see the *Scion*'s second-hand press, the cases of type, a rolltop desk, a couple of chairs, a kerosene lamp, and a dedicated editor at work. Although Sam Burwell was friendly, he did not at once sense young Cockerill's avid interest. The lad realized he would have to make the first move. Colonel Cockerill, years later, told how it happened:

"I remember well the drowsy summer afternoon when I strolled into the office and asked the editor to teach me how to set type. Mr. Burwell stood me on a candle-box in front of a case, placed a lot of wooden letters in the boxes, and showed me how to set the type in a stick." To the astonishment of Sam Burwell, before the afternoon was over the new pupil had mastered all of the boxes. Young John Cockerill was utterly and irrevocably fascinated. Then came the magic moment when Sam put a friendly hand on a boyish shoulder and asked: "How would you like to work on the *Scion*, John?" "That," recalled Cockerill, "was the beginning of my journalistic career."[10]

There was no drowsiness about the new apprentice as he raced home to tell the great news to his mother. Thereafter John Cockerill, editor, foreign correspondent, publisher, won acclaim from far and near, but Ruth Cockerill, from that moment, was her son's most devoted fan. Until her death in 1878 there reposed in the family sideboard a thick collection of clippings—all written by or about her editor-son.[11]

Sam Burwell was as much a teacher as editor. His interest in promising youngsters was a magnet that through the years drew many to the *Scion*'s humble shop. Eight of his pupil-employees were his own children: six sons—Orlando, Clay, Bickham, Samuel Jr., Cassius, and Bickman; and two daughters—Ella and Margaret. Clay and Bickham later joined the New York *World* and Orlando the Cincinnati *Times-Star*. Another protégé was Joseph P. Smith, historian and adviser to President William McKinley. But John Cockerill was Burwell's prize pupil and, with understandable hometown pride, historian Nelson W. Evans wrote unequivocally that "Cockerill became the most distinguished journalist in the United States."[12]

Having many mouths of his own to feed, Burwell did not keep young John Cockerill under his wing merely out of benevolence. He realized the lad's potential. In a matter of weeks John was proving himself adept at setting type, working the press, and writing news and advertisements, plus delivering the papers.

Years later the Colonel recalled the first story he ever wrote for a newspaper:

One day just as the Scion was about to go to press, a rural gentleman came into the office with an advertisement of a farm for sale. Mr. Burwell, my editorial preceptor, rushed to the case to put the notice in type. Then came my big opportunity. It was the rule to give each new advertisement a brief local mention—a sort of editorial endorsement. I asked for the privilege of preparing one . . . and it was granted. I sat down and wrote my first essay for print. It was as follows: "The attention of our readers is called to the advertisement of Farm for Sale in another column." This was the formula at the Scion. I was tempted to add a word or two about the excellence of this particular farm and the desirability of the location. But we were pressed for time. I carried my article to the case and carefully placed it in type. How I watched it upon the press and how I read and re-read it with a pride and sense of importance that I never felt since.[13]

For years a clipping of this initial effort remained with a dignity equal to the Colonel's more mature samples in Ruth Cockerill's collection. John had carried the paper home the day it came off the press and showed it to his mother. "She seemed happy," he recalled. "I remember more than once she referred to me as the 'young gentleman who is writing for the newspaper.' She probably thought she had seen brighter and abler articles but none more truthful, direct and concise than this."[14]

John was roller boy for the *Scion*'s ancient Ramage press. It consisted of immense wooden uprights and a clumsy "devil's

tail." Because the platen was only half the size of the bed of
the press, two pulls were required to print on one side of the
sheet. Cockerill later observed that the press that Ben Franklin operated in Philadelphia was scarcely more primitive.
The ink was applied with a short, hard roller. Each page had
to be inked in turn, the distribution being performed on a
piece of marble tombstone resting on a table. Despite the
limitations of equipment the *Scion* came off the press regu-
larly on Thursdays. Editor and publisher Sam Burwell, puffing
contentedly on a briar root pipe, and his young assistant
wrenched off an edition of 400 copies on this ramshackle
press. The circulation ultimately exceeded 1,100.[15]

Cockerill related that "once the paper was off, I would
help to distribute it through the village. That was a real delight in those quiet, prosy afternoons. With my bundle under
my arm I could wander listlessly and barefooted through the
side streets and alleys where cows ruminated and hogs dozed;
stopping here to fling a paper over a fence, thrust it under a
door, or climb upon a roof perchance. The route was not a
heavy one, but it never took less than three or four hours to
go over it."[16]

The *Scion* was a remarkably fine newspaper, above the
level of many of its weekly contemporaries in readability and
editorial content. Describing itself as "An Independent Dollar
Weekly Family Newspaper," it had expanded from a five to a
six-column sheet. It claimed the largest circulation among the
weeklies in Adams County. As with most such papers, collecting from delinquent subscribers was a perennial headache
to the *Scion*. It was taken advantage of so outrageously that
it solemnly warned, "Any subscriber wishing to discontinue
must first pay up arrearages."[17] For revenue the *Scion* depended on subscriptions, advertising at "75 cents a square,
liberal discount for yearly advertisements," and job printing.

The *Scion* was a news, literary, and marketing smorgas-
bord. It offered an amazing range of reading matter, from
anecdotes to long and profound essays on patriotism and

morals, from small advertisements of stores and professional
men to legal notices, from witticisms to political advice. Very
early in his apprenticeship young Cockerill noticed something
that puzzled and distressed him. In common with a practice
of the weekly press the *Scion* tucked its news items on inside
pages with small captions but plastered its front page with
material of a non-news nature. When Cockerill asked why
live happenings did not get on page one, he never could get
an answer that satisfied him. On a typical front page, such
as that of February 24, 1860, the following items were included: An unsigned poem, "The Place Where Men Should
Die"; a two-column reprint from the *Home Journal,* "Legend
of the Mississippi"; an unattributed essay on "Our Revolu-
tionary Heroes"; "Beauty of Woman," an essay in which the
Scion editor, quoting a battery of bards on the subject, observed that "none of them is able to withstand the sly smooth
witchcraft of a fair young face"; "Sands of Gold," a collection
of fifteen one-paragraph epigrams ("No one can love what
is not lovely"); "Witticisms" ("Can a big man ache harder
than a little one?" "Why is dancing like milk? Because it
strengthens the calves"); a rundown on the ages of national
government leaders; "War Horses," on the behavior of horses
wounded in war; and "Don't Be Frightened," eight paragraphs
of reassurance that the Union, though often threatened, has
always survived.

The *Scion*'s masthead emblazoning the American Flag
over a portion of the globe labeled "Our Country" crowned
a column of editorials vigorously Republican and pro-Union.
The lead editorial was a verbal cuff at "some of our weaker
brethren in the Republican party who are in a stew in regard
to our opposition. . . ."[18] The *Scion* carried notices of Republican party functions and, when Republicans held the county
offices, printed legal advertisements, always a proper means
of rewarding loyal party organs. It is unlikely that Sam Burwell tried to indoctrinate young Cockerill in the glories of
Republicanism. His protégé was initially a Democrat, reflect-

ing the influence of his father, although he would subsequently have reasons to switch political affiliation.

The *Scion* saw that items of feminine interest were not slighted. From Buffalo it printed an account of how a girl threw acid into the face of a young suitor who had the bad luck to admit that marriage was not the objective of his courtship. "This most barbarous result of a lover's disappointment," pontificated the *Scion*, "is we think without modern equivalent."[19] The *Scion* kept its readers informed of developments in health and medicine. It reprinted from the Rushville *Republican* a report of "A Remarkable Cure of Cancer of the Breast." Physicians, surgeons and dentists unashamedly advertised in the professional directory. Patent medicines bolstered advertising revenues. The advertisements hailed such attractions as *Everybody's Lawyer*, a home reference book; Sanford's Cathartic Pills; "Grain Wanted—oats, wheat, corn, barley, rye, white beans, flax seed, timothy and clover seed— T. J. McCutcheon," and the New Carriage Manufactory in West Union. It was customary to give an advertiser a free editorial boost now and then, as indicated in John Cockerill's first writing effort. When Caleb Flannagan of Manchester moved his store from Front to Second Street, John wrote: "Being a very tasty gentleman, our old friend has one of the handsomest and most extensive stocks of gentlemen's wearing apparel ever offered in the county. See advertisement."[20]

A healthy portion of the *Scion* and other weekly and daily newspapers was clipped from other publications. Newspapers therefore found it advantageous to swap subscriptions, a practice that survived far into the twentieth century. The arrangement enabled the *Scion* to publish some pretty lively if not always fresh material. Burwell let John share the task of clipping articles for possible use, and was astonished by the mature judgments reflected in the lad's choices. Burwell shortly began to notice that young Cockerill favored news stories over literary and miscellaneous material. In consequence *Scion* readers were fed a richer fare of national news than were subscribers of other area weeklies. In view of John Cockerill's rejoining the newspaper business after the war as an editor, it can safely be assumed that Sam Burwell entrusted him with a growing proportion of the paper's responsibilities.

The neophyte's sensitivity to news values may well have been affronted by the *Scion*'s failure to capitalize on local affairs. John Cockerill's subsequent reputation as an ace news editor makes it unlikely that it could have been otherwise. The shortcoming was not a total lack of local news. A casual look at representative issues reveals the death of a man killed under a collapsing house, the fatal burning of a fifteen-year-old girl whose hoop skirt was ignited at a fireplace, the editor's impressions of a dinner at Hopkins House, an optimistic forecast of the fruit crop, a listing of premiums offered at the Adams County Fair, notices of political meetings, obituaries, marriages, and accidents. It was their brevity that troubled the young assistant. Sam Burwell was moved but not convinced by Cockerill's temperate suggestions that more details should be given.

Editor Burwell appraised his paper in light of the times. Communication and transportation media of the 1850's and 1860's were such as to make the weekly press a peculiar institution. Not many West Union families took any of the few daily newspapers extant. Those who did got their news days, often weeks, late. Most people depended on their weekly papers for the news of their community and country and the world. Editor Sam explained that the *Scion* had to be more than a local newspaper.

There was one kind of local news no weekly paper could slight—that of war, mobilization of manpower, progress of the Union cause, casualties. This was a field in which the Cockerills figured heavily. There came the announcement on June 28, 1861, of volunteers accepted for three years' service. It listed brother Armstead Cockerill as a first lieutenant. There followed the notice of a giant basket-picnic honoring volunteers with Colonel J. R. Cockerill as officer of the day ("The

good people will not forget to bring their baskets well
stored . . .") and, on July 11, 1862, a complete listing of
Adams County volunteers with all three Cockerills—John,
J. R., and Armstead—heading the list from Tiffin Township.
The *Scion*, after John took up drums and musket, published
first-hand accounts of the Battle of Shiloh by John's colonel
father and of General John H. Morgan's raid by Private John
Cockerill. Of his experience in Paducah, Kentucky, Private
John Cockerill, in a letter dated March 6, 1862, wrote:

> Your readers will be surprised that we are here in the enemy's
> territory without the means of defending ourselves. . . . We are still
> without guns. The health of the regiment is not so good. Thirty-one
> are in the hospital, none dangerously ill. This morning sixty-seven
> were unable to report for duty. We have seen nothing of the pay-
> masters as yet. The Colonel has received orders to march south
> tomorrow but to what point my informant does not know. . . .

By coincidence John Cockerill's journalistic career began
just as a new wonder produced signs that it would revolu-
tionize the transmission of world news. On August 5, 1858,
shortly before Cockerill started work on the *Scion*, Cyrus W.
Field's Atlantic Cable was announced. The cable broke less
than a month later but its practicability was confirmed. On
July 27, 1866, cable communication between America and
England was resumed. Development of the cable linking
Europe and America broke the barrier of distance separating
two continents. The cable had miraculously shrunk the world
and made it the newsman's oyster. In New York George
Templeton Strong greeted the news in picturesque language
as the city celebrated:

> It's almost alarming to consider the amount of impious brag
> which the cable has generated all over the country. The triumphant
> pyrotechnics with which our city fathers greeted this final and
> complete subjugation by man of all powers of nature—space and
> time included—set the City Hall on fire. . . .[21]

Newspapers were not slow to reap the benefits of the new
partnership of cable and telegraph. The weekly newspapers

with which young Cockerill would be connected, and later
the *Scion*, depended for much of their news on metropolitan
newspapers. When by the end of the 1870's big city newspapers began flagging overseas news "By Cable," village editors wielded their scissors with renewed energy as they passed
on to their readers the fruits of this new medium. Young John
Cockerill had no way of knowing that this new communication wonder linking remote news sources to American news-
rooms would be the vehicle to carry him to fame as a foreign
correspondent.

Even after his death at ninety-three Samuel Burwell was
remembered as the editor from whom Colonel John A.
Cockerill learned the printing trade and the rudiments of
journalism. Yet Burwell was a unique figure in Ohio journalism in his own right. Of the colorful old editor Adams County
historian Nelson W. Evans, in 1900, wrote that Burwell's
habit of optimism about his community and his country is
a valuable trait in a newspaperman. "People like condiments
in the columns of a newspaper as well as in their food," he
observed. "He kept the *Scion* to a high standard of journalism.
We do not know of another newspaper in Ohio which has
remained for forty-six years under one management, nor do
we know of an editor in the state who has conducted the same
newspaper for forty-six years."[22]

In a tribute to Burwell written by an unidentified editor
and supplied by a granddaughter, Mrs. Beatrice Strauss of
Cincinnati, the West Union editor was portrayed as one of
the few men who linked the present with the past. "Measured
by sordid standards, by what he accumulated in worldly
wealth," said the writer, "his would not be pronounced a
successful life. He was too unselfish, too trustful of others to
amass great riches. But there remains behind him as a result
of his character, the certainty that he was honest and true,
warmhearted and genial; that his friendship once gained was
steadfast and enduring."

Under the inspiring guidance of Sam Burwell, Cockerill's

perspective and "know-how" broadened. He began to be sharply aware of his own potentials as a journalist.

IV. Hamilton, Dayton, and a Copperhead

During John Cockerill's two years at the West Union *Scion* under the friendly counsel of Sam Burwell, the lad learned his tasks well. The excitement of doing what so thoroughly absorbed both man and boy and the healthy ripening of the neophyte's talents made their association mutually rewarding. But as all things must end, this ended, too, when John joined the army as a drummer boy.

Along with Adams County fellow soldiers he returned to a hero's welcome. Young Cockerill's courage is verified by his war record as a "drummer boy of Shiloh" who also wielded a musket in that bloody encounter. He had borne well the proud Cockerill tradition of valor, lightly though he seemed to regard his military career. The war that had ended the Burwell-Cockerill association was a teacher, in its way, toughening and seasoning the young volunteer. The seeds of ambition had been planted. It can be taken without debate that John Cockerill began to think of himself as a future editor, a choice that soon would impose some pretty formidable barriers along the way.

The *Democratic Union* in 1860 had joined the chorus of Adams County political voices. It was founded by T. J. Mullen and John K. Billings to put a conservative rein on the brand of Democratic politics whipped up by the Adams County *Democrat*. It apparently succeeded; the latter disappeared within months.[1]

John A. Cockerill's newspaper proprietorship started as a

partner to John P. Patterson. Proudly nineteen-year-old John A. Cockerill, on a December day of 1862, inspected his own name at the top of the four-page, six-column weekly journal. There it was—"The Democratic Union, Published Every Friday by Patterson and Cockerill, Editors and Proprietors."[2] When Patterson on March 27, 1863, disposed of his interest to S. E. Pearson, he announced: "He [Pearson], in connection with my former partner, Mr. Cockerill, will continue the publication of this paper. And now, while taking leave of the Democracy of good old Adams, I do not hesitate to recommend the present proprietors as Democrats good and true. . . ." The April 3, 1863, issue displayed the names of the new partners, Cockerill and Pearson, Cockerill having moved up as senior partner.

Substantiation is lacking but Cockerill's father probably put up part of the money for his son's share in the venture. Young Cockerill had been promised a college education but the war intervened. He was now more interested in journalism than in a formal education. How much Pearson contributed is not known, nor is it important. An interest in a small weekly paper could be acquired for a pittance or a promissory note. Pearson's real interest in the *Democratic Union*, it was suspected, was as a front for his business interests. "Notwithstanding his editorial duties, S. E. Pearson," the *Democratic Union* announced, "will continue to practice law."[3] His advertisement in the *Democratic Union* billed him also as an insurance agent.

A perusal of the files betrays an early financial pinch. It was painful enough to prompt Cockerill, four months after his name appeared as a co-owner, to do some scolding: "Our subscription list is entirely too small. Let every Democrat at once take his county paper."[4] It was as if the mere suggestion of a small circulation was adequate cause for widespread party shame. Cockerill, to prick the conscience of the community, printed endorsements of the weekly press from other publications. At this time he found himself a political rival of his energetic mentor, Sam Burwell, and the staunchly Republican *Scion*. "From the fact that the opposition is using its utmost endeavors to suppress the publication of this newspaper," wrote Cockerill, "we are forced to the belief that we are either something 'big,' or that the opposition is very small. . . ."[5]

Democratic Union readers began to notice the often breezy, sometimes tough, ways in which Cockerill goaded the political competition. As the editor warmed to his task, the paper earned a growing welcome. Adams County looked forward to reading the Cockerill barbs. In less than two months after the *Democratic Union*'s complaint of its inadequate subscription list, the paper did some crowing: "Our subscription list is increasing very rapidly. Every day we are receiving accessions."[6] It backed its claims, frequently, by naming readers who had come to the office with subscription orders. When influential people subscribed, Cockerill saw that their names appeared. He also tried "sharing the wealth"—to every person who turned in ten subscriptions went a year's free reading of the *Democratic Union*. Within a year the partners, emboldened by a growing readership, raised their subscription price from $1.00 to $1.25 a year, "except when the old dollar rate is paid in advance." But in keeping with the practice of most weeklies the actual paid circulation figure was a well concealed piece of information.

As on the *Scion*, reprints were shrewdly picked to cover a wide range of interests; material of feminine interest was not overlooked; there were items to chuckle over; advertisers were handled with loving kindness; a high standard of fairness and morals prevailed. "A Bold Woman" verbally portrayed the girl to whom the Duke of Buckingham was engaged. "Female Life Among the Mormons" was revealed by the wife of a Mormon elder. Housewives could be cheered by "prospects of a fruit crop never, in our recollections, more favorable." Cockerill spiced up the reading menu with such titillating tidbits as this commentary on a kiss: "It fairly electrifies you; it

warms the blood and sets your heart to beating like a bass
drum and makes your eyes twinkle like a star on a frosty night.
It ain't a thing to be forgotten."[7] West Union was enchanted
by such intimate candor. Adams County girls were not above
the Cockerill reproach. When the soldiers sent word they
seldom heard from their friends at home, Cockerill got results
with a sentence-editorial: "Girls, can't some of you write to
the boys?"[8] One of the first issues under the Cockerill aegis
carried a note that the editor's mother, Mrs. J. R. Cockerill,
would receive gifts to be sent to the soldiers. If a businessman
bought an advertisement of sufficient size, he was accorded
editorial endorsement ("Don't fail to call on Kincaid &
Billings and get a picture while you have an opportunity . . .").
If the editor refused, the advertiser might take his business to
the *Scion*. No advertiser could boast kinder treatment from
the *Democratic Union* than Clement Laird Vallandigham, the
famous Copperhead. *Vallandigham's Record on Abolition,
Slavery and the Civil War* received wide notice because every
editor who gave his advertisement three insertions got three
copies of the book. Cockerill recommended the book to his
readers.[9] The *Democratic Union* reported the Copperhead's
trial before a military tribunal for treason, his exile to the
South, and his controversy with the Abolitionists.

But if there were similarities in practices and techniques
between the *Scion,* on which young Cockerill had cut his
journalistic teeth, and the Cockerill-Pearson weekly, John
Cockerill, obviously the working editor of the *Democratic
Union*, was no imitator. It was the *Democratic Union*'s differences that captured the community's interest.

Slowly but surely readers of the *Democratic Union* realized
they were getting a new kind of weekly newspaper. It was
reflecting a developing news sense in its young editor. This
evolution continued despite a puzzling notice that would
horrify a modern news editor. "Nothing of decisive nature
has transpired since our last issue," the *Democratic Union*
casually announced in one issue.[10] A week later it again ad-

mitted: "No news of interest this week."[11] Could this be the work of a young man who would one day edit a world-famous newspaper? Perhaps the *Democratic Union*'s utter lack of affectation helped it win the community's high trust.

However, the "no news" notices did not reappear. Indeed the *Democratic Union* thereafter became Adams County's "newsiest" weekly. In the selection and play of the news young Cockerill in a real sense was pioneering in journalism. There was no precedent in the weekly press for capitalizing on local news. As on the *Scion*, the *Democratic Union* prior to Cockerill followed tradition in filling its front page with long-winded dissertations on patriotism and morals. Cockerill started experimenting. When he transferred local news from inside pages to page one, he found the response encouraging. The shift of emphasis was slow. Other weekly editors thought the West Union editor was a little crazy.

News of real significance and great interest showed up on page one. *Democratic Union* subscribers read of the sacking of the Marietta, Ohio, *Republican* by an Abolitionist mob. Cockerill told of the burning of the Dayton *Journal* office. "The Journal is a Republican organ which has been conducted in an inflammatory manner against Democrats generally," the *Democratic Union* pointed out, "but whatever the cause, recourse to violence and destruction of property is not justified."[12] The paper recorded enactment of a law by the Ohio Legislature allowing soldiers on the field to vote, thus giving cognizance to an issue that would bother politicians decades later. Cockerill did not elaborate on any except important local news. A representative issue might include such local items as establishment of a school, a runaway horse, a minor fire, a basket picnic—with none running over a sentence. But when Cockerill deemed the news of importance, he let the story run. When Vicksburg was captured, a battle in which father J. R. Cockerill and many Adams County soldiers figured, the account was lengthy.

John Cockerill was feeling his way against tradition. The

guidelines he followed were his own. He could not break away abruptly, even if the suggestion occurred to him, from the accepted format of the village weekly. West Union did not have access to a big city daily except by delayed mail. The community newspaper could not be converted wholly to a medium for local news. Cockerill's responsibility was to deliver a full package of local, state, national, and world news plus the inspirational and entertaining features to which his readers were accustomed. The concepts of playing up the news, writing it tersely and colorfully and divorcing it from the profound and verbose style that characterized the press of the day, grew with Cockerill.

The oustanding trait of the *Democratic Union* was its uninhibited vigor in championing its causes and denouncing its critics. To an Abolitionist leader who had charged that just being on the Democratic side was traitorous, Cockerill hotly retorted:

If we are not to be allowed the full exercise of speech and are denied the privilege of expressing our sentiments upon questions of common interest, then away with self-government and let us have in its stead absolute monarchy. The word "traitor" comes from such Abolitionists with bad grace.[13]

Although he at times defended Vallandigham, he found a point on which he could agree with General Burnside, who brought the charge of treason against the Copperhead. Wrote Cockerill:

We rejoice that the General does not intend to stop free discussion of the policy and measures of the government, that he thinks such discussion should be done with candor and not in a manner to discourage and demoralize the Union forces. No man can render judgment under excitement. We urge coolness and profound reflection in the consideration of controversial issues.[14]

The national administration, *Democratic Union* readers were advised, had best keep on its toes. Cockerill was watching it every minute. "While we cannot agree with the present administration in many of its war and civil measures," said the *Democratic Union*, "we forever intend using our influence for the preservation of the Constitution and the Union. When the administration adopts a course ruinous and subversive to the rights and liberties of the people . . . then shall our voice be heard in warning our fellow men to rally to the ballot box and show they love and revere the Constitution and the Union."[15]

No thanks to partner Pearson, John Cockerill's first editorial venture was satisfying enough to kindle the flame of ambition. His editorship had given West Union a powerful Democratic voice. Furthermore the paper was solvent and making money. Although he could have stayed on, building up the *Democratic Union* and carving himself an important niche in the community, the young editor had committed himself to move on to the metropolitan newspaper field. This could not be done in West Union. After two years with the *Democratic Union*, Cockerill transferred his talents to nearby Hamilton. He had been obliged to do most of the work on the West Union weekly while sharing profits with Pearson, who lived up to his promise of not letting his connection on the paper interfere with his law business. The *Democratic Union* made a fine front for the inactive partner. This factor hastened Cockerill's decision to leave. Without the young editor's energy and direction the *Democratic Union* withered and died.

The new job Cockerill found in Hamilton was on the *True Telegraph,* which owed its genesis in 1861 to the political tug of war in Butler County. The weekly had been on the market three times when the West Union youth slid into the editor's chair on February 23, 1865. Cockerill had sold his equity in the *Democratic Union*, but the cash received was not enough to buy the *True Telegraph* when it became available eight months later. John persuaded his brother, Armstead Thompson Mason Cockerill, to join him in the purchase. On October 26, 1865, the brothers Cockerill announced themselves as the new proprietors. Their partnership continued until April 25, 1867, when John bought out his older brother's interest. He thus was owner, publisher, and editor of his own newspaper at twenty-two years of age.[16]

Cockerill's handling of the *True Telegraph* was a repetition of the *Democratic Union* story. The young editor played the news in progressively bolder fashion. The *True Telegraph* was Democratic in policy, but Cockerill appealed to readers of all political affiliations. "The True Telegraph," he announced, "stands for equal and exact justice to all men of whatever state or persuasion, religion or politics."[17] Under Cockerill the *True Telegraph* blossomed into one of the strongest Democratic newspapers in Ohio.

In the Cincinnati *Enquirer*'s newsroom a large, untidy heap of newspapers was piled upon a creaking table. Washington McLean, publisher and a political power in Ohio, and his editor, J. B. McCullagh, who was to become editor of the St. Louis *Globe-Democrat*, Pulitzer's morning rival, stood beside the table, whisking through the exchanges. Like other metropolitan newspapermen, their eyes were open for fresh talent. McLean plucked at the next paper and took a longer than usual look. His interest aroused, he turned to McCullagh as he pointed to the front page of an Ohio newspaper. McCullagh nodded agreement. The two talked for several minutes.

Within a week John Cockerill opened a letter postmarked Cincinnati. McCullagh wondered if he would like to be the *Enquirer*'s correspondent in Hamilton. The newspaper the *Enquirer* executives had spotted was the Cockerills' *True Telegraph*. McCullagh had checked to find that the editor was John Cockerill, son of Colonel Joseph Cockerill, the Civil War hero from West Union, and now a member of the state legislature. Young Cockerill accepted the offer, sensing a foothold in big city journalism.[18]

Brother Armstead's association as a partner had enabled Cockerill to be in Columbus, the state capital, for sessions of the legislature. He represented his own newspaper in the

capital where a close look at legislation provided background
for *True Telegraph* articles. Through his father he was appointed journal clerk.[19] In this post he was often a jump ahead
of rivals in sending news reports to the *Enquirer.*

In 1873-1875 Cockerill took another state assignment,
chiefly honorary, that of aide-de-camp of Governor White.[20]

One day in June, 1868, the strangest political figure of
the Middle West strode into the *True Telegraph* office at
Hamilton. Cockerill recognized him at once as Clement Laird
Vallandigham, Ohio's ex-Copperhead, now a Dayton lawyer
and newspaper publisher. His influence as an Ohio Democratic
leader had waned after a series of events in which Vallandigham had been castigated as a traitor and eulogized as a hero.

Clement Vallandigham was handsome, gifted as an orator,
and irrepressibly ambitious. Appraisals of the Copperhead
ranged from a "respectable rebel" to a "damned nuisance."
The label depended on where one stood politically. As a young
lawyer descended from a ringleader in the Whisky Rebellion
and sired by a stern Presbyterian clergyman, he inherited an
uncompromising belief in his own principles. As a jury lawyer
he was excelled by few. As early as 1845 he had served in the
Ohio legislature; two years later he was editing the Dayton
Empire. By 1856, after sale of the *Empire,* Vallandigham, a
"Peace Democrat," was in Congress, where his oratory and
his anti-abolitionist views quickly made him a controversial
figure. Highly critical of the Union cause, Representative
Vallandigham's speeches in the House and in Ohio were militant and intemperate. The Ohioan solemnly and repeatedly
affirmed his loyalty to his country but, as he put it, "I am for
suppressing all rebellions, the Secessionist Rebellion South and
the Abolitionist Rebellion North."[21]

Vallandigham had exerted influence in founding the *True
Telegraph* in 1861. With other anti-war Democrats, he had
been suspected of engineering a run on the Hamilton bank
of John P. Peck, outspoken supporter of the Union cause.
Peck was also publisher of the *Telegraph.* Peck's enemies, to

hurt him, withdrew their funds from his bank. Spurred on by Vallandigham, they instigated the establishing of the *True Telegraph*. The confusion of names, as planned, ruined Peck's paper. Peck could hold out no longer than late 1861, when his *Telegraph* was merged with the Hamilton *Intelligencer*. The *True Telegraph* then held the field free to denounce the administration.

A predecessor in the *True Telegraph*'s chair, John Mayo, had renewed Cockerill's fascination in the stormy Copperhead with his biography of Vallandigham.[22] Now as John Cockerill welcomed the man who had made headlines in two countries, he recalled some of the incredible high-lights in the career of his visitor.

The Vallandigham popularity among the anti-abolitionists reached its peak by 1863, the year of the famous exiling incident. Returning to Dayton after the congressional session, Vallandigham was tipped off that General Ambrose E. Burnside had vowed to put an end to the Ohioan's anti-Union ranting. The General, freshly installed as Commander of the Department of Ohio, had failed as a combat officer. As if to compensate, he issued his famous Order Number 38. It forbade citizens to "express or imply treason."[23] This order, fumed the volatile Vallandigham, was thought control, Civil War brand. Vallandigham's response was immediate and dramatic. In a speech at Mount Vernon he spat upon a copy of the order, ripped it to shreds, and tossed the defiled document over the platform, climaxing his act in a pantomime of washing his hands of the whole mess.[24] It was a crowd-pleasing performance that the Copperhead repeated in subsequent speeches.

The General could stand it no longer. Vallandigham was arrested in Dayton, accused of violating Order Number 38 by declaring sympathy for those in arms against the United States government, and found guilty on two of three counts. When Vallandigham was sentenced to close confinement in Fort Warren, Boston Harbor, it looked like the prize boner of the Lincoln administration. Many of his countrymen, including Union supporters, regarded the punishment as political persecution. A groundswell of sympathy for the prisoner swept across the country. President Lincoln was baffled until it occurred to him that Vallandigham, a potential martyr, could be stripped to Vallandigham, the goat. The President spotted in Order Number 38 a legal basis for commuting the sentence to exile in the South, "beyond our lines and inside the lines of his friends." And that, to the consternation of Vallandigham and his Copperhead cronies, was just what happened. Even the South was embarrassed; it had not invited the Northerner. The outraged Copperhead reiterated that he had never upheld the Southern cause and repeated his abhorrence of slavery. His supporters shouted that guarantees of free speech and trial by a civil jury were being circumvented by pushing the prisoner into the rebels' camp. They had a point, but the country seemed more intent upon enjoying the story of Vallandigham's Southern adventure.

Federal officers who escorted the flamboyant Copperhead to a Confederate outpost in Kentucky observed, "He don't look like no traitor." Vallandigham's arrival threw the Alabama line regiment, the exile's host, into nervous confusion.[25] The colonel could find nothing in the rule book about accepting exiles. The redoubtable Ohioan may have been of some use to the Confederacy by opposing war from political platforms in the North. As an exile in the South, he was useless to the rebels. Shortly after the maze of military protocol had been penetrated for a clue on what to do, a way was found to deport the Northerner to Canada as "an alien enemy of the Confederacy," giving the incident an international touch.

In June, 1863, the Ohio Democratic State Convention had nominated Vallandigham, "that incorruptible statesman and fearless patriot," for governor. The Republicans chose a Cincinnati *Enquirer* editor, John Brough, as their nominee. Union victories at Vicksburg and Gettysburg refuted the Democratic contention that the war was a failure. Though Brough won,

Vallandigham, with 185,000, polled more votes in Ohio than any other Democratic candidate for the post up to that time.[26]

In Hamilton, where John Cockerill now faced the stormy nonconformist, the Peace Democrats, through the *True Telegraph*, continued their fire. The paper went so far as to charge that any Democrats who had answered the Lincoln administration's call were hypocrites. Hamilton zoomed into the news on June 17, 1864. The district Democratic convention was in session when Vallandigham, without notice, appeared. His escape from his Windsor, Canada, "asylum" had been accomplished through his disguise as a fat man.

One delegate wrote that he "touched off cheering such as never before had been heard on this continent."[27] Lincoln let the returnee speak when and where he fancied. Vallandigham's popularity was immense, but the tides of war were running against him. At the National Democratic Convention he spearheaded a move that wrote into the platform a plank condemning the war as a means of preserving the Union. But General George B. McClellan was nominated for president and promptly repudiated the plank.[28] In the election Butler County, Midwestern hotbed of Copperheads, bucked the tide. It went heavily for McClellan and against Lincoln. Republicans won handily in the rest of the state, including Vallandigham's home county of Montgomery. While the Democrats' platform was branding the war a failure, the Union forces tightened the squeeze on the Confederacy. Vallandigham was no longer restrained; he was allowed to hang himself politically. He resumed law practice and editing a newspaper.

The Dayton *Empire* had been suspended by military order at the time of Vallandigham's arrest as a political incendiary. One editor, J. F. Bollmeyer, had been shot and killed in 1862 in an altercation over states' rights. The gunman was Henry M. Brown, a belligerent Unionist. William T. Logan, who had been Bollmeyer's assistant, edited the *Empire* for a few months until a party of Union soldiers, home on furlough, raided and demolished the office.[29] But Vallandigham, when he could spare the time from politics, rejuvenated the *Empire*.

The Democratic debacle of 1864 had written finis to his political career, but it took two more flings to convince him he was dead. In the first, earlier in the year of 1868, he had missed out on the Democratic nomination for the United States Senate. But he wasn't through. Although not a delegate, he wanted to attend the Democratic National Convention opening in a few days in New York. He was familiar with young Cockerill's work. The young man would be a useful fill-in editor while Vallandigham, who with J. McLain Smith was co-owner of the Dayton *Evening Ledger*, was trying to regain political ground.

Cockerill's visitor finally revealed his mission. Would Cockerill be interested in coming to Dayton to take over editing the *Daily Ledger*? In 1867 the *Empire* had swung from the weekly field and been renamed the *Daily Ledger*. Cockerill's "master plan" for reaching the metropolitan daily newspaper field called for another step-up. The *Ledger* would give Cockerill the experience of a daily operation. Continuing, Vallandigham spoke of the rich harvest that could be reaped with a young and aggressive editor at the *Ledger*. The rosy picture was capped with an offer for Cockerill to become at least a part owner. Vallandigham's partner wanted to pull out. There might even be an opportunity, said the Dayton lawyer, for Cockerill to gain a controlling interest. He himself might be withdrawing but he wanted to stay on during the election campaign. The proposition was intriguing. A vagueness over some aspects of the newspaper's financial situation did not seem important in the emanation of Vallandigham's gracious and persuasive manner.

In a matter of days Dayton *Daily Ledger* subscribers noted in their July 7, 1868, issue these words in the upper right corner of page one: "C. L. Vallandigham, J. A. Cockerill, Publishers and Proprietors." Cockerill's name replaced that of J. McLain Smith. In subsequent issues "J. A. Cockerill &

Co." appeared as "Publishers and Proprietors," indicating to the public that Cockerill had acquired control.

On July 2, 1868, Cockerill sold the Hamilton *True Telegraph* to Jacob H. Long.[30] The proceeds from the sale plus his own savings would have provided the invested funds. It is presumed that, in addition to buying out Smith, Cockerill gave Vallandigham a promissory note to be redeemed on the installment plan. The ease with which the controlling interest was conveyed to Cockerill was no doubt tempered by the fact that he was buying liabilities as well as assets. Whatever the details may have been, the new venture shaped up as a business challenge of serious proportions.

In the July 7 issue of the *Ledger* Smith, in a "Valedictory," announced sale of his interest to Cockerill,

late of the Hamilton True Telegraph, who in conjunction with Mr. Vallandigham, will conduct the paper. . . . Mr. Cockerill is a young gentleman of experience and ability who will, I feel assured, give complete satisfaction to the friends of the Ledger. He comes to us a comparative stranger, with a character for probity and courtesy which will win for him the respect and esteem of our citizens. He takes charge of the department I leave, and, I trust, will receive the same generous treatment I have always experienced, and a continuation of the patronage which has been extended to the Ledger during my administration . . . I leave the Ledger with a large and rapidly increasing circulation, a reputation for job work second to no office in the state and an advertising patronage that exceeds all expectations.

In response the new editor was brief. He pledged his best efforts

to the work of rendering the Ledger acceptable to the Democracy of Montgomery County and the state. I bring to my aid in this several years of experience as a publisher and thorough practical knowledge of the printing business. As to my antecedents, they are strictly Democratic—otherwise I would have no occasion to address the readers of the Ledger. . . . I enter the discharge of my duties confident of the success of the Ledger and its principles. . . .

Cockerill wasted no time jumping into political warfare. His first editorial blast, captioned "Republican Strength," was that the party "has no strength. . . . As represented by General Grant it is a negative one."

The *Ledger* tabbed itself the "official paper of Butler County," asserted proudly that it was read by the working people and, by its own claim, grew in circulation to become the top paper in the Miami Valley outside of Cincinnati.[31] For 20 cents a week or $7 a year the *Ledger* was published "every afternoon at 3 o'clock except Sunday and sent to all points by the railroads, by the first train after that hour." In addition an eight-page weekly edition was published Thursdays.

Cockerill soon found himself up to his ears in deadlines, editorial responsibilities, money worries, and the heavy demands made by Vallandigham's campaign for Third District Congressman. Gone forever was the leisurely pace of the weekly paper. And not to be forgotten was the political and business competition of the *Journal*, Butler County Republican newspaper.[32]

The *Ledger* published a wide variety of material. In an election year political news, along with a daily listing of local and state candidates, predominated. Cockerill's police court news was reported in a breezy fashion. ("Leonard Perin was found not only in a drunken condition but exceedingly belligerent. . . . He claims to be from Toledo but the Mayor thinks he is a canal loafer. . . . his knife was confiscated to prevent another display of its shaving qualities."[33] "A stranger, who seemed rather genteel in general demeanor, but whose over-indulgence made him depart somewhat from the rules of propriety, was arrested. . . ."[34])

Cockerill published a column of domestic news on the first page, provided every day by D. B. Williams with the "newest and most interesting items." A reader, consulting the advertisements, would have found dozens of services and a wide range of merchandise extolled in the *Ledger*, including carriages, patent medicines, furniture, wines and liquors, drugs, farms, saws, insurance, lumber, sewing machines, clothing, shoes, picture framing, stationery, books, stoves, groceries, mirrors, hair restoratives, tailoring services, wall paper, fruits, and candies. The *Ledger*'s service to its advertisers included the usual gratuitous mention of its larger accounts in the news columns.

Cockerill was given full sway in editing the *Ledger* with the one self-evident condition that the paper continue as the protector and champion of Clement Vallandigham. To the limit of the time that could be given to writing and editing, Cockerill's talents made the *Ledger* a more readable product. But as principal owner Cockerill had business tribulations. Circulation and advertising were gaining but income could not match disbursements. A New York *Herald* man, recalling Cockerill's Dayton experience, wrote: "He had plenty of work but very little honor or profit. . . . The work of editing the paper and getting it out devolved almost wholly on young Cockerill, who was quite unknown at the time and got but little credit. . . . He had not even the satisfaction of feeling that if he was not accumulating fame he was making money. Neither fame nor fortune was his at the time, and there were days when the future looked very dark and dreary to him."[35]

Cockerill did not find Vallandigham's political proclivities objectionable, at least in the early period of their association. The Dayton lawyer had accepted Lincoln's second presidential victory graciously. He was warm in praise of Lincoln's generous handling of the defeated, prostrated South. Upon Lincoln's assassination, he eulogized the Great Emancipator.

Nevertheless, the circumstances suggest that the politician's expectation of elaborate if not extravagant coverage of his speeches irritated Cockerill. For example the *Ledger* of August 10, 1868, reporting on a Vallandigham speech in Fort Wayne, Indiana, was made to say it was delivered before "the largest meeting ever held in that part of the state. Mr. Vallandigham's reception was a perfect ovation and his speech

is said to have been one of his ablest efforts." Apparently the
crowds were never small when Vallandigham spoke. On September 18 the *Ledger* claimed the Daytonian's speech at
Jackson, Ohio, drew the "largest political gathering ever held
in that part of the state." It may well be doubted, since the
lawyer, in his race for Congress, lost his own county, that the
home folks were as ardently pro-Vallandigham as the *Ledger*
professed to believe. Vallandigham was greeted with a barrage
of stones, according to the *Ledger*'s September 19 account,
when he spoke in Dayton. The *Ledger* charged they were
hurled from the direction of the Republican *Journal*'s office.
Vallandigham, in response, nobly exhorted his followers that
they must not interrupt Republican meetings. The *Ledger*
loyally bore the torch for its part owner: "Elect Vallandigham
and carry the state. Such a man . . . would be worth millions
to the workingmen and taxpayers of the country."[36] Cockerill
could not have enjoyed the self-serving position into which
Vallandigham's candidacy put him and the newspaper.

Vallandigham and the Democratic ticket were defeated.
Shortly after the November election Cockerill left the *Ledger*.
The familiar "J. A. Cockerill & Co., Publishers and Proprietors" appeared for the last time November 10, 1868. In its
place on November 11 came the names of the new owners,
James Kelly, H. Elliott, and Dennis Dwyer. The next day
Vallandigham announced he would spend all of his time in law
practice, having leased his half ownership to H. Elliott. This
would indicate that Cockerill either was unable to pay the
amount due Vallandigham, or simply walked out in disgust.
Absence of a farewell message from Cockerill suggests internal
friction. Whether a quarrel hastened an end to the Cockerill-
Vallandigham association is a matter of conjecture. Conceivably the lawyer, disappointed in one more political reverse,
was critical of the young editor. As far as any available record
is concerned, Cockerill was silent on the Dayton debacle; there
was no Cockerill complaint that, as one version put it, "he
fell into a trap by shrewd speculators and became so involved

by debts contracted by his predecessors that he lost every dollar of his investment."[37] Yet the truth seems to lean in that direction.

The four-month Dayton chapter in his career is symptomatic of Cockerill's ineptitude in business affairs. This shortcoming cost him heavily in the stormy years ahead. Cockerill, looking back upon his experience, may well have realized it would have been wise to hire a competent business manager so that he could have devoted all of his energies to editing.

Vallandigham, always a news maker, in 1871 made more headlines in death. In the course of defending Thomas McGehan, a bawdy scalawag, speculator, and onetime marshal in Hamilton, who was accused of a saloon killing, the Dayton attorney was explaining to another lawyer how he believed the shooting occurred. Grasping one of two revolvers lying on a table, he jammed the weapon into his right trousers pocket and pulled the trigger, fatally injuring himself. He had picked the wrong weapon, the loaded one. Upon the death of Vallandigham John Cockerill, by then an editor in Cincinnati, wrote that the Dayton politician had been "ferociously assailed and denounced as no other man of his day and generation had been." In their association the two often disagreed, "sometimes warmly and vehemently, upon party and individual matters," Cockerill recalled. "He espoused during the war the weak side. He combatted popular passion and prejudice, and risked his life, his property and character in behalf of what he considered right."[38] Referring to his differences with the controversial Daytonian, Cockerill's tribute concluded:

It is now to us a great satisfaction that just before the state convention we saw Mr. Vallandigham at Columbus and had a most cordial and friendly interview with him. There we finally disposed of any alienation or misunderstanding, if upon either side it had previously existed.[39]

v. City of Serenity and Sin

Out of funds and bruised in spirit, John Cockerill returned to Hamilton, where, for an unrecorded period of time, he presumably brooded over the Dayton fiasco. But soon he had a more exciting worry—how he would do as a reporter for the Cincinnati *Enquirer* in his first venture into metropolitan journalism. The offer came early in 1869 and he accepted jubilantly. This was the direction in which he wanted to go.

In Cincinnati young Cockerill found a city of sentiment and sin, of rascality and religion, of sordidness and beauty, its moods ranging from placid to volcanic. It was not unlike the socially ambitious matron who crossed over too quickly from the wrong side of the railroad tracks. To Michel Chevalier, a French visitor, Cincinnati seemed to be a city of working men grown rich without time to don their Sunday finery.[1] Cincinnati provided Cockerill the proving ground for a heavy arsenal of talents. It produced the "big story" with which the young editor lifted sensationalism to a fabulously profitable commodity. In John Cockerill, reporter and editor, Cincinnati found a "sort of furious young man, a hard master and a born journalist."[2] He worked with a dedication that would yield fortunes to publishers. He possessed an executive capacity that kept the newsroom humming.

The paper to which Cockerill reported at 247 Vine Street had been a leading Democratic voice in Ohio since 1841 when the brothers John and Charles Brough bought the Cincinnati *Advertiser* and renamed it the *Enquirer*. John sold his interest in 1843, becoming president of the Madison & Indianapolis Railroad. In 1863 he defeated Clement L. Vallandigham for governor of Ohio. Charles edited the *Enquirer* until 1846, when he became a colonel in the Mexican War. He sold the *Enquirer* in 1848 to James J. Faran, who had served in the Ohio legislature, as mayor of Cincinnati and as a congressman.

Washington McLean, the "Warwick of Democracy," became a partner with Faran in 1852. Although Faran at various times was editorial head of the paper, McLean was the dominant personality. Through their political connections Faran and McLean developed what was then described as the biggest job printing business in the world. But the newspaper side of the business was doing poorly. In circulation the *Enquirer* was anemic, having barely touched 16,000 in a rollicking city of 200,000. Editorially the paper was on the downgrade. To what extent J. B. McCullagh, who headed the editorial staff for a short period, and McLean had planned to push young Cockerill along in the organization is uncertain. Neither, of course, could have predicted the amazing "cure" which the young editor would shortly administer to the ailing newspaper.

Cockerill had not been on the new job long before he became aware of John R. McLean, son of Washington McLean. A warm friendship sprang up between the two. It is possible their association was a factor in Cockerill's swift upgrading on the staff. "Through young McLean's influence," one account says, "the young journalist was made city editor." A more convincing version of Cockerill's progress, starting as the paper's "humblest reporter," attributes it to his "enterprise in getting news and his bright, snappy way of writing it up. . . . [this] soon gained him promotion to city editor."[3]

McCullagh soon departed for Chicago, leaving Faran in nominal charge of the news and editorial departments. In 1870, with the aid of his father, John McLean acquired the majority of the *Enquirer*'s stock. Faran, involved in politics and business, could not measure up to young McLean's requirements for the paper. One day later that year, without warning, young McLean escorted Cockerill into Faran's office and introduced the young city editor as the new editorial head of the paper. Faran, taken by surprise, arranged his papers, grabbed his hat, and, wordless with rage, walked out, never to return to the *Enquirer* office. For this abrupt deposition he never forgave the son of his old partner.[4] Banishing the person was easier than banishing the name. Since Faran owned a block of *Enquirer* stock, his name stayed on the masthead until 1882.

An *Enquirer* reporter could get by knowing the city superficially as long as he was proficient in covering his own beat. As city editor and then as managing editor, Cockerill knew Cincinnati like a book. He made it a point to talk to as many readers as possible. Thus oriented, Cockerill made news assignments with authority. The freshness and vigor of his editorials reflected an ability to identify himself with Cincinnatians.

What kind of city awaited the young editor's exploration? Charles Dickens portrayed it as a "cheerful, animated city . . . lying in an amphitheater of hills forming a picture of remarkable beauty."[5] A British tourist was less rhapsodic; he called it a monster piggery. Cincinnati in 1869 ranked sixth in population among cities of the country, topped by New York, Baltimore, Philadelphia, Boston, and New Orleans. St Louis and Chicago would catch up in less than a decade. It was a virile metropolis of the rich, booming West, with a lack of restraint that drew an odd mixture of travelers and newcomers. Cockerill could spot the adventurers—loose women, gamblers, loan sharks, speculators, fortune hunters, crusaders, panhandlers, grifters, and pitchmen. Saloons dotted Sausage Row and Frogtown. In Bucktown roustabouts, thieves, and dope addicts fought and loved in a setting of tumbledown shacks, filth, and squalor. Vine Street was lined with beer parlors, dance halls, restaurants, theaters, opera houses, shooting galleries, dog pits, apple butter wagons, brothels, and nude figure studios. As if nature were ashamed of the Queen City, she had contrived to shut off the view by ringing the city with hills.

The steamboat traffic that brought bawdy characters from behind the hills also funneled in immigrants who gave the city political strength and culture. Down the river rode the mechanics who built the city's machine-tool industry. With them came refugees from political persecution in Europe who implanted a fresh, liberal viewpoint that tempered a Presbyterian stringency on one hand and a boomtown lustiness on the other. The voice of the city was marked by the German guttural and the Irish brogue. So many Germans found their way to Cincinnati that an Over the Rhine section sprang up. With six thousand Jews, the city was regarded as the center of Reformed Judaism in America.

River traffic in grain, with an assist from German brewmasters, produced the brewing and distilling industries. Cincinnati's packinghouses, slaughtering 600,000 hogs a year, won the title of "Porkopolis." Cincinnati-made wagons and carriages, soap, stoves, clothes, furniture, shoes, boots and other leather goods, combined with other products, grossed seventy-nine million dollars a year.

Older families with land holdings on the perimeter of the burgeoning young city bolstered their bank accounts. The wealthier Cincinnatians stretched for more breathing space and built lavish homes in surburban areas, industrialists needed factory sites, and merchants bought sites for more stores. Landowners subdivided their farms, at fabulous profit, into new additions. Real estate men, bankers, merchants, and speculators sat smugly atop the ladder of affluence.

The social whirl enhanced the popularity of the river packets. Swankily appointed sternwheelers were floating palaces for dining, drinking, dancing, and romancing. A contemporary description suggests the flavor:

The packets went to elaborate lengths to satisfy that critical organ, the human stomach. . . . Fabulous repasts were served in dining rooms luxurious in every detail. Over rich, soft carpets white-jacketed Negro waiters passed from table to table, bearing an array of savory viands. The tables bore the finest napery; the china was pure Haviland, the silver heavy and ornamental. While the passengers ate their fill, a stringed orchestra struck up its magic, and guests danced the minuet, the cotillion, the waltz, the polka and the mazurka.[6]

The packets lasted a long time because of sentiment but the river freight traffic was less durable. Those upstarts, the iron monsters, wielded a damaging blow to Ohio River traffic as the frontier shifted westward. Remote towns and villages, joined by rail, began to share boom-time benefits. Louisville for a while robbed Cincinnati of the bulk of its southern trade. Not until the Roebling Suspension Bridge spanned the Ohio River in 1867 did the Queen City begin to retrieve its losses. Under Cockerill the *Enquirer* promoted a series of industrial expositions which, managed by pompous but competent A. T. Goshorn, bolstered Cincinnati's prestige. Cincinnati was on the move in other ways. Horse-drawn street cars rolled into use in 1857. Gas street lights superseded oil lamps. Regular garbage collections were instituted. Cincinnati fielded the first salaried baseball team in the world, the Red Stockings.[7] The players drew from $1,000 to $1,500 a year. In off season they supplemented their earnings as bookkeepers, engravers, marble cutters and the short-stop doubled as Uncle Tom in performances of *Uncle Tom's Cabin*.

One of John Cockerill's earliest impressions was that the two halves of the city's soul, the better and the worse, were drawing apart. Wealth was more abundant, music and art richer, education more plentiful, entertainment gayer, but vice was wilder and political corruption more rampant.

In incompetence and graft city government dipped to its lowest point during John Cockerill's eight years in Cincinnati. Its streets and alleys were rubbish and filth ridden, touching off an outbreak of cholera that claimed up to seventy deaths a day in the early 1870's. Hoodlums presided in police court. Tom Snelbaker, who doubled as police chief and promoter of burlesque shows, fatally shot a special officer at the police station. The shooting was upheld as an act of self-defense. In 1870 so many prisoners escaped that Cockerill's headline renamed the county jail the "County Sieve." Cincinnatians found no restraints in quenching their thirst; 3,500 drinking places were at their service, many of them open all night.

Beer was three to five cents a mug plus all the buyer could eat. Under the administration of Mayor G. W. C. Johnston, the City Council found it convenient to "function" in two rooms. Officially its business was conducted in the council chamber. But adjacent was a room in which a keg of beer with cheese, bologna, and crackers was available to sustain flagging spirits. One chronicler relates that on a warm day two kegs were brought in. A quorum couldn't be kept in the council chamber but there was always a quorum in the other room.

Cincinnati was not without its virtues. When the Chicago fire reduced a third of the city to ashes, Cincinnati wired that it would take hundreds of the homeless, and every Cincinnati panhandler promptly became a Chicago refugee.

Womanly virtue was in constant jeopardy. The manager of the Crystal Palace on Elm Street was under a long sentence for operating a girlie show without a license. He was excused from serving time, due to City Hall connections, upon his promise to keep the show clean. When nude show girls brightened up the act, a politician defending the Crystal explained they were used for their artistic attraction.

With its wealth and prospering factories and business enterprises, the city welcomed competition. Bigness seemed more important than quality. Joseph Buddeke aspired to own the largest swinging bell in the world for his new church, St. Francis de Sales. When finally installed, the thirty-thousand-pound bell was swung by a wheel fifteen feet in diameter. When it rang Walnut Hills all but jumped out of its skin, the ground trembled, and windows nearby broke from the concussion.

Back of the rumble of political machines, the hum of factories, the vulgar clatter of honky-tonks and the chatter of high society, music, art and literary culture flourished. Critics pronounced Cincinnati's May Festivals incomparable. Libraries were numerous, most of them sponsored by genuine

book lovers. The thrill of listening to Jenny Lind inspired a
wealthy distiller to build Pike's Opera House.

Nor were the anti-sin brigades idle. By 1874 the Women's
Crusade had gathered force and opened up on Demon Rum.
Misgovernment had begot so many evils that mass meetings
were held and clergymen called for citywide prayers. Women
do-gooders invaded saloons, praying, singing hymns, and demanding a stop to the sale of intoxicating beverages. The
Volksfreund, a German newspaper, denounced the Crusade,
and this "prayer pestilence," as a nuisance.[8]

If Cincinnati suffered from delusions of grandeur, there
was good reason. In 1869 the New York *Times* proposed the
Ohio city as the best site for the nation's new capital. The
suggestion grew out of a rash of speculation about a substitute, in the interest of safety, for Washington. "Cincinnati,"
wrote the *Times*, "has the most metropolitan character of any
place but New York." The Cincinnati *Gazette* responded
modestly that if selected, "we shall acquiesce as a patriotic
duty."[9] Cincinnati was host to the Convention on the Removal
of the National Capital in 1870. The *Enquirer* reported that
every delegation was there to beat its own drums on behalf
of its city. Nothing came of the relocation scheme, but Cincinnati was thrust into the national limelight and loved every
moment of it.

VI. Murder a Profitable Commodity

It was early Sunday, November 8, 1874, when the word
reached the Cincinnati *Enquirer* office. A body had been
found late the night before in a furnace at Freiberg's Tannery,
Livingston Street and Gamble Alley, about two miles northwest of the *Enquirer* building. The crime happened too late
for the *Enquirer*'s Sunday edition.

To cover the story Managing Editor Cockerill sent, among others, a twenty-four-year-old, gnome-like, Greek-born reporter by the name of Lafcadio Hearn. He was a queer nonconformist with olive skin and a sensitive mouth hidden under a drooping mustache. One of his eyes, cruelly injured in a childhood accident and covered with a milky film, was utterly useless. The other, strained by vicarious functioning, was myopic and enormously enlarged.

In one account of the assignments to the story, Cockerill, "calling upon the indifferent gods for someone instantly to take up the matter," is described as "surprised by a timid request from the shy cub reporter who turned in daily market stuff to be allowed to deal with this tragedy, and after some demur . . . the editor accepted what appeared an inadequate answer from the adjured deities."[1] Cockerill may indeed have found Hearn to be one of the few reporters immediately available. But to suggest that the chief of the news room, out of desperation, would send a cub reporter on a story of such circulation potential is nonsense. Had Cockerill lacked confidence in the youth he could have summoned other reporters. In his two years on the staff Hearn had impressed Cockerill with the vividness and beauty of his writing. The editor chose Hearn because doing so gave the reporter an opportunity to apply his special talents to a crime that gave early promise of many sensational facets.

If assigning Hearn was a gamble, so was Cockerill's decision to sidestep a stodgy rule. The use of news illustrations in weekday issues was all but unheard of. Yet this story could have enormous circulation-building possibilities. Back to the office he called Henry F. Farny and Frank Duveneck, young artists. His orders went something like this:

I want you two to sketch the scene of this murder, any suspects who may be rounded up and anything else that helps tell the story. John Chamberlain, you will pick up the routine details; Hearn, you will do a feature story. And Hearn, this just might be the chance you've been waiting for. Gather every scrap of information, every rumor you can pick up.[2]

Enquirer readers were startled the next morning to see the Tanyard murder story, under a gaudy caption, "Violent Cremation, Saturday Night's Horrible Crime," spread over five columns of the front page. Illustrating this gruesome homicide were the five unprecedented drawings—of Andreas Egner, Fred Egner, George Rufer, the suspects; Freiberg's Tannery, the murder scene; and a diagram of the area indicating locations of the death furnace, Schilling's bedroom, the gate leading to Egner's harness room, stable, tan-bark sheds, water tank, and carriage room.

Noting that the *Enquirer* had just recorded one of the city's largest fires in years, Hearn wrote that "we are called to describe the foulest murder that has ever darkened the escutcheon of our state. A murder so atrocious and so horrible that the soul sickens at its revolting details—a murder that was probably hastened by the fire, for, though vengeance could be the only prompter of two of the accused murderers, FEAR OF A DREADFUL SECRET coming to light may have been partly the impelling motive that urged on the third to the bloody deed. . . . The story, as near as we can obtain it, and divested of unnecessary verbiage, is as follows. . . ." Whereupon Hearn, in five and three-fourths columns of deftly chosen phrases, set before *Enquirer* readers a picture so grim that it must have caused the flesh to crawl upon their bones.[3] In a remarkable understatement Cockerill found it expedient to point out editorially that "our extended story of the murder, accurately illustrated, will command attention, though it provokes shudders." In the Tuesday, November 10, 1874, issue the *Enquirer* proudly noted that its Monday edition was sold out and that "there has been no cessation of calls for it."[4] Hundreds of curious visitors milled around the scene of the crime, comparing what they saw with drawings in the *Enquirer*. Four days after the murder the *Enquirer* commented that "the tannery horror continues to burden our local columns. The morbid appetite is fed today with a continuation of the Coroner's inquest and the confession of the younger Egner. . . . We are not the special advocates of the Christian gallows but society demands an example—a sacrifice. . . ."[5]

If the story was a "burden," it was joyfully and profitably tolerated. Newspapers over the country quoted the *Enquirer*'s account. From the moment of the sellout of all editions and extras November 9,[6] the *Enquirer*'s rejuvenation, already stirring under Cockerill's aegis, shifted into a faster gear. From a miserly circulation that had fluctuated between the 10,000 and 20,000 levels in his first year, the *Enquirer* spurted phenomenally in readership. By 1877, when Cockerill took another assignment, circulation was well on its way to the 90,000 mark.[7]

What made the Tanyard Murder the crime that was different? It had all the elements for sustained interest—sadism, conspiracy, jealousy, sex, color, and suspense. But it had deeper implications. It was human drama that exposed an unflattering side of Cincinnati, opening civic eyes to the wretched conditions that tainted some segments of industry, particularly the leather-making business.

The victim, Herman Schilling, was a young employee who slept in the tannery. Accused of the crime were George Rufer and Andreas Egner and his son, Frederick Egner. The Egners had sworn to kill Schilling because of his affair with Julia Egner, daughter of Andreas. At Egners' Saloon and cooper shop at 153 Findlay Street just west of the tannery, Andreas thought it would be good business to have Julia help wait on customers. She was just under fifteen and already showing a robust promise of womanhood. Her eye-catching figure brightened up Egner's place, a center of leisure for brewers, tanners, and coopers. Julia shortly was found to be as proficient in drawing admirers as in drawing beer. She began yielding to the blandishments of young men, apparently with little discrimination. One of these young men was Herman Schilling. Since Herman then occupied the room next to Julia's, it was not difficult to arrange a clandestine affair in which the two could pursue their amours to their satisfaction.

Julia's shame was discovered. Andreas Egner was a parent of stern tradition, but his moral code, as it turned out, did not deny him the luxury of committing murder. Upon discovering that Julia had entertained well but not wisely in her room, he beat his daughter and drove her out of his house. He vowed vengeance upon Schilling, who, he mistakenly assumed, was his daughter's only lover. Herman was ousted in the same vengeful thrust but remained in the neighborhood, continuing to toil for Henry Freiberg, the tanyard proprietor. Julia paid a heavy price for her dereliction. Seven months pregnant and suffering from cancer, she died in a hospital August 6, 1874. Upon hearing the news the Egners—Andreas and Frederick—thrashed Schilling mercilessly with barrel staves. They failed to kill him then only because bystanders intervened. Schilling had his assailants jailed, fined, and put under a peace bond, insisting he was innocent of any offense to Julia.

George Rufer, like Schilling, worked for Freiberg. Between the two employees a smouldering animosity flared into quarreling. It culminated in Rufer's discharge on the very day of the murder. Out of Rufer's dismissal there was born with the Egners an alliance of hatred toward Schilling. Between ten o'clock and midnight of Saturday, November 7, the trio found Schilling currying a horse used to grind tanbark for fuel. They beat him on the head with clubs, perforated his body with a fork, and thrust him into the tanyard furnace. It was never established whether the victim was dead before he was cremated. When Cockerill's men reached the scene, the police had just removed the half-charred body from its fiery container. Traces of blood could be seen from the boiler room to the stable one hundred feet away. A five-pronged fork with blood and hair and a heavy stick of pine and a broom, blood-soaked, were found on the scene. Police were lacking neither suspects nor motives. The three suspects were quickly arrested, Andreas and his son in the Egner saloon, Rufer nearby.

George Rufer and Andreas Egner were found guilty of first degree murder. The younger Andreas testified against his father, who insisted his son was not a party to the crime. Both Andreas Egner and George Rufer were sentenced to be hanged July 13, 1875, but their date with the gibbet was never kept. The Supreme Court of Ohio reversed the judgment of the Mailton County Court and remanded the cases for new trials. Fred Egner, who had never been brought to trial, languished in jail for two years, charged with nothing but valued as a witness. Andreas was tried again, convicted on the same charge, and sentenced to life in prison. He served a few years, became ill of tuberculosis, and was granted a conditional pardon. Rufer eventually was found guilty of second degree murder. He, too, was pardoned ten years later by William McKinley and promptly disappeared.

There were so many ramifications to the Tanyard Murder that Cockerill found it easy to keep it alive for many months. It was a gruesome, brutal crime, but even more fascinating to *Enquirer* readers were the motivations and the characters of the principals. By an odd circumstance Schilling suffered from an eye defect, enabling *Enquirer* reporter Hearn to identify himself with the victim. A man of deep compassion, Hearn could see through the sordid outer events and reveal the hearts of the pathetic people whose livelihood stemmed from the industrial jungle of a growing city. Julia Egner as the feminine lead in this tragedy lost nothing in the *Enquirer*'s portrayal:

She was very fair, with that waxy, mezzotint complexion almost peculiar to American-born German girls; very plump, bright and playfully saucy, and possessing quite a graceful and womanly figure, although only between fifteen and sixteen years of age. Her father was never very kind to her . . . and it is well known that he made use of her beauty to decoy customers to his saloon.

It is not to be wondered that the poor girl, thus exposed by her own father to every possible temptation, should in her youth and giddiness and affectionate disposition fall as hundreds of young women, far more carefully brought up, have fallen. . . .

Julia had many lovers, long before Herman was found in her bedroom. They used to climb in at night through the window of her bedroom. The guilt of her seduction does not lie upon the memory of the unhappy man who was so terribly sacrificed; and the father is not less to blame than the real criminal.[8]

Cockerill's "big story" held strong social implications skilfully emphasized by the managing editor. In a Sunday feature following the murder story Hearn, at the Colonel's request, did a story describing the district in which Schilling had been stuffed into a furnace. The candor of "The Quarter of Shambles,"[9] a word picture of slaughterhouses, rendering plants, candle factories, hog pens, tanneries, the atmosphere heavy with the stench of animals, rats in dung heaps, street lights at night hanging over the slimy pavements like yellow goblin eyes, shocked Cincinnatians. Serene Cincinnati began to see beyond the murder. Leading citizens outside the City Hall clique were outraged; the result was a tortuously slow reform movement yielding improvements in sanitation and other health measures.

If John A. Cockerill had left written impressions of those whom he started on distinguished literary or journalistic careers, we could draw on a priceless commentary on the editor's adeptness in spotting and nurturing talent. He did leave a brief account of his hiring of perhaps the most colorful, exotic, and gifted of all Cockerill recruits—Lafcadio Hearn. It is possible the Colonel may have foreseen a greater future for Hearn than for any other Cockerill protégé. Since Hearn's death in 1904 several biographies have appeared. O. W. Frost's *Young Hearn* finds that appreciation of Hearn's novels is growing. Other biographers say he will be ranked alongside that other romanticist Edgar Allan Poe. Cockerill, after a talk with Hearn in Japan twenty-three years after their first meeting in Cincinnati, wrote that the author is "as remarkable in literature as Goldsmith, Keats or Shelley."[10]

Recalling their first interview in 1872, the Colonel filled in some details: "One day there came to my office a quaint, dark-skinned little fellow, strangely diffident, wearing glasses of great magnifying power, and bearing with him evidence that Fortune and he were scarcely on nodding terms."[11] Tense and wretched with shyness, Hearn had paced up and down the hall outside Cockerill's office at the *Enquirer*, seeking courage to go inside—and failing. It was only when the Colonel opened the door and found him there that in a soft, shrinking voice Hearn asked whether the editor ever paid for outside contributions. Recalled Cockerill:

I informed him that I was somewhat restricted in the matter of expenditures, but that I would give consideration to whatever he had to offer. He drew from under his coat a manuscript and tremblingly laid it upon my table. Then he stole away like a distorted brownie, leaving behind him an impression that was uncanny and indescribable. Later I looked over the contribution. I was astonished to find it charmingly written in the purest and strongest English.

I printed the article and the next day the writer called for his money, which, as I remember, I paid from my own exchequer. He wrote more. I paid him inadequately. Later he had a steady job for a salary so ridiculously low that I am ashamed to recall the fact. But those were the days of cold, small things. ... His great bulbous eye would rest as closely to the paper as his nose would permit while he scratched away with beaver-like diligence, giving me no more annoyance than a bronze ornament.[12]

Cockerill shrewdly nurtured the scholarly tone his new find was lending the *Enquirer*. Among Hearn's initial offerings paid for at space rates was a long review of the Gareth and Lynette episode of the *Idylls of the King*. This infusion of literary flavor was unusual if not new to Midwestern journalism. Cockerill encouraged it and Publisher McLean, in the wake of spiraling circulation figures, overcame whatever misgivings he may have had. By the summer of 1873 Hearn was installed as a regular space-rate contributor. His high output was made to order for the *Enquirer*'s Sunday edition, started in 1854 and widely regarded as the first in the country. "I have known him to write twelve to fifteen columns of matter for a single issue," Cockerill recalled.[13]

Upon the basis of his performance in the Schilling murder story Cockerill raised Hearn's salary to $25 a week, a sum large enough to signify superior rating as a reporter. This status had not come easily. The Colonel found his recruit initially so shy that he assigned him a desk in his own office. "He was sensitive as a flower," the Colonel said. "An unkind word was as serious to him as a cut from a whip lash."[14] Under the Colonel's wing young Hearn was tranquil and prolific. But his diffidence was a serious barrier. The little reporter did not mind mingling in a crowd to gather information, but "if Hearn was sent to interview anyone, the person would have to come out into the street and invite him in or he would come back empty-handed."[15] Cockerill was obliged to put him for a period on market reports, civic meetings, and feature assignments. He was soon aware that Hearn could not write what reporters call a "straight news story." He was at his artistic best in the off-beat approach. "The classics were at his fingertips," the Colonel said. "He was poetic and his whole nature seemed attuned to the beautiful, and he wrote beautifully of things that were neither wholesome nor inspiring. As a member of the city staff his descriptive powers developed. He prowled dark corners and from gruesome places he dug out charming, idyllic stories. . . ."[16]

But always there was that shyness—or almost always. Cockerill, finding that Hearn was responsive to unusual assignments, suggested a daring subject. Would Hearn care to visit a studio and write a story of an artist painting a nude? He expected the young reporter to decline the order in embarrassment. To his surprise Hearn uttered not a word of dissent. Later in the day there lay on Cockerill's desk a glowing appreciation of a nude female model. While it was mildly sensational, the word picture was entirely lacking in improprieties or innuendoes.[17] The story appeared the next day captioned

"Beauty Undraped." It was the first time any Cincinnati newspaper had breached conventionality to that extent. Cockerill half expected a summons to the publisher's office, but not a word of official protest was uttered, and circulation continued its merry upward trend.

Behind the comfortable façade of the city, Cockerill knew, there lay poverty, cruelty, destitution, low wages, crime, superstition, corruption, exploitation, and ignorance that should be exposed. Hearn's reading of Poe, Bulwer-Lytton, and the French romanticists had turned the reporter's interests "toward the quivering fantasy underneath life's prosaic vestments" but in Cincinnati what lay underneath was no fantasy. Cockerill possessed a driving curiosity to see what that lower layer actually was.

His name established by the Tanyard Murder story, Hearn became the Colonel's eyes and ears in assignments that opened the eyes and ears of *Enquirer* readers. He sent the young journalist to probe the privations of poorly paid women in the clothing industry, to expose fakes in spiritualism, to portray life in the city dump. In potter's field he interviewed a sexton found to be conspiring with body snatchers from a medical school. He horrified readers with a story on abortionists, and he inspired public contempt of chicanery among dealers in second-hand tombstones. *Enquirer* word pictures spread into many areas to reveal levee life, opium haunts, slaughter-houses, fertilizer plants, and medical-school dissecting rooms. The *Enquirer* enlightened its readers on butlers, laundry workers, firemen, undertakers, policemen, actors, opium smokers, saloon keepers, leech doctors, bird stores, and suicides. Material was gathered from pickpockets, counterfeiters, and escaped convicts.

About a reporter with limited vision an intriguing question poses itself: How much information came from what Hearn saw and how much was fabricated by imagination? While myopia blurs outlines and details, experts say it lets color come through undimmed, giving it greater comparative value. As a myope Hearn had adjusted to a dimness of vision quite effectively. There is no record of his visual accuracy having been challenged by those viewing the same scene. Indeed it appears that Hearn "saw" too much. A biographer contends that it was his adeptness in exposing religious fanatics, bigots, quacks, charlatans, and corrupt politicians, rather than his affair with a mulatto, that led to his discharge.[18] He wrote so well that many readers became uncomfortable; he was stripping Cincinnati down to its unqueenly worst.

If Hearn's exposures brought embarrassment to the city fathers, his private life conspired to make Managing Editor Cockerill and the *Enquirer* management even more uncomfortable. At the Haslam boarding house he had met Althea Foley, a handsome mulatto of seventeen who served the household as cook. A waif just as Hearn had been, she was born into slavery. She drifted to Cincinnati with her quadroon son, who was born out of wedlock when she was fourteen, a souvenir of an encounter with a white man. Hearn, to whom race prejudice was as irrational as religion, found Althea a girl with whom he could feel at ease. Barred from associating with his mental equals by a near-psychopathic feeling of inferiority caused by his small stature and defective eyes, Hearn possessed a strong sexual drive that made the cook seem desirable.

Both were pariahs, both had known hunger, both knew what it meant not to be wanted. As their acquaintanceship grew, they were drawn together in a recital of experiences in troubled youth. Althea felt attracted to the olive-skinned reporter with the gentle voice, beautiful words, and evident interest in her. It was inevitable that in the dead of a Plum Street night the two strays should find themselves in each other's arms. Hearn wanted to marry Althea but there were obstacles. It was illegal for a white to marry a Negro. He knew there would be social condemnation. But hadn't he been disapproved of all his life? He refused to consider what the marriage might do to his job. Cockerill and other colleagues, learning of his intention, sought to dissuade him.

Accounts differ on what happened. One source says the two were married after Hearn obtained a marriage license by withholding the fact that Althea was partly Negro, and that a colored Episcopal minister performed the ceremony. Yet after Hearn's death Althea's claim to a widow's share of his estate was denied. The court said such a marriage was performed by fraud. Whatever the facts, the report was soon out that Hearn had married a Negro. Hearn did not help his case by displaying a waspish temper when the subject came up in the office. His temper affected his writing. Exposures became diatribes.[19] Hearn could not understand that he had become a public figure and that his private life mattered.

A dilemma confronted Cockerill. Something had to be done to tone down the writing of his star reporter, who became resentful, even defiant. Deletions and revisions of his copy increased. Trying to reason with Hearn was unavailing. Cockerill found his ace reporter with no appreciation of the awkward position Hearn's reported marriage to a mulatto and his intemperate prose had created for Cockerill and the *Enquirer*. With a heavy heart Cockerill, in July of 1875, fired his finest writer.[20] Despite the dismissal the Colonel and Hearn remained close friends.

In the Colonel's appraisal of newspaper personnel the reporter held the top role. Editors, circulation men, advertising salesmen, the business office are necessary, but without reporters who can dig out the news and write it accurately and colorfully, newspapers, in Cockerill's view, could not exist. No one more than the *Enquirer* editor realized Hearn's contribution as reporter to the newspaper's success. Conceivably Hearn, with all of his eccentricities, would have been the Colonel's choice of reporters who had most to do with Cockerill's individual achievement in guiding the little known *Enquirer* to national prominence. Cockerill had found in Hearn the reporter who made it possible for the *Enquirer*, as no newspaper had so effectively done prior to the Tanyard Murder, to capitalize on sensationalism. And all the while readership was building up to give Cockerill a massive audience for a powerful and respected editorial page, a realm in which he exercised the master's touch.

At the Cincinnati *Commercial*, under editor Murat Halstead, Hearn resumed his newspaper career. There he persisted in writing with frightening candor. Rumors reached the *Enquirer* that Halstead was likewise obliged to wield the blue pencil on Hearn's copy. Hearn, although he stuck with Halstead for nearly three years, could not produce the circulation gain the *Commercial* counted on. In 1878 he fled to New Orleans, ostensibly to cover a political story for the Cincinnati *Gazette*. He never returned. There his prolific pen began to interest book publishers. After a tour of the West Indies and a period in New York he went to Japan, where, having been estranged from Althea, he married a Japanese girl. At Tokyo Imperial University he took over the professorship of foreign literature and continued what he loved most—to write, write, write.

VII. Fortune Made—Exit Editor

What kind of person was the furious young man who was masterminding the Cincinnati *Enquirer* before he had turned thirty? John Cockerill, pushing the six-foot mark, seemed curiously to be both compact and tall. He weighed about 180 pounds, and in the twenty-odd years left to him his weight varied little from this figure. The editor is shown in *Enquirer* pictures to have acquired a mustache that all but concealed his mouth. His dark hair, parted in the middle, lay flat over an expansive forehead. Penetrating eyes set beneath bushy, well-arched eyebrows gave visitors an impression that his mood could shift instantly from deep compassion to stern impatience. A discerning observer could sense in the Colonel's manner a readiness to dispose quickly of timewasters, crackpots and

promoters who habitually descend upon editors. Socially the
Colonel was popular. A dominant figure in the newsroom,
Cockerill could be debonair and amusing at the dinner table
or on the dance floor. On the infrequent occasions when the
pressures at the *Enquirer* office lightened, the Colonel and the
girl he chose to squire around—always a beauty—drew ad-
miring glances. After the Tanyard Murder story the Colonel
was increasingly in the public eye. Inevitably his dashing,
elegantly attired figure, showing up in Pike's Opera House,
Debalt's Restaurant, in saloons or hotel lobbies, produced
a little hush as curious eyes took him in.

Nothing endears public figures to newspapermen more
than color. The Colonel himself possessed that indefinable
quality. But some of his traits would be poorly rated in a
Sunday School discussion. In his years as a Cincinnati editor
Cockerill developed a flair for ribaldry to the point where
he could mix sarcasm and blasphemy with hair-singeing effect.
Woe to the blundering reporter or subeditor who might draw
the Colonel's wrath! Cockerill was brought up by a church-
minded family but at an early age was exposed to rough and
unschooled men in the extremes of suffering and conviviality.
The Civil War enriched the Colonel's off-color vocabulary.

Editor Cockerill enjoyed fastening pseudonyms on Cincinnatians whose names were in the news. The more prominent
they were the more likely were they to find themselves with
new titles. The Colonel's friend, Jacob Aug, became "Cardinal" Aug; A. C. Sands, a United States marshal, was "Arch-
bishop"; Thomas Hartshoren, sportsman, took his nickname
"Thomas Ammonia" to the grave.

Among his associates at the *Enquirer* Cockerill was more
admired than loved. He exercised a ceaseless drive over members of his staff but never spared himself. He was an efficient
human dynamo capable of emitting sparks of rage. Many
seasoned reporters were afraid and neophytes were terrified
of him. Their greatest apprehension lay in bringing down a
fierce contempt of some mark of incompetence. The hottest

sparks erupted from "dynamo" Cockerill when he encountered resistance to his vows to shake the *Enquirer* out of its traditional concepts in presenting the news.

The Colonel learned much from the mushrooming circulation growing out of the Tanyard Murder case. In the protracted coverage of this celebrated crime the editor saw the birth of a new pattern in handling the news—in pictures and in writing style. The pioneering tanyard sketches and diagrams had heightened interest immeasurably in stories of the crime. While other papers remained skeptical, the *Enquirer* stepped up its use of illustrations. As his career advanced, so did the evolution of newspaper art, moving from the painfully slow and awkward sketching process into the half-tone method of reproducing photographs. Colonel Cockerill realized the possibilities of tempting newsstand buyers by spotting front-page pictures above the fold of the newspaper.

But it was still an era not of picture-lookers but of readers. Aware of this the Colonel resolved that the *Enquirer* should capitalize on the surge of interest in the Schilling cremation. He set in motion what cannot be termed less than a revolution in news-writing style. Writing for the *Journalist*, the newspaperman's bible, ten years later when Cockerill was in New York, O. H. Rothacker dubbed the Colonel the best news editor in the country. "Much of the new birth of the Cincinnati *Enquirer*," he wrote, "was due to John Cockerill's keen instincts. He is the best exponent as he is also the father of the peculiar school of journalism to which both the *Enquirer* and the *World* belong."[1]

Cockerill was convinced that readability would be enhanced by an unorthodox style. Newspaper prose had been labored, opinionated, and packed with tortuously long and stilted sentences. Exponents of the modern short-sentence cult, reading the Colonel's prose, may wonder where the improvement lay until they compare Cockerill's style with the news-writing that characterized the daily press up to the Cockerill revolution. The Colonel's exhortation to reporters may well have gone something like this: "Cut down on the length of your sentences. After all, there is a limit to the reader's patience. If you're determined to ramble, don't write." Dull and ponderous stories were returned to the reporters' desks with curt memos asking that they be "brightened up." Reporters who could not make the grade in the new school of journalism were asked to withdraw from the *Enquirer*. The Colonel's formula was profitable. The *Enquirer*'s counting-house at 247 Vine Street well before the middle seventies testified that the newspaper's rebirth was no fluke.

But to the dismay of the editor the *Enquirer*'s prosperity heightened the political ambitions of his friend, John Ray McLean, the young publisher. Washington McLean, in preparation for conveying his interest in the paper to his son, had sent the young man to Harvard and Heidelberg for culture. He hoped to send young McLean through the lower echelons of the newspaper to get the feel of the business. Young McLean had other ideas: he wanted to be a professional baseball player. Out of the father's persuasive methods came what must have been the first "bonus" ever paid a player not to sign up. The bonus, in cash, was a tidy sum. The unhidden persuader delivered John Ray McLean into journalism and deep involvement with Colonel Cockerill. John McLean was not a great editor or publisher. But, vested with his father's interest and reaping the profits of Colonel Cockerill's regeneration, he was eventually able to buy out James Faran's stock.[2]

John McLean aspired to his father's political prestige. To the distress of Cockerill he chose to advance his personal objectives through the columns of the *Enquirer*, thus sowing the first seeds of distrust in the mind of his managing editor. Alvin F. Harlow, a student of the Cincinnati scene, wrote that "for forty years the *Enquirer* was the voice of John McLean the politician yearning for office . . . governor, senator, anything, which he never won."[3] In 1889 he was the unsuccessful Democratic candidate for governor of Ohio. In the 1896 Democratic National Convention he polled 54 votes as a candidate for the presidential nomination and 296 for the vice presidential nomination.

McLean, although not brilliant, was not stupid. He leaned heavily on Cockerill's editorial skills and executive ability. The Colonel did not hesitate to keep a steady, sane hand at the helm, trying and usually succeeding in toning down McLean's nightmarish schemes for promoting McLean. The *Enquirer*'s irrepressible proprietor started stoking his political fires in forthright fashion. He would stand in front of the *Enquirer* building to let the passersby know who he was. They saw a stylish dresser and, except for oversized eyes, a handsome man. In this posture of affluence McLean, when the mood struck him, would hand out coins. To the "gentlemen of the road" he passed quarters; men who looked worthy got half-dollars; needy men with families could count on dollars while the money lasted.[4] One day Cockerill, en route to lunch, stepped out of the building. He was all but mobbed by a large and noisily angry group of decrepit-looking characters. "Where's our money?" shouted the spokesman. Among the world of ne'er-do-wells word of McLean's share-the-wealth program had spread at rocket-like speed. Before all of the would-be beneficiaries could assemble, the publisher had either tired of his game or emptied his purse. Cockerill had caught the overflow of growling late-comers.

McLean managed to attain a political prominence of dubious value. As a Democratic leader, he formed an alliance with a shyster criminal lawyer and rising Republican boss, Thomas C. Campbell. The city had soured on the disgraceful administration of Mayor G. W. C. Johnston. The McLean-Campbell coalition was huckstered as a reform movement. With the two parties in an amiable but nefarious partnership the election thus resulted in a siege of lawlessness and graft that made the Johnston regime look lamblike in comparison. The new mayor was Robert M. Moore. He wore a rose on his coat; he was a gracious City Hall host serving crab apple cider (applejack to those of stronger tastes), but he had no idea of what a mayor was supposed to do. He was owned by McLean and Campbell.

McLean's peculiar political ties posed an uncomfortable barrier for John Cockerill that he never surmounted to his own satisfaction. Street-walking and prostitution, for instance, thrived in the Moore regime. Because of the *Enquirer* publisher's involvement, Colonel Cockerill was obliged to read in a competing newspaper exposés that should have been reported in his own paper. The rival *Gazette* not only designated Longworth Street between Plum and Central Avenues as a red light district, but printed the names and addresses of twenty brothels. A reporter accompanied two policemen on a tour of the area. The officers went, not to preserve the peace, but to accept a "monthly tithe" from every madam on the street. Collections were made as casually as any landlord picking up the monthly rent. This was part of the payoff that swelled the political grafters' coffers. The administration was expert in collecting tribute but negligent in service to the city. The streets were so persistently neglected that on some thoroughfares merchants took up collections for their own clean-up programs.

John McLean's political aspirations were blocked, locally, for a time by the rise to power of a young Republican saloon keeper, George Barnsdale Cox. The son of an English immigrant, Cox was a party poll watcher at eighteen, a city councilman at twenty-four, and a tower of party strength at thirty. He knew how to win city elections. The Cox machine sidetracked the Campbell-McLean combine but without discernible benefit to the city. Colonel Cockerill was relieved when McLean no longer had a personal political interest in city government. It meant a termination of reporting restraints that prevailed when the *Enquirer*'s publisher was involved in the administration.

McLean's political hopes did not die easily. In 1895, long after Cockerill's departure, with an eye to promoting his political objectives in New York, he acquired the *Morning Journal* from Albert Pulitzer, the younger, less gifted brother of Joseph Pulitzer. Sources differ on what the Cincinnatian paid for the paper, one says a million dollars, another $360,000. The *Journal* appealed to McLean as the vehicle on which he could ride politically in grander scale than he deemed possible in Cincinnati.

As a one-cent paper the *Journal* had somehow managed to survive since 1882 when Albert Pulitzer founded it on capital of $25,000. McLean made his first mistake when he jumped the price to two cents per copy. His biggest mistake was having no John Cockerill at the editorial helm. McLean found himself outclassed in the fast company of the *World, Sun, Tribune, Herald* and other New York journals. His ardor cooled fast as week after week he diverted from *Enquirer* profits funds to cover *Journal* losses. When a buyer offered $180,000 for the ailing *Journal*, the gout-ridden McLean winced but accepted. The sale set up a young, rich publisher from California in establishing the mightiest newspaper empire in the world. The new owner was William Randolph Hearst. John McLean's New York fiasco put the Cincinnatian's political ambition on permanent skids, but he made up for his setbacks in other ways. His holdings in banks, utilities, and railroads were enormous and lucrative.

Cockerill was forever finding himself in association with men ranging in flavor from the eccentric to the brilliant. In the latter category was Joseph Burbridge McCullagh, whose influence upon the Cockerill career, while incalculable, must have been considerable. The Irish-born journalist, three years Cockerill's senior, was a nationally known war correspondent, a Civil War hero, and had been a confidant of Andrew Johnson. He had been printer and reporter in New York, St. Louis, and, of course, Cincinnati. McCullagh's passion for editorial independence could not have escaped young Cockerill's attention. In subsequent years in St. Louis McCullagh is said to

have barred the editorial department to any business office
man, lest his staff become commercially tainted.

McCullagh's political background intrigued Cockerill. He
had been General John C. Fremont's body guard. As a lieutenant aboard a gunboat he had been under fire at Fort
Donelson. As a correspondent for the Cincinnati *Gazette*, he
had written battle reports unflattering to the Union forces.
When the *Gazette* deleted the adverse portions, he switched
to the Cincinnati *Commercial,* where his reportorial skills were
more warmly appreciated. As a Washington correspondent he
became a favorite of Andrew Johnson, who often used the
McCullagh dispatches to Cincinnati as political trial balloons.

Young Cockerill was fascinated by McCullagh's stories of
life in the capital. He relished the one pertaining to Andrew
Johnson's difficulties on the day he became vice president of
the United States. McCullagh and another newsman, in a
Senate committee room prior to the ceremony, watched as
Johnson poured himself a half tumbler of whiskey. Johnson
downed it and unsteadily made for the Senate chamber, where
the inauguration was then conducted. As the oath was administered Johnson responded with a dazed look and half-
audible words. The new Vice President was plain drunk, but
McCullagh always insisted he was not a drunkard. In the
subsequent feud between Johnson and Congress, McCullagh
championed the President's cause, he said, out of sympathy
for the underdog.

In a poem "Little Mack," by Eugene Field, Cockerill
found himself mentioned in a tribute to McCullagh:

> I've heard 'em tell of Dana, and
>   of Bonner, and of Reid,
> Of Johnny Cockerill, who, I'll own, is
>   very smart indeed;
> Yet I don't care what their renown
>   or influence may be,
> Our metropolitan exchanges are
>   quite enough for me.

So keep your Danas, Bonners, Reids, your
   Cockerills and the rest,
The woods is full of better men, all
   through the woolly West.
For all the sleek, pretentious eastern
   editorial pack
We wouldn't swap the shadow of
   our Little Mack.[5]

McCullagh remained at the *Enquirer* only a few months after the Colonel's arrival. Cockerill and McCullagh would later find themselves in St. Louis as rival editors. With his brother, John W., McCullagh moved to Chicago, where the latter was in charge of the *Republican* until the 1871 fire destroyed his newspaper. By 1875 he was installed as editor of the St. Louis *Globe-Democrat*. There he resided until his death in 1896 in a fall from a bedroom window.

In May, 1872, John Cockerill met a young Missourian by the name of Joseph Pulitzer. As representative of the St. Louis *Westliche Post*, a German newspaper, the tall, gangling, red-mustached Pulitzer was in Cincinnati for the national convention of the disgruntled liberal wing of the Republican party. Pulitzer's boss, Carl Schurz, *Westliche Post* editor, and B. Gratz Brown, governor of Missouri, had inspired a Republican rump movement bent on unseating President Ulysses S. Grant. Its platform was reconciliation with the South, civil service reform, and reduction of the tariff. Editors, rather than politicians, composed the core of the split-off. Pulitzer was at the convention as delegate, convention secretary, and newspaper correspondent. It was in the latter two capacities that he was confronted by Cockerill, representing the *Enquirer*. Within minutes they had discovered mutual interests—in politics, in journalism. Their Cincinnati association ended with unspoken but deeply felt admiration for each other.

Nominated for president by the Liberal Republican convention was Horace Greeley, renowned editor of the New York *Tribune*. Ticketed for vice president was Pulitzer's friend,

Governor Brown of Missouri. The convention of the Democratic party, convinced its only chance to gain national power was to back Grant's opponents, swallowed its pride and also nominated Greeley for president. The *Tribune*, which had espoused many contradictory political positions represented in the Liberal Republican party, in 1866 had branded the Democrats as "the traitorous section of Northern politics." The anti-Grant movement was a dud almost from its inception. The Liberal Republicans could agree on nothing except their opposition to Grant. It was under this handicap that Cockerill's *Enquirer*, editorially, and Pulitzer, on the platform of sixty political rallies, tried futilely to sell Greeley and the liberal program. In the election Grant and the Radical machine carried all but six states. Pulitzer withdrew from the Republican fold and thereafter was a Democrat, like his new friend John Cockerill.

John Cockerill's first taste of presidential politics had occurred shortly after his arrival in Cincinnati. Publisher Washington McLean hoped to win the nomination for "Gentleman George" H. Pendleton and thereby assure himself, if Pendleton was elected, of a seat in the White House inner circle. John Cockerill was necessarily a key man because he wrote the stories of Pendleton's candidacy. Pendleton had served in the United States Senate and House of Representatives. He was credited with a heavy assist in Civil Service reform. The genial, colorful Cincinnatian made good copy but a defection of strength in Indiana forced his withdrawal. Pendleton, who was married to Alice Key, daughter of Francis Scott Key, author of "Star-Spangled Banner," was subsequently appointed U. S. minister to Germany.

To those who frequented Aug's Clubhouse, where the Pendleton strategy was mapped, the Colonel was a more interesting figure than Pendleton or McLean. As the years rolled on they took pride in noting the Colonel's newspaper proclivities. One of them, in a nostalgic bit for the *Enquirer*, wrote:

Always connected with Aug's Clubhouse must be the personality of John A. Cockerill. His abilities in newspaper business were so conspicuous that other great owners of papers in other cities . . . secured his services after his several years as editor and correspondent for the *Enquirer*. . . . On the *Enquirer* he did much fine writing, with a diction interspersed at times with fascinating humor and at others with a bitterness of invective startling to Cincinnati. . . .[6]

For Cockerill the *Enquirer*'s seven-column editorial page provided a vehicle for his developing writing and editing talents. It was in this role that the power and punch of the Cockerill editorial paragraph first came into their own. Below its one-column masthead at the upper left-hand corner the *Enquirer* prefaced its editorials with a quotation, two paragraphs on markets, and the weather forecast. It printed up to forty-five editorials per issue, opening with one-sentence thrusts and continuing with increasingly longer discussions. The three right-hand columns were a potpourri of terse comments lifted from other publications and letters, often followed by editor's notes. Cockerill realized that letters increased readership, but he used only those that were short and to the point.

The *Enquirer* files of 1876 and 1877 reveal its vigorous support of the Democratic cause in what was then the closest presidential election in American history. The paper backed Samuel J. Tilden in his race with Republican Rutherford B. Hayes. The *Enquirer* portrayed the Republicans and Hayes as the party and spokesman of wealth and privilege. The opposition, said the *Enquirer*, kept open the wounds of the War between the States, boasted of a false prosperity, and rendered itself unfit to hold the reins of government. As the *Enquirer* bore down upon its political foes, the Colonel loosed such verbal missiles as:

A solid North elected Mr. Lincoln in 1860, but the whole country will elect Mr. Tilden next Tuesday.[7]

The Republicans had another big street demonstration last night. They have money in abundance and are not afraid to use it.[8]

The Republican statesmen in Ohio and Indiana will try the effect of money upon a disconsolate people this week. Big meetings, big noises and big swindles constitute this program.[9]

The United States government, we presume, never borrows any money in Europe. The capitalists of Europe simply loan money to the Republican party.[10]

If the Republican party can only succeed in arresting Democrats enough, with high-handed lawlessness, they may carry a few doubtful precincts in the country. But the purpose of the people cannot be arrested.[11]

For "the Republican party's pet stumper" the Colonel had a few acid words:

Robert G. Ingersoll declares that of "all the religions that have been produced by the egotism, the malice, the ignorance and ambition of man, Presbyterianism is the most hideous." Their synods he calls shebangs and the Saviour they worship he calls a bastard. He also has an ill opinion of the Democratic party.[12]

The rhetorical cuffing of Ingersoll subsequently took an ironic twist. John Cockerill later would find himself on the Republican side of the fence and, as president of the New York Press Club, entreating Ingersoll to address that organization.

Colonel Cockerill's sense of fair play moved him at times to censure the intemperance of Democratic partisans. A reader in an open letter wrote: "Don't vote for a man [Hayes] who, if he enters the White House, may be jerked out and rammed into the penitentiary." Managing Editor Cockerill wrote that "Mr. Hayes' tax returns were very faulty. His blooded cattle listed at $12.50 [a reference to an appraisal per head] may return to plague his conscience. But we do not believe he has been guilty of a penitentiary offense. Mr. O'Connor should use milder language."[13]

The *Enquirer* pecked away at what it labeled the Republicans' false prosperity theme. "People know whether they are prosperous," wrote the Colonel. "No amount of newspaper sophistry can convince the voters that times are not hard. And the beauty of it is they know whom to hold responsible."[14]

The *Enquirer* saved its heaviest bludgeons for Cincinnati's two Hayes-supporting journals, the *Commercial* and the *Gazette*:

The *Commercial* was in the business of manufacturing prosperity again yesterday. Tomorrow the *Gazette* doubtless will shout, "The mills are roaring. . . ." While investigating this prosperity on paper, let us turn over a page and look at the commercial reports in those Republican journals which say the land floweth with milk and honey. They will furnish better evidence . . . that pig iron is selling at $20. . . . When [Republicans] were protesting that Greeley's election would ruin business, pig iron sold for as much as $60 per ton.

As further signs of the pseudo-prosperity the *Enquirer* took pains to point to pork at 7 cents per pound, flour at $3 per barrel and corn at 48 cents per bushel, "all scandalously low." Realizing the "hard times" theme might have local repercussions, the Colonel clarified the *Enquirer*'s position:

It is not our business to decry our city. . . . we prefer to build our party up without putting our city down. Cincinnati is as prosperous as any city in the West. But our business men do not fail to see that the prosperity literature in the Republican press is an electioneering trick. Readers of the *Commercial* and *Gazette* do not suppose that any sane man of affairs would, when interviewed, tell his competitors and the world that he was running tremendously behindhand. This element in human nature robs these interviews that exhale wealth of some significance. It is suspicious, too, that those interviewed are Republicans.

In another jab the Colonel cited "history":

Four years ago the country listened to the appeal of the bankers, and elected Grant. The bankers said that there would be no business security, no general prosperity, if the Democratic party succeeded. Grant was elected, and six months after his inauguration came the panic of 1873.[15]

During the campaign the Boston *Post* was an admirer of the *Enquirer* and did not hesitate to say so. "A good newspaper exercises a far more potent influence in a political campaign than a score of stump speakers, however eloquent," wrote the *Post*'s editor. "As such a paper we recognize the Cincinnati *Enquirer,* which has distanced its Ohio contemporaries by the vigor, enterprise and ability with which it is helping on the campaign."[16]

A count of the popular vote justified the *Enquirer*'s confidence, as the presidential election campaign ended, that Tilden would win. Tilden's popular vote was 4,284,757 to Hayes' 4,033,950. Not until March 2, 1877, did the *Enquirer* and the nation learn that Rutherford B. Hayes was the new President. Some historians to this day contend that Samuel J. Tilden was robbed of the presidency. The twenty-two electoral votes of Florida, Oregon, Louisiana, and South Carolina were disputed. Congress created an Electoral Commission that ruled, by a straight party-line vote (eight Republicans to seven Democrats), that Hayes had won the electoral votes in question. The decision gave the Republican nominee 185 electoral votes to 184 for Tilden.

Politics did not monopolize the editorial page. Some nonpolitical topics claimed attention:

"The Pope [intermittently ailing and recovering] is very sick again." Brush up those obituary notices.[17]

A boy in Jersey City was teasing the monkey which accompanied an organ grinder. The animal became infuriated and bit the boy severely. The organ grinder was locked up.—New York *Graphic.*

That's the way with American justice. Why wasn't the monkey sent to prison?[18]

The *Enquirer* is a good organ. It ought to have a post office [an allusion to a popular form of political spoilage].—Columbus *Journal.*

We prefer journalism to post offices. We have no time to waste, setting up traps for dishonest clerks.[19]

Editor Cockerill through the *Enquirer* hit hard at two targets, the Prohibitionists, whom he derided as ill-advised crusaders, and bigots. We return to a political angle only to illustrate, in two items, the Colonel's disaffection with the two groups:

The Cincinnati *Enquirer*, having failed to prove that Milton Barnes [a Republican candidate for office] is a Prohibitionist, has started the report that he is a drunkard, that he was intoxicated at Zanesville during a recent visit, and, in short, that he is a wine-bibber and a beer-drinker who chips in with Republicans and sinners.—Columbus *Journal*.

Comment by the *Enquirer*: Mr. Barnes is a Crusader and a bigot of the worst stripe. Finding himself losing caste among the liberal men, he attempted to "square himself" by drinking a little wine at Zanesville. . . . It is quite common with sneaks and hypocrites of the Barnes school to do this sort of thing, but it only serves to bring them into contempt.[20]

The editor of the *American Israelite* was quoted on the Milton Barnes controversy thus:

We think a man with such perverted and theocratic notions of government is unfit for public office. If those who nominated him and hold him up for public support knew all about this, then they ought to be politically shunned as an undemocratic and corrupt element, as they must know that no republic with a religious test can exist in this century, and that the letter and spirit of the Constitution of the United States are hostile to all the theological tests and all legislation against personal freedom.[21]

To which the Colonel editorially agreed, adding: "It is the narrowness, the bigotry, the prejudices of the party that nominates such men which should be rebuked more than Barnes himself."

Although Cockerill used strong language freely and continuously, there is no record that he ever involved the *Enquirer* in a libel suit. Skins apparently were not so tender then and rarely needed the balm of damages through litigation.

Once the younger McLean's political irons were out of the fire, the *Enquirer* under Cockerill did not hesitate to dig into and expose unsavory government practices. One such revelation dealt with "professional" jurymen. It revealed how unqualified citizens were chosen for jury duty through favoritism. The disclosures resulted in greater care in checking on the qualifications of veniremen.

The Colonel won the affections of Cincinnatians with his civic pride. A slight to the city's prestige made the *Enquirer* indignant. It happened, to borrow Cockerill's words, "when some ignorant and ill-paid herder from the plains, who holds a position on the Chicago *Tribune*," used a belittling figure of 200,000 as Cincinnati's population of 1876. "The last federal census showed a population of 218,000," wrote the Colonel, "and more than 20,000 people have since been added by annexation. These facts should be kept prominently before the citizens of the Mortgaged City" [referring to Chicago as the city of floundering finances].[22]

In the thick of the Hayes-Tilden campaign the *Enquirer* was capable of a change of pace. Using as a news peg the opening week of plays at the Grand Opera House, the *Enquirer* was an ardent, even eloquent, exponent of the drama:

We have called it [the drama] a teacher; it is the greatest of instructors, being the most comprehensive. It summons all the arts to its aid—architecture, sculpture, music, pictures, poetry, romance, oratory. The high errand of the drama is its contributions to literature. The geniuses among poets have been the dramatists from Aeschylus till today. History and poetry and love have found their way from the soul of genius to mankind through the avenue of the drama and the stage. Virtue never triumphs on that miniature world that the audience does not applaud; vice is never punished that the hearts in front do not throb quicker with delight. The stage is travel, history, biography, society, as well as poetry and romance. It is palace and hut, splendor and squalor; it is life and love and death, the monotonous but ever-changing story of the human race.[23]

One might have supposed, in light of this lofty defense, that the drama had been assailed and rescued in the nick of time by the *Enquirer* mounted on a white charger. The length and prominence of the editorial suggest an interest in the stage that later on involved the Colonel's personal life.

It is small wonder that the Cockerill-edited newspaper

increased its readership. A student perusing the files is tempted to read on and on.

During Cockerill's transformation of the paper into one of the most prosperous publishing concerns of the West, the Colonel and Publisher John McLean remained close friends. When McLean took over control of the paper, he provided Cockerill with adequate if not excessive funds to hold a competent staff and to produce a well read paper. If there was ever reluctance to put up the required funds, it vanished as the *Enquirer*'s cash register rang up increased sales. McLean's instincts as a businessman eclipsed his editorial talents. Therein probably lay the key to the successful working relationship between the publisher and his dynamic editor.

But the day came when John McLean viewed Colonel Cockerill's assurance and popularity with more envy than admiration. It looked pretty simple; why shouldn't he step into the Colonel's shoes? But how? McLean had let Cockerill alone, except to pull the reins occasionally when he was involved in the city administration, for seven years. In that period the *Enquirer* had built a fortune for McLean. Colonel Cockerill was well established. Easing the Colonel out of the editorial chair could be awkward. A valid sounding approach had to be contrived, else the ever-alert editor might smell a rat in the publisher's woodpile.

An "out" was suggested to McLean by a headline on the Russo-Turkish War. He called the Colonel into his office. "John, you've been working pretty hard," he ventured. "What do you say to a breather?"

McLean's voice sounded friendly; the "breather" to Cockerill sounded good. "What do you have in mind?" he responded.

"We would like you to go to Europe for a few months to report the war," said McLean and, fearing as he spoke that the Colonel might see through his scheme, added: "Your job will be waiting for you when you return."[24]

Colonel Cockerill accepted the arrangement in good faith.

Within days he was en route to his first assignment as a war correspondent. Soon the Cockerill dispatches were keeping *Enquirer* readers abreast of developments in the Russo-Turkish War.

There appears to have been a business deal between the *Enquirer* and the New York *Herald* in the use and transmission of the Colonel's reports. They carried no byline in the *Enquirer* but each was credited as a "Special Dispatch to the *Enquirer*," by "Cable Telegram to the New York *Herald*." Occasionally the designation, "the *Herald* correspondent," appeared in the text. A plausible explanation is that in exchange for optional use of the Cockerill dispatches the *Herald*, whose publisher, James Gordon Bennett, Jr., operated an extensive cable and telegraph service, made a concession to the *Enquirer* on toll rates. In any case this arrangement first brought Cockerill's reportorial ability to the attention of the *Herald*.

The Colonel's European and Near Eastern experience tossed him into another phase of pioneering in American journalism—reporting by cable. By the time Cockerill started tracking down the Turkish army, cable service, though still in infancy, was fairly dependable. At the standard rate of $5 a word, the sheer necessity of packing maximum information in minimum wordage exercised a healthy discipline on Cockerill the writer.

Not only was the magic of the cable bringing America and Europe into closer relations, it was also inducing a belated conciseness of newspaper style. The New York *Herald* saw in the new terseness a welcome contrast to "the long-winded style of the magazine school, which rendered the leading articles almost unendurable. The telegraph will bring us back to that succinct, simple and condensed method of expressing our ideas which prevailed in ancient times. . . ."[25]

A few passages drawn at random from Cockerill's dispatches to the *Enquirer* illustrate his flair of pairing compactness with color:

Constantinople is under a reign of terror. Great crowds of desperate and lawless soldiery are on the streets. Bands of Circassians and Zebecks range at will about the city, robbing and murdering with impunity.

This line is defensible for the Turks, if they are active. Their most vulnerable point is near the Tchernavoda end of the railways. Kustendje may be cut off but it can hardly be captured.

Turkish officials declare the Russians have burned alive the inhabitants of Jonis, near Tirnova, who had taken refuge in a mosque.

A great battle has been fought at Febditch, south of the Balkans. The Russians met with a decided check. Nicopolis was virtually captured on Sunday by the taking of the heights commanding the town. The consternation of the Turks at the dashing advance of their enemies seems to be very great throughout the Empire.[26]

From the thousands of words the Colonel wrote of the Russo-Turkish War none excels his story of the capture of Nicopolis by the Russian forces as they pushed toward Constantinople. His grasp of the tactical factors involved, his perspective of the battle as a whole, and the vividness of his narrative may be appreciated in excerpts from his July 17, 1877, account in the *Enquirer*:

A crossing at Nicopolis possesses many advantages over that at Sistova. The river's current is not as strong, and a number of small stands fronting Turna-Maguerilli are favorably located for bridging purposes.... Nicopolis had been reduced to ruins, but the two hills on which the town was built completely sheltered the Turkish forces from Russian fire.

Therefore it became necessary to attack the town and position from the Bulgarian side of the river. For this purpose a force of infantry was massed west of Sistova, and during the concentration these troops served to cover the crossings. When the two corps established themselves in the direction of Bjela and Tirnova the crossing body was prepared to move on Nicopolis; but in the meantime the Turks were strengthening their position and preparing to defeat the very apparent object of their enemy. The indications, therefore, pointed to a bloody struggle for possession of Nicopolis, and neither side seemed anxious to begin it. The threatened failure of the Sistova bridge, and the frequent interruptions of traffic necessitated by repairs, forced the Russians to make the attack. . . .

Finally the order for the Russian advance was given, and after an arduous march around the lake west of Sistova and toward Nicopolis, the contending forces collided.

The Turks had taken the precaution to cover their position by double lines of pickets, supported at intervals by several companies of picked troops. This was to guard against the raids of the Cossacks, whose enterprise has impressed itself upon the Turkish mind. . . . As soon as the Russians came within effective range of the Turkish position they were met by a severe artillery fire, which, however, did not check their advance, and to which they replied with a still more formidable fire. The Turks, being posted in a commanding position, had a considerable advantage, and as the Russians approached frightful gaps were made in their ranks by the Turkish artillery. With surprising valor, however, the Russians continued to approach the heights. . . . when they came within rifle range they opened fire on the Turks. For half an hour this musketry duel continued, the Russians in the meantime developing their front so as to approach their left in the direction of the Osern River.

This was the movement which threatened the Turkish line of retreat. . . . About midday on Sunday . . . the whole Russian line . . . stormed the heights occupied by the Turks. During this awful climb, in the face of deadly fire, the Russians suffered terribly, while the defending Turks sustained equal losses. The onset was so impetuous that the Turks could not withstand it, and were driven headlong over the crest of the hills toward Nicopolis, followed by the Cossacks and detachments of light infantry. After taking the heights commanding the town—at a terrible cost—the Russians virtually had Nicopolis at their mercy. The Turks, finding their line of retreat threatened, abandoned the town, which the Russians entered this morning. It was filled with Turkish dead. . . .

Correspondent Cockerill did not remain to see the fall of Adrianople early in 1878, which all but knocked Turkey out of the war. The Russian victory virtually shattered European Turkey. Out of the Treaty of Berlin there emerged from Turkish soil three new independent states, Serbia, Rumania, and Montenegro. The capture of Nicopolis, described by Cockerill, proved to be a turning point in the war.

After six months Cockerill, his assignment concluded and his stature enhanced, sailed for America. How or why his stay was terminated after this comparatively short period is unexplained. It can only be surmised that someone in authority at the *Enquirer* instructed him to return to Cincinnati. "His graphic dispatches from the scene of hostilities as a special correspondent," in the New York *World*'s appraisal, "materially added to his reputation."[27] Enlightened and refreshed, Cockerill was eager to get back to his editorial post at the *Enquirer*.

In New York City disturbing news shook the Colonel. Despite McLean's assurance that the Colonel's old job would be awaiting him, the publisher had slid into the managing editor's chair—to stay. He had not even troubled himself to notify the Colonel, who was believed to have read the notice in a trade journal. Thus ended the long friendship of Cockerill and McLean; thus came another of the disillusionments that were to plague the Colonel's life and career.

VIII. Summons from St. Louis

Colonel Cockerill resumed his newspaper career in Washington, D. C., but there are no records explaining the circumstances under which as editor he paired with founder Stilson Hutchins to start the Washington *Post* on its crusading way. The Colonel may have taken on the Washington proposition out of desperation, for the city was considered a graveyard for newspapers. At any rate he was idle for only a short time after the termination of his connection with the Cincinnati *Enquirer* late in 1877. It is probable that Hutchins, who once owned the St. Louis *Times* and knew of Cockerill's work on the Cincinnati *Enquirer,* invited the Colonel to team up on the new paper. It seems likely the Colonel had a financial stake in the venture. Whatever the circumstances, the first edition of the *Post* hit the streets on December 6, 1877.

Despite its prestige as the national capital, Washington bore marks of a frontier town. At the site of the Lincoln Memorial was a malarial swamp; the Tidal Basin was non-existent; a railroad crossed what is today the Mall; the northern boundary of the city was Florida Avenue, Dupont Circle was out in the "sticks," and the Federal Triangle was a red light district. Washington Monument was one third erected; quipsters said it looked more like an Egyptian tomb than a memorial to the first President. Residents drew their water from the impure liquid of the Potomac River. Politically the city was equally unsavory. General Grant's graft-ridden administration ended shortly before the *Post* came to life, leaving another Republican, Rutherford B. Hayes, in its line of fire. Hayes was in the White House by the grace of one vote in the electoral college.

It was a setting made to order for a crusading newspaper; Cockerill and Hutchins seized their opportunity. The Colonel put his know-how to work. The *Post* cried for civic improvements and exposed crime and corruption on a pattern for which the Colonel's piloting of the *Enquirer* so well prepared him. Plain people read the *Post* with admiration; conniving politicians with apprehension.

The *Post,* like Cockerill, was Democratic, but it was no party mouthpiece. On its first anniversary, thriving with 11,875 customers, the *Post* explained its success: "It has been independent. . . . No man has been able to say that he owned it except the owner. . . ." In four months the newspaper moved from its small plant at 914 Pennsylvania Avenue, N. W., to larger quarters at 339 Pennsylvania Avenue and two years later transferred to still larger accommodations at Tenth and D Streets.

Information is sparse on Cockerill's brief tenure at the

Post. From its soaring readership it may be assumed that his aggressiveness and ingenuity made their impact on a journal that spoke to and for the people. With a fine contempt for orthodoxy, he set editorial tongues wagging by hiring Calista Halsey, one of the first girl reporters ever to crack the "male barrier" in American journalism.[1]

The year-and-a-half old *Post* was robust and prosperous and still growing when Cockerill, for reasons that are buried in obscurity, disposed of his interest in the paper and accepted the editorship of the Baltimore *Gazette*, owned by George Colton. Since this was not the first time the Colonel had left a newspaper after a comparatively short stay, one line of speculation seems plausible. Although he usually performed as a well controlled executive, the Colonel could be explosive, even truculent, when provoked. His repertoire of sulfurous epithets was overshadowed only by his skill in arranging them in new and devastating combinations. It is possible that he and Hutchins, normally good friends, fell out over some phase of the paper's operations. What else, unless Colton offered him a salary he simply could not afford to turn down, would induce Cockerill to leave a newspaper that was doing so well?

In 1888, nearly a decade after Cockerill's departure, Hutchins bought the Washington *Daily Republican*, the *Post*'s morning rival, and announced that the *Post*, which had been strongly Democratic, would be independent. Hutchins sold the paper in 1889 to Frank Hatton, a Republican and former member of the Cabinet, and Beriah Wilkins, a former Democratic congressman. In 1893 the *Post* moved to 1335 E Street, where it remained until 1950. In 1905, after the deaths of Hatton and Wilkins, a familiar figure moved into the Washington newspaper picture. John R. McLean, Cockerill's publisher-boss at Cincinnati who had ousted him, bought the *Post*, which managed to survive under his ownership. McLean, again with no Cockerill to run the show, was an undistinguished publisher. The *Post* lost much of its zip and lost even more when son Edward B. McLean, upon his father's death, took over in 1916.[2]

In Baltimore the *Gazette* became the third major newspaper to sail under the Cockerill colors. It was "aggressively but independently Democratic." This, piously explained the *Gazette*, meant that it was "thoroughly Democratic in its teachings and tendencies, but independent of all corrupt rings, cliques or factious oligarchies."[3] The *Gazette* made no secret of its intention to place the Democratic party in power and, as its new editor phrased it, "bring about a much-needed change in the administration of the government. . . . A great struggle for political mastery is coming on. In 1880 another battle for the Presidency will be fought. The importance of such a newspaper as the *Gazette* in educating, organizing and preparing the people for this contest cannot be overestimated."[4]

It is worth noting that, consistent with the Colonel's growing distaste for the rambling prose that prevailed in contemporary journalism, he pledged in the *Gazette* upon taking over that "opinions will be expressed in terse and pointed English."[5]

While engaged in rejuvenating the Baltimore paper, Cockerill was unaware that he was to become the prize "quarry" of a nationwide manhunt initiated by a restless Western publisher. Joseph Pulitzer, at a sheriff's sale in December, 1878, had acquired the tired and creaking St. Louis *Dispatch* for $2,500. Two days later he merged it with John A. Dillon's *Post*. Pulitzer and Dillon had continued as partners for a year when, as Don Seitz put it, Pulitzer's speed overwhelmed Dillon, who sold out to his partner late in 1879.

In the *Post-Dispatch*'s gain in power and the circulation war with the *Globe-Democrat* there rose the need for an editorial associate to replace Dillon. Because nobody in St. Louis filled Pulitzer's exacting requirements for a managing editor, he canvassed news editors of the nation.[6] Cockerill's first inkling of the result of the hunt came when he stopped to pick up his room key at Barnum's Hotel in Baltimore. "Here's a telegram for you, Colonel Cockerill," the room clerk mumbled. The wire, from Joseph Pulitzer, asked whether Cockerill would be interested in becoming managing editor of the *Post-Dispatch*.

As he read and reread the telegram the Colonel recalled his meeting with Pulitzer in Cincinnati at the Republican "rump" convention of 1872. That encounter now took on new significance in light of the job offer. Pulitzer, Cockerill reasoned, must have been sizing him up. The Colonel remembered the St. Louis publisher as a tall, gaunt figure topped by a bulbous head with a small, pointed chin tufted with a few strands of red hair. A guttural accent lingered but, the Colonel noticed, Pulitzer spoke in precise if studied English. Engulfing the man was a restless fervor that seemed to say, "Let's get on with it!" The Colonel's first impression, never altered in all the years the two collaborated in producing profitable newspapers, was that while the publisher was not without a sense of humor, he was too often in nervous haste to let it function. Although Cockerill recognized this as a facet of the Pulitzer personality, it in no way detracted from his admiration of the man who was now proposing a new challenge. The Colonel had heard enough of Pulitzer's work in St. Louis to be convinced of his high-minded concept of a newspaper's purpose, particularly in the exercise of community leadership.

It cannot be determined, in the absence of anything except brief published references by Pulitzer to his new associate, what qualities attracted him to Cockerill. There is no doubt that he wanted a Democratic editor who would not be a lackey to St. Louis politicians. There were strong resemblances between the political postures of the Baltimore *Gazette* and the *Post-Dispatch*, both of which vowed they would repudiate party, if necessary, to serve people. Pulitzer was impressed by what he knew of Cockerill's conversion of the Cincinnati *Enquirer* into a leading newspaper. Nor could he have overlooked what he knew was more than a coincidence—every newspaper under the Colonel's editorial direction started bear-

ing constructive influence and harvesting profits. From this
and other evidence, he knew Cockerill was his man.

The Colonel took little time to ponder. He accepted the
St. Louis offer because he was powerless to resist the prospect
of exposure to Pulitzer's crusading zeal. By early 1880 he was
installed as the *Post-Dispatch*'s new managing editor and a
full-fledged Pulitzer disciple.

From the moment he stepped into the newsroom the
Pulitzer-Cockerill team clicked. Their partnership lay not in
joint ownership (although the *Journalist* years later said
Cockerill had an interest in the paper),[7] but in the fierce
dedication to what both were trying to do—publish a fearless,
factual and provocative newspaper. "Cockerill settled into the
St. Louis field with the same ease in which he took command
in Dayton, Cincinnati, Washington and Baltimore," Pulitzer
biographer James Barrett wrote. "He caught the Pulitzer spirit
[and] for nearly three years cooperated in building the *Post-
Dispatch*." Seitz wrote that Pulitzer had found "a man after
his own heart and one who had wit, quick decision and willingness to face the music on all occasions, no matter how loudly
it played." It was not surprising that Cockerill soon ran the
paper in the publisher's absence, possibly the earliest hint that
Pulitzer had a serious health problem. Already the fury with
which he drove himself was taking its toll.

As Cockerill took over, the real nature of the new managing editor unfolded. It soon became evident why the Colonel
owned a national reputation as a news editor. He appeared
inexhaustible, his news sense was razor sharp, he was aggressive if not pugnacious, and he could write tersely, forcefully,
even militantly. He was a pungent paragrapher to be feared.
The story goes that when his presence became known in St.
Louis, Joseph B. McCullagh, once Cockerill's boss in Cincinnati and now editor of the *Globe-Democrat*, shrewdly avoided
any offense to the *Post-Dispatch*. McCullagh spared nobody
else, but he had no taste for the Colonel's shafts.[8] One theory
is that Pulitzer, in screening the field for an editor, knew he

must come up with one who could match the redoubtable
McCullagh.

On the job Cockerill was all business. Outside of working
hours he knew how to relax. He was cordial, good-humored,
and an easy spender. He seemed to be the curious combination
of city gentleman and frontiersman. His gregarious nature and
fluency as a conversationalist made him a popular figure,
particularly at the Elks Club. But intimates also knew he
could be merciless in denouncing a hypocrite or a cheat and
could, upon occasion, be needlessly brusque.

The Colonel found St. Louis to be a corruption-plagued
city crying for reform. Well before his arrival Joseph Pulitzer
had laid the groundwork for a newspaper that would serve
the public instead of an interest. Don Seitz analyzed the situation well. "The public soon learned where its welfare lay," he
wrote, "and support was never lacking." Initially thousands of
Missourians subscribed out of curiosity to read a nonconform-
ing journal, and remained, many out of sheer weariness with
the dutiful party organs and others from admiration of the
new brand of journalism. It was inevitable that the *Post-
Dispatch*, full of the vigor of reform and exposure, would make
powerful enemies. This did not deter Messrs. Pulitzer and
Cockerill.

In order to portray St. Louis exactly as it was, John
Cockerill's reporters roved the city from Grand Avenue
to the Mississippi River levee where the packet trade thrived
and Negro stevedores sang and laughed and quarreled; from
the water tower in North St. Louis to Carondelet, the French
quarter to the south. There was then little of interest in this
city of 300,000 west of Vandeventer Avenue. As one historian
saw it:

What there was of St. Louis was wide open. Along Chestnut
Street and Market Street the gambling joints and bawdy houses
prospered cheek by jowl with doors ever hospitable to friend or
stranger. Touts picketed the sidewalks in front of their craps or
faro games and openly tipped off the passersby. The girls sat with

opulent bosoms in the lace-curtained windows, or leaned in the doorways, calling the males, joking, flattering, naming the price. There were variety houses going day and night, usually run in connection with saloons. Sharp-faced dapper fellows, known to City Hall, infested these places selling tickets for the protected lottery rackets. On a short stretch of downtown Lucas Avenue— once fashionable in the '60s—the pleasure haunts were quieter and more dignified; life went on more elegantly behind drawn curtains; black, shiny carriages lined the street, and the champaign and chandeliers rivaled those of swell Vandeventer Place where the ex-senators, ex-governors and ex-generals lived, the men who ruled the town but didn't want it known and behaved with aloof innocence. The new whisky and railroad barons, enriched by the easy-going General Grant, had lately built mansions there, too.[9]

In the heart of St. Louis lay Kerry Patch, the Irish quarter, bounded by O'Fallon and Morgan streets west of Twelfth Street. In the railroad slot south of Mill Creek Valley a German settlement burgeoned. The bookshops where the intellectuals gathered and the German cafés where the beer guzzlers clustered surrounded the old Court House, on whose steps slaves once had been auctioned.

It was along the river, near the steamboat docks, that sin in its more primitive forms thrived. On Valentine Street girls paraded in front of swinging doors and rows of low-partitioned cubby-holes. In and out the traffic of river men, back from extended voyages, was heavy and persistent. To the north along the river teemed the areas of Negroes ranging in type from "blue-gum" Africans to pretty quadroons living in luxury. Along the Mississippi the ward heelers herded votes and built their political power. Rival bosses wanted those votes and murder at an appallingly low cost per head was not considered too high a price.

Cockerill briefed himself through his reporters and the newspaper files, by frequenting saloons and cafés and, as at Cincinnati, by strolling through a dozen areas to get the feel of the city. St. Louis, he quickly learned, was a giant octopus of greedy political bosses grasping for that prize bonanza—control of vice and gambling.

Editorially the *Post-Dispatch* lashed out against sin. It now had two articulate voices. Until Cockerill's arrival, Pulitzer had carried the load. An editorial expressing a sense of outrage at a powerful gambling ring bore the Cockerill trademark:

The pollution of its bribery has silenced the servile press; has corrupted an obsequious police; and has defiled the very seat of justice itself. The congenial alliance between the gambling hall and the brothel; the convenient service of the pander and the capper; the coercion of the spy and blackmailer—these have been the influences which have ruled St. Louis, mocking at honesty, insulting purity, defying decency.[10]

The *Post-Dispatch* suspected that collusion between the gambling-vice interests and police was responsible for a rash of murders. The paper, through the Colonel's pithy pen, spoke its mind:

Our very streets are red with blood. They are thronged nightly with brutal creatures who feel that they have perfect immunity and who are ready to kill at the slightest notice. . . . Murder must be made odious in St. Louis.

The crusading partnership of Pulitzer and Cockerill through their newspaper:

1. Publicly embarrassed wealthy and prominent St. Louis citizens who had dodged taxes by failing to declare, as required by law, all of their property and investments. Cockerill used the effective gimmick of publishing in parallel columns property listings of rich and poor taxpayers. The exposures brought reforms.

2. Brought about a prison term for Alanson B. Wakefield, head of a gambling ring, and enactment of a state law making big-time gambling a felony.

3. Won a campaign to clean and improve streets, which had been rivers of mud from one end of the city to another.

4. Sparked the start of St. Louis' park system.

Reform and improvement, wrote Don C. Seitz, "were not done easily or without friction and rattling of dry bones." The *Post-Dispatch* sought to shake the city out of its complacency. When the 1880 census returns showed that St. Louis slipped from fourth to sixth in population, it blamed the decline on "backwardness, lawlessness, mossback business methods and Bourbonism."[11]

In the Pulitzer-Cockerill era St. Louis editorial jousting was a rough affair. Modern newspapers would have winced at the name-calling that rattled between the *Post-Dispatch* and its rival, the *Republican*. The latter, founded in 1803, despite its name, was also a Democratic newspaper. In a typical thrust Cockerill wrote that "when the shadow of the upas tree of the Republican falls across a public man, he withers like a detached cabbage leaf in a cowboy's hat." The Colonel's reference was to the practice of cowboys in stuffing their ten-gallon hats with cabbage to protect the wearers from the sun. The *Republican* was variously tabbed as "the gamblers' organ," the "poor old misery *Republican*," the "somnolent *Republican*" and "the awful squid of American journalism."[12] Back of the *Post-Dispatch*'s ferocity was knowledge that the *Republican* was the voice of the aristocrats and the older families. The diehards in this segment, unable to control popular majorities in elections, sought to control the men who were elected. The *Post-Dispatch* was determined to see that they did not.

Kate Pulitzer was delighted with her husband's managing editor. She hoped now to see more of Pulitzer, a feverish, intent worker who often toiled far into the night. Pulitzer, though near exhaustion, would never admit it. He developed tension that produced the mannerism of rubbing his forehead as if he could make the headache go away. "It hurts me every time I see him do it," Kate confided to a friend. "Perhaps John Cockerill can take complete charge for a while and we can have a vacation."

Cockerill kept the editorial fires blazing. He could match

the boss in editorial thundering. He absorbed the Pulitzer spirit with such enthusiasm and effectiveness that when Pulitzer was away, it still seemed to be Pulitzer roaring, though the words were Cockerill's. Some of the Colonel's admirers insist that Pulitzer learned much from Cockerill; that Pulitzer was in some ways an emulator of his managing editor. Who can really know? The important fact is that each complemented the other; where one was weak the other was strong. The results were far beyond what either man could have achieved single-handedly.

A contemporary wrote that the extraordinary success of the *Post-Dispatch* was due to Cockerill's performance as head of its editorial staff. "Colonel Cockerill is a man *sui generis*," he said.

In his early years he had unusual opportunities owing to his father's leading position in Ohio for the study of social and political affairs; and being possessed of a quick mind, a nimble wit and a temper that would rather strike than be quiet, he developed into one of the remarkable journalists of the day. . . . His power results from extraordinary editorial judgment and audacious incisiveness in paragraphing, combined with a style of the finest literary quality. This latter shows admirably in his more lengthy articles, while no one knows better than he when and how to apply the lash.[13]

On December 31, 1881, the *Post-Dispatch* blossomed out in its new home at 515-517 Market Street. Two Hoe presses were installed to handle its soaring circulation. First in the evening field, the *Post-Dispatch* was nipping at the heels of the morning *Globe-Democrat*. Before the year 1882 was half gone Pulitzer could see that if the present rate of gains continued, *Post-Dispatch* profits would top the $85,000 cleared in 1881. The fall of 1882 seemed just the time for Joseph and Kate Pulitzer and children to treat themselves to that vacation visit to California.

Then disaster struck.

IX. Homicide with Honor

At the time of the 1882 congressional campaign Colonel James O. Broadhead was one of St. Louis' most prominent attorneys. Born and educated in Virginia, he served as representative and senator in the Missouri Legislature, as a United States district attorney and as a delegate to the Missouri constitutional convention. His title was a holdover from his Civil War days as a lieutenant-colonel. He represented the government in the famous Whiskey Ring cases in St. Louis. Broadhead's prestige was enhanced when the American Bar Association elected him president. Colonel Broadhead was fond of high-minded platitudes. Another "colonel"—John A. Cockerill at the *Post-Dispatch*—recalled one in particular. It went like this:

No man without an upright mind, or who has not preserved his integrity, has ever died leaving the reputation of a great lawyer.[1]

There was no question of the Colonel's popularity. Nor up to this period had there been the slightest taint upon his integrity. Now he wanted to go to Congress. His party had chosen him as the Democratic nominee. His prospects were favorable.

Then one day the roof all but fell in on the candidate; and ironically a tragedy growing out of a vengeful act by a law partner saved him from political defeat.

Colonel Broadhead had been retained by the City of St. Louis as counsel in litigation against the Laclede Gas Company. This was not unusual. Broadhead's firm represented many prominent institutions and citizens. But one day a report reached Colonel Cockerill that Broadhead had dumped the city as a client to become attorney for the utility firm. This curious switch of clients disturbed the Colonel. "If this report on Broadhead is true," Cockerill told his city editor, "he is not a fit person to represent the people of this district in Congress. Get on this fast and let me know the moment you confirm it." Corroboration quickly followed.[2] Cockerill's course was obvious to him. The newspaper's platform, announced upon the merging of the *Post* and *Dispatch*, was "to serve no party but the people." Broadhead was a Democrat and Pulitzer leaned in that direction, but an issue bearing so heavily on the public interest superseded partisan consideration.

Cockerill was appalled that a lawyer, seeking a position of public trust, would, after learning the facts on the city's side of the case, desert his client and defend the gas company. And this by a man held in such high esteem! This was not merely shady ethics; to the Colonel it was sheer perfidy. Nor was the odor improved by Colonel Cockerill's play of the story in the pages of the *Post-Dispatch*. With the news of the discovery of Broadhead's act the *Post-Dispatch* published stinging editorials that portrayed Broadhead as a modern Judas. Cockerill was not content to let off steam in print; in high indignation he took to the stump to denounce what he considered to be a sell-out by the candidate for Congress.

Shortly after the *Post-Dispatch*'s blast was published Sam Williams, an editorial writer, walked into Cockerill's office wearing a worried look. "John," he said abruptly, "I think you had better carry a gun."

"Me carry a gun?" Cockerill roared in laughter. "What on earth for?"

"Well," Williams, dead serious, persisted, "you know what that fire-eater is saying, don't you?"

The "fire-eater" was Alonzo W. Slayback, Broadhead's loquacious and hefty partner and a veteran of the Confederate Army. He was among the dwindling number who clung to the tradition of avenging one's honor with violence, if necessary. The *Post-Dispatch*'s attack upon Colonel Broadhead was a blow to the law firm, collectively and individually. Broadhead shrewdly "played it cool," permitting, perhaps encouraging, Slayback to carry the "war" to the *Post-Dispatch*. Slayback did so with such belligerency that one might have supposed he was the aggrieved. Slayback's tone was as sharp as it was indiscreet. He began to berate the *Post-Dispatch* in public and in private. Rumors reached Cockerill that Slayback had threatened to kill him. He didn't take them seriously. Now Sam Williams was alerting the Colonel to his personal danger. "I don't believe you appreciate what Slayback will do," he continued. "He will meet you in a public place some time. He will taunt you, threaten you, humiliate you and he won't hesitate to kill you."[3]

Cockerill was persuaded that afternoon to obtain a revolver, which he reluctantly carried in an inside coat pocket. A couple of days later he complained to Williams that he was "damned tired of toting this thing around." He poked the gun into a desk drawer.

Slayback made Cockerill, rather than Joseph Pulitzer, the prime target of his oral broadsides. Apparently he knew that, in Pulitzer's absence, the managing editor was in editorial charge and responsible for leveling charges of unfitness at Broadhead, the candidate for Congress. Slayback expected a violent encounter with Cockerill. As if to size up his adversary, he approached General William Tecumseh Sherman, who was then a St. Louis resident. "What kind of man is Cockerill?" Slayback queried. The answer was not reassuring. General Sherman, who cited John Cockerill's father for valor, told Slayback that father and son saw action in the Civil War; both, he added, served with distinction. "Have no doubt," warned the General, "John Cockerill will fight, if he must."[4]

Walt McDougall, the New York *World*'s celebrated cartoonist, once described Cockerill as just the sort of man to be selected Exalted Ruler of the Elks.[5] The Colonel performed in that very role on the night of September 30, 1882, at the St. Louis Elks Club. The Elks's benefit show went well. The most surprising development of the evening had nothing to do with the minstrel show, the Colonel reflected as he ambled serenely toward the Lindell Hotel where he lived. He had finally shut off the loud-mouthed Slayback.

After the show Cockerill was relaxing in the club lounge when he overheard voices. Glancing around, he saw Henry Moore, his city editor. Seated beside Moore was a heavy-jowled, grisly man wearing a showy watch fob across a checkered vest. He recognized Alonzo W. Slayback, who was not aware that the Colonel was seated within earshot. Slayback was bending the city editor's ear: "The *Post-Dispatch* is a lying, blackmailing sheet and everyone connected with it is a liar and a blackmailer—and you can tell Colonel Cockerill I said so. . . ."

Now was the time to rise in indignation and invite Slayback to deliver the "message" personally. But Cockerill demurred. Confronting the detractor, reasoned the Colonel, will do the paper no good if this thing develops into an open brawl. Perhaps if he could talk to Slayback alone—

Minutes later Moore left; Slayback remained. Cockerill rose and approached the lawyer. In the meantime Slayback's abusive remarks had caught the ears of a number of other men. They read the *Post-Dispatch*. They knew there could be trouble. Cockerill's movement therefore attracted notice. A dozen pairs of eyes were glued upon the two men. As Cockerill neared his taunter, the room was hushed in silence. Would one or the other administer the conventional slap across the cheek that prefaces a duel?

Those who expected something dramatic were disappointed. The Colonel, looking friendly, made himself known. The two withdrew to the library and conferred behind the locked doors. A tenseness prevailed as brother Elks waited for something to happen. Half an hour later the two emerged, chatting amicably. "Come on out to the bar, Colonel Slayback," Cockerill invited, "and let's drink to it." Whatever they were drinking to, it sounded friendly. The charged atmosphere cleared. The curious onlookers lost interest as the pair strode to the bar. The dove of peace had fluttered in and smothered what could have been some interesting fireworks.

As soon as the two entered the library, Slayback closed and locked the door. Without any preliminaries he accused Cockerill of bringing him there to bulldoze him into letting up in his attacks on the *Post-Dispatch*. When the lawyer ran out of breath, Cockerill assured Slayback that he merely wanted an explanation of Slayback's intemperate language. The *Post-Dispatch*, Cockerill reminded him, was not attacking Slayback. Except to mention his name in connection with the Broadhead law firm, the paper had not further cited Slayback. Broadhead was the real target, said Cockerill. What kind of a congressman would he make—a lawyer who, after accepting a $10,000 fee to represent the city, would then turn around and become counsel for the city-sued utility company?

Cockerill informed him that about a year ago the *Post-Dispatch*, on Pulitzer's order, stopped its presses at great inconvenience and expense to kill the Glover card addressed to Slayback. "Cards," as preliminaries to duels, were intended to bring personal antagonisms to a head. If the feud seemed to warrant, either principal could insert in the newspaper a card at regular advertising rates—payable in advance for obvious reasons. The card was an accepted medium for accusing one's enemy of anything from cheating his grandmother to being a plain scoundrel. John Glover, a young attorney, in his card was adequately insulting; he wrote that despite his name Slayback was a coward. The card appeared in only a small portion of the press run and so Slayback, until the Elks library interview, had never heard of it. The interview pacified him somewhat. The Glover card could have meant violence or even death for one or possibly both of the principals. The Glover card would be heard from again.

Cockerill and Slayback discussed their differences. As Cockerill surmised, Slayback was directing his diatribes at the Colonel principally because as the managing editor he had stirred up the charges against Broadhead. He insisted that he was not doing so as a personal slap at Cockerill but would hold Cockerill responsible for anything and everything the paper might say. Cockerill replied that in Pulitzer's absences he was obliged to assume such responsibilities but, he emphasized, the publisher stood back of him in the Broadhead campaign. He would give "satisfaction," he assured Slayback, should the latter elect a more forceful means of settling their differences. "I have never written an unkind word about you, Colonel," Cockerill added. "And I hope I never have to." This seemed to calm Slayback. The two shook hands.[6]

And now, Cockerill, walking thoughtfully through the Lindell Hotel lobby, was cautiously optimistic. There was no pledge, in so many words, that Slayback would desist from ill-tempered attacks upon the *Post-Dispatch*, but surely he would tone them down. Pulitzer was in New York, to be gone several weeks. Despite some peaceful signs, the situation could erupt again. Back in his room, John Cockerill wrote furiously for half an hour. Pulitzer should know the whole story.[7] Cockerill posted the letter that night.

After the Elks Club reconciliation Slayback held his fire for a few days. Then, on the morning of October 13, 1882, City Editor Henry Moore addressed Cockerill: "Have you seen the morning paper?"

"No, Henry. Why?" Cockerill responded.

"Better get a grip on yourself," Moore cautioned.

There it was. Slayback, in a meeting of Democratic ward politicians, denounced the *Post-Dispatch* and its editors as a gang of blackmailers.[8] Cockerill made a fast check with several persons who had heard Slayback's latest outburst to confirm the report. He pondered his course. The paper's crusades had made many enemies, among them the rival *Republican*. Joseph Pulitzer had been physically assaulted by Colonel W. B. Hyde of the *Republican*. The attack had not intimidated the *Post-Dispatch*. Sometimes an insult was better ignored, reasoned the Colonel, but not when the charge was blackmail, the blackest smear of all. As he searched his mind for the answer, Cockerill recalled his remarks to Slayback pertaining to the withdrawn card of John M. Glover, who had been a candidate for Congress. Why not publish the card which would present the public an appraisal of Slayback other than his own?

Having adopted this line of action, Cockerill reprinted the Glover card on the editorial page of October 13, 1882, prefacing it with a reference to Slayback as an "individual whose chief claim to distinction rests upon the fact that he is the law partner of Colonel James O. Broadhead." Slayback, without personal provocation, wrote Cockerill, had applied "a string of vile and virulent epithets to the *Post-Dispatch* and its conductors, making charges which he knew to be false." This was the same A. W. Slayback, said the Colonel, concerning whom the card had been written and published November 11, 1881.

Because of the explosive results it set off, the Glover card is reprinted here in its entirety:

In your account of yesterday's proceedings in a trial now pending you quoted certain language used of myself by Colonel Alonzo W. Slayback, to-wit: that I was "an impertinent young puppy," coupled with a statement on the Colonel's own authority that he had pocketed a great many insults from me the day before; also, that the presence of the court and the ladies in attendance had alone induced him to pocket said insults. The Colonel also assured the court that he was a brave man.

Now in simple justice to the Colonel it must be stated that he did not use the language quoted until I had told the court several times that I had no respect for him, and as he correctly says, had induced him to discontinue a certain line of remarks by telling him that I would slap his face at any time and place he might appoint except that court-room. That he declined this invitation and pocketed those "insults," as he misnamed these expressions of abstract truth, he will be able to prove, as he says, by every one in the court-room, and candor compels me to make the same admission. But when he says that the presence of the court and the ladies restrained his valor, perfect frankness required me to say that, on the contrary, they account for it. In fact, so far from being a brave man, the Colonel, notwithstanding his military title, is a coward. He dare not be brave except in a courtroom or a church and he will beg or cringe out of any difficulty into which his vaporing humor may have gotten him. Anyone who remembers the published correspondence a year or two since between him and a gentleman whom he had called "a creature" before the City Council, will see to what extremities cowardice may go after a vaporing insult. In fact I have so often seen the calf drubbed out of that lion's skin that the process would lack both novelty and originality. Now the "Colonel's" title I believe is "Colonel Alonzo W. Slayback." The word Alonzo is of Etruscan origin and means "coward," the middle name is never printed in full as having the same significance, and the title "Colonel" is never applied except in derision and originated in the gallant manner in which the "Colonel" once marshaled a female sewing society.

John M. Glover[9]

About five o'clock on the day the card was published, Colonel Cockerill was in his office chatting with Business Manager John B. McGuffin and Victor C. Cole, foreman of the composing room, when angry voices knifed through the city room. Two irate visitors brushed past startled reporters on their way to Cockerill's office.

"Is Colonel Cockerill in?" snarled Slayback's voice.

The trio in Cockerill's office broke off their conversation—to listen and to wait. The tread of heavy, ominous footsteps grew in volume, attesting that the visitors knew their way to Cockerill's office. Into the room barged the pair. And into the life of Joseph Pulitzer's top editor walked a tragedy that would rock the city and send a wave of political reverberations to be heard for years. There was Slayback, a pistol in his hand and blood in his eyes. Close behind was burly William H. Clopton. In Clopton Slayback had chosen, as partner in his mission, a talented and experienced bruiser. Also a lawyer, Clopton, in less than a year, had horse-whipped and mauled two members of the bar whom he accused of malpractice.

Cockerill was confused. So were his colleagues. He had not expected action so soon. The presses were still rolling.

Slayback must have been handed one of the first copies off the press. It is tempting to speculate that even in this crisis a fleeting moment of satisfaction comforted the Colonel. People were reading the *Post-Dispatch*!

His first impression, the normal one under such circumstances, was that Slayback had come to arrange "satisfaction" at an appropriate time and place. Then Cockerill's eyes found the pistol grasped in Slayback's right hand. Another glance caught a weapon in Clopton's hand. Cockerill had had a few close calls in the Civil War in which he had been a target of the Confederates at Shiloh. This was different. This was no peaceful mission to arrange a duel. These two intended to gun him! The action was confused and fast. No two accounts tell the same story but they all agree that Cockerill, almost too late, remembered the gun in his desk, in the upper lefthand drawer. This was the moment Slayback started to take off his coat. Slayback's friends made much of this detail, contending the lawyer planned only to give the editor a sound thrashing. When Cockerill grabbed his revolver, Slayback forgot about removing his coat. Instead he asked, "Is that for me?"

In the meantime Clopton, with Slayback, was advancing menacingly toward Cockerill. Clopton was armed but he had not yet pointed his gun at the editor. The two were closing in; Cockerill was backing away. In response to Slayback's question, Cockerill shouted, "No!" and "No" was what he meant. He hoped it would not be necessary to pull the trigger; but the law of survival was working. At this point both visitors had crowded in on Cockerill. Slayback leveled his revolver at Cockerill, who was by now against the wall. Slayback's finger was on the trigger.

McGuffin up to that point had been only an astonished witness to this incredible drama. But now, with catlike swiftness, he grabbed Slayback's weapon in such a way that the hammer caught his hand between the thumb and forefinger. This act probably saved Cockerill's life. And it was a movement Cockerill could not anticipate. But he did anticipate what he took to be Slayback's attempt to fire at him. Almost simultaneously with McGuffin's snatching movement, Cockerill's gun went off. Slayback slumped to the floor.

Clopton had not counted on this development. He had agreed with Slayback that the editor could be intimidated. Neither of the intruders expected Cockerill to have a gun. "Why you murderer!" roared Clopton and he started to point his pistol at Cockerill. But McGuffin, who had wrenched Slayback's weapon from the fallen man, was quicker. He held the revolver to Clopton's head. Clopton desisted.

The law of the jungle had taken over; tragedy lay in its wake. Four men—Cockerill, McGuffin, Clopton, Cole—stood in stunned silence. Quickly they sensed the import of what had happened. Cockerill, with the others, tried to minister to Slayback. As the editor knelt to detect a waning pulse beat, the blood of his fallen critic soiled Cockerill's sleeve. A few lingering gasps and the lawyer was dead. It had all happened in less than a minute.

A half hour later the coroner was examining the bullet-pierced body of Alonzo W. Slayback.

Cockerill quietly left the *Post-Dispatch* building.[10]

X. Ordeal and Exoneration

News of the fatal shooting of Alonzo Slayback spread like a prairie fire. A small gathering of men at the entrance watched sullenly as the coroner entered the *Post-Dispatch* building. By the time Colonel Slayback's body was carried from the premises, the group had grown to an ominously large crowd. The word was that Slayback was killed in cold blood without a chance to defend himself. The slain lawyer's cronies circulated the blackest version of what happened. It was soon evident the mob believed that the target of their wrath was still in the building. Their shouts penetrated the late afternoon air: "Where's that murderer, Colonel Cockerill? Let's go in and get him! Let's burn the God-damned place to the ground."[1]

Watching from a third-floor window, Sam Williams, sensing what might happen, sent for the police. No one doubted that had the front doors not been locked, the mob would have wrecked the newspaper offices. Rowdies were wielding a battering ram at the front door and hurling lighted pitch-pine torches at the windows when police arrived. Even then it was a hopeless battle until an extra detail of police was dispatched to the scene. After three hours the mob was dispersed, but having been thwarted, the hecklers left in an ugly mood. The motivation of the attempted lynching went beyond a desire to avenge a lawyer's death. It stemmed from the *Post-Dispatch*'s crusades against vice, gambling, collusion and corruption. In the mob were ward heelers, shysters and political lackeys who stood to lose by the newspaper's disclosures. Here was their chance to hit back.

For John A. Cockerill it was the beginning of a campaign of abuse that showed him no mercy for many years.

As an editor, Cockerill had often "served up" homicide to his newspaper readers. Now, as he walked rapidly toward the Lindell Hotel room where he lived, he found himself a principal in the biggest homicide story of the year. He felt remorse in taking another man's life, but, he told himself, it was a matter of shooting or of being shot. He would see it through. He would not run. He remembered that Pulitzer was out of the city. How should the story be handled? There was no hesitation. The city must be told what happened. There must be an expression of sorrow for the tragedy, and sympathy for the bereaved. He would send the word to his city editor, Henry Moore.

In his room, Cockerill changed into another suit and hung up the blood-spattered garments. He rejected as stupid the idea of concealing or destroying them. There could be no question of his next steps. He would see his attorneys and insist on

going voluntarily to the authorities. He had committed no
crime. An hour later, after consulting the law firm of Johnson
and Lodge, John Cockerill was in Four Courts, placing himself
at the disposal of the law.[2]

The *Post-Dispatch* on October 14, 1882, the day after the
shooting, told (up to a point) a straightforward story of the
tragedy:

In regard to the terrible tragedy which occurred yesterday evening the *Post-Dispatch* has nothing to say but words of sorrow for
the dead and sympathy for the bereaved, and of simple justice to
the gentleman, who is one of the chief sufferers by this sad affair.

The paper reiterated that it had the kindest regards for
Colonel Slayback, that the proprietor and Colonel Cockerill
had sought to preserve cordial relations with the slain lawyer.
It recalled that nothing personally offensive to him had ever
been published "until after he had denounced, in a speech,
with opprobrious epithets, everybody connected with the *Post-
Dispatch* and had denounced the paper itself as a slanderous
and blackmailing sheet." The *Post-Dispatch* described its brief
editorial refuting his attack as "mild as the nature of the
remarks permitted."

In its version of the encounter the newspaper reported:
"While Cockerill was crowded against the wall and almost
on his knees, regarding himself as assailed with apparently
murderous intent by two men, he fired the fatal shot." With a
significance that could not be missed, the paper pointed out
that McGuffin and Cole were present as witnesses to the fact
that Cockerill "fired in necessary self-defense."

Then Colonel Cockerill, reading from a copy rushed to
him at the county jail, winced. "We ask only," pleaded the
Post-Dispatch, "that the managing editor be known as one as
tender-hearted as a woman, a man of peace whose life has
been full of generous and kindly deeds, a man who abhors
injustice and is ever ready to repair a wrong." The passage,
fumed the Colonel, might be appropriate for an obituary notice

but such ingratiating words would only infuriate his enemies. The boys in the newsroom, the Colonel concluded, had got carried away with their good intentions. The prediction was accurate. The clamor for punishing Cockerill and the *Post-Dispatch* grew. All but forgotten was Colonel Cockerill's charge of improper conduct against lawyer Broadhead, the congressional candidate. Broadhead's prospects for election took a turn for the better. As the shooting victim's law partner, Broadhead was gratefully reaping the benefits of Slayback's "martyrdom."

At the inquest the coroner's jury heard two versions of the shooting. William H. Clopton, the only witness on behalf of the victim, Colonel Slayback, testified that Cockerill had goaded his antagonist beyond endurance and then wantonly killed him. Slayback, he said, had merely come to demand an apology of Cockerill. The testimony of McGuffin and Cole on behalf of Cockerill was that Slayback, "with blood in his eyes," had come to the office "armed and with a mortal purpose." Cockerill, they said, killed in self-defense. Cockerill testified that "Slayback invaded my private office with the avowed purpose of assaulting me and fell with a weapon in his hand. I obeyed the common instinct of humanity in defending myself."[3]

The coroner's jury found only that Slayback died at the hands of John A. Cockerill. It did not rule upon the culpability of the act. Cockerill was ordered remanded to jail. Under pressure of Slayback's and Broadhead's friends and the taunting of the *Republican,* the *Post-Dispatch*'s bitter rival, a charge of second degree murder was filed against Cockerill in the Court of Criminal Correction. Cockerill was released on bail. The case went to the Grand Jury but from the first it was a farce. Whether Slayback had actually pointed a gun at Cockerill became academic. Slayback, armed, accompanied by an armed crony, had invaded Cockerill's office. Their purpose was obviously unfriendly. After two weeks of what Cockerill later described as "a patient ex parte investigation," the Grand Jury failed to indict the defendant. On December 6, 1882, assistant prosecuting attorneys Krum and Seward moved that the case be stricken from the Court of Criminal Correction record. The judge granted the motion. John Cockerill's slate, officially, had been wiped clean.[4]

But the troubles of John Cockerill, editor, were far from over.

Cockerill, back at his *Post-Dispatch* desk, was feeling better. Had he not been exonerated by the court? Consoled by such reflections, he was startled several days later by a sharp rap at his door. The caller was a briefcase-armed lawyer representing Mrs. Slayback. The Colonel, he said, was being sued in Circuit Court for $5,000 in damages for depriving her of her husband. A mood of depression enveloped the tough, incisive editor. Would this thing never end? How should he handle this latest attempt to defame him? He turned to Alexander Carpenter Howard, with whom he had become friendly during the organization of the St. Louis Lodge of Elks. It was a friendship that endured through the years. Months after the shooting Alexander Howard, in an attempt to build up the editor's still-battered morale, asked permission to use the name of Cockerill when christening the Howard offspring.

Now, with a damage suit hanging over his head, Cockerill at the Elks Club was confiding in and seeking advice from a friend. Alexander Carpenter Howard asked one question: "What has been your policy in all of this tragic happening so far, John?"

"Why, I guess it has been just to tell what is happening, Alex."

"Then go right on telling the truth," counseled Howard, adding, "And don't be afraid to defend yourself. Your political enemies will crucify you if they can."[5]

Another friend and adviser with whom Colonel Cockerill talked of the shooting incident was Charles F. Joy, a young and brilliant lawyer, later elected to Congress. "By nature

Cockerill was fearless and unswerving," Joy recalled. "Even though the consequences were terrible, he did not reproach or condemn himself, as other more irresolute persons would have done. But he did regret the incident." Joy was with Cockerill for several hours after the editor surrendered to police. Cockerill was not immediately released and the two discussed the shooting from many angles. It was Joy who as friend counseled the Colonel to stick to his contention that he shot in self-defense. He later reported Cockerill as saying, "But I wish I might have been the one to fall. Would that I had not been the unhappy instrument of adding to the sum of earthly woe, the grief of widowhood and orphanage." But to his last day, Colonel Cockerill's belief was that his act of firing the fatal shot at Slayback was fully justified.

Cockerill, in the *Post-Dispatch*, acknowledged he had been served notice of the suit, explaining:

When a Grand Jury decided I had been guilty of no crime, I presumed that my vindication was morally complete. But I find that the enemies of the Post-Dispatch and myself are determined that I shall have an opportunity to more fully justify myself before the bar of public opinion, and I accept the situation.

From the beginning of this regretful affair, I have been pursued with almost inhuman malignancy by the proprietors of the Republican and such persons as they have been able to incite and control. These men have a deep-seated business hostility against the Post-Dispatch—a hostility which they were reasonably careful to conceal until they believed I had been forced into a position . . . from which I could not easily extricate myself—and then the processes of hatred peculiar to them were put into play.

From the very outset they accused me of the most heinous crime in their paper; they accused every witness who was in a position to testify to the justness of my act, of perjury and conspiracy.

My counsel were equally accused and this fiendish malignancy did not even spare those whose name I bear. A more unwarranted abuse of journalistic power certainly was never manifested in this country—and all this in the face of pending judicial investigation.

Not content with this the Knapps [owners of the *Republican*], through their newspaper, are now seeking to arraign before the public the conscientious members of the Grand Jury who failed to find in the testimony before them cause for charging me with a crime.

That this present suit and claim for damages is instigated by them is evidenced by the fact that it is brought by their stock-holder-attorney who has access to their columns, and who had been exceedingly active in hounding me.

It is due to the public to say that I shrink from no investigation. There is no responsibility that can be forced upon me that I am not willing to meet.[6]

The Colonel had borne patiently much persecution, he said. He had been connected with journalism for twenty years, and was justly proud of his "record for peacefulness and fair dealing." He wished to maintain that record. "This harassment," he supposed, "was part of a pattern of the feeble few who have proclaimed the benevolent purpose of denying me a home in St. Louis." Concluding, the Colonel hoped that his friends and the public would understand the motive behind the damage suit but warned that "whatever the eventuation of this form of persecution, the responsibility will rest with those who devised it." These were brave words from a fighting editor but they did not quell the agitation against Cockerill and the *Post-Dispatch*.

Pulitzer, returning by train from New York, was concerned but not alarmed by the shooting. The latest sequence in the affair, given to him behind closed doors in his office immediately upon his arrival, left the publisher's faith in his managing editor unshaken.

Pulitzer could understand the situation in which Cockerill found himself. Pulitzer had shot a man with far less provocation. He was recalling the incident now as he discussed the Slayback killing with his managing editor. Publisher Pulitzer in 1869 had become Representative Pulitzer in the Missouri Legislature. He had introduced a bill to abolish the county court because of the court's actions involving the poorhouse and insane asylum. Construction of a new asylum had begun; a juicy million-dollar contract had been awarded Captain

Edward Augustine, a political conniver of the first water and a grafter of considerable success. Augustine thought well of the court. It was not surprising that he should try to kill the Pulitzer bill, nor was it unusual that the publisher-legislator, in his *Westliche Post* of St. Louis, should report the development. The conflict led to a startling outcome.

Augustine, muscular and menacing, confided to one of his St. Louis County political henchmen that he planned to insult Pulitzer publicly and get him to drop his support of the obnoxious measure, a stratagem that seems to have placed too high a premium on an insult. At the Schmidt Hotel in Jefferson City "Augustine," according to the St. Louis *Post-Dispatch*'s account, "mildly told Mr. Pulitzer he was a liar [in reference to the county court's conduct]. Pulitzer cautioned Augustine against such strong language. Mr. Pulitzer left the hotel. He returned with a pistol and went for Mr. Augustine. Had not Pulitzer's pistol been knocked down, Missouri would have been in mourning today for a slaughtered loyal son." Pulitzer fired two shots at close range. The first took effect in Augustine's leg. In retaliation Augustine struck Pulitzer on the head with a derringer, cutting his scalp and ending the encounter. The second shot had missed, boring through the floor of the hotel lobby. Pulitzer was arrested, released on bond, found guilty of assault and fined $100 and costs. His bill passed, the Augustine contract was nullified, and the corrupt county court was deprived of its power.[7] Pulitzer could view his editor's experience with unusual understanding.

Although no record exists of the conversation between publisher and editor, Pulitzer is known to have praised Cockerill for exposing Broadhead's acceptance of a retainer from the city to handle its suit against the gas company and the lawyer's deserting the city to defend the company. We may assume that Pulitzer called this real journalism and that he reaffirmed his confidence in his managing editor.

Nevertheless, while assuring each other that they could weather the storm, both men realized that the gravity of their dilemma was something that could not be talked away. Pulitzer could understand a drunken mob incited to irrational conduct. But what hurt the *Post-Dispatch* owner in a manner from which he never fully recovered was that so many people in St. Louis were turning against the newspaper. He believed, as did Cockerill, that the *Post-Dispatch* meant much to St. Louis. That so many people did not accept the newspaper's account of the shooting baffled Pulitzer. Cockerill had an explanation. He held that the people were good and decent but did not recognize what was happening as a politically inspired campaign. Many did believe the *Post-Dispatch* but, as the editor may well have phrased it, "the West is growing up. People are weary of settling disputes by gunfire. They want a government of law, not pistols." Although there is no evidence to back it, Cockerill conceivably would have preferred that his case had gone to trial before a jury so that he could have been cleared publicly of the "murder" with which he was accused.

As always Pulitzer felt the urge to do something; in this case it was to write an editorial exonerating his editor. He led off, on December 18, by assuring *Post-Dispatch* readers that its opposition to Colonel Broadhead was based solely on his record as a public official. There was no personal motive. Pulitzer revealed that two weeks before the shooting, Cockerill had written him about the Elks Club "peace" conference with Slayback and how, despite the truce, the lawyer had excoriated the paper. The publisher asserted he had instructed Cockerill to reprint the Glover card if Slayback persisted in his attacks.

"The charge of blackmail," wrote Pulitzer, "is the worst that can be preferred against any honest paper or editor. If Mr. Cockerill had remained silent under it, he would, by his silence, have confessed its truth and invited its repetition. The publication of the Glover card under the circumstances was purely in self-defense, justified, invited and made inevitable by Colonel Slayback's own provocation." Then Pulitzer put on the clincher: "If Mr. Cockerill had allowed the public stigma of blackmailing to go unresented, he would have been unfit for his position, and would have ceased to be managing editor of this paper."[8]

Thus Pulitzer backed his editor all the way. Indeed there is reason to suspect that Pulitzer was extra generous in his defense of his managing editor. Although the *Post-Dispatch* owner announced it was he who ordered the Glover card inserted, the circumstances suggest otherwise. It is doubtful that Pulitzer, out of St. Louis at the time, would have thought of doing so. The provocative act has Cockerill's impulsive hand written all over it.

Lacking evidence to support it, the civil action filed against Colonel Cockerill on behalf of Mrs. Slayback was dropped. The Colonel felt his exoneration was complete. Slowly the depression that had gripped the editor since the shooting lifted. Yet the tragedy, despite its aspects of self-defense which Pulitzer and Cockerill thought were well established, induced a feeling of resentment against the newspaper that persisted in St. Louis for many years.

James O. Broadhead was elected to Congress for the short term; his opponent, Dr. J. H. McLean, won the long-term assignment. Broadhead later was appointed by President Cleveland as minister to Switzerland. William H. Clopton, Slayback's strong-arm companion on the ill-fated visit to Cockerill's office, became, of all things, U. S. District Attorney.

The immediate effects of the shooting upon the *Post-Dispatch* were detrimental, as will be seen; but the long-range effects were beneficial. The newspaper not only survived the aftermath of harassment but ultimately emerged as a journal with increasing influence and crusading zeal. There is risk in being a fearless newspaper, if not from a Slayback pistol, from the threat of libel suits. In 1953 a former managing editor of the *Post-Dispatch*, in the proud tradition of his paper, stressed a newspaper's responsibility to its community:

If it is doing a good job, it is not only unafraid of a libel suit; it should deliberately invite a libel suit if it is sure its facts point to a disservice to the community. If your newspaper is sued on an important campaign story, take heed of your advantage. Your advantage is that the suit may serve to bring out facts which would establish your case and that otherwise would not be available to you. . . . The privilege of publishing depositions in advance of a trial usually can be arranged through the newspaper's attorneys . . . at least that is true in Missouri. Dishonest officials do not relish getting caught in that net. There is a chance that in taking depositions you might catch some other crooks whose heads are beneath the surface. . . . Of course no newspaper and no editor wants libel suits, except when it or he invites them. There were times in my work on the Post-Dispatch when I wished certain characters would sue me. . . . In any case seek out the facts and print them without fear or favor.[9]

Subsequent to the shooting a capable young woman bearing a resemblance to Colonel Slayback quietly went about her duties as society editor of the *Post-Dispatch*. The impression prevails that she was hired at the suggestion of Colonel Cockerill. After her retirement she remained for the rest of her life on the newspaper's payroll. She was the daughter of Alonzo W. Slayback.[10]

XI. The Colonel Bows Out

One day early in 1883 a young man who, it soon became evident, did not know the meaning of the word "no" asked to see Colonel Cockerill. This was no ordinary interview because out of it grew the versatile career of one of the *Post-Dispatch*'s leading editors. When Colonel saw who his visitor was, he greeted him with extra warmth. The caller, George Sibley Johns, twenty-seven, as publisher of the weekly St. Charles, Missouri, *Journal*, had been one of the few country newspapermen who had supported Cockerill and his newspaper in the Alonzo W. Slayback affair.

Johns quickly explained his errand: he was job-hunting.

"The *Post-Dispatch* is the only newspaper I want to work for," said young Johns. "I've sold the *Journal* and I'm available." As grateful as the Colonel was to Johns, he had to say there were no openings at the time, but Johns continued as if he had not heard: "I would like to get acquainted with the city and work directly under you. I have some money and I won't need any pay." What could a man do in the face of such earnestness? Cockerill relented: "Hell, son, I can't keep you from working if you want to. Go ahead."[1]

Johns quickly demonstrated two attributes that Cockerill required of every reporter—strong legs and a legible, lucid pen. The newspaper was not served by the communication facilities that have induced a pathetic laziness among some modern reporters who favor the telephone over foot power. After Samuel F. B. Morse in 1837 proved the practicability of transmitting messages by electric impulses, the telegraph was hailed as a miracle for sending news from city to city. But the telegraph was no help in gathering news in sprawling St. Louis. Nor in the Cockerill period was the telephone of more than token assistance. In 1878 the city's first public telephone line with twelve subscribers was inaugurated. When Cockerill rode into town two years later to become Pulitzer's right hand man, six hundred telephones had been installed in the homes of a few rich men, in offices of prominent businesses and in key government agencies. At this crude stage the telephone inspired more blasphemy than confidence. A contraption known as a typewriter had become available in 1878 but it was not in general newspaper use until the 1890's. The *Post-Dispatch* owned a couple of machines, but reporters scrawled their stories in longhand. There was neither a telephone nor a typewriter for the *Post-Dispatch* reporter. The reporter's beat could not be covered by sitting cozily with telephone in hand contacting news sources while taking it down on the typewriter. Cockerill's reporters kept their feet on the pavement rather than on top of their desks.

Johns did not spare his legs. He tramped up and down

St. Louis streets gathering news. The freshness of his copy quickly caught Cockerill's eye. In a couple of weeks the Colonel summoned the young staff member to his office. "Reporters overlook a lot of what's right under their noses," said the managing editor. "I've been looking for somebody to do just what you are doing. We are using your items. I can't let you work any longer without paying you. Here's an order for $12. That's your weekly pay until there's a regular place on the staff. You'll get the first one that occurs." A week later there was still no vacancy but Johns was on the payroll regularly and, with the exception of two short periods, remained with the *Post-Dispatch* until his death in 1941. In that period Cockerill's protégé wore every important editorial hat—dramatic critic, city editor, managing editor, editor in charge, editor of the editorial page, and associate editor.

The first interview of consequence was one in which Cockerill assigned Johns to ask General William Tecumseh Sherman a loaded question. The "Scourge of Georgia," a big, brusque, heavily-bearded, fearsome gentleman, had been welcomed joyfully to St. Louis. When he decided to make it his home, jubilant citizens bought him a fine house. Up to the time of the Johns interview, General Sherman had lived quietly enough. Cockerill saw him often at the Elks Club. The General was known to have patronized one of the currently popular massage salons. At some salons women helped give the Swedish style treatments. Sly gossip said this part of the service was the one most enjoyed by the Civil War hero. The mischievous managing editor thought it might be interesting, even explosive, to have young Johns ask the General if he engaged the services of lady masseurs. Accordingly, the reporter, after a preliminary exchange in which Sherman was most cordial, put the question. The effect was like tossing a lighted match into a barrel of gasoline vapor.

"That's none of your paper's God-damned business," roared the General. "You go straight back and tell John Cockerill and Joe Pulitzer I'll be massaged where and by whom I damned please." It was not long until General Sherman, in high indignation, vacated the mansion presented by patriotic St. Louisans. As a final fillip of disdain for accusations that he had kissed and been kissed by a stage girl, the General retorted: "I'll kiss any damn kissable woman I damned please . . . as long as the woman I'm kissing doesn't object." The General departed St. Louis in a huff in favor of New York City.

Henry Ward Beecher had been dubbed the swearing preacher. When Beecher's tour brought him to St. Louis, a Cockerill-inspired mission was to have Johns ask whether the evangelist used "hell" and "damn" as expletives or as nouns. Beecher responded

I use them as expletives. Why not? They're good words. 'Hell' ought to be the favorite word of a preacher. And 'damn' is a common word among men. You can't get at men, sir, without using their words. I'm not a very orthodox preacher and sometimes you have to use strong language. When I want to say something I think ought to be said, I use any word at all that fits. You can tell them that, young man.

Cockerill, impressed by the young reporter's trustworthiness, made Johns his private secretary. Johns did not relish the job but out of fear of offending the Colonel stuck to it until an ingenious method of escape occurred to him. Johns's penmanship, normally quite legible, mysteriously worsened until the Colonel had trouble making it out. Cockerill took the hint and released him to full-time reporting.

One day Cockerill told him: "George, you have a flair for the unusual. I wish you'd write a column every Saturday about personalities, oddities, features—anything that attracts your interest you think people would want to read." The experiment was successful. Under "Jingles"—Johns's pseudonym—the feature appealing to a wide range of interests was so popular it showed up in some New York papers. It may have been the very first newspaper "column" of this type. It was produced in connection with Colonel Cockerill's building of the

Saturday edition in which the managing editor pioneered in a weekly magazine section.

Orrick Johns, son of George Johns, draws on his father's recollections for a vivid portrayal of Colonel Cockerill:

He was a gifted editor. He had been a war correspondent in the Crimea in 1877, and proved his ability and courage under the tremendous difficulties that civilian writers met with in those days of belligerent zones. He was a first-class news man, with cool and quick judgment, overflowing spirits and a fluent, free, entertaining style. He was an adroit phrase-maker, and a master of the short and deadly paragraphs, the equal of J. B. McCullagh of the *Globe-Democrat*. . . .

The *American Journalist* revealed that *Post-Dispatch* circulation had more than sextupled since the consolidation of the *Post* and *Dispatch*. "That, with its enormous advertising patronage," the publication concluded, "makes it perhaps the most valuable piece of evening property, outside New York City, in the country."[2]

George Johns, reminiscing many years after Cockerill hired him, attributes this candid portrayal of the *Post-Dispatch* publisher to the Colonel:

Joseph Pulitzer was the damnedest best man in the world to have in a newspaper office—for one hour in the morning. For the remainder of the day he was a damned nuisance. He would come to the office chock full of ideas and energy. He would start a dozen things in the way of news and editorials . . . and would become meticulously critical . . . change plans, hold up a story until it was written to suit him, and thus become somewhat of a drag carrying out his own ideas. He would stop the press to insert a paragraph or change a word. . . .[3]

Weeks of discouragement followed the Slayback shooting. Exoneration by Joseph Pulitzer bolstered the Colonel's morale but not the newspaper subscription list. Finally John B. McGuffin walked into the Colonel's office wearing a deep frown. The business manager sat down across the desk from Cockerill and began thumbing through figures on a ledger sheet.

"John," he began cautiously, "the paper is losing. We know you're doing everything possible to counteract the dirty work of the Slayback people to undermine the *Post-Dispatch*. But you can't argue with the story these figures tell, John. Our subscription list is shrinking and our advertising is down. Joe's worried. What do you think?" Cockerill suspected that Pulitzer had sent McGuffin. Was this a hint of some kind? Interrupting the reverie, McGuffin tried a consoling note: "I was there and saw what happened. You are not to blame. You had to shoot to save your own life. Still—"[4] McGuffin's words trailed off in silence. Cockerill glanced over the figures. They were disturbing but he was confident the *Post-Dispatch* could ride out the storm; time is a wonderful healer. But, he reasoned, would it be fair to Joseph Pulitzer if he, the "editor with the itchy trigger finger," as some political enemies were dubbing him, stayed on?

A decision had to be made. Cockerill withdrew from the paper. How the decision was arrived at is not clear. The most plausible explanation is that the Colonel, feeling his usefulness had been impaired, stepped out voluntarily. There is no indication of a Cockerill-Pulitzer quarrel. James Barrett's version, lacking details, was that "J. P. acted decisively. He told Cockerill he must go." But Don Seitz wrote that "Pulitzer stood by Cockerill through the storm but it was soon apparent that neither owner nor editor could hold his former standing in the city and that the paper required another pilot."[5]

John A. Dillon, Pulitzer's former partner, for whom the Pulitzer pace had been too dizzy, nevertheless was recalled as general manager. The *Post-Dispatch* eventually turned the tide of opposition. Henry Moore, city editor, moved into the managing editor's office, although the title denoted no such sweeping editorial authority as that wielded by Cockerill. The circulation and advertising slump ended and the newspaper regained its "respectability."

Nevertheless the tragedy imposed a heavy toll. Its effect was to drive Pulitzer and Cockerill from St. Louis, neither to return as a resident. Thereafter Pulitzer visited the *Post-Dispatch* rarely, and not at all after 1890. And incredible as it may seem, this biographer has found that to this day some resentment against the two newspapermen lingers in the city because of the gunfire death of a belligerent lawyer.[6]

Thus Colonel Cockerill found himself an unemployed editor. His late boss, it is true, made some vague reference to the probability the two would pair up again, but the Colonel dismissed the remark as a consoling gesture. He told himself that had he remained at his post the paper could have recouped its losses. He had been utterly devoted to the job. Pulitzer had treated him well. In case Cockerill had failed to bring the journal around, the fiasco would have been on his conscience. The departing editor welcomed a few days of leisure—he hoped it would not be more. He could catch up on his correspondence and perhaps visit relatives in Ohio.

The telegram that arrived at the Lindell Hotel early in May, 1883, ended such diversions.

XII. Park Row Invasion

After the Slayback affair Joseph Pulitzer's ill health worsened, aggravated by a feeling he was no longer wanted in St. Louis. He could not sleep, he was plagued by a racking cough, he had severe headaches, and his eyes bothered him. About May 1, 1883, his doctor ordered him to stop work for a while and take a cruise to the Mediterranean. Although he did start on the trip with Mrs. Pulitzer and son Ralph, then four, the three stopped off at New York City. That was as far as he got. The Pulitzers planned to tarry a few days in the city, presumably at Kate Pulitzer's suggestion that some shopping and sightseeing would soothe her nervous, run-down husband. Pulitzer dutifully escorted his wife to a few department stores, the theater, and the art gallery—and was bored every moment. His mind seemed to be far away.

It was different the next day on a ride down Park Row. As their rig rolled along Ann Street from Broadway, the Missouri publisher, now bubbling with interest, was entranced as he squinted at the buildings flanking the thoroughfare. From Broadway and Ann Street to a tiny triangle at Nassau Street stretched world-famous Newspaper Row. North of Printing House Square loomed the plaza entrance to the Brooklyn Bridge, nearing completion. Within a pistol shot of Benjamin Franklin's statue at Nassau Street a score of newspapers had been published, outlasting dozens more that could not meet competition. Housed in a nine-story edifice across from City Hall nearby was the late Horace Greeley's *Tribune* with its majestic clock tower, an architectural marvel rising 285 feet. The Tribune Building provided office space for the *Morning Journal,* published by brother Albert Pulitzer. As his carriage moved slowly on, Pulitzer identified the newspaper edifices: the white marble structure housing James Gordon Bennett, Jr.'s *Herald*, arrogant and prospering; the *Sun,* edited by Charles A. Dana; the *Mail* and *Express*, respected but undistinguished; the *Commercial Advertiser*, whose editors went all the way back to Noah Webster in the 1790's; the *Daily News*, an undersized sheet that saucily thumbed its nose at its smugly respectable competitors; the *World*, a worrisome liability owned by Wall Street financier Jay Gould, housed in the old Western Union Building; the enfeebled *Times*; the *Star*, at Park Place and Broadway; the *Evening Post*, Broadway and Fulton Street, and the *Staats-Zeitung*, a German language newspaper destined to be the last to desert Park Row. Dominating the field were the *Herald*, the *Sun* and the *Tribune*. Park Row was a colorful segment of a city which, like Cincinnati and St. Louis, was caught in the throes of growing pains, a city where romance thrived in doorways, where vice, horrible yet fascinating, stalked the byways, where life was freer, more wicked, and bolder than anywhere else.

Immigrants pouring into New York had swollen its population to a million and a half. Under the impact of newcomers, old families, to avoid contacts with the alien residents, were moving uptown. Small family neighborhoods sprang up all over Manhattan Island. The major business district was below Fourteenth and Canal Streets. Park Row was strategically situated to give newspapers access to City Hall and the criminal courts from which flowed the juiciest of the day's news. The Bowery, where most of the crime originated, lay conveniently nearby. Behind the Bowery was the ghetto district of the lower East Side. There in the dank and dirty slums Russians, Poles, Irish, Italians, Germans, Bohemians, Greeks, Negroes, and other national groups eked out a miserable existence. In the overpopulated tenements frustrations and cruelty were partners. Drunken fathers beat their wives and children. The number of homeless waifs was matched by droves of girls soliciting on the streets. Along Sixth Avenue and Broadway, extending north from Twenty-third street, was the city's lusty district of sex and sin, the Tenderloin. More than half a century later a Park Row reporter, Samuel Hopkins Adams, would re-create the flavor and mood of this area in his novel *Tenderloin*. In 1886 Bishop Simpson of the Methodist-Episcopal Church admitted there were more prostitutes in New York than Methodists. Their "business" was boosted by veiled advertisements of houses of prostitution in some newspapers. Respectable men idling in parks could expect to be accosted. The bolder girls did not hesitate to solicit men squiring their wives or girl friends, quickly whispering addresses into the ears of their startled prospects and flitting impudently away. Wages were pitifully inadequate. An immigrant arriving fresh with hope of a new and easier life, if he were lucky, earned one dollar for a day of twelve drudging hours. Small wonder wives and daughters were forced into sweatshops or onto the streets to entice gentlemen who would pay for their pleasure.

New York City reeked with all of the vice and corruption Joe Pulitzer and John Cockerill had railed at in St. Louis, plus some large-scale sinning exclusive to itself. Cheap labor was caught in the squeeze for easy profits. The city cried for reform. The opportunities for a great newspaper were abundant.

A few years previously Pulitzer had come close to owning a New York newspaper. He had nibbled at Benjamin Wood's *News* and John Kelly's *Star*. He was involved indirectly in that he owned a small stake in the one-cent *Morning Journal*. He had put up part of the $25,000 brother Albert needed to found the paper.[1] Now, vacationing, he pored over the city's journals, one in particular. He had heard that Jay Gould's moribund New York *World* at 31-32 Park Row was for sale.

The *World* sprouted as a one-cent sheet in 1860. Edited along religious lines, it was merged later with the *Courier and Enquirer*. During the Civil War it served as a mouthpiece for New York Copperheads. It was a vehement opponent of the government's war policies. In 1864 it printed a bogus proclamation, purported to have been signed by President Lincoln, appointing a day of fasting and calling into military service 400,000 men. In 1876 it fell into the hands of railroad magnate Thomas A. Scott, with whom it languished until Scott's death. Under Jay Gould, who bought it from the Scott estate, circulation had dipped to a notorious low of 10,000 by 1883. The undernourished journal could boast one asset— an Associated Press membership.

Not until he spent a sleepless night of indecision did the invader from the West agree to Gould's terms. When Pulitzer confided to his brother the possibility of taking over the *World*, Albert received the news frostily. One Pulitzer in Park Row, he retorted, was enough.[2] In the showdown Kate Pulitzer took the honors for helping her husband reach an agonizing affirmative decision. Pulitzer has been portrayed as so gloomy before the deal was closed that he announced they would sail for Europe the next day. But his wife calmed him down and talked away his fears.[3] The next morning Joe Pulitzer was on hand— strolling over the creaking floors of the Western Union Building in which the *World* had managed to survive.

When the word was out that Pulitzer had met Gould's price of $346,000 for the *World,* skeptics said the wily financier had unloaded a lemon upon the thirty-six-year old greenhorn from St. Louis. Many agreed that if the indefatigable Missourian was to make a success of the newspaper he "would have to divorce the old *World* from the new World."[4] Undaunted, his European trip forgotten, Pulitzer set about his task in whirlwind fashion.

The sedate and polished William Henry Hurlbert, whom Pulitzer inherited as editor, composed for the May 10, 1883, issue a notice that the entire control of the newspaper had been transferred to Joseph Pulitzer. It was the editor's last official act. Pulitzer, in an editorial, wrote a friendly goodbye to Hurlbert, who, seeing it for the first time in the paper, was first to feel the axe. On the way out he bumped into John Gilmer Speed, general manager, also fired. Gone forever was the quiet routine the old *World* staff loved so much. No one could count on keeping his job. The office seethed with Pulitzer's cyclonic operations.

In a fashion that was to become a Hearst trademark, J. P. invaded his brother's office, hiring as managing editor E. C. Hancock. The bewildered Hancock's tenure was one of the shortest on record, less than a week. But before his departure, in Don Seitz's account, he performed one great service— "he pestered the excited owner . . . to make some sort of an announcement proclaiming the change." This is doubted by some students, who say all new owners ran such declarations of policy. At any rate the announcement included Pulitzer's oft-quoted credo:

The *World* . . . will be different in men, measures and methods . . . in purpose, policy and principle . . . in objects and interests . . . in sympathies and convictions . . . in head and heart. Performance is better than promise. Exuberant assurances are cheap. I make none. . . . There is room in this great and growing city for a journal that is not only cheap but bright, not only bright but large, not only large but truly democratic—dedicated to the cause of the people rather than that of purse potentates—devoted

more to the news of the new than the old world, that will expose
all fraud and sham, fight all public evils and abuses—that will
serve and battle for the people with earnest sincerity. . . .[5]

Under Hurlbert the newspaper may have been the most
polished but least read New York newspaper. For Pulitzer
there could be no leisurely stylist as top man in the newsroom. After the lightning fadeout of E. C. Hancock the new
owner prepared to play his trump card—John A. Cockerill,
erstwhile editor of the St. Louis *Post-Dispatch*. It is likely the
"Come at once" telegram was on its way to the Colonel by
May 11, 1883, Pulitzer's first full day at the *World*. Seitz
wrote that within the first week of the new ownership Cockerill
had taken charge of the news end of the paper. The choice
could scarcely have been more dramatic. Cockerill was a
hard-fighting, extroverted, tireless, and talented editor. The
curiosity and perhaps even apprehension with which Newspaper Row awaited him were enhanced by the pistol encounter in which the Colonel had shot Alonzo A. Slayback to death.

Pulitzer may have had Cockerill in mind the moment he
decided to plunge into Park Row. He had intimated as much
when Cockerill withdrew from the St. Louis *Post-Dispatch*.
The partnership had a ring of inevitability. For this relentless pair their production of the *World* was in a sense a cul-
mination of dress rehearsals in St. Louis. Not only did the
Pulitzer-Cockerill teamwork on the *Post-Dispatch* yield the
money for the down payment on the *World*; it provided the
cherished opportunities to develop their own concept of a
daily journal on the mightiest stage of all—New York's Newspaper Row. Seven years after the Pulitzer-Cockerill duo encamped on Park Row the *World*, in a bit of self-eulogy, said,
"The foundation was laid in St. Louis. The battle of new ideas
and theories was fought there under the banner of the *Post-
Dispatch*."[6]

The Colonel was warmly welcomed by his boss.

To bind their bargain with "sweetness," Pulitzer is said
to have allotted Cockerill a few shares of stock in the *World*

(the exact number was never publicly reported). Pulitzer inserted a condition; if Cockerill wanted to sell, Pulitzer would have first option. The story, plausible at least, is that Cockerill cheerfully agreed.[7] If there was such a deal, it was in no sense a shrewd one on the managing editor's part. Joe Pulitzer was the smarter business man. Cockerill was naïve about money matters, a trait compounded in this case by his complete trust in Pulitzer, who, he was sure, would reward him adequately for services performed. But now John Cockerill's passion was the *World*'s news department. His personal finances seemed a remote worry.

Soon the word filtered through Park Row that the redoubtable Western editor had arrived. As he took command of the news department the contrast between the Colonel and Pulitzer was instantly apparent. Pulitzer's energies burned within so that they threatened to burst out all over while Cockerill's energies were better contained. It is quite true their talents complemented each other, but it is inaccurate to portray Cockerill exclusively as a front-page man and the *World* owner as interested only in the editorial page. The Colonel, as we shall see, was remarkably versatile as an editorial writer, while Pulitzer, until illness forced him from on-the-spot supervision, read the news pages with meticulous care and was prolific in suggesting stories.

In no phase of his "own show" was Pulitzer the star performer. Biographer James W. Barrett put it thus:

> As a newspaperman, he was a good artisan. He could write a story, edit copy, write heads, make up the paper, carve out a strong editorial, even keep the accounts if necessary. But he discovered other men could do all these jobs better than he. As a writer of editorials, his ideas were definite, challenging, but his style was not brilliant . . . his efforts were labored.[8]

Yet Joseph Pulitzer was matchless in his ability to inspire other men. The publisher's genius held its spell over the *World*'s managing editor, who excelled in transmitting it to the staff.

Even more than his employer, Cockerill had been annoyed by the lofty style of contemporary journalism. Long involved sentences were the curse of most news writing. The first impact of the new editor's regime was soon noticed by readers of the *World*. One can easily imagine the editor's indoctrinating a reporter thus: "Instead of trying to be literary or to impress Mr. Pulitzer, write your story as you would tell it to a friend." Was it surprising, then, that among the first comments on the new *World* was the frequent one that "the newspaper seems to be talking to us rather than writing over our heads"?

If style was important in achieving the popularity the *World* sought, so was the choice of subject matter. The *World* dispensed an endless stream of sensations. In a few weeks after Cockerill's arrival front page headlines proclaimed such bizarre subjects as "A Bride but Not a Wife," "A Mother's Awful Crime," "Screaming for Mercy," "A Mystery of the River," "Love and Cold Poison," and "The Wall Street Terror." The *World* also made frequent use of alliterative captions such as "Bachelor Bang's Bridal," "Terrible Times in Troy," "Baptized in Blood," "Jim-Jams in the Jury," and "Duke Meets His Doom." This technique was new with the *World*. Since the Cincinnati *Enquirer* under Cockerill's editorship had used this technique, it is probable that the Colonel introduced it on the *World*. Reporters were sent foraging for stories that would excite, infuriate, fascinate, and inform. Human comedy and human tragedy were fair game, to be dissected and exposed in the glare of the *World*'s front page "show window." Malfeasance and corruption in high places were fuel to fire up the *World*'s championship of the masses against the privileged classes. The *World* brought about the conviction of a builder of firetrap tenement houses. It crusaded against a police officer who had criminally assaulted a little girl and a custodian who had murdered a young woman. It exposed a pseudo-astrologer. It delighted in capitalizing on stories the *Times*, *Tribune*, *Sun* and *Herald* out of laziness or a sense of dignity had slighted or ignored. To brighten its image as a crusader against the privileged classes the *World* proposed taxes on luxuries, inheritances, large incomes, monopolies, and great corporations, a tariff for revenue, reform of civil service, punishment for corrupt officials, penalties for vote-buying and punishment for government officials who coerced their employees in elections. Nothing pleased Cockerill and Pulitzer more than the prospect of a story which would convey the image of the *World* as a fearless champion of the masses.

Its crusading magic bore fruit, with a tragic twist, shortly after Colonel Cockerill picked up the editorial reins. The new Brooklyn Bridge, oddly, had rated scant notice in the other papers. This factor plus the spectacular character of the bridge as an engineering feat prompted the *World* to give it extra play.

To the horror of economy-minded John B. McGuffin, who had been transplanted from St. Louis as business manager, Pulitzer and Cockerill had laid out plans McGuffin considered wildly extravagant. Cockerill was, in his view, getting out of hand with his idea of "opening up" the paper with more white space. "We need every bit of space we can get for news, and you're talking about white space!" McGuffin snorted. Cockerill looked over at Pulitzer, murmuring, "Wait till you hear Joe's plans." Pulitzer's plans—for plastering the front page with stories and a drawing of the forthcoming bridge-opening— were actually Cockerill's plans. "That's right," Pulitzer responded. "We'll go all out on the bridge celebration."

Even before the bridge was put into use, the *World*, catering to popular whim, urged doing away with the five-cent fare for foot passengers and later on, the charge for vehicles. Both fees were eventually abolished.

On May 24, 1883, while other New York papers were absorbed in the birthday anniversary of Queen Victoria, the *World*'s page of background stories greeted readers on the day the Brooklyn Bridge was formally opened. In a sense the

World did its work too well. So many people thronged to the
bridge that a dozen pedestrians were killed. They were crushed
in the panic growing out of a rumor that the bridge was
weakening under the load.

From the foregoing it might be concluded that the *World*
was interested only in sensational material. This was not true.
In preserving balance Cockerill's hand can be seen. Journalism
historian Edwin Emery finds that much of the success of the
news policy is credited to the Colonel. He describes the managing editor as "adept in both playing up human interest
stories and in maintaining a solid presentation of significant
local, national, and international news; for despite the attention given to sensational material, the *World* tried to give its
readers full coverage of the day's events."

In 1885 the *World* added momentum to its surge as a
journal of influence.

As a friendly gesture France had presented the United
States the Statue of Liberty. But a pedestal for its Bedloe
Island site was lacking. The inspiration for raising the money
for the pedestal has been erroneously attributed to Pulitzer. A
fund drive was already in progress when he bought the *World*,
but it had raised only $150,000 of the $250,000 needed.
It was neither Pulitzer nor Cockerill who suggested that the
World put the necessary "steam" into the lagging campaign—
it was John R. Reavis, a promising newcomer from Missouri.
Cockerill recognized this as a made-to-order opportunity to
goad the rich and champion the poor, particularly the immigrant population to whom Miss Liberty meant something
special. Walt McDougall leaves the impression that it took
some urging to get Pulitzer's approval for what undoubtedly
was to be the *World*'s most popular exploit. To his credit the
World owner, once sold on the plan, threw the newspaper's
resources unsparingly into the campaign.

Pulitzer was in Europe much of the time and so the responsibility of publicizing the drive fell to the Colonel, who
took to the task with his usual fire. The *World* excoriated the

rich for their failure to contribute the needed funds. "Let us not wait for the millionaires to give this money," the *World* stormed. "Let us hear from the people. . . . Give something, however little."[9]

The *World* appealed to modest wage earners and farmers and schools all over the country. It was a rewarding effort. Small donations poured in from school children, working people, shop girls, and artisans. Their gifts, the *World* took pains to point out, made up the bulk of the pedestal fund. By June, 1885, all but $10,000 had been raised. When the $300,000 statue, designed by the famous sculptor, Auguste Bartholdi, was shipped to the selected site in New York harbor and officially received by the American people, it was a proud moment for the newspaper. All of the additional $10,000 needed was eventually contributed. Colonel Cockerill in a letter to Joe Pulitzer in Kissingen, Bavaria, reported on the great day:

> Of course, you will see by the papers how we received the Statue of Liberty. It was really a grand success, despite the indifference of other newspapers. I am sure no newspaper ever had a greater triumph than the World had on that day. One of the World steamers—the Emmons—was my own private enterprise. I took with me Sutton, Fiske, Graham and their families, together with all the boys in the office who could be spared. . . . Our program was carried out to perfection. In fact, I never saw such a complete success. And the World was the only newspaper heard of that day.[10]

The Colonel wrote Pulitzer that "the Herald, by its foolish treatment of the Statue of Liberty story, has driven another nail in its coffin."[11] Other newspapers belatedly picked up the story. The *Sun*, reported Cockerill, was still failing, adding: "Last Saturday, when there certainly ought to have been some demand for the story of the reception [of the statue], they could not get above 98,000."[12]

President Cleveland accepted the statue for the country.

In a sense the *World* could claim both the statue and the President as its very own.

In 1884 Grover Cleveland, governor of New York and former mayor of Buffalo, drew favored notice from the *World*. Pulitzer, possibly sensing his potential as a king-maker, predicted in the *World* that a "candidate like Cleveland" would sweep the country as effectively as Cleveland did in the gubernatorial contest.[13] In that test Cleveland carried New York by a 200,000 margin. The *World*'s artful reference to a "candidate like Cleveland" was a leading factor in the National Democratic Convention's choice of the New York governor to oppose James G. Blaine, the Republican nominee for president.

The campaigns of both candidates were rocked by scandal. The *World* managed to hoist its candidate out of the mire, due to some ingenious master-minding in which Cockerill as managing editor played a heavy hand. Blaine could never get out of a defensive position. The first blow to Cleveland's candidacy pertained to his romance with a statuesque Buffalo woman. The Democratic nominee admitted readily enough his friendship with the widow but, he added, he wasn't at all sure that he was the father of her child. His political enemies pointed out this was mighty peculiar, since Cleveland was paying for the child's care in an orphanage.[14]

The *World* was stunned, momentarily. Its course of action bore the stamp of Cockerill's counsel. Instead of an angry denial of the rumor, the possibility of Cleveland's fatherhood was conceded. Indeed, the Cleveland supporters capitalized on the scandal, doing so through pungent comment by the *World*:

It is true that Governor Cleveland once had a sporadic association with a middle-aged female. Is such an offense unpardonable? If Grover Cleveland had a whole family of illegitimate children . . . he would be more worthy of the office than Blaine, the beggar at the feet of railroad jobbers, the prostitute in the Speaker's chair, the lawmaking broker in land grabs, the representative and agent of the corruptionists, monopolists and enemies of the Republic.[15]

The *World* published a report of an inquiry made by a group of prominent clergymen shrewdly captioned "Endorsed by Clergy."[16] It held that Cleveland was more "sinned against than sinful." The *World*'s strategy portrayed Cleveland as a good, brave man who if not infallible was on the side of the people against Blaine, "the captive of venality and political corruption."

Politically, Cleveland's indiscretion was minor when compared to Blaine's imprudence in attending a banquet at Delmonico's given in his honor by Jay Gould, former owner of the *World*, Russell Sage, and several wealthy backers. The candidate's attendance against the advice of close friends was seized upon by the *World* to deliver its heaviest punch at the Republican nominee as a tool of the vested interests. Spread across the front page of the *World* of October 30, 1884, was a cartoon depicting "The Royal Feast of Belshazzar and the Money Kings." The Republican candidate was shown flanked by diamond-studded millionaires feasting on Monopoly Soup, Lobby Pudding, and Gould Pie while a poor man, his wife, and child stretched out hands for crumbs from the rich men's table. Some historians say it was the most effective political cartoon ever published.[17] Blaine found it futile to deny the implications of the caricature. From that moment the tide swung in Cleveland's favor.

Colonel Cockerill had a hand in both the cartoon and in hiring the cartoonist who created it. Months before, Walt McDougall, a young and frustrated cartoonist, had done a cartoon for *Puck*, which was rejected. On a hunch the young artist walked into the Western Union Building and, lacking courage to see anyone in authority, thrust his cardboard into the hands of an elevator operator. "Give that to the editor," he shouted and fled. The cartoon landed on the Colonel's desk. Cockerill examined it, casually, then with growing interest. He laid it across the top half of a newspaper. It matched.

Minutes later, in Pulitzer's office adjoining his own, Cockerill excitedly tossed it on the publisher's desk. "Joe, take a good look at this," and the Colonel pointed out the similarity in size between the drawing and a news page. "Are you thinking what I'm thinking?" The cartoon was not distinguished but since it took a slap at Blaine it was a political attention-getter. Pulitzer was intrigued. A five-column engraving was made and the cartoon appeared the next morning on page one. The Colonel suggested they summon McDougall; Pulitzer agreed; McDougall arrived, breathless, from his Newark home and within minutes he was the *World*'s political cartoonist. The twenty-six-year-old McDougall, starting on a fifty-dollars-a-week salary, was around for sixteen years.[18]

Cockerill occasionally suggested, as editors do, a theme for the daily cartoon. McDougall wrote that Cockerill was one of only two *World* editors who ever suggested usable ideas to him.[19] It is possible the editor suggested the Belshazzar idea.

McDougall once drew the Colonel's censure. When the cartoonist turned in to Cockerill a snappy photograph of a curvaceous actress with seven inches of shapely calves exposed, the managing editor blue-penciled a line across the young lady's ankles. "This cannot be published in a respectable journal like the *World*," he said with a twinkle and exaggerated emphasis on the word "respectable." "We'll crop off the bottom of the picture to make it decent. We don't want another double-exposure scandal in this office. We'd have all the God-damned ministers in town down on us."[20] The pair roared in laughter. Their mirth was reminiscent of a curious double-exposure. It happened in the operation of the *World*'s new sixty-dollar "instantaneous" camera. McDougall, in his first try, thought he had photographed an antique buggy—but the picture also revealed a bare-legged woman.[21]

When Grover Cleveland was elected president for his first term, the *World* quickly placed the credit where the paper thought it belonged. "While claims for the defeat of Mr. Blaine and the preservation of the republic are coming from every quarter," it crowed, "permit us to say that the New York *World* did it."[22] Cleveland agreed. "If the contest had lacked the forceful and potent advocacy of democratic principles provided by the *World*," wrote Cleveland nineteen years later in an anniversary message to the *World*, "the result might have been reversed."[23]

A curious switch during Cleveland's first term found Colonel Cockerill vigorously opposed to the President's bid for re-election in 1888.[24] Thus Cleveland lost the supporter who, as Pulitzer's top editor, had done so much to elect him. Cockerill's disenchantment with Cleveland lay in the President's action in pushing for a lowering of the tariff. Cleveland had not measured up to the Colonel's expectations in other areas, such as civil service reform. President Cleveland had tried to please both reformers and spoilsmen. But it was the tariff issue that most disturbed the Colonel. Cleveland contended that high protection was a bane to the farmer and laborer and a cause for monopoly. Cockerill regarded Cleveland's "free trade" policy as a threat to American industry and a betrayal of the American laboring man to the pauper labor of Europe. Under pressure of tariff reformers in his cabinet, the President had devoted an entire state of the union message to his pet program—the lower tariff. Cleveland's obsession with his reform proposals served to unite the defenders of high tariff duties.

In the Republican National Convention of 1888 the high protectionists bowled over the tariff reformers and nominated a conservative corporation lawyer, Benjamin Harrison of Indiana, a staunch supporter of high tariffs and sound money. Cleveland was renominated by the Democrats for a second term.

For John Cockerill, switching political allegiance to the Republican party was a matter of personal conscience. Yet the fact that he turned Republican has created the impression that Cockerill fought Cleveland in the news pages of the *World* while the editorial page, under Pulitzer's direction, ardently supported Cleveland. One account goes so far as to say that Pulitzer, because he considered Cockerill among his few close friends, decided to practice true freedom of the press and permitted the situation to continue. An examination of the *World* files for the period of the 1888 campaign does not support this assertion. Indeed some of the political stories in the news columns seemed more vigorously anti-Republican than the editorials. In the first six days of November the *World* published several exposé-type stories detrimental to the Republican cause. On November 2 the *World*'s lead story was a glowing account of a Democratic rally in which Democratic Governor David B. Hill was the chief speaker. Elsewhere there was news of a big Democratic rally, but a reader would search in vain for word of a Republican rally.

The *World* on November 3 revealed that Colonel W. W. Dudley, treasurer of the Republican National Committee, had begun suit against the paper for $25,000 damages "for what he calls libel." The "libel" was the *World*'s report that Dudley had promised Republican county leaders in Indiana that their committee "will certainly receive financial assistance to hold our floaters and doubtful voters, and gain enough of the other kind to give Harrison and Morton a 10,000 majority." The suit never came to trial, a healthy sign that Cockerill's reporters had documented their charges.

If there was Republican slanting by Cockerill, it did not show through a November 5 story captioned "Begging for His Father." A Chicago datelined report said Harrison's son was trying to raise $100,000 from Western businessmen to aid the Republican candidate's cause. The next day the *World* charged a Republican plot by the U. S. Chief Supervisor of Elections "to arrest Democratic voters in order to keep them away from the polls." Stories about Democratic rallies and party activities outnumbered those of Republican functions. Full coverage was given Cleveland's low tariff policies, which Cockerill believed would damage the American economy. On this issue Cleveland was the defender, always a political disadvantage.

Not all of the breaks fell for Cleveland. Reporting the New York visit of two Canadian ministers to confer with prominent Republicans, the *World* played up the incident as a "Canada-Wants-Harrison" feature.[25]

It would be difficult to draw on another situation that demonstrates more forcefully that a competent reporter or editor, while embracing personally strong political convictions, can remain objective in reporting a highly partisan campaign. Colonel Cockerill, it may be added, was editing a newspaper that, despite its claims of independence, was regarded as a Democratic journal. Of necessity it carried much Democratic news.

The *World's* more discerning editorial page readers might have noticed a difference between the 1884 and 1888 campaigns. In 1884 the *World* was ardently pro-Cleveland. During the 1888 campaign Pulitzer, although in control of the page, was pulling the strings from his yacht. He was in touch through a battery of secretaries who read the news to him, but it was William H. Merrill who wrote most of the editorials and got out the page. Not that the *World* had lost its affection for Democracy. "The Democrats deserve success," it said on election day morning. "They have displayed the full courage of right convictions. And . . . if such a course shall meet its just reward, the result will be the re-election today of President Cleveland and a Democratic House of Representatives."[26] Yet the name of Cleveland appeared far less often in editorials, and those extolling the President lacked the fire of the 1884 campaign. Some *World* readers may have sensed in its November 6 editorial a note of faltering enthusiasm. "There is a fair choice between the parties. The *World* earnestly believes that Democratic success would promote the public welfare. But," the newspaper added graciously, "a government of the people is safe in the hands of any majority of the people." The editorial seemed to be saying that it would be no disaster if Harrison were elected.

Since Harrison won the election, although Cleveland won a majority of the popular vote, perhaps it was not surprising that Colonel Cockerill, a Republican sitting in the sensitive chair of managing editor, should have been accused of slanting the news for his man. A careful study of the files, however, would indicate he did the Republican cause far more good by keeping the news as objective as the role of Democratic paper would allow. Indeed one scholar's impression was that the newspaper, "with a fine impartiality, embarrassed both parties on occasions."[27]

Colonel Cockerill was drawn into a stormy repercussion that followed the *World*'s support of Cleveland in 1884—an intensification of the feud between Pulitzer and Charles A. Dana, editor of the New York *Sun.*

In 1884 scholarly, belligerent Dana was miffed by Cleveland's snub of the *Sun* editor's request for the promise of an appointment for a friend. In consequence Dana turned his wrath upon the Democratic nominee, joining forces with the Greenback Labor party's choice, Benjamin F. Butler. When Cleveland won, Dana suffered prestige pains. The *Sun*'s circulation dropped from 137,000 to 85,000.[28] The crowning humiliation came the day the *Sun,* which had printed its circulation daily on page one, ceased to do so. It was a pathetic tip-off of the paper's decline.

Other New York newspapers felt the hot breath of the *World* upon their necks. Within a year the "new" *World,* at two cents a copy, forced the *Times* to trim its figures from four cents. The *Herald,* slicing its three-cent rate to two, bought space in the hated *World* to advertise itself. Cockerill took exquisite pleasure in noting the fact editorially. The *Tribune* dropped from four to three cents. By August 11 of its first year under Pulitzer and Cockerill, *World* circulation shot up to 39,000.[29] When the figure touched 100,000 in 1884, Pulitzer ordered a 100-gun salute fired in City Hall

Park. Jubilant *World* staffers wore tall silk hats, courtesy of the management. In less than two years the total was up to 125,000. By September, 1886 the *World*, with over 250,000, claimed the largest circulation ever attained by an American newspaper.[30] Just as it shoved back the *Sun*'s circulation, the *World* as early as 1884 overtook the *Herald* in advertising lineage. *World* advertisements stretched to fifty and sixty columns a day in a 14-page edition. Four years after Pulitzer and Cockerill invaded Newspaper Row the *World* proprietor wrote a friend that newspaper earnings exceeded half a million dollars for one year. Jay Gould had been paid off. By 1886 the *World* was the most profitable newspaper ever published up to that time.

In the savage Pulitzer-Dana editorial feud the decisive chapter grew out of the famous boodling case exposed by the *World*. When the Board of Aldermen, over the veto of New York Mayor Franklin Edson, in 1884 granted a franchise for a horse-car railway on Broadway to Jacob Sharp for half a million dollars, Cockerill suspected bribery. The *World* protested that the franchise fee was absurdly low. Cockerill sent reporters digging. Irate property owners slapped a temporary injunction on Sharp's company but it was vacated the next year by the courts. Sharp's workers started laying tracks from Fourteenth Street to City Hall. Editor Cockerill, fortified by public indignation, demanded answers to some pertinent questions: Was money paid to any member of the Board of Aldermen? How much was paid and who paid it?

Pressures from the *World* bore fruit. In April, 1886, the New York County Grand Jury indicted all except two members of the Board who voted for the franchise. (It is an interesting question whether the Pulitzer-Cockerill exposures were ultimately in the public interest. Their effect was to toss the corrupt franchise into the greedy hands of William C. Whitney and Thomas Fortune Ryan. The latter were thus enabled to make millions by building a colossal pyramid of high finance that smashed the Metropolitan Street Railroad.)

Assigned to prosecute the grafters was young, energetic De
Lancey Nicoll, an assistant district attorney. Several of the
accused aldermen, including Sharp, were convicted; but Sharp
was granted a new trial. He died before he could be tried
again. Impressed by Nicoll, the *World* backed the young attorney in his race for district attorney. So did Dana's *Sun*,
initially, then reversed itself, thus starting a hassle between
the *Sun* and the *World*. The *Sun* joined Tammany and the
Democrats in support of Nicoll's rival, John T. Fellows,
another district attorney. The incongruous lineup found the
World bolting the Democratic party to promote Nicoll.

The extremes of vilification in which Pulitzer and Dana
engaged have seldom been matched in a newspaper war. Dana,
in the Nicoll-Fellows campaign, reached for his most vicious
weapon, a personal attack upon Pulitzer, with pointed reference to his ethnic background. Pulitzer, said the *Sun*, was a
renegade Jew who denied his breed, adding:

The insuperable obstacle in the way of his social progress is not
the fact that he is a Jew but in certain offensive qualities. . . . his
face is repulsive, not because the physiognomy is Hebraic, but
because it is Pulitzeresque . . . cunning, malice, falseness, treachery,
dishonesty, greed, and venal self-abasement have stamped their
unmistakable traits. . . .[31]

Pulitzer's father was part Jewish, his mother German-Catholic;
the Pulitzer family was identified with the Protestant Episcopal
Church. The publisher was married in an Episcopal church
and buried in that faith. Pulitzer ignored all references to
his ethnic background. But when Dana shifted his attack to
Colonel Cockerill, the *World* returned the fire.

In its resurrection of the St. Louis tragedy, the *Sun* loosed
this barrage:

Col. Alonzo W. Slayback was shot and killed, under shocking
circumstances, in the editorial rooms of Mr. Pulitzer's paper, the
Post-Dispatch, by Colonel John A. Cockerill, then as now Mr.
Pulitzer's managing editor. It has been charged that the reason
the St. Louis Grand Jury failed to indict Colonel Cockerill for

murder was that such was the degree of Mr. Pulitzer's hold upon the district attorney of St. Louis and his administration that the indictment was frustrated.

We can see no avoidance of the truth or the effect of these statements, but it is our manifest duty to take account of them in the light of the unprecedented, frantic and astounding effort which the same men are now making to obtain what is virtually the control of the district attorney's office.[32]

It was out of such distrust of these *World* men, explained Dana, that he had withdrawn the *Sun*'s support of Mr. Nicoll. It was too bad, he added, that such a young and promising lawyer was associated with the *World*.

In an editorial that Cockerill may be assumed to have composed because of his obvious knowledge of the St. Louis shooting, the *World* countered: "In seeking an apology for his sudden change from an active supporter of Mr. Nicoll . . . to a position of malignant hostility, the vicious editor of the Sun assumes that it will not do to have a man elected . . . who enjoys the support of the World." Turning to the St. Louis affair, the *World* declared that raking up this old chestnut was in character for Charles Ananias Dana. Such a revival, it said, is worthy of "an assaulter of women and a mortgaged, broken-down calumniator in the last agencies of humiliation." The *World* reviewed the Slayback affair, reminding New York that in St. Louis two grand juries had investigated and refused to present a bill. "A St. Louis newspaper clique," said the editorial,

actuated by the same kind of motives to be found on the surface of the New York *Sun*, sought by every means to create prejudice and misuse of the machinery of the law. The clique even tried forgery, perjury and conspiracy to compass the discomfiture of one who was cruelly forced to defend himself against the premeditated assault of an armed man, backed by an armed villain, in his own office, after an unsought quarrel had been foisted upon him. Every fact that could then be distorted was distorted; and we all know something of the venomous malignity of a decaying newspaper, as exemplified in the case of the New York *Sun*. In the face of all this and the prejudice incident to it, the vindication of Mr. Cockerill was complete.

The *World* recalled that a civil suit against Cockerill was dismissed. It denied using any influence upon the prosecutor, who, "though elected against the *Post-Dispatch*'s opposition and a Republican, being an honest, intelligent man, did not assent to the persistent proposition to have his court converted into an instrument of persecution." The editorial concluded with a blast that impugned Dana's financial solvency, tagged him a hate monger, challenged his veracity, questioned his sanity, and branded him an unmitigated scoundrel.[33]

The vehement defense of Colonel Cockerill did not have much to do with the election of a district attorney. Nor did it produce a victory for De Lancey Nicoll. He was swamped by a combination of Tammany politicians who had no taste for Nicoll's crusading talents. Fellows won by 20,000 votes.

Charles A. Dana was not a gracious winner. Joyously concluding that Joseph Pulitzer was finished, the *Sun* addressed itself to the *World*'s owner: "We could wish, Pulitzer, that St. Louis had possessed a greater stomach . . . then we should have been spared the infliction of your presence here. . . . It may shortly please the inscrutable Providence, which has chastened us with your presence, to give you that stern and dreadful signal—'Move on, Pulitzer, move on!' "[34] The *World* took its defeat good-naturedly. It had hoped to have a district attorney who would carry on the prosecution of the boodling aldermen. It knew Mr. Nicoll could have done it; it hoped Mr. Fellows would do it. If he does not, said the *World*, he will be spanked; if he does the *World* will be as generous in praise as it has been frank in its opposition. The *Sun* had won the battle but lost the war. Dana hoped to turn the Fellows victory into a tide of resentment against the *World* and a resurgence of popular favor for the *Sun*. Instead the *World* emerged stronger than ever, in circulation, advertising, and popularity.

The newspapers that once bore the imprints of Pulitzer and Dana today are housed under the same roof and published under the masthead of the New York *World-Telegram and Sun*. If it has become possible in the mysterious realm of eternity for these two intrepid editors to discover that fact, they must be shuddering at the very thought.

XIII. Gal Reporter

Prior to the invasion of a pint-sized, hazel-eyed, auburn-haired girl of twenty, the *World* newsroom was a stronghold of tough, proud masculinity, its atmosphere polluted by cigar smoke and profanity. Placed strategically among the desks, chairs, wastebaskets, and littered papers were brass cuspidors that occasionally provoked tests of marksmanship. The misses added nothing to the cleanliness of the room. A decent girl had to be a little mad just to show up. The prevailing view was that respectable girls stayed home until they were married, or failing to snare husbands they could teach or take up nursing. There had been stirrings of discontent in feminine circles but trouble makers like Susan B. Anthony, Belva Lockwood, and Elizabeth Cady Stanton were not to be taken seriously. Womanhood was noble as long as home ties held it in check. If such bonds gave way, in the orthodox male view, the whole fabric of society could be ripped to shreds. This meant, of course, that hiring women to gather news was simply out of the question.

It was assumed that Colonel Cockerill held this conventional view. So on a lazy late-summer day in 1887, it was taken for granted that when a demure job-seeking girl finally badgered her way into the Colonel's office, she soon would emerge, perhaps under the editor's angry escort. Those who awaited the outcome could not know that behind the managing editor's door Colonel Cockerill was ready to ignore an absurd professional prejudice against girl reporters. Nor could they guess that the crusty Colonel was plotting with this strip of a girl one of New York City's most spectacular exposés.

The girl who had braved the awesome city room gave the name of Nellie Bly. Three hours earlier she had walked to the railing that fenced in the news department and in as calm a voice as she could muster, said, "I want to see Mr. Cockerill."

"Sorry, miss," a snippy copy boy informed her. "Nobody can see Mr. Cockerill today. That's orders."

"I intend to see Mr. Cockerill if I have to stay here all day and all night and all day tomorrow—I mean to see him. This is a matter of life and death for me."[1]

A few more words of insistence and refusal were exchanged and the copy boy walked away. Nobody paid much attention. The hope was that the girl would go away if ignored. Nellie, in a thin summer dress of gray lawn trimmed with coral braid and a gray straw hat with white veil, stood her ground—for an hour. As she lingered, looks that had been casual turned into curious stares. One of the first to notice a bulldog persistence written in this pert little face was Bill Nye, the *World* humorist. Nellie was gathering increasing notice from reporters and subeditors. In the second hour of waiting, two more attempts to persuade her to leave failed. The copy boy joined a cluster of reporters and advertising men. Among them was the business manager, who volunteered "to get rid of her." He turned toward the gate. Nellie wasn't there. She had headed toward the stairway that led to Cockerill's office.

"Here, you can't go up there," shouted the surprised copy boy. The girl was limp with fear but she kept going. The copy boy overtook her but, to her relief, not to eject her. Instead he pointed at the door bearing the words "John A. Cockerill." Everybody waited and watched. The explosion would come soon enough. A few moments passed; nothing happened. Then

a minute. Two minutes, three . . . four. Still there appeared
no brash young lady being ousted from the busy man's office.

Colonel Cockerill was intent upon his work when the
timid rap on his door distracted him. "Who is it?" His clipped
words betrayed annoyance.

"I am Nellie Bly," said the intruder. "I want to be a reporter for the *World*. I waited down there for three hours to
get to see you. I don't intend to go away until I have talked
to you."[2] The words poured out. John Cockerill looked up
in astonishment.

He saw a trim, slender, neatly dressed girl. Set in an attractive face were melancholy eyes that seemed to look straight
into one's mind. To the Colonel the girl did not seem as
frightened as she should have been under the circumstances.
Indeed with a major obstacle of getting into the managing
editor's office overcome, she was recovering her poise.
Cockerill rose, walked around in front of his desk and offered
Nellie a chair. Something about this youngster intrigued him.
She had seemed timid, yet her words revealed no fear. With
one icy "No" Cockerill could have turned her away. He restrained himself.

"What did you say your name was?"

"Nellie Bly," she replied.

Cockerill frowned. Something familiar about that name.
Then it clicked. "Oh, yes," he recalled. "You wrote me a letter
offering to cover the balloon ascension sponsored by the St.
Louis *Post-Dispatch*. (Cockerill had acknowledged her letter,
informing her that another reporter—a man—had been assigned to cover it.) You didn't mean YOU would have gone
up in that balloon?"

Nellie Bly felt a flutter of hope. Here was the managing
editor of the greatest newspaper in the country showing interest in her! It couldn't come too soon.

As Nellie Bly, Elizabeth Cochrane had been a sensation
in Pittsburgh. It all began two years before. Editor George A.
Madden of the *Dispatch* had published an editorial on "What

Girls Are Good For." It was not good, said the *Dispatch*, for girls to work in offices or to try getting into politics. They should not get out of bounds. An indignant reply came, signed "E. Cochrane." The writer asked for an interview. Madden was surprised that E. Cochrane turned out to be Elizabeth Cochrane, but he liked her answer to the editorial, "Girls and Their Spheres in Life."[3] He published and paid for it and, to spare her the indignities expected to befall a girl reporter, gave her the pen name "Nellie Bly" (From Stephen Foster's "Nelly Bly, Nelly Bly, bring de broom along"). Nellie's success was immediate and spectacular. She exposed the miseries of slums, the paltry wages and the hazardous working conditions of Pittsburgh factories. She cajoled Madden into sending her on a reporting trip to Mexico. She was admitted to the Press Club, petticoats and all.

Ultimately Nellie, armed with clippings of her Pittsburgh conquests and full of misgivings, decided to invade New York. The *World* was her objective, to her a reporter's paradise. Her first call there was a fast brushoff. The other newspapers were equally brusque. Nellie Bly and her press clippings meant nothing to Park Row. Fear of failure began to haunt her. Perhaps she should have stayed in the friendly atmosphere of her Pittsburgh job. Then came the minor incident that can influence a lifetime. A vagrant snatched her purse as she sat on a park bench. It left Nellie penniless. It forced upon her the "life-and-death" aspect of getting a job without which she might never have had courage to return to the *World*.

With the question of whether she would really go up in a balloon, Nellie was certain Cockerill was testing her. She was ready for him. "I certainly did mean it." As Nellie met the Colonel's gaze, her words fell with all the emphasis of a spinster saying yes to a belated marriage proposal.

"What kind of things would you like to write for the *World*?" The Colonel was exploring.

Nellie reported on the kind of stories she had done in Pittsburgh for George Madden.

"Oh, yes," Cockerill said. "I had a letter from Madden about you. He's a good man. George isn't afraid to scuttle a tradition now and then—"

"Then you must respect his judgment," Nellie cut in quickly. "He hired me, didn't he? I know you have all the good reporters you need, Mr. Cockerill. I also know that to get a job with you I'd have to offer something different. That's exactly what I'm going to do. I can give you stories that you have never published."

It is at this point in the conversation that in some accounts Miss Cochrane is supposed to have sprung her sensational proposal of feigning insanity, having herself committed to the Blackwell's Island asylum to find out how the inmates were treated, and writing her story for the *World*. Referring to this as Nellie's own idea, Ishbel Ross in her *Ladies of the Press* wrote that the *World* decided to let her work up the idea. One of the more romantic versions says that in response to the impersonation proposal "blue flames shot out of Cockerill's eyes" and when the *World*'s owner heard it later "Pulitzer's nostrils quivered . . . The lass had hit home. Insanity was a feared subject in the newspaper world."[4]

Elizabeth Cochrane herself disputed the theory that it was she who made the proposal to feign insanity. "On September 22, 1887," she wrote in her *Ten Days in a Mad-House*,[5] "I was asked by the *World* if I could have myself committed to one of the asylums for the insane in New York, with a view of writing a plain and unvarnished narrative of the treatment of the patients therein and the methods of management." Who then asked her?[6]

Miss Cochrane's visit was timely. Her entreaty for a job came at a time when the *World* was cudgeling its collective wits for a new sensation with which to startle its readers and shake its competition. This sense of urgency supports the more plausible explanation that the impersonation plan was hatched in the Colonel's fertile brain. As the applicant told of her expeditions in and exposés of slum and working conditions in Pittsburgh, the bolder idea may have occurred to the managing editor that a girl of Nellie's pluck and initiative could become a "mental patient" and write a revealing story. Miss Cochrane knew little about New York and presumably nothing of the disturbing reports of mistreatment of patients and poor management at the Blackwell's Island asylum that the Colonel had been hearing.

Whatever the truth of its origin, the proposal was tailored to the *World's* concept of news enterprise. As plans took form the Colonel's thoughts were diverted momentarily. As he sized up his young listener he found himself asking an unspoken question: Why should editors discriminate against women in journalism? The Colonel himself had hired a girl reporter, Calista Halsey, on the Washington *Post*. Miss Halsey had made good. If Miss Cochrane joined the *World* staff she would not be the first woman reporter, a distinction often but erroneously attributed to her.[7]

Cockerill, excusing himself, consulted Pulitzer briefly in an adjoining office. Returning with Cockerill to the Colonel's office, Pulitzer listened to the proposal. There is not the slightest evidence that the *World's* owner did anything more than approve the plan and the hiring of Miss Cochrane. She was the Colonel's find.

Thereafter the Colonel apprised Nellie of the risks involved, both to Miss Cochrane herself and to the prestige of the *World*. If the *World's* scheme were to be discovered prematurely, the newspaper would become the laughingstock of the city. He questioned Nellie further, reassuring himself that the girl could be trusted. The Colonel preached accuracy. He told her that if a sensational story resulted, it must be factual. The inner workings of the asylums for the insane, he warned, are kept hidden from the press and the public. Her mission would not be easy. "We do not ask you to go there for the purpose of making sensational revelations," Miss Cochrane was told. "Write up things as you find them, good or bad. Give praise or blame as you think best, and the truth all the time."

"I had some faith in my own ability as an actress," Nellie recalled, "and thought I could assume insanity long enough to accomplish any mission entrusted to me."

Cockerill had one misgiving about his new recruit. "I am afraid of that chronic smile of yours," he told her.

"I will smile no more," Nellie responded. "But how will you get me out after I once get in?" The Colonel admitted he did not know, but assured her, "We will get you out even if we have to tell who you are."[8]

As Nellie strode buoyantly from Cockerill's office, the copy boy who had tried to thwart her was idling at the railing. His face betrayed the obvious question: How did this girl manage to stay in the managing editor's office for nearly an hour? Masculine eyes followed her girlish figure in disbelief. Nellie, producing a slip of paper, decided to give the staring men something to "chew on." "You are to direct me to the cashier's office," she chirped saucily to the copy boy. "I want to get this voucher cashed." A voucher, as everyone within eavesdropping distance knew, was a salary advance on a job. Nellie was now one of them.

On October 8, 1887, Nellie Bly's bomb—the opening salvo of her series, "Behind Asylum Bars"—left New York reeling. Nellie had succeeded in impersonating an insane girl so expertly that all but one of the examining physicians had been duped. The delicious mystery of "Nellie Brown, the unknown insane girl with the Spanish accent," which kept the other newspapers in a dither, was solved. The public was fascinated and horrified by Nellie's first-person account of her experiences inside the asylum and her poignant description of cruelty and neglect in the care of her fellow inmates. And with Nellie's disclosures of inhuman practices public indignation rose.

Cockerill derived great personal satisfaction in Miss Cochrane's achievement and, with Pulitzer, glowed over the play given Nellie Bly in competing newspapers. As the *Sun* phrased it, "Nellie Bly was too sharp for Island doctors."

A member of the Board of Charities called on Cockerill. "We need your help," he said. "For years we've been begging for more appropriations so that the Blackwell's Island asylum could have more competent doctors, good nurses, more research and more adequate facilities. But we never get enough money. Now we would like to have your Nellie Bly—there is such a person, isn't there?—go back there and point out the conditions she wrote about."[9]

Nellie in testimony before the grand jury had already elaborated on conditions described in her stories for the *World*. She named names and was specific in her charges of mistreatment. For example, she made the acquaintance of Bridget McGuinness, who seemed to Nellie to be sane. "The beatings I got there were something dreadful," she told Miss Cochrane. "I was pulled around by the hair, held under the water until I almost strangled, and I was choked and kicked. . . . It was hopeless to complain to the doctors, for they always said it was the imagination of our diseased brains, and besides we would get another beating for telling. . . ."[10] Nellie herself said she always made a point of telling the doctors she was sane and asking to be released but, she added, "The more I endeavored to assure them of my sanity the more they doubted it."[11]

Cockerill took his caller to Nellie and his caller took Nellie back to Blackwell's Island, there to join members of the grand jury in an inspection of the institution. No one there was to know of the impending visit, but the word leaked out. "A mysterious change had come over the institution," Miss Cochrane reported. "The kitchen was clean, halls in order, beds improved, no fault could be found. The patients about whom I had written had disappeared. I hardly expected the grand jury to sustain me, after they saw everything different from what it had been while I was there. . . ."[12] Cockerill, Miss Cochrane, and the *World* staff feared their crusade might be discredited. But on October 28 the *World* reported that the Board of Charities had been granted a million dollars more than ever before in appropriations for city asylums; better food was being served; more doctors would be allocated. The grand jury's report endorsed every recommendation made in the *World* as a result of Nellie Bly's stories. "I have at least the satisfaction of knowing that the poor unfortunates will be the better cared for because of my work," Nellie concluded.[13] Cockerill's newest find possessed a compelling desire to right the wrongs of the world. With this attribute she combined a clear and readable style that Ishbel Ross insisted has never been duplicated by any other woman in journalism.

The series uncovered one other angle that disturbed Cockerill. One examining physician had not believed "Nellie Brown" to be insane, but he lacked the courage to protest against her confinement. What, reasoned Cockerill, was there to prevent unscrupulous doctors in conspiracy with relatives from having "undesirable" but sane relatives committed to mental institutions? Newspaper editorials, following the *World*'s lead, alerted the public to this insidious possibility.[14]

XIV. Outfoxing a "Fox"

Too often Edward R. Phelps could make good his open boast that he could kill any bill that might be tossed into the Albany legislative hopper.[1] He was New York State's wiliest lobbyist, so elusive that he was called "Foxy" Phelps.[2] John Cockerill of the *World* had long pondered how to trap the "fox." Exposing him would require documentary evidence. He needed some tasty bait. Nellie Bly had proved herself an actress in the Blackwell's Island disclosures. Edward Phelps had his price. Perhaps he could be duped into doing business with a wealthy matron. If Nellie could impersonate a mental patient, why not a respectable married woman? He summoned Nellie.

After the asylum series the Colonel had given Nellie a change-of-pace assignment. He had sensed that *World* readers would appreciate Nellie in a lighter role. He could not have been more correct. She became a ballet dancer and reported her experiences in a spicy three-column story of tribulations in the ballet that was a circulation builder.[3] The Colonel delighted in Nellie's willingness and adeptness in poking fun at herself. He was as charmed as *World* readers by her breezy approach. She wrote of her embarrassment when she was obliged to cavort on the stage garbed only in a tunic, her legs unhidden by the long skirts typical of the period. The ballet story encouraged Cockerill to convert Nellie into a chorus girl.

Nellie was a flop as a chorus girl, but her first-person account was a knockout in the news columns. The audience had seen the chorus line of thirty girls, all dressed in silver tights and helmets and carrying spears and shields, do their stuff. All except one girl kicked and danced in perfect rhythm. When they went one way, she went another; when they kicked, she whirled. She lost her helmet; her wig went askew. She drew angry looks from the stage manager. The audience sensed something unusual. Whatever it was, it had not been rehearsed; it was funnier than if it had been planned. Nellie's confusion finally left her in the center of the stage where even the hero could not suppress his mirth.

Cockerill had given her several other assignments tailored to Nellie's light-handed touch.[4] She had taken up fencing; she had exposed a mesmerist. She even had time to be a girl. She could indulge in some of the pretty clothes that James Whitcomb Riley once urged her to buy. The Hoosier poet knew that Nellie's natural charms, complemented by the right clothes, would open many doors to her.

Tough, untiring John Cockerill was proud of Nellie. He did not hesitate to give her the privileges and compensations she deserved—as a craftsman, not as a woman. In liberalizing restrictions on a feminine reporter he did more for "women's rights" than a stack of resolutions adopted at a convention of suffragettes. Shortly after the asylum exposé he gave her a desk in the city room. This did not sit well with some of the *World* men. Petty jealousy reared its head. Besides that, some of the men were annoyed by feeling restrained. They feared some of the talk common in a newsroom would have to be censored in deference to feminine sensibilities. Their worries were groundless, according to one story, as a reporter discovered one day when he edged over to admit their predicament. "We've been wondering if we shouldn't watch our language," he confided to Nellie. "But I notice you don't seem to mind."

"What was that?" Nellie responded, then pulled a wad of cotton from each ear.[5]

Despite a few friendly gestures, animosity deepened as it became apparent Nellie Bly would be around for a long time. Finally a *World* reporter who opposed the "desegregation" movement decided to teach Nellie a lesson. He invited her to the Albion, a dimly lighted nearby restaurant frequented only by men. Nellie didn't know that until she was inside. She began to notice surprise and resentment registering on the faces about her. There was no escape. Her escort pretended not to notice her distress. Nellie for a moment considered stalking from the room in maidenly disgust. But that, she told herself, is just what he wants. She would give no hint of her humiliation. Frustrated in his scheme, her companion suggested they leave.

"Oh, I wouldn't think of it," Nellie responded gaily. "I'm having a wonderful time." Beckoning the waiter, she startled those sitting at nearby tables by ordering tea. "Tea" in such an alcoholic atmosphere was a strange word. John Cockerill wandered in with Bill Nye. He surmised what Jim Cole, her companion, had done to Nellie. Just like him. As the two joined Nellie, Cockerill under his breath asked, "What in the world are you doing here, Nellie?"

Nellie did some quick thinking. Why expose Cole and make him an enemy? "This was kind of a dare," she lied sweetly. "I thought how interesting it would be to write a story on 'How Men Act When They Think No Woman Is Watching.'" This spur-of-the-moment proposal did not fool the Colonel. He spotted other *World* men who, in response to his silent command, joined the table. And pretty soon Cockerill ordered—of all things—tea; and so did all the other *World* men. Cockerill appreciated her embarrassing situation; he appreciated even more her resourcefulness. Nellie Bly could have hugged the Colonel. It was the *World* against the rest of the smug habitués of this male fortress![6]

Now, as Nellie sat expectantly in front of his desk, Cockerill reflected on all that had happened since she became the *World*'s first woman reporter. She had adjusted well to the tribulations that beset a trail blazer. Nellie Bly was becoming a household phrase wherever the *World* was read. Now came her biggest, most dangerous assignment to date. "You have done very well so far, Nellie," Cockerill assured her. "Now we have a job, a risky one, for you in the political field." Cockerill gave a fast rundown on the Fox. "Phelps has a good thing," he continued, "and there isn't anything he won't do, murder included, to hang onto it."

The managing editor told her that while little was known of how Phelps got his start, he had cut a thick slice of Andrew Johnson's patronage during the war; he made thousands selling the Army shoddy goods; he had been in the pay of the railroads and oil companies. Cockerill, recalling his clash with a utility firm and its lawyers in St. Louis, added: "We know for certain that he made a hundred thousand from gas companies in having killed a bill that would have lowered their prices and slashed their profits."[7]

Phelps would be staying at the Kenmore Hotel in Albany, the state capital. Nellie would go see him, disguised as a wealthy married woman. She would take with her a proposed patent medicine bill. This measure was designed to eliminate quack remedies. As the wife of a patent medicine manufacturer, Nellie would ask Phelps to block the measure and, as opportunities afforded, gather evidence against the Fox. Cockerill described the matron Nellie would impersonate. "Can you manage it?" he asked. "Oh, sure," she responded. "I'll use padding on my hips. I'll wear a conservative black bombazine dress and silk sheen. I'll be a frightened wife asking for the help of this big, strong, handsome—did you say he was handsome?—man."[8]

Three days later an apologetic Mrs. Brown was admitted by a secretary to the Kenmore Hotel suite that Phelps used as an office. Moments later she was looking at the "Fox," a fifty-five-year-old, self-assured, smiling man, neither robust nor slight, with gray hair, side whiskers and a faint resemblance to a minister. Nellie "introduced" herself. "Mrs. Brown" then pulled out a copy of the bill Cockerill had supplied her. Her husband had been ill, she explained. This bill would ruin their business. She had been advised by friends to see Mr. Phelps. So expertly did Nellie portray her role, so skilfully did she play up to his vanity that the Fox appeared to suspect nothing as Nellie put this all-important question: "Do you think you could kill this bill?"

"Never fear," beamed Phelps; "I'll have this abominable measure killed . . . but it will take money, you know." Yes, $2,000 should do it. He would have to pay some assemblymen.

With this naïve, trusting lady, Phelps forgot to be adequately cautious. Nellie's story said he looked into her record and found her to be honest. Some men would not be crooks if being so did not involve stupidity, and Phelps, with all his cunning, was satisfied with a superficial inquiry. He produced a sheet of names on which he had written numerous notations. The names included those of twelve committee members who would consider such a bill. There was Crosby of New York, "a rich man who can't be bought." But there were Gallagher of Erie, Tallmadge of Kings, Prime of Essex, De Witte of Ulster, Hagan of New York, and McLoughlin of Kings. They had their price.[9]

Mrs. Brown left Phelps with the understanding she would see him in New York the next Friday—to pay off. What is more, at her insistence, Phelps handed her the list of legislators, taking care to cross out the incriminating "price" notations. But the marks showed on an accompanying blank sheet, a fortuitous circumstance on which Nellie and the *World* capitalized.

Nellie notified Cockerill of her appointment in New York to settle with Phelps. The Fox had indeed blocked the patent medicine bill in committee. He could be expected to be insistent about collecting. Cockerill switched signals. He decided no money would be paid. Rather than write a check, Nellie would meet Phelps in his office and plead that her husband would not let her risk writing a check. She would then try to lure Phelps to the St. James Hotel, where the lobbyist was told the cash awaited him. Waiting instead would be a reporter Cockerill had posted as a lookout in the lobby.

Nellie started with Phelps to the hotel. But as they left the building housing Phelps's office, Nellie suddenly sprinted away, boarded a cab, and dashed to the *World* building. Her story was slated to appear the next day if it could be wrapped up. Cockerill wanted Phelps deceived as long as possible. A furious Phelps and his son showed up at the St. James, looking for Nellie. She was nowhere to be found. And there was no pay-off.

On April 1, 1888, Cockerill had another news scoop, thanks to his faith in a girl reporter. The *World* told the world how the Fox had been snared in a neatly laid trap, prefacing its revelations with a bit of verse designed to torment its prey:

> For I'm a pirate king!
> I'm in the lobby ring!
> Oh, what an uproarious
> Jolly and glorious
> Bid for a pirate king!

Nellie wasted no words getting to the point:

I was a lobbyist last week. I went up to Albany to catch a professional briber in the act. I did so. The briber, lobbyist and boodler whom I caught was Mr. Ed Phelps.[10]

The *World* story was embellished by a cartoon depicting Phelps as a lobby king, his feet on a desk, money piled high around his chair. The Cockerill-Bly coup hit home. The edition was a sellout. The public was up in arms. Lawmakers were swamped by indignant letters. The exposure made all legislators, many of them unfairly, suspect. An investigation was demanded.

The *World* gave Phelps space for a long denial and "explanation." But he could not refute Nellie's bribery charge. Cockerill kept the issue alive. One follow-up story at Albany, as might have been expected, reported the "denials" of the legislators who Phelps had said could be "bought." Some demanded that their good names be cleared. In a subsequent hearing conducted by the House Judiciary Committee, Nellie took the stand to repeat for the record what she had reported in the *World*. Also present was a much subdued Phelps. Pale and trembling he rose and, pointing at Nellie across the committee table, screamed, "Did I say buy? Did I say buy?"

To Cockerill it soon was evident that trapping the Fox was not total victory. The committee decided to restrict its inquiry only to Phelps's claim that he could buy off legislators. Lobbying practices in general would be excluded. Irate citizens and decent lawmakers called to commend Cockerill. One committee member said the upheaval would enable his group to break up the illicit lobby gang. He was too optimistic. Crooked lobbyists were not eliminated and never will be.

Cockerill had insisted on sending a bodyguard with Nellie when she went to Albany to testify. She laughed at the idea. "Don't argue about it, Nellie," he said. "It would mean a great deal to those men to keep you from appearing on the stand." What he didn't tell her was that he had received letters threatening her life.[11]

He had other news for her, unpleasant. The fatherless

Colonel knew how to be fatherly. He walked around his desk
and gently said what had to be said: "Nellie, we ask a lot of
you. It is the sort of thing you wanted to do. But assigning
you the Phelps story may have been a mistake." Nellie was
disturbed. How had she failed? It was nothing like that,
Cockerill admitted, and continued: "It's the men. They are
behaving like a bunch of spoiled children. They were pretty
sore about my assigning you this story. They can't realize
that the world is changing, our *World* and the whole world.
A delegation was in to see me. They want you to stay out of
what they regard as their field." Nellie reacted as Cockerill
had hoped.

"Their field, eh?" she echoed sharply. "Didn't I handle the
assignments—"

"Don't worry," Cockerill responded, calmly. "I told them
I would go right on assigning you stories that I think you can
handle."[12]

He did just that. Under Cockerill's direction she exposed
the seamy side of New York. Incognito, she visited the slums;
she posed as a factory girl; on the basis of her stories the *World*
demanded better housing, more sanitation facilities, more
effective public health measures. Nellie let herself be picked
up by a scoundrel who recruited girls for brothels, then wrote
a story charging that police were paid not to interfere.

The Colonel sent Nellie to interview Mrs. Ulysses S. Grant
and the wives of several Cabinet members.

Nellie would have been an invaluable exponent of the
women's crusade for equal rights. She had cracked the male
barrier. Nellie was invited to throw in with the movement.
The proffer came from Belva Lockwood, the candidate for
president on the Women's Suffrage ticket. The *World*'s ace
woman reporter declined to be enlisted. "As one of few news-
paperwomen," she explained, "it is difficult enough now. If I
became a suffragette, I would play into the hands of my critics.
They may not like me but they respect me. Joining your group

would identify me as a partisan. I can help your movement best by putting into practice what you have been preaching."[13]

The excitement stirred by Nellie's famous trip around the world could not have been less than the furor touched off by the Russians' first satellite put into orbit in the mid-1950s. Nellie, attired in a blue broadcloth dress trimmed with plaid camel's hair cloth with matching cap and carrying only a checked wool coat, a second cap, and a small traveling bag, sailed from New York on November 14, 1889. She was home on January 25, 1890. Her time was seventy-two days, six hours, and ten minutes. She had realized the *World*'s goal of circling the globe in less than the eighty days required by Phineas Fogg, the hero of the Jules Verne novel. With characteristic candor Nellie told the world that "any American girl could have done it."[14] Another girl at the same time almost did. Elizabeth Bisland, circling the earth in the opposite direction, made it in seventy-six days, without fanfare. The future biographer of Lafcadio Hearn published her impressions in the *Cosmopolitan* magazine.

Colonel Cockerill engineered the plans for Nellie's round-the-world trip.[15] It was he, editor in charge, who over the opposition of Julius Chambers, managing editor, and Morrill Goddard, sold Joe Pulitzer, who was away in Europe, on the idea. One source says a delay of three weeks occurred because a secretary thought the proposal too unimportant to bring to Pulitzer's attention. Cockerill's urgent cables swung the decision in Nellie's favor. As Chambers put it, "Cockerill thinks there's no one like Nellie."[16] Yet the Colonel regarded Nellie's trip as far less significant than many of her other accomplishments. He would have agreed with Nina Brown Baker, who thus concluded her biography of the reporter:

Yes, Nellie Bly went around the world in less than eighty days. But she also got decent treatment for the insane, and heating stoves for sweatshop workers, and an end to dozens of evil rackets. If something must be forgotten, let it be the eighty-day junket. Nellie Bly has a nobler claim to our remembrance than that.[17]

xv. Conflict: Cockerill vs. Smith

After three years at the *World* Colonel Cockerill agreed with Joseph Pulitzer that a competent assistant managing editor was needed to lighten the editor's mounting responsibilities. Ballard Smith, a vigorous, arrogant, Hoosier-born editor, was lured from the New York *Herald* in a shift that angered the flamboyant James Gordon Bennett, Jr. It was Bennett's boast that he never fired a reporter, and when a good man resigned the Commodore considered it a blow to the *Herald*'s prestige. In retaliation the irritated publisher swore any man could fill the vacancy and gave the job to a baseball writer. Then he had another idea: he would abolish the position. Doing so helped him let off steam.

Pulitzer considered Smith a "find." Cockerill was less enthusiastic. The newcomer was competent but painfully obvious in his ambitions. Friction began on the day Smith tried to countermand Managing Editor Cockerill's orders. Cockerill made no issue of the lesser incidents of insubordination, but Smith felt the sting of the editor's fury when the countermanding affected major assignments. Nevertheless, the principals managed to keep their differences under control. Remarkably, it was in this supercharged atmosphere that the staff produced some of the *World*'s major crusades and sensations in which Cockerill was the creator, Smith the doer.

Then Pulitzer abruptly made Smith the managing editor and designated Cockerill "editor in charge."[1] The Colonel thought the order meant that he was to be top man, but the division of authority was never spelled out. Cockerill chose to give his title a literal definition; Smith, with his new title, resisted the Colonel wherever he could. Yet each knew that an appeal to Pulitzer for clarification could cost his job. Here was a forerunner of a cruel stratagem. Put two promising, strong-willed men at work in close proximity, leave their

responsibilities purposely vague, then see what happens. The
theory is that the stronger, abler man will survive, but experience in this technique was costly to Pulitzer. Indeed, it often
resulted in driving out good men who by temperament were
not equipped for personal feuds. Yet curiously Pulitzer continued to apply it.[2]

In the protracted animosity in which Cockerill and Smith
worked, a circumstance which Pulitzer, had he been possessed
of an administrative awareness, could have eliminated with a
word, the *World* nevertheless continued to prosper. But it was
in spite of, not because of, the incompatibility between the
editor and his assistant. The fierce, internal warfare impaired
morale and prevented both men from achieving their potential.

Among those who saw at first-hand the results of Pulitzer's
clumsy staff maneuver was Elizabeth Jordan, novelist and
playwright. In an account of her involvement in the Smith-
Cockerill affair is a warm, personal impression of Colonel
Cockerill as an editor skilled in spotting and nurturing talent.

Elizabeth Jordan's first encounter with Colonel Cockerill,
unlike that of Nellie Bly, was memorable because she chose
to approach the famous editor "cold." The young Milwaukee
secretary had edited the women's page for Peck's Milwaukee
Sun. She had sold a few stories to the Chicago *Tribune*. In
her possession was a glowing recommendation from her former
boss, humorist George W. Peck. But she didn't use it. With
nothing except her own personality to smooth the way, she
asked to see the editor and—possibly because she arrived at
the after-lunch lull—was ushered into that dignitary's private
office. There to greet her was Colonel Cockerill. To the pre-
cocious applicant he was "a big man, six feet tall, weighing
about two hundred pounds, with a massive head of graying
hair, an expression suggesting power combined with a valiant
kindliness." The editor had "strained, tired eyes that usually
held a friendly twinkle. He was coatless and cigar ashes flowed
in and out among the crumpled folds of his waistcoat."[3]
Cockerill was leaning back in his chair, reflectively smoking,

when "Miss Milwaukee" entered—without intercession from
a soul. Like Nellie Bly, Elizabeth Jordan, in her first breath,
babbled out her wish to be a *World* reporter.

What started as a fearsome interview with a famous editor
quickly melted into a heart-to-heart talk. As Elizabeth Jordan
recalled it, "the entente between us was perfect." The Colonel
sensed in this young woman the potentials that in a matter of
weeks would deliver a great news beat to the *World*. The
Colonel asked questions. He elicited the girl's account of her
meager experience and background. She was on vacation from
her job as secretary to the superintendent of the Milwaukee
public schools. She knew nothing about New York. She had
done no reporting. She had never conducted an interview, and
she said so. What prompted the Colonel to promise a tryout
to this pretty, lithesome brunette who had apparently so little
to recommend her? Was it her unflinching gaze, or that dainty
but firm chin?

"You know, young lady," Cockerill warned, "it is a serious
thing for one so far from home to build up hope only to find
she doesn't fit in this business."[4] Miss Jordan assured the
Colonel that she would gladly take that risk. The fact that
Elizabeth Jordan was fighting for her chance and leaning on
nobody was not lost upon the editor. Ultimately the editor and
his visitor concluded their business. Miss Jordan would get a
tryout. She was to resign her position as secretary to the
Milwaukee superintendent of schools and to report to the
World the following April. Yet even as interruptions prolonged the interview, Cockerill seemed in no hurry. Not wishing to encroach upon the great man's time, several times she
rose to go; each time the Colonel detained her. Another
edition of a great newspaper was in the feverish pitch of preparation. Yet here was its editor in no haste to be rid of her!

Among the interruptions was that of a secretary who
occasionally placed cards on the editor's desk, a silent testimony to other callers cooling their heels. A grinning office
boy handed the Colonel a note which touched off a barrage

of vituperation. Could the sender of the note have been Smith? "The twinkle in the tired eyes disappeared," Miss Jordan recalled, "and the editor sent up a fountain of profanity that made me stare. The Colonel swore as naturally and as easily as he breathed. It was held by his admirers that he could swear ten minutes at a time without repeating a phrase."[5] One of the Colonel's idiosyncrasies, according to Elizabeth Jordan, made his speech even more picturesque. That was to insert oaths between syllables of a word, as if he could not wait until the entire word was pronounced. Now as he reacted to the message, Elizabeth heard its sender portrayed as a man who was "too-inde-—God-damned—pendent."[6]

Curiously Walt McDougall, the *World* cartoonist, attributed the same idiosyncrasy to Joseph Pulitzer and cited the same example—"inde-God-damned-pendent"—of splitting a word to insert an oath. "Pulitzer and Cockerill," wrote McDougall, "were the most profane men I have ever encountered. I learned much from them, for their joint vocabulary was extensive and, in some respects, unique. When J. P. was dictating an editorial upon some favorite topic, such as Collis P. Huntington's extremely ill-gotten wealth, Jay Gould's infamous railroad-wrecking or Cyrus Field's income, his speech was so interlarded with sulphurous and searing phrases that the whole staff shuddered."[7] But since both were skilled practitioners in the "art," perhaps each enriched the other's vocabulary.

Another incident recalled by Miss Jordan pertains to the Colonel's propensity for rough language. One night the Colonel woke a sleeping office boy and gave an order the boy was too dazed to understand. For five minutes "blue language" rent the air ending in Cockerill's discharge of the lad. The bewildered boy stumbled out. "He doesn't even know what happened," the Colonel grumbled. Minutes later the boy, sobbing bitterly, returned to ask whether he had been fired. Told that he had been, the youngster replied, "Well, what I want to know is why in hell you did it?" Shaken, the Colonel glanced at Miss Jordan and, fully repentant, muttered: "Is it possible this kid learned that from me?"

"Who else?" Miss Jordan responded.

The boy was promptly restored to his job with the Colonel's warning that "the next time I hear an oath out of you, you'll stay fired. Nobody under twenty-one swears in these offices. And that's an order. Now hustle."[8]

In contrast to characterizations by other contemporaries of the Colonel as an editor feared by his staff and one who seemed to dwell in perpetual fury, Miss Jordan wrote: "Nobody was afraid of him. His staff, from the smallest office boy to the most impressive of his editors—always excluding Ballard Smith—really loved him. . . . He was frequently disgusted and often annoyed but rarely angry."[9] To her the furious, swearing, cigar-smoking editor was a god—"the kindest, biggest-hearted man in the newspaper world, with abilities and idiosyncrasies that made him one of the most discussed journalists of his day."[10]

This is a propitious time to point out one of the Cockerill specifics in handling new reporters. He assigned them "home work."[11] To Elizabeth Jordan he suggested a long reading list that would acquaint her with the bustling, raucous and complex city of New York. Veteran reporters were constantly amazed by the knowledge of the city that Cockerill's out-of-the-city protégés demonstrated, knowledge that often exceeded their own.

Seven months later Elizabeth Jordan reported for work. One look at the Colonel's face told her something had happened. To her he seemed older and very, very tired. She was chilled by a vagueness and uncertainty in the Colonel that defied definition. The two talked, but now Cockerill's words, in contrast to their bristle and fire of last September, were spoken in weary resignation. She would soon understand why. Since her September interview Pulitzer, as noted earlier, had promoted Cockerill to "editor in charge" without officially implanting in him the authority that goes with the title. The power scramble was on.[12] Cockerill, although friendly enough, turned the recruit over to a subeditor. Managing Editor Smith wanted to do the hiring. He had filled some jobs close to him in the newsroom. Consequently, as a slap at Cockerill, he had the city editor, a Smith hireling, give her trivial chores. Smith expected that nothing noteworthy would result, and Cockerill's poor judgment in taking on this unknown from Wisconsin would be exposed. Cockerill watched this little game and did not interfere for a while. It was frustrating to the newcomer, but she did not complain.

Two months passed in which the Colonel's assignments to Miss Jordan were sometimes struck out by Smith. Cockerill made his move. He had his newest find transferred to the Brooklyn office. There Elizabeth Jordan wrote a series of articles for the Brooklyn edition about Long Island summer resorts and hotels. The proprietors and managers were ecstatic over the publicity.[13] Elizabeth had capitalized on her "home work," which familiarized her with the locale.

This was not journalism in the sense of the sensational exposés that made the *World* the brightest star on Park Row. But they stamped Elizabeth Jordan as an able reporter. Moreover they brought requests of resort and hotel people for thousands of copies of the *World* for distribution. When the circulation of the Brooklyn edition boomed and advertising based on more subscribers took a healthy jump, the business office, along with Pulitzer, took notice. Cockerill helped this reaction along. Vincent Cook, managing editor of the Brooklyn edition, elated by the success of Elizabeth's resort "puff" stories, told Cockerill about them. Cockerill seldom missed on a fledgling but he was not prepared for the Jordan feat to come so soon. He saw that the circulation and advertising figures came to Smith's attention. The young reporter was given a salary boost to $30 a week and expenses.

In company with the ace reporters of other New York newspapers the *World* staff had failed on a coveted opportunity. The President of the United States, General Benjamin

Harrison, had moved his family from Washington to a seashore cottage at Cape May, New Jersey. It was rumored that philanthropist George W. Childs of Philadelphia had turned over his summer place to the President's family. Was Childs seeking favors from the Harrison administration? If a newspaper could reveal the intimate details of the presidential family's life in the cottage environs, it would have a sizzling "exclusive." None had succeeded. The Harrisons, by order of the President, barricaded themselves from the press.

It occurred to Ballard Smith, however reluctantly he had noted the evident quality of the Jordan stories, that the girl reporter might be able to do what no other newsman had done—crack the Cape May "iron curtain." Smith's secretary was cynical. "We've had half a dozen of our best men on that Cape May doorstep for two weeks," he pointed out. "What chance would this dame have?"[14] He was overruled. Back to the *World*'s newsroom hustled a surprised Elizabeth Jordan. Smith briefly told her the situation and sent her to Cape May. There is no point in elaborating upon Elizabeth Jordan's successes, at Cape May and elsewhere, which are narrated vividly in her *Three Rousing Cheers*. It is sufficient to report that she did what more experienced reporters had failed to do.

On the Harrison assignment Elizabeth merely used the direct approach. She calmly rang the doorbell at Cape May, asked the butler if she could see Mrs. Harrison, and, because the First Lady chanced to overhear the caller, the *World* reporter was admitted. It is probable that Elizabeth Jordan didn't look like a reporter. Minutes later the two were chatting like long-separated sisters. They visited on the beach while a grandson cavorted on the sand. Mrs. Harrison gladly answered every question. The First Lady capped the Jordan coup by writing her unsolicited guest a complimentary note on her story.[15]

Miss Jordan remained on the *World* staff for ten years. The most vivid thing about it all, Miss Jordan reminisced later, was the warmth of John A. Cockerill's handshake in welcoming her. Miss Jordan rose to the editorship of *Harper's Bazaar,* wrote several novels, and left her mark in Hollywood and Broadway. Never did she forget that here, in the office of an editor who found time to encourage her, was where it all started.

Cockerill had played the game the hard way. Rather than imposing his authority on Smith and forcing the managing editor to accept an untried reporter, he had contrived the opportunity for Elizabeth Jordan to make good on her own. The incident produced a thaw in the frigid Cockerill-Smith atmosphere, although the storm signals never wholly disappeared. Smith thereafter gave the Cockerill recruits a better break. The feud dragged on for several years. It ended when Smith became indifferent to his duties and, according to Pulitzer biographer Don C. Seitz, was sent, ironically, to Brooklyn to take charge of the edition devoted to that city. Thereafter he shuttled between the Manhattan office and Brooklyn and was, for a time, acting editor in chief. A mental breakdown clouded the last seven years of his life. He was finally sent to London as the *World* correspondent but after a year his mind gave way. He died in 1900 in a sanitarium.

XVI. For the Good of the World, Mostly

Among the men of the *World* hired by John Cockerill none ended a brilliant career more pathetically than humorist Bill Nye. The managing editor had chuckled at Edgar Wilson Nye's contributions to *Puck* magazine. Nye, in his early thirties, had been doubling as magazine writer and editor of the Laramie, Wyoming, *Boomerang,* a small newspaper. The nation was still laughing over Nye's *Forty Liars and Other*

Lies, published in 1882. Cockerill brought some of Nye's work in *Puck* to Pulitzer's attention, suggesting that the *World* ought to sign up Nye, or someone just as funny, to meet the competition of the *Herald*'s author-humorist, Mark Twain.

Pulitzer agreed. Luring Nye to New York posed a problem. He was already in wide demand. To Cockerill fell the task of enticing the humorist. This was fortunate. Bill Nye had heard of Cockerill and, according to his son, Frank, "was an admirer of Colonel Cockerill, a newspaper executive whom he liked perhaps more than any other."[1] Cockerill's invitation to Nye to work for the *World* tempted the humorist, but he was suspicious of the big city. While pondering the offer, Nye sought the advice of Melville E. Stone, editor of the Chicago *Daily News.* Stone, who knew Cockerill, told the humorist to grab the job. He knew something about the *World*'s readiness to pay generous salaries.

Yet Bill Nye stalled. "He was afraid," recalled Cockerill. "He thought that his homely humor would not be appreciated in New York. He feared he would lose touch with things rural. I convinced him that the metropolis was made up of country-born men, and that our active, potential citizens loved the smell of dog-fennel, the hum of the bees and the sweet incense of the haymow on wet days."[2] The editor's portrayal of New York as an overgrown hick town impressed the humorist. The Colonel himself was just a country boy from the backwoods of Ohio, he reminded Nye. "It was only when satisfied that there was a great deal of human nature in the metropolis," related Cockerill, "that he consented to come at all, and even then he took a place on Staten Island where he could romp with his kids and keep a cow."[3]

The *World*'s new jester, whom John Dewey called a great satirist exposing pretense and superstition, brought enjoyment to *World* readers with such paragraphs as:

Many people in the United States and Canada who were once as pure as the beautiful snow, have fallen, but they did not attract the attention that the falls of Niagara do.

GENERAL JOSEPH R. COCKERILL

A born soldier, a superb conversationalist

RUTH COCKERILL

"Hers was a holy womanhood . . ."

CLEMENT LAIRD VALLANDIGHAM

Ohio's No. 1 Copperhead

JOSEPH PULITZER

as he looked to Colonel Cockerill
at their first meeting.

NELLIE BLY

whose round-the-world adventure was
supported by Colonel Cockerill.

BILL NYE, *Humorist*

Tragedy wrote the final act.

PARK ROW

James Gordon Bennett, Jr.

Last week I visited my birthplace.... I waited thirty years for the public to visit it, and as there didn't seem to be much of a rush this spring, I thought I would go and visit it myself.

Fox hunting combines the danger and the wild, tumultuous joy of the skating-rink, the toboggan slide, the mush-and-milk sociable and the straw ride.

Responding to an invitation to a county fair, Nye wrote:

I would like to be excused from any duties as a judge of curly-faced stock or as an umpire of ornamental needlework. After a person has had a fountain pen kicked endwise through his chest by the animal to which he has awarded the prize, and later on has his features worked into a giblet by the owner of the animal to whom he did not award the prize, he does not ask for public recognition at the hands of his fellow-citizens.

Nye's observations of a run-down hotel which he called a swaybacked wigwam and its personnel were typical of the humorist's resourcefulness in finding material practically anywhere at all:

A pale chambermaid wearing a black jersey with large pores in it warbles a low refrain as she nimbly knocks loose the venerable dust of the centuries and sets it afloat throughout the room. All is bustle about the house. Especially the chambermaid.... She is versatile and waits on table while not engaged in agitating the overworked mattresses and puny pillows upstairs. In this way she imparts the odor of fried pork to the pillow-cases and kerosene to the pie.

She has a wild, nervous, apprehensive look in her eye, as though she feared that some herculean guest might seize her in his great strong arms and bear her away to a justice of the peace and marry her. She certainly cannot fully realize how thoroughly secure she is from such a calamity ... she is just as safe as she was forty years ago when she promised her aged mother she would never elope with anyone....

Everywhere I go I find people who seem pleased with the manner in which I have succeeded in resembling the graphic pictures made to represent me in the World. Many seem to suppose that the massive and undraped head shown in these pictures was the result of artistic license or indolence and a general desire to

evade the task of making hair. For such people the thrill of joy
they feel when they discover that they have not been deceived is
marked and genuine. These pictures also stimulate the press to
try it themselves and to add other horrors which do not in any
way interfere with the likeness, but at the same time encourage
me to travel mostly by night.[4]

Bill Nye quickly won the affection of his *World* colleagues.
His popularity, through the increasing readership of his dry
brand of humor, soared. The tall, well-proportioned, blue-
eyed humorist moved with a lounging gait, he wore a sweet,
wry smile and, as McDougall, the *World* cartoonist, recalled,
was slightly stooped as if from bending down to lesser mortals.
Bill Nye looked, spoke, and behaved as a humorist should.
Many thousands of Americans flocked to hear him when he
teamed with the Hoosier poet, James Whitcomb Riley, in
lecture halls throughout the country. Both had a fondness for
the convivial cup. To Nye it brought shame and ruin.

The *World* humorist was scheduled to lecture to a Pater-
son, New Jersey, church audience. If not inebriated, he tot-
tered in that direction while performing. His listeners deeply
resented this kind of conduct by a man of his fame. En route
to his train, Nye was pelted with eggs and vegetables tossed
by his less restrained critics. When he woke up to what had
happened, he was humiliated beyond recovery. He was dead
in six months, the victim of a broken heart, his friends said.
He left a huge fortune, which his widow is said to have
promptly lost.[5]

Colonel Cockerill was not immune to errors in judgment,
and nothing endeared him to Pulitzer more than his readiness
to admit his lapses. The Colonel's fallibility was dramatically
laid bare by a monstrous deception engineered by a *World*
reporter. The fraud perpetrated upon the Colonel ironically
helped boost Richard Farrelly to a top editorial post.

In one version, Farrelly showed up in Cockerill's office
during the blizzard of 1888. Would the Colonel be interested
in a series of reports on the storm by an intrepid writer-

explorer of the frozen North? Farrelly happened to be wearing a fur headgear and carrying a pair of snowshoes. Cockerill surveyed the applicant hopefully. This could be the fresh angle needed on the storm story. He handed Farrelly a fat voucher for an advance and a carte blanche assignment. Farrelly departed to the comfort of a nearby hotel. Bolstering his spirit with a suitable quantity of whiskey, Farrelly fabricated a series of blizzard narratives so vivid that the imposter was embraced as the *World*'s hero of the North.[6] Worldly-wise in so many respects, Colonel Cockerill, too late, finally caught on. In hardly any time at all Farrelly had nailed down a full-time reporting job, from which he rose to become city editor of the *Evening World*.

But such errors on the Colonel's part were rare. More typical of his career were his pioneering efforts in building up the Sunday edition of his paper. In the late 1880's the Colonel's hand in editing the Sunday *World* again demonstrated the Midas touch. Almost from the day the Sunday *World* was enlarged from 36 pages under Cockerill, it was a circulation builder and money maker. By the time the Colonel was installed in his eleventh-floor office in the golden dome of the new *World* building in 1890, he had taken on, in addition to his other responsibilities, editorship of the Sunday *World*. The phenomenal success of the Sunday edition is all the more remarkable in view of the Colonel's tribulations in producing it. It began as simply an enlarged daily edition. There was no regular Sunday staff. Cockerill's weekly notice on the bulletin board warned that every member must furnish at least one article.

In the Colonel's concept the Sunday edition must appeal to the family as a whole, to children and their parents, to a wide range of adult interests. It must find a place with women, upstate farmers, the Fifth Avenue drawing room set, East Side tenement dwellers, millionaire club members, suburbanites of Flatbush and New Rochelle, college students, professional classes and workers, the idle and the rich, all walks of life.

Advertisers supported the Sunday edition, knowing people
had more time to read on Sundays. The *World* brashly raised
its advertising rates; the advertisers took it in stride and multiplied, taking up, in Cockerill's tenure as Sunday editor, about
50 per cent of the space.

Morrill Goddard, who succeeded Cockerill as Sunday editor when the Colonel left the *World*, has been tabbed as the
editor who brought the Sunday paper, first under Pulitzer and
then with Hearst, to its epitome of sensationalism. Under the
Goddard rein the Sunday edition, in one appraisal, grew into
a frenzied amalgam of surgery, nudity, monster ape men,
exotic criminals, and society scandals. But the foundation of
the Sunday edition was solidly laid by the Colonel,[7] who was
by no means averse to the use of "shock and shiver" material.
The Sunday circulation had touched the quarter-million level
before Goddard arrived.

As an editor Cockerill was an avid advocate and, in a
sense, a pioneer of pictures as a reporting aid. His recognition
of the potency of the editorial cartoon and his shrewd use of
news illustrations gave the *World* a decided advantage over
its competition. He foresaw a future in which pictures would
be employed increasingly to capture the attention of readers;
he did not overlook the large segment of illiterates who would
buy newspapers only if profusely illustrated. Cockerill's use
of page-one illustrations in the Cincinnati *Enquirer*'s coverage
of the gruesome Tanyard Murder marked him as perhaps the
nation's first editor to capitalize on this type of pictorial
reporting.

Cockerill's enthusiasm for pictures, however, was tempered by misgivings. The misuse of a picture was no more to
be excused than verbal inaccuracies. Before the halftone became standard engraving procedure, artists scampered about
New York City like scared ants sketching trial figures, criminals, chorus girls, fires, celebrities—anything in the news that
lent itself to free-hand artistry. These methods often led to
distortion and exaggeration. Cockerill once cited five morning

newspapers that had published pictures of Jack the Ripper caught red-handed with a victim, each portraying the villain in a different posture of ferocity. "What public good," he wrote, "can come from such illustrations?"

In his second year as managing editor of the *World*, Cockerill encouraged an experiment that touched off a boom in daily newspaper illustrations. This was accomplished in the face of indifference, if not opposition, by Joseph Pulitzer. Documenting the Colonel's role in this phase of newspaper pioneering is the account of Valerian Gribayédoff, a *World* artist.[8] "It was early in 1884 that I came in contact with the proprietor of the *World*," wrote Gribayédoff. "I found him little disposed to listen to any suggestions on a subject that had caused him no little expense. Not so Colonel Cockerill. He readily agreed to give me a trial in the matter of outline drawing at the earliest opportunity." The first experiment produced a series of designs representing the crests of well-known American families. The Colonel was pleased, but Pulitzer remained skeptical. Cockerill gave the green light to the next effort, with startling results. Subsequently, readers were startled by eighteen caricatures on page one captioned:

WALL STREET "NOBILITY"
Some of the Little Men Who Control Big
Millions[9]

The list included Jay Gould, John W. MacKay, C. P. Huntington, Russell Sage, Sidney Dillon, Cyrus W. Field, William H. Vanderbilt, and Rufus Hatch. "Few have seen these great leaders of Wall Street," said the *World*, "yet their names are household words throughout the length and breadth of the land. They may only be seen behind oak or cherry doors and the imposing 'Strictly Private' signs."

By twentieth-century standards the drawings were crude. Yet their novelty compensated for imperfections. The money lords, drawn with oversized heads and in characteristic poses, were recognizable, painfully so, to their friends. For the masses the rich have an irresistible fascination. With this collection of figures, in the text written by the financial editor, the *World* gave its readers an inside, unflattering view of the richest men in the country. As always there was the implication that the *World* itself was virtuously outside this grasping circle. It seemed irrelevant at the moment that Joseph Pulitzer was accumulating millions—he was to leave a gross estate of $18,645,249.

The Gribayédoff experiment was rewarding beyond expectation. *World* readers loved the caricatures. The *World* circulation leaped ahead and continued upward week after week. In their turn city fathers, politicians, the militia, and other public figures were lampooned. Letters of inquiry on the preparation of the cuts streamed into the *World* offices. Other newspapers asked Gribayédoff to illustrate their editions. The nurturing of an experiment by Colonel Cockerill started a picture boom that spread all over the country. It was implemented by the rejuvenation of the moribund American Press Association. The APA supplied small country papers with stereotyped plates of news matter pirated from big city dailies. The *World*'s success prompted the APA to supplement its plate material with a large variety of outline cuts. An engraving company was established for producing cuts by the faster, more reliable method of zinc etching. The *World* could now get engravings in four hours, regarded as a remarkably short interval.

Not all of the Colonel's pictorial adventures were for the good of the *World*. When the novelty of portraying politicians and other public figures in grotesque shapes wore off, there ensued some editorial head scratching. When someone suggested, "Why not give the fair sex a picture whirl?" the Colonel imprudently nodded approval. There blossomed a series of drawings of Brooklyn society belles so poorly done and so ineffectually reproduced that a jaundiced colleague of the Colonel dubbed them "counterfeits in soft metal and printer's ink." A society matron was made to look as if she

wore a beard. There were other horrible disfigurements. The
Colonel learned the hard way what he should have known—
the feminine hide is too sensitive for satire. The uproar was
immediate and accompanied by threats of violence. An infuriated parent vowed he would visit the editor armed with
a horse-whip; the district attorney's office warned that the
World had left itself open to indictment for criminal libel.
None of these dire things happened.[10]

There were other repercussions to the new "art." Some
critics said that illustrations, except in cases of rare adapta-
bility, killed the text. Fear was voiced that this pictorial outrage would destroy literary features. John Cockerill clung
stubbornly to the concept that pictures support and enliven
the text, that the two go hand in hand. Cockerill, with Pulitzer
in agreement, evinced a new wariness of long-winded articles.
Although Cockerill was often obliged to return lengthy
articles, sometimes by close friends of Pulitzer, the *World*
turned more and more to pictures as a complement to the
written word. Cockerill realized that the articles without illustrations must compete with the growing profusion of pictures
and cartoons.

Illustrations posed another problem. Without editorial
discretion pictures could become tools of personal vanity.
The managing editor was constantly pestered by politically
and socially ambitious persons contriving to get their pictures
into the paper.

Development of the zinc etching process enabled the
World to accelerate its picture policy. Election campaigns
presented the opportunities to vary column-wide portraits and
caricatures with wider cartoons of a political nature. Already
described is the cartoon of "Belshazzar's Feast" satirizing the
dinner at Delmonico's indiscreetly attended by presidential
candidate James G. Blaine and given by Jay Gould and other
rich Republican backers. The cartoon with twenty figures
was drawn in less than two hours and reproduced for the
next day's paper. Large reproductions of the cartoon were

ordered by the Democratic National Committee and carried in parades. The cartoon was widely reprinted, handing the *World* an abundance of free publicity.

Possibly no other contribution to the *World*'s phenomenal circulation gain exceeded Cockerill's use of pictures. Within a year after his arrival, the *World* was publishing diagrams illustrating murders and feature stories in the Sunday edition. Illustrative of Pulitzer's lukewarmness toward pictures was the order he left to Cockerill before leaving for Europe. The *World* was to get rid of its woodcuts. Reluctantly and undoubtedly swearing at his departed boss, Cockerill started carrying out the dictum on a gradual basis. When, not to his surprise, he found that circulation fell as the number of pictures was reduced, he reversed the order. He published more illustrations than ever and "circulation rose like a thermometer on a hot day, until it reached over 230,000 on the day of Grant's funeral."[11] Here, again, was an example of Pulitzer's inclination to shun new methods; here again was evidence of the Colonel's trail blazing.

Just as Cockerill was wary of making friends for the paper, he was loath to ask favors. But as distasteful as it was, he occasionally requested a "service," sometimes with Joseph Pulitzer's tacit approval. In a note of June 22, 1885, to William C. Whitney, Secretary of the Navy, the Colonel wrote on behalf of Dr. Montrose Pallen of New York, "an old friend of Mr. Pulitzer."[12] Dr. Pallen wanted to be United States Consul-General in Paris. Cockerill would consider it a favor, he said, "and I know Mr. Pulitzer would also," if Secretary Whitney would speak to the President in regard to the matter. The Colonel defended the request by pointing out that "inasmuch as a brother-in-law of the *Herald*'s proprietor has received a foreign mission and the *Times* has secured an appointment for one of its staff, an old Democratic paper like the *World* may be allowed to inquire as to the disposition of an application which its editor has endorsed."

Colonel Cockerill's relatives, his correspondence indicates, did not share his reticence about asking favors. Two letters to Whitney in 1888 pertain to assistance given by the Secretary of Navy in getting Cockerill's nephew admitted to the Naval Academy. The nephew was Joseph Randolph Campbell, son of Cockerill's sister Esther and Dr. Campbell. On August 22 the Colonel in a note of thanks to Whitney made this revealing comment:

I felt a delicacy about asking a favor in his behalf though more than once urged to do so by his father. This feeling grew out of no distrust of you but was due to Mr. Pulitzer's well-known desire to keep the *World* from any sort of obligation to public officials. I recognized his personal friendliness to you and hesitated to tax you lest my act should be misunderstood.[13]

On October 2, 1888, the Colonel in a follow-up note to Whitney, confirmed that his nephew had matriculated at the Naval Academy and expressed his thanks to the Secretary for his "kindness in this matter."

Cockerill apparently felt there was considerable difference in lending a hand to a nephew trying to get into a military academy and interceding for a relative in quest of a political plum. On July 17, 1885, Cockerill wrote to Daniel S. Lamont, President Cleveland's private secretary, these second thoughts:

I had a letter the other day from Mr. S. S. Cox in which he said that before he left Washington he spoke to you about an application for a Kansas postmastership made by a relative of mine, Mr. Eylar.

I wrote to Mr. Cox as much as two months ago asking him to withdraw the papers in this case. I have no idea that Mr. E. will receive the appointment asked for or that his application will even be considered but I am not willing that you should be charged even with the annoyance of remembering it on my account. I, therefore, trust that the matter will be dropped, as it was with great reluctance in the first place that I permitted my name to be used in forwarding the necessary documents. This without prejudice to Mr. Eylar.

I merely wish to convey the idea that I am asking no favor.[14]

XVII. Leonora Barner

Out front in the Grand Opera House the audience buzzed expectantly. In five minutes the curtain would rise on Bartley Campbell's popular melodrama *The White Slave*. John Cockerill, seated a few rows from the stage, was unaware that through an aperture of the curtain a pair of feminine eyes were peering at the *World*'s managing editor. Only a few minutes before being led to his seat the Colonel had met his young observer backstage. He liked the pre-makeup view.

The introduction was managed by Billy Connor, friend of the Colonel and manager of the famous American trage-dian, John McCullough.[1] Connor, cognizant of Cockerill's bachelor status, persuaded the Colonel to accompany him to the Opera House. His motive was simple enough—the Colonel needed feminine company. The actress to whom he presented the Colonel was Leonora Barner. She was obviously young and even more obviously a gorgeous, bosomy creature with green eyes, perfect teeth, and the most exquisitely formed lips Cockerill had ever seen. Her profile was delightfully feminine; her figure, of medium height, denoted both supple-ness and gracefulness. Leonora's alertness impressed Cockerill. He had the curious impression of having been tested and, in the three or four minutes in which they chatted, approved, pending further inquiry.

Billy Connor had said Leonora was a native of Peters-burg, Virginia, the daughter of Mr. and Mrs. W. T. Barner of an old plantation family. Leonora was in her third season before the footlights, having started as a chorus girl. Since opening in Haverley's Fourteenth Street Theater in April, 1882, *The White Slave* had played to enthusiastic audiences in Brooklyn, Harlem, Williamsburg, and London prior to its week's run at the Opera House in August, 1884.

Although not blessed with talent, Leonora gave the production all she had, and in physical charms she had considerable. Her spontaneity, her gregariousness, and her flawless performance from the technical viewpoint kept her name high on casting rolls. Her name does not appear in press notices of the day or among the stars listed in theatrical histories, but she was known to love the attention a stage career would bring her.

The White Slave[2] portrays the story of Liza, the supposed octoroon who turns out to be white. As the melodrama unfolded, John Cockerill's mind was not primarily on the story. His eyes were glued to Leonora during her brief appearances. His attention was arrested by these lines, planted deliberately by Campbell for their effect: Lacy, the hated owner of Liza— "I can send you to the fields to work all day among common niggers, a hoe in your hands, rags upon your back." Liza (her voice ringing with righteous indignation)—"Rags are a royal raiment when worn for virtue's sake and rather a hoe in my hands than self-contempt in my heart." The passage seldom failed to evoke shouts of approval and prolonged applause. Except for Leonora's few lines, the play failed to divert the Colonel's mind from his anticipation of his after-theater supper date with the young actress. Cockerill could not be sure of Leonora's age; he would guess she was about half his age—but on that night the editor did not feel half his forty-two years.

After the last curtain call members of the cast noticed an immaculately dressed gentleman idling near the stage door. Moments later they saw Leonora, fully changed and primped, appear, her eyes starry and searching the area. Spotting her target, Leonora walked swiftly toward the man. Colonel Cockerill greeted her and the two walked out, arm in arm and blissfully, it seemed to those who watched.

The Colonel was known to several members of the cast. The playwright, a former reporter on the Cincinnati *Enquirer* before the Colonel joined that staff, was a friend of Cockerill. Soon the word spread that John Cockerill was romancing

the pretty and—a few added—designing Leonora Barner.
It was a delicious morsel for the gossips' tongues. Even in
sophisticated New York a mild sensation was compounded
when a middle-aged man of Cockerill's affluence—his salary
in all likelihood had topped the $10,000 mark[3]—started
squiring around a young girl. In some circles there were serious
reservations about show people. But neither Leonora's age
nor her stage career deterred the romance.

Colonel Cockerill's marriage to Leonora later that year
left the *World* editor's cup full and overflowing. The bride,
bright, warm, companionable, was the complement Cockerill
felt he needed to the pressures and frustrations at the *World*.
The Colonel and his wife took a suite of rooms at the Astor
House. Life, professionally and domestically, looked rosy.

The Colonel was so deeply in love that he was eager to
show off his bride to the folks back home in West Union,
Ohio. A flock of relatives gathered at a dinner where Leonora
ostensibly was the guest of honor. It did not come off well.
Nothing unkind was said in her hearing—no one cared to
risk the Colonel's wrath with any such indiscretion—but a
frosty atmosphere chilled the bride's reception. Leonora tried
hard to win them over, but her association with the stage, the
disparity of their ages, and suspicions of the bride's motives
were too much to overcome. More than ever the Colonel
missed his parents, by then deceased. He was certain Joseph
and Ruth Cockerill would have understood and given their
blessing. The flatness of the visit palled upon the Colonel
and his subdued young bride. They returned to New York
in relief.

The Colonel made one more try with his sister, Esther
Elizabeth, who had not met Leonora. The Colonel and
Leonora visited Esther and her husband, Dr. John Campbell,
in Torresdale, Pennsylvania. Esther's reaction followed the
West Union pattern. She was polite, but her disapproval was
poorly concealed. As if by instinct Esther and Leonora from
the moment of their first meeting nurtured a bitter dislike of

each other. When Esther maneuvered her brother for a few minutes of private conversation, she was cruel and blunt. Her first jab was at their disparity in age. Then came the real dig: Surely John could see Leonora was after his money—and a show girl at that!

The Colonel insisted that he was lucky to have Leonora and that they would be happy. Hettie, as subsequent events revealed, remained suspicious of her sister-in-law.[4]

The Colonel and his wife, without family blessing, apparently were happy just as Cockerill had said they would be. Their names occasionally appeared in society news and Press Club reports of social activities. In 1888, when Cockerill drafted a will leaving all of his possessions to Leonora,[5] there seemed no doubt at all of their wedded bliss.

How long it would have continued had Leonora not met Walter Louis Lineau no one can say. In such a marriage there were risks in any case. The Colonel, in giving up bachelorhood, was obliged to make adjustments that were not easy. His hours at the *World* were long and arduous; his temper often short. Leonora missed the attentions which had been hers on the stage. Her youthful beauty and impetuosity loomed as marital hazards. She attracted the attention of men wherever she went. The Colonel was at first inclined to bask in the pride of possessing a prize package younger men coveted. As long as Leonora was all his, he welcomed the admiration his young wife attracted. Forbearance turned to misgivings the day he heard that Lineau, a friend, had been seeing his wife more often than propriety would permit. He found them together at Delmonico's restaurant one day, and though the Colonel tried to make his appearance casual, it clearly flustered them. The Colonel greeted the pair warmly but Lineau excused himself quickly and disappeared.

Cockerill eschewed the melodramatics of the outraged husband, although one may suspect he was cursing his rival under his breath.

Leonora half expected her husband to fly into a rage.

His quiet demeanor nettled her. She explained icily that Lineau
had to go to his office. Lineau, head of the silk department
of Frederick Victor & Achelis at 65 Leonard Street, was
younger than Cockerill, even younger than Leonora.

When the Colonel ventured that Lineau may have felt the
pinch of a guilty conscience, Leonora "blew up." In one
version, apocryphal but plausible, she snapped: "What do
you expect me to do all afternoon and most of the night,
John," snapped Leonora, "sit up there in our rooms and
dry up?"[6]

The Colonel, stung by the implication of his wife's words,
had no words in reply. Leonora, as a mother, might be a different person, a better wife, he realized. A child would fill
the empty hours. No man wanted more to be a father than he.

But while the pair waited for parenthood that never came,
Leonora's impulsive inclinations, her yearning to be with
younger companions, her restlessness in the long, tense hours
the Colonel spent master-minding the *World's* newsroom persisted. Minor irritations ballooned into distrust and sharp
words gravitated into bitter quarrels. Cockerill reluctantly recalled his sister's gloomy predictions. His marriage looked
hopeless. He finally told himself what he would not admit for
months—he could not hold Leonora. The breaking point
occurred in 1894. To Hettie, according to her subsequent
petition contesting the Colonel's will, he confided his misgivings and his decision. Believing his wife wanted her freedom, the Colonel suggested a settlement. To Leonora he gave
$5,000—$3,000 of it in gold—upon the understanding she
would go to South Dakota for a divorce decree. He did so
as one reluctantly letting go of a treasure too dazzling to keep.

In confiding to Hettie the Colonel added fuel to a feminine
feud that would have appalled him had fate not spared him
that humiliation. The unhappy story, while foggy in details,
emerges in court developments.

Leonora did not, as her husband assumed, seize the
opportunity to win her freedom. For reasons that may be

conjectured only, she did not go to South Dakota for a divorce. Why, in view of the $5,000 settlement,[7] a generous sum by prevailing standards and one that would have enabled Leonora to maintain herself on a luxurious level, did she elect not to do so? Leonora, it may be assumed, knew of her husband's will. She must have known Cockerill was one of the highest paid editors in the country. Did she deliberately avoid the divorce, looking to the day she might become a wealthy widow? Or was she, after all, still in love with the Colonel?

At any rate the two were estranged; and adding a further note of mystery was the affidavit of Hettie, who became a litigant involving the Colonel's will. She swore that the Colonel, through his lawyer, T. C. Campbell, petitioned for an absolute divorce decree in New York City.[8] Was this action taken, as Hettie wanted the court to believe, so that the Colonel would be rid of his wife? The petition was not acted upon because of an assignment that took John Cockerill half way around the world.

The question of the legatee popped up later, adding difficulties in the execution of the Colonel's will. It could be suggested that the confusion surrounding these developments merely confirmed the editor's lack of business acumen. Lest it be concluded that he bungled even in arranging his own will, an unusual situation must be taken into account. All available data indicate that what rarely happens to any man happened to the Colonel—he died not knowing whether he was married or unattached. Despite assertions of his sister to the contrary, there is no evidence that the Colonel changed his will. Under the law a man cannot disinherit the woman who is still his wife. The Colonel's curious dilemma returned to becloud events following his unexpected death.

XVIII. Press Club Prestige

On the afternoon of December 4, 1872, three New York newspapermen sat around a table in Schalk's Restaurant, 120 Nassau Street, mulling over a proposed club for the press. Two decades later their brain child, the New York Pless Club, had become the world's largest social organization of newspaper workers. Through its quarters flowed a steady stream of politically, economically and culturally important visitors. Authors, statesmen and militarists, stimulated by the image of favorable publicity, cherished invitations to address its gatherings. A key figure in enhancing the prestige of the New York Press Club in that era was John A. Cockerill.

The founding trio, James Pooton of the New York News Association, Howard Carroll of the New York *Times,* and Jeremiah J. Roche of the New York *Herald*, on that afternoon of 1872, took a solemn vow to form such a club, despite previous failures. When the word sifted out, some publishers were horrified. They visualized such fraternizing as ruinous to competitive news-gathering. James Gordon Bennett threatened to fire any member of the *Herald* staff who joined.[1] But Pooton, Carroll, and Roche stuck to their guns. The emerging "Journalistic Fraternity," with Pooton as president, adopted a constitution in March, 1873.[2]

Pooton was dubious over the prospects of enlisting more than a handful of the braver scribes. For some journalists, joining could mean dismissal. Even so, many newspapermen seethed at being catspaws in the shabby competitive tactics engaged in by some journals. For some of them, at least, their bread and butter depended upon their ability to make their employers believe they were endeavoring to cut their rivals' throats whenever opportunity afforded. The new organization was primarily a protest against such conditions. Surprisingly, the charter membership appeal produced sixty-eight joiners, including a number of New York's crack reporters. Publishers' resistance subsided.

The room at 6 Centre Street, above the *Staats Zeitung* Building, rented in December, 1873, as club quarters, was a shabby locale for the genesis of a club that ultimately would enchant the high and mighty. Its equipment included a few wooden chairs and unpainted tables, the gift of the United States marshal. Early financial troubles forced a committee, tin cup in hand, to canvass the publishers for help. Convinced by now that the club was not a sinister plot to rob news competition of its zest, the publishers were co-operative. Donations from Charles A. Dana, James Gordon Bennett, and Horace Greeley enabled the club to add two rooms, to paint the walls, to carpet the floors, and to buy a billiard table, a piano, and a shelf of books. Horace Greeley, invited to inspect the new quarters his money had helped provide, took a jaundiced view. "You boys are damned nicely fixed here, the rooms are very clean," he quipped. "But how the hell can you write copy here, after being accustomed to the dust and litter of a newspaper office? I couldn't do it."[3]

When the club, continuing to thrive, promoted itself in 1878 to more central headquarters in the Wood Building, 119-121 Nassau Street, the housewarming drew such celebrities as Thurlow Weed, Walt Whitman, and Henry Ward Beecher. By January 6, 1881, membership had swollen to 385 and the treasury bulged with $1,800. The club celebrated with a banquet graced by the presence of General Ulysses S. Grant. Most speakers courted the newsmen's favor by tossing compliments. The General made a hit by twitting his listeners. "The newspaper fraternity," he said, "is ready to take any office that might be tendered it, from mayor to president . . . and I have been astonished that our citizens have not given it to them."[4] As it prospered the club moved on to more luxurious quarters. Its next address was 120 Nassau Street, across the street from the Wood Building. Members rested, read, dozed, gambled, lunched, talked, or cursed their employers in their new, well-appointed quarters that included a parlor, restaurant, reading room, library, and a billiards room.

John Cockerill found the atmosphere of the Press Club to his liking. He joined shortly after arriving at the *World* and Park Row. Before his marriage he divided his leisure time, which was little enough, between his Astor House room and the Press Club. Later his beautiful young actress-wife often accompanied her debonair editor-husband to social functions. One of the nation's top news editors, the Colonel was well received in the club. His genial manners and his capacity to make friends were assets to the organization. He was not a back slapper, but he could be jovial and entertaining.

Nine years before he joined the group, a burial plot in Cypress Hill Cemetery was presented to the club. But it remained unimproved. Cockerill, despairing of the neglect, decided to act. Money was needed for a suitable monument. In the club's fund-raising proclivities Cockerill's gift for promotion asserted itself. In the benefit program of May 9, 1886, every seat at Wallack's Theater was filled. Colonel Robert Ingersoll and Henry Ward Beecher, both friends of the Colonel, topped the lecture bill. The Colonel's promotional flair took the club into happier financial days. The club coffers were enriched by $3,775. On June 12, 1887, a granite obelisk thirty-eight feet high, with the words "New York Press Club" on its pedestal, was unveiled before a gathering of five thousand people. Another friend of the Colonel, Chauncey M. Depew, dedicated the monument.

In the Press Club plot today rest the remains of many newspapermen. Alfred Trumble was moved to pen a few lines in tribute to the fallen journalists:

> Dead lies old Rome, sepulchred in the past,
>   Her tumbled glories to decay the prize;
> But fame, that must all mortal deeds outlast,
>   Still makes it honor high in mortal eyes
> To die in harness, with an armed band.
> So died these all, but wielding pen, not brand.[5]

Ironically, John Cockerill was not destined to rest in the plot he had helped groom.

One evening late in 1887 John A. Greene joined Cockerill for a glass of beer. Greene was president of the club. "John," he offered, after the two had engaged in small talk for a few minutes, "we want you to take over the club next year. I'm stepping out."

The Colonel was pleased. "I'd be glad to help in any way I can," he responded.[6] He was elected by acclamation at the club's annual meeting.

Thus began for Cockerill the first of five successive terms—1888 through 1892—as president of the New York Press Club, a tenure matched only by Joseph Howard, Jr., at various times with the *World*, the *Herald* and the *Star* (1895-1899).[7] Cockerill's administration, said the New York *Times*, raised the standards of the club. He resented the encroachment of outsiders who for purposes of prestige or influence sought to buy their way into the company of newspapermen. The club dispensed associate memberships to lawyers, doctors, merchants, and politicians. The Colonel saw that abuse of the practice would cheapen the Press Club in the eyes of the newspaper profession. He curtailed the number of associate memberships granted and recommended only those he considered of the highest character.

A dinner arranged by his fellow Press Club members to honor their president drew a large gathering of newspapermen and New York celebrities. Joseph Pulitzer, in Monterey, California, for his health, sent a personal note of regret that he could not attend. It deprived him, wrote Pulitzer, of a desire "to pay public tribute to Colonel Cockerill's talents and charming amiabilities of character." The *World* publisher garnished his accolade with the observation that he knew of no one more devoted to the highest mission of the press than John Cockerill.[8]

Under Cockerill the Press Club's legitimate membership neared the one thousand mark. It was evident the Nassau

Street quarters would soon be inadequate. Strong pressure developed for new, plushier, more expansive accommodations. An appeal to businessmen for a building was decided upon. The response was helpful. Joseph Pulitzer, mostly out of his regard for Cockerill, gave $5,000. During the last year of Cockerill's administration $100,000 was raised toward the $247,500 purchase price of a property at Frankfort and William Streets, proposed site of new quarters. But the club could not swing it, and Pulitzer, who held the mortgage, reclaimed the property. In 1895 (Cockerill by then was on a foreign assignment) the club took over a four-story brownstone building at 34 West Twenty-sixth Street.

Without the Colonel's firm hand on the gavel, the New York Press Club thereafter appears to have degenerated into an era of imprudent use of its considerable influence. Its ardor for funds with which to finance its luxurious quarters impaired its judgment. The late Samuel Hopkins Adams joined the Press Club during the last year of Colonel Cockerill's presidency. "Under Colonel Cockerill and what he represented," Adams recalled, "the club would never have descended to the expedient of broad-gauge beggary. . . . Colonel Cockerill's own reputation was entirely free from the taint of Press Club grafting." Although, in Adams' words, Cockerill was in a higher echelon of the newspaper business than he, the novelist had some acquaintanceship with the *World* editor in the Lotos Club, another organization to which the upper levels of Park Row personnel belonged. Adams resigned from the Press Club when its membership became "too inclusive (any sort of cheap gambler of Broadway merchant could get in)." "Before the club moved into new quarters," Adams recalled, "it sent forth a deluge of begging letters to prominent citizens in no way identified with the club. The veiled implication was that the recipients might find it advisable to cultivate the good will of the newspaper fraternity. This aroused the wrath of Daniel Kellogg, then city editor of the New York *Sun*. Kellogg took his pen in hand and invaded the editorial page of the *Sun* with a slashing attack upon the Press Club's fund-raising campaign. The title was something like 'Sturdy Beggary and Self-Respecting Newspapermen.' That editorial became a sort of declaration of faith in the better circles of Park Row."[9]

Reviewing its granting of memberships to persons outside the newspaper profession, the Press Club in 1905 insisted it had never been prodigal in the distribution of honor memberships. In thirty-eight years up to 1905, wrote a club historian, it conferred the honor upon only eighteen men.[10] They included John Jacob Astor, William Waldorf, General Howard Carroll, Chauncey M. Depew, Levi P. Morton, Judge Henry Hilton, Henry M. Stanley, George F. Williams, Andrew Carnegie, Theodore Roosevelt, and William J. Bryan, most of whom were friends of Cockerill. Associate memberships were another matter. After Cockerill's departure they were made available to a large number of men who, although in no way connected with journalism, showed a "special interest" in the club and a willingness to part with the required fees. The revenue helped to finance the club. It was Adams' contention that these associate memberships were tossed shamelessly as bait to the affluent.

Later dissension split the organization. A segment that opposed moving to the Twenty-sixth Street quarters formed a competing group, the Newspaper Club. Ultimately the Press Club realized it should return to the vicinity of Park Row. But not until 1900 was the consolidation with the Newspaper Club effected. The Press Club returned to the fold. The merged groups established quarters in the Morton Building.

Whatever its shortcomings, the Press Club possessed a brighter side. It spent thousands of dollars to help needy members of the newspaper profession and their families. It provided newsmen with facilities for recreation, entertainment and study. It was equipped with a large newspaper reference library. It endowed beds in several New York hospitals and in thirty-two years gave $50,000 to charity. It exposed the absurdity of fears that a social medium for reporters and editors would stifle newspaper competition. It gave receptions in honor of such celebrities as Henry M. Stanley, Thurlow Weed, Henry Watterson, Mark Twain, and William Butler Yeats, and thus provided the means for establishing rapport with leading news figures—from police commissioners to presidents of the United States.

The Colonel held a deep affection for the club. Upon his death in 1896 the Press Club was foremost in lauding Colonel Cockerill as a friend and eminent member of the profession.

XIX. Walkout on the "World"

A quiet death is long overdue for the myth that Joseph Pulitzer, and only Pulitzer, made the New York *World*. The image of a yacht-bound publisher masterminding by cablegram every move of his newspaper is a popular but erroneous one. Situations constantly arose that could not be handled by an absentee owner. Someone had to be there, in the flesh, to make fast and astute decisions, to dream up new crusades and story ideas, "to mind the store." John A. Cockerill, for much of his eight-year tenure on the *World*, filled that role. The Colonel could not have lasted merely as a Pulitzer "yes" man; he had also to be creator and activist.

In view of Pulitzer's extended absenteeism this was an enormous responsibility. Pulitzer, from 1887 to his death, visited the *World* offices only three times.[1] His election in 1885 to Congress from the Ninth District of New York, combined with a never-ending siege of ill health and near blindness, precluded his being an on-the-spot newspaper executive. To be sure, he cabled his office frequently and profusely regarding problems and issues that interested him. But the *World* had to go on between messages. As Don Seitz put it, the *World* was managed by its managers and edited by its

editors. Pulitzer suggested freely but ordered little. Final judgment was always with the office.

It was in his capacity as first in command in Pulitzer's
absence that a valid claim can be made for Cockerill's large
share in making the *World* the most profitable and perhaps
the best read newspaper of the late 1880's. An insight into
the Colonel's status in *World* management is provided in
Cockerill's communications with his superior. In a note signed
"J. A. C." Cockerill in 1885 wrote Pulitzer thus:

> I infer from the tenor of your last letter that you at least give
> yourself no anxiety about affairs here and that to me is an ample
> reward. Everything is going well here—so much better than I had
> reason to expect—that I am really happy. Many thanks for your
> kind and appreciative words.[2]

The *World*'s affairs had not always gone happily, nor
would they in the future of this booming enterprise. As he
scrawled one of his numerous reports to the *World* owner,
Colonel Cockerill recalled the printers' strike, first of its kind,
in the early weeks of the "new" *World*. The surface wrangle
was over soap and ice. The deeper issue was the Typographical Union's drive to convert the *World*'s composing room into
a union shop. When Cockerill arrived at his office on the eve
of the formal opening of the Brooklyn Bridge, not a printer
was on duty. Fuming, Cockerill stalked through the composing
room and, finding the men nonchalantly idle, demanded to
know why they were not on the job. "How can we keep cool
and clean without ice water and soap?"[3] one of the printers
responded. The penny-pinching John B. McGuffin, business
manager, who had been transplanted from the St. Louis *Post-
Dispatch*, had cut off the supplies. Shrewdly the strikers timed
their walkout to coincide with the hours when the publisher
and managing editor would be seething to get on with the
next morning's edition on the bridge dedication ceremonies.

There ensued no long period of negotiation; there was no
call for mediation or arbitration; the printers did not even

leave the premises. After a hurried conference with the president of the Typographical Union and the Colonel, Pulitzer resolved the matter simply enough: "You say all they want is ice water and soap? I say, hell, yes, give it to them and fast. We got a newspaper to get out."[4] The obstinate McGuffin tried to "fudge" by "forgetting" to order ice for the next weekend. The maneuver backfired. Pulitzer ordered rectification when he himself drew a warm swallow of water from the shop spigot.

Although the identification meant different things at various times, John Cockerill's title most often mentioned at the *World* was that of managing editor. Various Pulitzer biographers also attributed to him the titles of editor in charge and Sunday editor. A biographical sketch of Cockerill, presumably approved by the Colonel, says Pulitzer offered him the position of editor and that afterward he became both editor and managing editor.[5] At his death the *World* listed Cockerill as its managing editor from 1883 to 1891.[6] Cockerill signed his letters as managing editor.

Whatever Cockerill's titles might have been technically, his management went beyond the news and editorial departments. He was in constant touch with the printers: he could speak "their language," having learned their trade on Ohio newspapers. Avoiding friction between newsroom and composing room, as any astute managing editor through the decades of American journalism has known, is essential to a smooth-running newspaper. The Colonel carried the aura of a fighting editor in the literal sense of the word. Had he not shot to death a St. Louis lawyer who tried to assault him? If Editor Cockerill wanted a quick proof of a story or a headline revised, he had only to ask.

The prospering *World*'s dilemma was not unlike that of a boy growing out of his pants. The pains of expanding faster than old equipment and crowded accommodations would gracefully allow were multitudinous. Cockerill, in a memorandum to Pulitzer, projected a typical problem:

As to appearance of the paper, I have sweat and suffered more over that than anything else. You know what a pride I take in the printing. The paper is simply a compound of wood pulp and white clay—with clay predominating. The types are absolutely worn out and sometimes I wonder that we do as well as we do. I have hopes of the new man we have in the press-room. He has energy and intelligence and is learning. I will get some estimates for a new dress from the type founders and have them ready by the time you return.[7]

Later Cockerill reported that "the stereotype department has been moved quite successfully and a new system of delivering the Brooklyn edition established—to prevent mixing."[8] Cockerill had gone to Brooklyn looking for a new building for the *World* offices but reported "no conclusion arrived at."[9]

In another phase of the physical vicissitudes of the *World*'s stepped-up production, Cockerill reported a weather problem:

Last Sunday's edition was crippled somewhat by the intense heat in the press-room. The thermometer registered a part of the time 109 degrees. We melted fourteen rollers though we had 20 new ones to start with. The heat was so great that several of the men were exhausted. The presses were running steadily from 10 o'clock in the evening until 5:30 in the morning. The run on the main sheet was delayed by the constant changing of rollers. . . . The printing was bad. I have had a new blowing machine rigged up—or rather an old one put in shape—and during the hot weather will use the street steam instead of our own boilers. There is nothing to be gained in saving on steam and wasting on rollers which cost about $5 apiece. The printing of the paper, which you justly complain of, I am doing everything to improve. The heat . . . may be responsible for some of it but bad type and poor paper cannot be overcome in combination. I have had an estimate made of the amount of type needed for new dress and will see some of the type founders this week. The new dress should not be delayed. . . .[10]

Memoranda from "J. A. C." to "My dear Mr. P." are enlightening on other particulars. Since they are the most revealing memorabilia on the Cockerill-Pulitzer personal and working relations, we quote further from these hitherto unpublished notes. In mid-1885—that would be roughly about the end of the *World*'s second year under Pulitzer—Cockerill wrote:

We are all well and getting along as nicely as possible. Not a jar has occurred and everybody appears to be happy. The politicians with axes to grind bother me a little but I manage to keep them at arm's length.

I feel that the paper was never better grounded in its popularity. Our editorial mail is more than twice what it was when you went away and never a fault-finding letter—nothing but praise.[11]

Like any news editor Colonel Cockerill was sensitive to "news droughts." "There is a very general complaint of dull times from all parts of the country,"[12] he wrote Pulitzer on one occasion. On another he sought to console the *World* proprietor, pointing out that "in view of the fact that we have been absolutely without a 'sensation' for a month, the keeping up of the circulation is really a marvel to me."[13]

Cockerill and Pulitzer occupied adjoining offices. One day in November, 1887, the Colonel walked in on the publisher to retrieve some proofs. He found the publisher bent over them, a dazed look on his face. "John, something's wrong," he said. "I can't read these."[14]

Cockerill called Kate Pulitzer. Pulitzer's eyesight, although further impaired, survived this bout, but a specialist advised his patient, in order to stave off the threat of blindness, to take a trip to California. From California Pulitzer sent regrets that he could not attend a New York Press Club dinner honoring Cockerill, its president. In that message he said he could neither read nor write.[15] There followed through the years a series of voyages to Europe as the stricken publisher sought to regain his eyesight and his strength.

At Wiesbaden, Germany, Joseph Pulitzer was ministered to by the world's top oculist, Dr. Hermann Pagenstecher. Nothing that money could buy or hire was denied the publisher in his quest for a cure. At Constantinople the publisher

was about to sail when he casually remarked to a secretary
that it had become dark very fast. The surprised secretary
blurted out that it wasn't dark at all.[16] Joseph Pulitzer had
walked into the world of shadows that would surround him
to the end of his life. The detachment of the retina had
scrambled the mechanism of his eyes. Thereafter Pulitzer remained painfully sensitive to certain sounds, of which none
was more irritating to him than that of voluble soup eaters.
From that day on Pulitzer's eccentricities multiplied, but in
semi- or total darkness Joe Pulitzer seemed more alert than
ever.

The *World*'s housing at 31-32 Park Row was becoming
painfully cramped as the newspaper galloped and snorted to
new circulation and advertising records. To meet the demands
for the morning, evening, and Sunday editions, a new building
was a foregone conclusion. On his forty-first birthday anniversary Pulitzer, for $630,000 in cash, bought French's Hotel,
Park Row and Frankfort Street. The deed, signed on April 10,
1888, was a prized possession, not only because the site would
be graced by the tallest, most elegant business structure in
New York City. The document was meaningful because
twenty-three years earlier a porter had kicked a young ex-
cavalryman out of the lobby because the visitor could not
produce the fifty cents needed for a room. The boot had been
applied to young Joe Pulitzer. Pulitzer consulted Cockerill
on the style and plan of the building. But he credited George
W. Turner, the business manager, with "ingenuity and devo-
tion" in its construction.[17] The Colonel was not impressed by
the business manager, with whom he was obliged to work on
business problems. At one point he observed to Pulitzer,
"Turner is doing well but he is too nervous to have so much
responsibility."[18]

Into the contract with the architect, George B. Post, Pulitzer inserted an unusual provision. The *World*'s new home was
to be "at least as good as the *Times* building." The result was
a magnificent sixteen-story edifice. The gold dome and the

great archway over the entrance were Pulitzer touches. The *World* in its new quarters installed new Hoe presses, which gave it a decided if temporary edge over its competitors in production, printing and color. At opening festivities on December 10, 1890, Cockerill had a feeling of loneliness. For missing among the attending celebrities was the proprietor of the *World*. Pulitzer had sailed for Europe the day before.

After six and one-half years under the Pulitzer-Cockerill team the *World* "flexed its muscles" in this towering $2,500,000 structure, a symbol of a remarkable achievement. The *World*'s earnings made it possible to pay off all construction costs without a mortgage.

Joseph Pulitzer was undistinguished as an administrator. Had he continued to rely upon Colonel Cockerill as the *World*'s top editorial executive, rather than confounding him with confused authority, the little wars under the gold dome might never have happened. Frictions occurred prior to the completion of the new building. The publisher's worsening illness and prolonged absences aggravated them. In an atmosphere of bafflement and frustration *World* executives found themselves in a struggle for survival.

On October 16, 1890, Cockerill wrote and published an announcement requested by Pulitzer: upon his physicians' advice, he was withdrawing from an active role in the *World*. Control was vested in an executive board of principal editors, but "the change is more nominal than otherwise."[19]

In the creation of a three-man regency, Pulitzer betrayed a fallibility that plagued the *World* incessantly thereafter. Pulitzer did not know how to delegate authority. He thought three heads were wiser than one. Ignoring the hazards of nepotism, Joseph Pulitzer brought in his brother-in-law, Colonel William L. Davis, to be vice-president. Davis, Cockerill, and jittery George W. Turner constituted the regency.[20] Out of what brand of reasoning had Pulitzer decided that Davis, a competent mining engineer, could shift conveniently into a newspaper executive? Only the *World* owner could have explained. Conceivably Pulitzer was betting on the loyalty of a member of the family. Pulitzer made three-man rule sound so sensible and easy. In November, 1889, in a note to Davis, he put it this way: "Any question that can be settled at the office should be settled there, and for that very purpose you, Cockerill and Turner should have a regular daily sitting and consultation. . . . You three gentlemen have ample power and discretion to settle any of the ordinary questions that may arise during my absence." Pulitzer did not want his travels spoilt by ordinary bothers, he warned, but on "any extraordinary thing I want you to cable me fully . . . even if it costs forty dollars a word." He suggested in lieu of "ordinary bothers" as "many pleasant and agreeable reports as possible."[21] But more often than not, Davis sent tales of woe. The regency floundered in its own impotence. And while it floundered, Pulitzer pursued his roaming existence. Over the years he lived alternately on his estates in Lakewood, New Jersey; Bar Harbor, Maine; Jekyl Island, Georgia; and Cap Martin, France.

On Park Row the towering *World* building housed a dynamic, influential, and prosperous newspaper but, paradoxically, under its roof suspicion and animosities headed toward a showdown.

John Cockerill in the comic opera of scrambled authority fought to make his voice heard as the editor in charge. Prior to the regency he had suffered through a conflict with Ballard Smith. Now the long dormant hostility between Turner and the Colonel was coming to a head in a feud of the first magnitude. The disagreement, it was said, arose over office arrangements in the new building, but the basic clash, according to Don Seitz, was "over who was really IT in the establishment."[22] Cockerill was caught in a power squeeze. The Colonel was highly trusted and deeply involved as Pulitzer's right hand man. Now he felt his authority slipping away. As to quarrels over office arrangements in the new building, it is doubtful that Cockerill was interested in any physical details beyond assurance of smoothly operating news and editorial departments. There seems even less doubt that had Pulitzer kept the Colonel endowed with full and undisputed jurisdiction over the news and editorial functions no such disruptions would have occurred.

The picture was complicated by a suspicion shared by both Turner and Cockerill. There was no question of the *World*'s financial success. Under the impetus of the new building, enormous advertising and circulation gains were made. The prospects for 1891 looked even brighter. Both men realized the *World* was making Pulitzer a fabulously rich man. Each thought he was due a larger share of the profits. Turner was infuriated; Cockerill felt let down. In the spring of 1891, reasoning that direct action was the more effective course, Turner flatly demanded a "controlling share" of the business.[23] He was promptly dismissed. Turner's case had not been improved by the long periods of time spent on his yacht away from the cares and worries of making Pulitzer rich.

Colonel Cockerill, the man closest to Pulitzer's elbow since the pair took over the old *World* in 1883, now started reflecting upon his lack of foresight in failing to protect his interests. This, he told himself bitterly, he could have achieved with the right kind of contract. Then his thoughts mellowed. Pulitzer had been like a brother prior to the plushy era under the gold dome. The two saw eye to eye on newspaper problems, even though Pulitzer was now behaving like an estranged relative. He seemed unaware of the jealousies and bickerings his dubious administrative methods created. His near-blindness and his absenteeism had drawn a curtain between the two. Yet Pulitzer was still Pulitzer. How could he so easily forget what the two had been through? The Colonel presumably decided to take up the problem with the boss, reminding him that he had worked very hard to implement Pulitzer's ideals on the *World*. He would continue doing so. But in view of the *World*'s substantial earnings would Joe like to make a more realistic and equitable financial arrangement with his managing editor?[24]

As pointed out earlier, Pulitzer is supposed to have allotted Cockerill a few shares of stock in the *World*,[25] but there is no corroboration for any such action. There is reason to doubt such a gesture was ever made. In a letter to Professor Thomas Davidson, an occasional book reviewer for the *World,* Cockerill wrote that "I am not a stock-holder in the company; consequently I defer to Mr. Pulitzer's judgment and wishes in all matters."[26] Was the story of shares given to Cockerill a biographical gesture of kindness to Pulitzer?

In one biographer's version the Colonel was reported spending most of his time in Room 1 at the Astor House.[27] Picking up this unconfirmed tidbit, other writers have enlarged upon the reference to portray the Colonel as an editor brooding over his beer and neglecting his job. These statements do not square with plausibility. It was out of character for the Colonel to take his responsibilities lightly. It happened on no other newspaper, in no other job. There is no available record of Pulitzer's ever having found his right hand man derelict in judgment or performance. Cockerill, for his part, once admitted to a *World* writer that his position was a "peculiar one," but made it clear that "I have no ambition beyond carrying out Mr. Pulitzer's ideas in the conduct of the paper."[28] Their compatibility on most basic policies was never in doubt.

A more convincing explanation of their cleavage is that in the transformation of Pulitzer the working publisher to Pulitzer the wealthy newspaper proprietor, Pulitzer's perspective suffered. Apparently he lost sight of the value of a trusted editor. An unsubstantiated report says the final break came when Cockerill, in requesting a more equitable arrangement, wrote an impertinent note to Pulitzer. The communication, if it ever existed, was not preserved. A probable theory is that, since both were strong-willed men, a noisy quarrel ended their association. It may well have occurred when Pulitzer, ignoring the obvious injustice to his colleague and longtime friend, ordered the Colonel to St. Louis once again to take over the prospering *Post-Dispatch*. At any rate, whatever the circumstances, the suggested transfer was distasteful to Cockerill. Disappointed, disenchanted, the Colonel, in May 1891, walked out of the *World* forever.

John A. Dillon was summoned from the *Post-Dispatch* to succeed George Turner as business manager. Turner fled to the faltering New York *Recorder*. Don Seitz wrote that "Colonel Cockerill was never replaced on the *World*, although many were called and some were chosen. That is to say, no one ever came into the editorship who fitted in so well with Mr. Pulitzer and at the same time was able to rally men to himself and inspire them with his zeal and energy."[29]

Ballard Smith was temporarily elevated to editor in charge and Colonel George B. McLellan Harvey became managing editor. Smith lasted barely a year, having too ardently supported, in Pulitzer's view, the Homestead, Pennsylvania, strikers in the riot of 1892. Smith was shipped to London as correspondent and was finally and tragically the victim of a mental breakdown.

There followed a bewildering parade of editors, none capable of filling Colonel Cockerill's shoes except Kansas-born Frank I. Cobb, whom Pulitzer hired away from the Detroit *Free Press*. With a penchant for bringing in outsiders, Pulitzer in his blindness became partial for a time to confident, flowery conversationalists. He liked men who sounded sure of themselves and under their spell would decide that finally he had spotted just the editor to save the *World*. Legend has it that in time the *World* staff dreaded the appearance of flashy looking, fast talking strangers clutching notes the publisher had written on his pale blue stationery. Each would function for a time as editor in charge until Pulitzer caught up with his inadequacies, which was always soon.

It was said of Colonel Harvey that the new editor would sit in impressive silence in conferences until every possible suggestion had been made. Then, seizing the ideas that ap-

pealed to him most, he would calmly and solemnly comment
upon them at length as if they were his own. Some recollections have it that Pulitzer also used this technique, but it
required a master of audacity to get away with it. Pulitzer
could do it but not Harvey.

Still less successful as a successor to Cockerill was Colonel
Charles H. Jones, whose appearance with one of the familiar
blue letters caused one reporter to report that the astonishment
of the shop was not so much at the Colonel as at the wide scope
of authority seemingly given a man with no knowledge of the
newspaper field. Resented also was Pulitzer's complete disre-
gard of those who had done so much to hold the *World*
together. Jones was immediately an unpopular executive,
so much disliked that Walt McDougall caricatured him and
his wife in *World* cartoons without either apparently catching on.

On one occasion Pulitzer summoned S. S. Carvalho, a
World executive, to berate him because of the paper's dull-
ness. Carvalho suggested another shakeup. Pulitzer rejected
the proposal, then made a surprising suggestion:

> I think it's because the staff is stale. I think it's because no-
> body in the place gets drunk.... When I was there someone
> always got drunk, and we made a great paper. Now ... find a
> man who gets drunk and hire him.[30]

Pulitzer's suggestion was acted upon. The business manager encountered near City Hall Park a brilliant writer who
had been dropped from other newspapers because of his propensity for the bottle. He was nailed to the *World* pay roll
for life, despite one narrow escape from a permanent separation from his salary. He thought he saw a blue dog in the
ground-glass door of the managing editor's office and threw
a punch in self-defense. Only prompt attention by a doctor
prevented his bleeding to death. He survived this and every
other hazard normal to the regular imbiber.

Contemporary newspapermen regarded as a serious mis-

take Pulitzer's release of Colonel Cockerill.[31] It is tempting
to speculate on what course Cockerill's career would have
taken had he been retained at the *World* and given the un-
wavering support that Pulitzer accorded him in St. Louis and
in the early years of the *World*'s rejuvenation. If in that
capacity his life had been prolonged sufficiently to meet the
challenge of the Hearst blitzkrieg, the circulation war between
the *World* and Hearst's *Journal* might well have taken a turn
more favorable to the *World*.

XX. Pulitzer's Portrait

When John S. Sargent was commissioned to paint Joseph
Pulitzer's portrait, the publisher was told the artist's genius
lay in conveying to canvas the innermost weaknesses and
strengths of his sitters. "That is what I want," Pulitzer replied,
"to be remembered just as I really am. . . ."[1] Sargent responded
with a portrait in which one side of the face looks benign and
scholarly while the other has a Mephistophelian cast. Told
that Dr. George W. Hosmer intended writing his life story,
the publisher, in the same vein, urged his prospective biographer to tell the precise truth.[2] (Hosmer died before he could
complete the biography.)

Unfortunately a strong distaste for personal reminiscing
deterred Pulitzer, despite many requests, from writing his
autobiography. The "precise truth" about him is elusive and
fragmented. His image as portrayed by contemporaries ranges
from that of a tyrant to that of a demigod. It is ironic that
there should be so much disparity in the appraisals of a man
who insisted that he be known just as he was. A formidable
task awaits the biographer who presents fully and factually
the real Pulitzer. Sixteen years after the publisher's death Walt
McDougall found that the "misty clouds of myth are already

dimming the outlines of the man who made the *World*."³
Little has been written since to clear away the fog. If ever a
definitive biography of Pulitzer is published, a serious void
will have been filled in the literature of journalism.

Even the physical aspects of the Pulitzer image bring forth
contradictions. Pulitzer regarded himself as an ugly man. He
once admonished a barber not to make him look like an orang-
utan. But Arthur Brisbane insisted that Pulitzer possessed
the best kind of good looks, "those which indicate character,
concentration of purpose and the capacity for strong feeling."⁴
A less flattering description shows Pulitzer as a tall (six feet
two and a half inches), gangling, carelessly attired, almost
knife-thin man whose flying mop of black hair contrasted
oddly with a tuft of reddish brown beard.⁵ He was lean and
loose-limbed. He had broad, slightly stooped shoulders, a flat
chest and long arms, a long nose, prominent cheek bones,
strong jaws, and a forehead that well bespoke the intellect
behind it. To conceal a small but powerful chin Pulitzer wore
a beard after he was thirty. "His complexion was as delicate
and beautiful as that of a tender child," one contemporary
remarked. "His hands were those of a genius with long, slender
fingers, full of warmth and magnetism. The eyes before they
became clouded were of a grayish blue. Always weak, they
never lent much expression to the face, yet his visage was
animated and attractive. Pulitzer's nose, a delight of car-
toonists, vexed him and if there had been any way of modify-
ing its prominence, he would have greatly rejoiced."⁶

Although he outlived John Cockerill, his robust managing
editor, Pulitzer was destined to be plagued by ill health and
faulty eyesight for much of his life. Consulting distinguished
medical specialists became a passion with him. Many passed
in review, doing what they could, taking lavish fees, but leaving no cures. The loss of Pulitzer's eyesight was not total,
according to biographer Seitz, but his vision was so dim that
it became a greater strain than if he had been wholly in gloom.
In bright light he saw nothing; when the sky was cloudy he

could perceive his surroundings but not the printed page, except for a time the larger headlines. His right eye was totally eclipsed by the detachment of its retina; the other suffered from a suffusion that all but completed the disaster.

Irvin S. Cobb wrote that when he joined the *World* as a reporter in 1905, Pulitzer was totally blind. "His mistreated nerves had frayed until the smallest alien noise was a monstrous torture to the captious recluse," Cobb recalled. "He abode in inner compartments of sound-proofed houses or took long voyages aboard a private yacht having quilted bulkheads and padded floors for the owner's quarters—a yacht which privately we called 'the prison hulk' because of the existence his bullied underlings were presumed to endure while aboard her."[7] When Pulitzer brought in a musician to soothe his taut nerves, no third person could be present. A rustle or a creak might distract the listener. Cobb said his cowed subordinates crept about trying to anticipate what neurotic whim might next possess the master. To Cobb Pulitzer was a "giant intelligence eternally condemned to the darkest of dungeons, a caged eagle furiously belaboring the bars."[8]

Alleyne Ireland, one of Pulitzer's secretaries, found it impossible to give an adequate description of his chief's extreme sensitiveness to noise. Wrote Ireland: "To him even the sudden click of a spoon against a saucer, the gurgle of water poured into a glass, the striking of a glass, produced a spasm of suffering. I have seen him turn pale, tremble, break into a cold perspiration at some sound which to most people would have been scarcely audible."[9] It became a test of supreme ingenuity for the Pulitzer entourage to arrange transportation and hotel accommodations with a maximum of efficiency and a minimum of decibels.

Pulitzer was no recluse in the sense of excluding himself from recreation. A staff of secretaries in his darkened world read constantly to him, from the classics, current magazines, and the newspapers. Much of the reading was for sheer entertainment to while away sleepless hours. Two other diversions, horses and chess, weighed heavily in the Pulitzer career, although poker occasionally engaged his attention. In the early days of the Pulitzer "exile" Brisbane took on his boss in poker with a pack of very large cards. The arrangement ended when Brisbane won $500 at one sitting. Pulitzer's fondness for chess was of long standing and had served him well in the Civil War. For knocking down an officer brutal to his men, Pulitzer was arrested and held for court-martial. A general seeking a chess opponent heard of Pulitzer. He was amazed by the young man's intelligence; and though the general never won a game, Pulitzer was never tried. On an earlier occasion Pulitzer found himself watching a game of chess in St. Louis, and could not resist suggesting a move. The player was Dr. Emil Pretorius, who with Carl Schurz published the *Westliche Post*. The incident led to the kibitzer's joining the newspaper staff.

Perhaps no one has surpassed James Creelman, a star reporter for the *World*, in this colorful glimpse of the Pulitzer temperament and personality: "He is tremendous. No other word quite describes him. He thinks dramatically. . . . There is no stage-manager like him. A man of tempestuous emotions, abnormally sensitive, beset with sudden rages or enthusiasms, alternated with cold moods of cruel analyzing; one hour candid to the point of brutality, violent in word and gesture, the next hour subtle, suspicious, evasive, intuitive; a mingling of occident and orient; recklessly brave, honest, intractably cunning; mystic, iconoclast, persistent, inconstant, generous, unforgiving. . . ."[10]

Arthur Brisbane saw in Pulitzer a publisher "who made the American idea stronger; he seized the opportunities that were offered to him; he used his brains and his ability to promote the idea that liberty and equality should be a reality." But Brisbane, who deserted the *World* to work for William Randolph Hearst, is less rhapsodic in appraising the effects of financial success upon Pulitzer. "His attitude toward the world," wrote the columnist in 1902, "is perhaps not that which it was before the *World* had begun to pay him a revenue of a million dollars annually. He takes too kind a view of an imperfect social system, now that that social system gives him everything he wants and more. . . ."[11]

That the genesis of most ideas for crusades and exposés in the *World* lay not in Pulitzer but in Cockerill and other editors is indicated by at least two of the publisher's contemporaries. "I am convinced," wrote cartoonist Walt McDougall, "that very few 'big ideas' ever germinated in Pulitzer's harassed brain. I know that certain memorable achievements when first submitted as suggestions were greeted with scorn and often stubbornly opposed, while others of lesser importance, even trivial and silly schemes, were hailed as genuine whales."[12] Seitz wrote that "strange as it may appear, his initiative was not extraordinary, and he frequently showed hesitancy that verged upon timidity in adopting policies urged upon him by his juniors."[13] If Pulitzer could not create an original situation, he was effective in seizing upon an old situation and breathing new life into it. In this forte lay his special genius.

Aware of his enormous impulses, Pulitzer warned his aides not to be swept off their feet by any order he might issue. Directives from headquarters were to be tempered by information which he might not possess, an "iffy" arrangement that at times could be more confusing than helpful.

Because McDougall was a contemporary of both Cockerill and Pulitzer, the cartoonist's impressions of the *World*'s proprietor are more pertinent to the period concerned in this book than the generally favorable commentaries on Pulitzer published in periodicals since the publisher's death. "The writings of some of Pulitzer's former employes," McDougall complained,

are creating a demigod out of a highly commercial gentleman who knew exactly what every cent in a dollar was worth and what sort of printed matter would at least expense extract pennies from the lower classes. That was his job, and he went to it with enthusiasm and haste. In his first years at the *World* he was very approachable . . . even companionable, when not irritated by fear of disaster or the increase of expense. He was almost absolutely devoid of any sense of humor, save of a certain banal sort. . . . He was so obsessed by the dread of libel suits that he read almost every paragraph of the paper nightly. This practice eventually cost him his eyesight. He was haunted by a fear of dishonesty among his employes, and any detected or suspected commissions received by his business agents drove him to extremes of passionate indignation. . . . I early gathered that he had little of the personal courage of Cockerill, but as a writer he was as rashly bold and reckless as a rhinoceros.[14]

We are indebted to McDougall's reminiscences for a "sobering" incident that appears to have diverted Pulitzer permanently from a political career. A moderate drinker, the publisher could not handle more than three man-sized "samples" without breaking into a boisterousness and boastful garrulity that contrasted sharply with his usual testiness. One night, soon after Tammany district votes sent him to Washington, Congressman Pulitzer and McDougall were strolling from the Capitol grounds. They had just indulged in several cocktails. Pulitzer found it progressively difficult to propel himself in a straight line. His erratic course prompted a policeman to investigate. As the officer started escorting him to the police station, Pulitzer lisped out a protest: "Look here, othifer, I'm a Congrethman. You can't arreth me!"

"That doesn't cut any ice with me," the cop replied, hustling his prisoner along.

McDougall shuddered at the prospect of glaring headlines chronicling the arrest of Joseph Pulitzer! And on a public intoxication charge! "You don't want to jug this gentleman," McDougall remonstrated. "He is Joseph Pulitzer, editor of the New York *World*."

"Holy Cheesus!" bellowed the cop. "Why didn't you say so? I'll get you a carriage and you can take him home without anybody seeing him."[15]

When he realized what had happened, Pulitzer was both

impressed and horrified. Being the owner of the *World*, he decided, was more important than being a legislator, even a great one. Pulitzer's brief and undistinguished legislative career was abandoned.

Shortly before his death in 1959 Samuel Hopkins Adams, novelist and onetime Park Row reporter, told of his brief employment by the *World* as a special writer to do color pieces of the McCoy-Corbett championship prize fight and the Harry K. Thaw murder trial. Earlier, when Charles A. Dana fired him (for three days) from the *Sun*, Adams asked the *World*'s city editor about a job.

The city editor—I think it was Charles Edward Russell—told me, "I'll take you on tomorrow if you like," Russell said. "But I warn you against it, Sam. You're a *Sun* man; you are used to being treated like a gentleman. You wouldn't stand *World* methods and manners for a month."

I took his friendly advice. How much the atmosphere of the *World* office was a reflection of Pulitzer's own lack of decency in his relations with underlings, I do not know. I should think there was some relationship. He was notoriously ill-tempered and abusive. There is a legend of a new editor who, after listening to Pulitzer's diatribe for ten minutes, thus addressed him, "If you weren't blind, you son of a bitch, I'd punch the hooked nose off your face."[16]

McDougall recalled that members of the staff received many gratuities. "But I suspect that J. P. was not so freely favored," he said. "One day he came into my room and remarked that I occasionally put a trade name on a bottle in my cartoons. Then he asked me what I got out of it. 'Oh, that's a champagne sold by friends of mine, the Somborns,' I admitted. 'They send me a case, now and then.' " At this point, so the McDougall story goes, Joseph Pulitzer looked wistful as he complained, "Well, I never get any champagne."[17] Then he walked out. McDougall promptly tipped off his friend, Eddie Somborn. The next day, elated as a child, the publisher of the *World* stepped in to tell his cartoonist someone had remembered him with a case of the finest vintage.

Despite gratuities, it was the *World*'s proud claim that it had no friends. Pulitzer once had to correct a secretary who used the phrase "your friends." "I have no friends," J. P. interposed quickly.[18] In Cockerill the policy found a staunch supporter. At least one incident illustrates how the Colonel kept it in force. The managing editor engaged William King, a Naval expert, to write an article on disciplinary methods that had created a maritime scandal. "Write what you believe to be right," ordered Cockerill. "The *World*, Mr. Pulitzer and I have no friends . . . nor any policy that interferes with the facts."[19]

Advertisers who expected large accounts to buy favors quickly became aware of the "no friends" policy. Indeed, if a department store executive, pointing meaningfully at a half-page advertisement, suggested that a transgressing relative's name be withheld from court news, the *World* staff made sure the miscreant's name was printed with extra prominence. A vow of dismissal hung over the head of any *World* man who suppressed news to please an advertiser.[20]

Both Cobb and McDougall took notice of Pulitzer's clumsiness in handling personnel. There was nothing new in Pulitzer's three-man board of managers (at times it included Cockerill), wrote Cobb; the Caesars of ancient Rome used the stratagem. Three senators were commissioned with equal power to conduct imperial affairs in the absence of Caesar. Just one wouldn't do; he might seize the empire. Nor would two; the pair might plot to the same end. But three—they would do nicely. If two conspired for power, the third, moved by jealousy, could be counted on to tattle to Caesar. "This was an excellent policy of accident insurance for any absentee seignior of a domain to carry; not perfect protection . . . but fairly safe," commented Cobb.[21]

As in the case of John Cockerill and Ballard Smith, the *World* owner was fond of pairing business and news executives without clarifying their responsibilities but with the idea apparently that one would watch the other. "The plan was unproductive, mean and clumsy," wrote McDougall. "It produced a condition of suspicion, jealousy and hatred, a maelstrom of office politics that drove at least two editors to drink, one into suicide, a fourth into insanity and another into banking. Even those of his employes who were kindly and of generous instincts were compelled in self-protection to resort to unseemly tricks."[22]

With the exception of Hearst, Pulitzer's name has been linked to sensationalism more often than that of any other American newspaper figure. To command wide readership, contended Pulitzer, the newspaper must lean on methods that catch the public's eye. Thus the sensational material served a virtuous end; it provided a forum in which Pulitzer's *World* could shout for reforms. The *World*, as Frank Luther Mott viewed it, was a paradox in its union of sensationalism in the news with an editorial page of remarkably sound character. Such ambivalence, however, wrote Mott, suggests a hula performing in front of a cathedral to attract attention. Oswald Garrison Villard was less charitable. Pulitzer, wrote Villard, deliberately stooped for success. The *World* at times touched lower depths than the *Herald* under the elder James Gordon Bennett, Villard contended, adding: "Pulitzer was willing to out-Hearst Hearst in shameless and unwarranted sensationalism, lest the Hearst organization do his papers irreparable damage."[23] Harry Thurston Peck, writing in 1906, stressed that "sensational journalism was not new, only Pulitzer's development of it was. He not only sought news but created it. . . . Anything that could startle and cause talk was eagerly caught at by what presently became known as yellow journalism."[24]

Pulitzer's *World* shared with Hearst's New York *Journal* the dubious distinction of inspiring the term "yellow journalism." In one version of its origin a London periodical known as *The Yellow Book* was publishing questionable material; at the same time the *World* and the *Journal*, in their battle for readers, were depicting the adventures of rival cartoon characters, those famous Yellow Kids. It seemed perfectly natural that these yellow phenomena, in New York and London, together with the lurid efforts to grab public attention, should be dubbed "yellow journalism."[25]

Even Cockerill, as we shall see in another chapter, regarded the *World*'s brand of sensationalism as "a spectacle which should make good men shudder and angels weep." Did Pulitzer feel that his own image as a fearless liberal editor and publisher was tarnished by accusations that he was a purveyor of sensationalism? As an answer Pulitzer's long speech to a secretary elaborating on the *World*'s evaluation and play of the news may be cited. Although he referred to "sensational topics" and "the matter of sensationalism," at no point did he acknowledge there was any misuse or impropriety in the *World*'s choice and presentation of news. Modern newspapermen will be interested in the following passages from Pulitzer's exposition because it takes cognizance of criticisms of the press that are as prevalent today as when the *World*'s publisher addressed himself to the subject in the early years of this century:

The criticisms you hear about the American press are founded on a dislike for our headlines and for the prominence we give to crime, to corruption in office, and to sensational topics generally; the charge of inaccuracy is just thrown in to make it look worse. I do not believe that one person in a thousand who attacks the American press for being inaccurate has ever taken the trouble to investigate the facts. Now about the matter of sensationalism: a newspaper should be scrupulously accurate, it should be clean, it should avoid everything salacious or suggestive, everything that could offend good taste or lower the moral tone of its readers; but within these limits it is the duty of a newspaper to print the news. When I speak of good taste and of good moral tone I do not mean the kind of good taste which is offended by every reference to the unpleasant things of life. . . . Some people try and make you believe that a newspaper should not devote its space to long and dramatic accounts of murders, railroad wrecks, fires, lynchings, political corruption, embezzlements, frauds, graft, divorces, what you will . . . they are wrong. . . . We are a democracy, and there is only one way to get a democracy on its feet in the matter of its individual, its social, its municipal, its state, its national conduct, and that is by keeping the public informed about what is going on. There is not a crime . . . a dodge . . . a trick . . . a swindle . . . a vice which does not live by secrecy. Get these things out in the open, describe them, attack them, ridicule them in the press, and sooner or later public opinion will sweep them away. Publicity may not be the only thing that is needed, but it is the one thing without which all other agencies will fail.[26]

The success of the *World* in the Cockerill era appears to support a theory offered by George Sibley Johns, longtime editor of the St. Louis *Post-Dispatch*. Johns said the Pulitzer newspapers found an effective road between the personalized school of journalism represented by Horace Greeley and his editorial page and that represented by the James Gordon Bennetts of the *Herald* in their elaborate news-gathering facilities. "Pulitzer believed that aggressiveness and leadership as well as news sold the paper," wrote Johns. "He wanted his newspapers to be a moral force in civilization; they should never be satisfied with merely selling news. The newspaper should take the initiative, organize its own campaigns of investigation and exposure; but it should also try to build when the opportunity affords."[27]

In his comprehensive history of journalism Edwin Emery sees Joseph Pulitzer as "one of those many immigrants who helped to build the new America of the post-Civil War period. In so doing, he both gave and received: the two great newspapers which he established won for him the honor of being named as the leading American editor of modern times (as determined by a poll of U. S. editors conducted by *Editor & Publisher* in 1934), and they also built for him a fortune . . . one of the largest ever accumulated in the newspaper field. The story of Joseph Pulitzer's journalistic success climaxes the story of the emergence of the modern newspaper born of the new national environment."[28] Dr. Emery credits Pulitzer with contributions to the creation of the "new journalism," but "more importantly, he achieved his leadership by being receptive to the ideas of others." Pulitzer's true greatness, Emery feels, lay in his high-minded concept of a newspaper's objective, particularly in its exercise of editorial leadership, and in the way in which he kept alive that concept in his newspapers.

In the early, decisive years of the *World*'s regeneration the team of Pulitzer and Cockerill struck an extremely effective balance. Cockerill's broad and diverse newspaper background exceeded Pulitzer's; his flair for colorful and breezy writing, his resourcefulness and drive in supervising the *World*'s crusades and campaigns, complemented well the *World* owner's talents as a shrewd businessman. But Pulitzer wanted to be remembered as a journalist, not as a newspaper proprietor interested in profits. His passion was for the newspaper's opinion department. Not long before he died Pulitzer insisted "that feeble, invalidish activity is my only thought. . . . my heart was and still is in the editorial page and will be in spirit."

No one knew better than Frank I. Cobb Joseph Pulitzer's affection for the editorial page. As Cobb, who succeeded William H. Merrill as the *World*'s editorial page editor, phrased it, the editorial page to Pulitzer was the expression of the paper's conscience, courage, and convictions.

Sick or well, it was never wholly absent from his thoughts. When he was well he had it read to him every day and expressed his opinion about every editorial article, the style in which it was written, the manner in which the thought was expressed, whether the editorial was strong or weak, whether it served any useful public purpose, whether it said the thing that a great newspaper ought to have said. . . . Nothing was ever allowed to interfere with its independence and its freedom of expression. There were certain questions about which he became convinced that in spite of all his efforts he was possibly prejudiced. In these matters he exacted a pledge that . . . no instructions from him would ever be followed, but that the paper would always say what an independent, untrammelled newspaper ought to say in performing its duties to the people. This pledge was never violated. . . .[29]

A theory exists that Pulitzer became jealous of Cockerill's reputation as the real secret of the *World*'s early success, a state of mind that is supposed to have intensified as Pulitzer's health deteriorated and his suspicions were more easily aroused. Cockerill was tremendously popular—a gay blade seen everywhere and active socially. Furthermore, he was a journalist who had the common touch and commanded the respect of reporters.

Dr. Julian Rammelkamp, whose Harvard doctoral thesis was an extensive study of the St. Louis *Post-Dispatch*, has suggested the plausibility of this theory. He believes that Pulitzer resented the credit Cockerill received from the working press. "Yet Pulitzer," according to Dr. Rammelkamp, "had what Cockerill never displayed—business capacity. This was Pulitzer's long suit, although he seemed ashamed to admit it. He was the business genius in making the *Post-Dispatch* and the *World* what they were. Pulitzer was a turgid writer with a high-pitched, rather hurried style. But he was not really a great editor in the writing sense of the word that Cockerill was."[30]

Joseph Pulitzer expected the tradition of leadership and enterprise to sustain the *World* indefinitely. In his will he enjoined upon his descendants the duty of preserving, perfecting, and perpetuating the *World* "in the same spirit in which I have striven to create and conduct it as a public institution. . . ."

The *World* did not survive as an independent newspaper. But, James W. Barrett, its last city editor, insisted, "the *World*, thank God, never failed. Though enfeebled, battered, kicked about and ridiculed, there was the breath of the Almighty in it even to the very last . . . still beloved by its workers . . . still a fighting institution . . . aye, every inch a king of newspapers."[31] Its "very last" was brought about by its sale to the Scripps-Howard newspaper organization. While women cried and men tried to drown their sorrow in drink, the last issue went to press on February 27, 1931. The next issue in which the famous name appeared was the "hybrid" New York *World-Telegram*. Its loyal family contended that the *World* could have been rescued. "The trouble was," wrote Barrett, "there was no Joseph Pulitzer to save and revive it."

Curiously the St. Louis *Post-Dispatch,* always second in Joseph Pulitzer's affections, was forging ahead strongly in the Pulitzer-Cockerill tradition as this was written. There, under the leadership of Pulitzer's grandson, Joseph Pulitzer, Jr., *Post-Dispatch* staff members have taken seriously Joseph Pulitzer's counsel first published in the newspaper's masthead of April 10, 1907:

I know that my retirement will make no difference in its cardinal principles, that it will always fight for progress and reform, never tolerate injustice or corruption, always fight demagogues of all parties, never belong to any party, always oppose privileged classes and public plunderers, never lack sympathy with the poor, always remain devoted to the public welfare, never be satisfied with merely printing news, always be drastically independent, never be afraid to attack wrong, whether by predatory plutocracy or predatory poverty.

XXI. Cockerill and the "Advertisers"

As John Cockerill thumbed through an afternoon newspaper one early spring day in 1891, a news story caught his eye. It reported that the faltering New York *Continent* was back in the hands of its owners, Collis P. Huntington and Mark Hopkins, Western Pacific Railroad magnates. As the Colonel pondered the New York newspaper situation, an idea began to germinate. Cockerill was eager for another New York newspaper opportunity in which he, not some absentee overlord, would be calling the shots. As a later chapter sets forth, the publication of Colonel Cockerill's views in contemporary magazines reflects some disillusionments in his experience with the *World* and his association with Joseph Pulitzer. The Colonel also left his mind open to the right kind of assignment as a foreign correspondent, having had a taste of such a role in the Russo-Turkish War. He could not foresee that such a challenge would be offered him.

But now the Colonel, in the quiet of his Astor House room, pursued his reflections on the ill-fated New York *Continent*. Before Cockerill walked out of the *World*, the Huntington interests had purchased the New York *Star*, a money-losing morning paper. Frank A. Munsey, flushed with the success of his weekly *Argosy*, had taken a six-month option on the *Star,* establishing an office at Broadway and Park Place. The *Star* "went into orbit" when a group of *Sun* employees, irked by salary differences with the *Sun*'s management, decided to edit a paper of their own. It was successively a disappointment to Joseph Howard, Jr.; Boss Tweed, who fed it with legal notices; John Kelley, who used it as a "detergent" on Tammany Hall; and Munsey. The latter had often noticed annoyed passengers on the Elevated trying to manipulate full-sized newspapers. He reasoned that a tabloid which could be read without its poking the eyes of neighbors would be welcomed. He took over the *Star,* renamed it the *Continent* to dissociate it from earlier failures, and resumed its publication as a tabloid. The experiment drew some initial interest, but New York was not ready for a tabloid, at least not Munsey's kind. So the *Continent* was returned to its reluctant owners.

Cockerill could appreciate the predicament of the law firm of William Allen Butler, Thomas Stillman, and Thomas H. Hubbard, which was handling the affairs of owners Huntington and the Hopkins estate. The *Continent*, Cockerill reflected, might be the means of helping to carry out an idea that kept buzzing in his mind. It was when the Colonel, well posted on the fortunes and foibles of New York newspaper properties, realized that the faltering *Commercial Advertiser,* one of New York's oldest newspapers, was on financial rocks and for sale, that his idea took definite form.

Under proper circumstances perhaps two "losers" could be "parlayed" into a winner.

The *Commercial Advertiser* boasted a distinguished genesis. It started in 1793 as the *Minerva* with a pledge from editor Noah Webster of dictionary fame that it would be "chaste and impartial." Early contributors were Alexander Hamilton and Rufus King. Webster published a series of letters in defense of Jay's Treaty with England that won the warm praise of Thomas Jefferson. In 1797 the *Minerva* became the *Commercial Advertiser*. It was popular among financiers and businessmen, whose support, however, was not sufficient to keep it "off the block." It was limping bravely under Harold Godwin, grandson of William Cullen Bryant, in a modernized Park Row plant when John Cockerill resolved upon a bold plan. Why could not those Huntington millions be tapped to purchase the evening *Commercial Advertiser* and convert the *Continent* into a one-cent edition of the *Morning Advertiser*? This would leave Sunday open to the competition. So, why not a *Sunday Advertiser* too?

The Colonel, whose portfolio included the credentials of an editor who had made newspaper fortunes, was well received by Messrs. Butler, Stillman, and Hubbard. Undoubtedly it was Cockerill's unique qualifications that, after the pros and cons were debated, convinced Huntington and his colleagues that acquiring another ailing journal could be good business.

Apparently Cockerill fully appreciated the odds against his converting a couple of sickly journals into a successful enterprise, both professionally and financially. He warned his new associates of the costliness of such a venture. He was promised "sufficient funds" for the undertaking,[1] although there is no record defining precisely how much would be "sufficient." Cockerill felt his work at the *World* had been an important factor in its resurrection. He not only cherished a chance to prove it was no fluke; he hoped the *Advertisers* could be forged into a competitive threat to the *World*. Cockerill assumed the firm could spend in such amounts as he and Pulitzer had expended to inject new life into the *World*. *Cockerill* took comfort in the fact that Collis P. Huntington, his financial angel, was one of the richest men in the United States.

By late May, 1891, the name of John A. Cockerill appeared as editor of the *Commercial Advertiser*, 29 Park Row. Charles E. Hasbrook was listed as publisher. In some sections of the press Cockerill was reported as the purchaser.[2] Cockerill is thought to have invested an undisclosed amount, which probably accounted for the report. Although not the sole owner, the Colonel stipulated himself as the executive in complete editorial control.

To set the tone for the *Advertiser*, the Colonel announced:

It will aim, first of all, to be within its lines, a liberal newspaper, free from prejudice, free from factionalism, free from outside dictation. It will maintain at all times a wholesome independence. It will be found on the side of the honest man as against classes, upon the side of honest democracy as against the growing tendency of aristocracy, active for economical government—in fact, without cant or creed, a sincere newspaper for the people. It will place accuracy above all else in gathering and setting the news before the public, and, cherishing the institutions which have made this republic the happiest and most prosperous on earth, will be at all times American in every bone and fiber.[3]

In the masthead Cockerill left undisturbed the editorial announcement of the *Commercial Advertiser* that had run in every edition since October 2, 1797: "This Paper Will Be the Friend of Government, of Morals and of the Truth, Independent of Party or National Prejudice." The *Commercial Advertiser* was a member of the Associated Press. In addition to its Park Row address, it had branch offices in Union Square, uptown, and Harlem.

Other papers took notice of its aspirations. "If Colonel Cockerill can make a success of a paper with a record of disaster so remarkable as that of the *Continent*," said the Rochester, New York, *Post-Express*, "his reputation as an editor will be second to none."[4] Cockerill hired as managing editor the brilliant Foster Coates, who assembled under the Colonel's direction a staff starring Joseph Donelly, city editor, and James Clark, telegraph editor. Early signs of progress were promising. The *Journalist* late in 1891 saw in the *Advertiser* building at 29 Park Row

that sure sign of prosperity, a new press. The *Morning Advertiser* . . . was the first issue printed on the giant. With a capacity of 96,000 per hour, this triumph of modern ingenuity is modestly declared by Colonel Cockerill to be sufficient for present needs, but he hints that the rapidly increasing circulation of the bright new penny sheet may soon require another press.[5]

There was excitement, too, in the news departments of the *Advertisers*. They all but outdid themselves in covering the four hundredth anniversary celebration of the discovery of America and in the spectacular opening of the luxurious Waldorf Hotel, garnished by a reception for Eulalie, aunt of the King of Spain. The Colonel, attending the Columbian Exposition of 1893, filed colorful accounts of the visit by the Duke of Veragua, a descendant of Columbus.

It was on the editorial page that the Colonel's pen was most in evidence. Park Row could boast of no editorial page brighter or wittier, or one that more persistently prodded the political opposition. Its readership appeal ran the gamut from those with earthy tastes to the level of sophistication. As on other papers under his editorship, letters to the *Commercial Advertiser* flowed freely. Cockerill insisted on one inflexible rule—lengthy letters were condensed to a mere one to three paragraphs.

One of Cockerill's innovations was a popular column of shorts that he called "Gossip of the Flying Day." Grover Cleveland, whom the *Advertiser* opposed in his third bid for the White House, was a favorite Cockerill target, and a subject of gibes all over the page. In "Gossip," for instance, the Colonel wrote that: "Cleveland obviously agrees with his chum, Tim Campbell, that he ought not to 'allow a little thing

like the Constitution' to stand between him and the White
House."[6] Since the Colonel was not feeling benevolent toward
the *World*, the editor found it possible to combine both targets
in the same thrust:

The World is frank enough to confess that when Cleveland
shall be again seated in the White House, it will not matter much
through what process his election was secured. There you have a
naked statement of the attitude of all the idolaters, canting hypocrites and Pharisees. They would gladly steal it to gratify the
Prophet's inordinate ambition.[7]

Referring to a measure that would have permitted a build-up
in political patronage, the *Advertiser* in another "Gossip"
item, observed: "Any Democrat who opposes this bill must
try to curb his appetite for pie."[8] By openly tagging the column
"Gossip" the Colonel left himself a wide, unfenced field for
shrewd guesses and political trial balloons. But the column
was not all political. "One of the burning questions which have
survived the recent celebration is whether Columbus had red
hair," observed the Colonel.

The *Advertiser* capitalized on "name-dropping." In what
was perhaps the first "Good Afternoon" column the editorial
page presented a non-political array of people and places.
("An interesting man is J. E. Rowland, who worked long
and hard for the pardon of a Northampton bank robber. . . .
A talented and energetic artist is Miss Alice Donlevy, a moving
spirit of the Ladies Art Association. . . . A stylish, new figure
often seen on Park Row is Willis B. Troy. . . . Michael J.
Mulqueen, the talented son-in-law of Mayor Gilroy. . . .")[9]
It was a gain in status for a rising young lawyer, actress,
socialite, merchant or even a clergyman to find his or her
name in "Good Afternoon."

The massive average word-volume of the *Commercial
Advertiser*'s editorial page would dismay the modern reader
who is lured to his newspaper through flashy captions, eye-
catching typography, nine-point (or larger) body type, and
pictures galore. Except for the Colonel's occasional use of

half-column cuts, the seven columns of six- and eight-point type filled the page. Yet the perceptive journalism student today would find Cockerill's editorial page fascinating, despite its quaintness of style by modern standards.

The editor's technique was calculated to catch the reader's attention and, if possible, hold him through the entire seven-column course of enlightenment, indignation, persuasion, and amusement. The technique worked this way: The first column was a teaser of brief quips designed to entice the reader to begin. It started with a sure-fire attention-getter of one brief sentence. There followed paragraphs of increasing length intended to warm up the reader for bigger things to come. By the time the reader had finished this column, he was ready to plow through the longer, heavier editorials and full-fledged discussions of current issues.

For appreciating the full impact of the *Advertiser*'s editorial page upon the life and times of Colonel Cockerill, there is no substitute for a leisurely perusal of the files. However, it is possible, through representative excerpts, to sample its flavor. For instance the Colonel might lead off with this gem: "Mayor Boody's decision to quit politics does not bring him into violent opposition to public opinion."[10] Cockerill quips often left the reader looking for hidden meanings, such as when he observed that "The proposal of an Ohio legislator to correct football abuses by law is fresh evidence of the theory of evolution, though calculated to suggest doubts as to whether the right animal has been identified as the common ancestor of us all."[11]

Always a champion of the press, the *Advertiser* made it evident in declaring:

The truth bubbles up from the bottom of the well. It was the press that saved the Chicago Fair and not George Francis Train. This brings Mr. Handy and Mr. Train face to face on a great issue. And our advice to Citizen Train is to lapse into that silence of his which at times is so dense and beautiful you can slice it with a knife.[12]

Sarcasm was a weapon used with such withering effect that it became a Cockerill trademark, as when he aimed this verbal dart at President Cleveland:

When Mr. Depew sent a Monsignor within to ask the Pope if any ceremonials were to be observed during their interview, word came back that Mr. Depew was at liberty to bear himself precisely as if he were being received by the President of the United States. That was courteous; but we trust His Holiness does not wish to imply that his greatness is for a moment to be compared to that of our own Grover.[13]

In figures of speech, particularly the metaphor, the Colonel was a master:

What New Jersey needs is pure water and pure politics, and it cannot have either as long as the Democracy is permitted to defile the springs of both.

Viewed in its physical aspects the Cleveland-Croker ticket is much the larger at the head, but it is the little cracker or Croker on the end which counts at the ballot box.

Diagnostically considered, Mr. Wayne MacVeigh's open letter to Minister Egan is of value as shedding light upon the causes which separated him from the Republican party. It indicates a condition of hepatic abnormality that clamors constantly for calomel.[14]

The Colonel took note of feminine politicians:

From the way the Southern press assails Mrs. Mary Ellen Lease—the Atlanta Journal calls her the "paid petticoat protector of James Bandit Weaver" and a "Republican wolf in People's party sheep's clothing," which clothing is the "mask she wore" and subsequently "lifted"—we fear the sweetness and light infused into politics by lovely women's participation are more imaginary than actual.[15]

And another feminine note of interest:

There is grave possibility that ex-Queen Liliuokalani will be placed on the witness stand in a libel suit between a citizen of Honolulu and an editor. The case grows out of a publication which left a taint on the ex-Queen's reputation for chastity and sobriety.

It is thought that under cross-examination a sidelight may be
thrown on high life . . . in Honolulu. Perhaps so. But isn't this a
case where the fair, the chaste, the unexpressive she may decide
to perjure herself like a lady?[16]

Having run through a dozen or so opening quips, the
Advertiser reader could count on a half-dozen full-length,
often angry editorials. The once pro-Cleveland editor remained militantly anti-Cleveland after the 1888 election when
Cleveland failed in his bid for re-election. Cleveland in his
successful third try in 1892 was opposed by the *Commercial
Advertiser,* which harassed the candidate unmercifully. Early
in his second term Cleveland chanced to use the phrase "noise
and clamor" in reference to his political opponents. Cockerill,
with alacrity, pounced upon the phrase:

"Noise and clamor" have done much for the world. If the
ponderous President has any regard for history other than that
made by himself, he might look backward and observe that "noise
and clamor" have been tolerably busy ever since the world began,
and to the great benefit of mankind. Nearly all the great reforms,
and especially those in politics, either have been entirely brought
about or materially assisted by "noise and clamor." In all likelihood
it will assail to some purpose the wonderful ears of Mr. Cleveland
himself.[17]

Perhaps remembering Charles Dana's mud-tossing at the
Colonel when Cockerill was at the *World,* the *Advertiser*'s
editor aimed a blast at the *Sun* publisher:

The *Sun* boasts of "Mr. Cleveland's success in turning down
malcontents in New York City." We are inclined to accept Mr.
Dana on this subject as one who speaks with great understanding
and personal, painful experience. . . . we do not recall one who
was more miserable in his malcontentedness than was Brother
Dana. . . . how bitterly he poured forth his spirit touching the
"Stuffed Prophet" prior to the Chicago convention. . . . Yet observe
how completely Mr. Dana is now "turned down." The fat man
from Buzzard's Bay has not only turned him down but has rolled
him over and booted him until his spirit and his back are both
broken. . . .[18]

The "religious issue" was a problem that disturbed Colonel
Cockerill in the nineties just as the "religious issue" exerted
immeasurable weight in the 1960 presidential election. But
bigotry, if no more prevalent in the Colonel's day, was less
subtle. Cockerill's editorial page injected the issue with reference to an organization known as the American Protestant
Association. An APA member swears, said the *Advertiser*,
that

> he will do all in his power to retard and break down the power of
> the Pope; that in all grievances he will seek only Protestants and
> counsel with them . . . and will not countenance the nomination
> in any caucus or convention of a Roman Catholic for any office
> in the gift of the American people; and will not vote for nor coun-
> sel others to vote for any Roman Catholic; that he will endeavor
> at all times to place the political parties of this government in the
> hands of Protestants. . . .[19]

The APA was a secret organization, despite which the Colonel
exposed its oath, asserting editorially that such principles
embraced in secrecy were abhorrent. The Colonel, however,
pointing out that there were instances in which some denomi-
nations sought civic domination, asserted:

> The opponents of alliances of every character between Church
> and State are rallying their forces and will make themselves felt . . .
> but to espouse this laudable cause it surely cannot be necessary
> to violate this very principle as to the churches and the State by
> attempting to annihilate a certain class of citizens who belong to
> one of the churches.[20]

Another kind of religious note emerged in the report of
a sermon by the ever-aggressive pastor of the Madison Square
Presbyterian church, the Reverend Charles H. Parkhurst. "The
uptown movement of various New York churches," said Dr.
Parkhurst, "is dastardly cowardice. The church that picks
itself up bodily and moves uptown to a life of chilly, easy
inactivity away from the densely populated downtown dis-
tricts, where there is work to be done, has lost its holy spirit
and is no longer a church but a religious club."[21]

Dr. Parkhurst made good copy in other ways. His relentless crusade against vice and corruption prompted the famous Lexow inquiry of 1894. His charges of police corruption blazed a hot trail toward Boss Richard Croker. The *Commercial Advertiser*'s handling of the investigations produced what has been dubbed New York City's first banner headline. In a scorching denunciation of Croker, Dr. Parkhurst hinted that the political chieftain, his conscience smarting, had fled the city. To make his point, the clergyman quoted Proverbs 28:1: ". . . the wicked flee when no man pursueth." Croker had done no such thing up until the time he read the pastor's accusation. He had merely left his office for a few days of relaxation. On a hunch Cockerill's newspaper captioned the story with a page-wide streamer. It read:

THE WICKED MAN FLEES WHEN NO MAN PURSUETH—
BUT RUNS FASTER IF SOMEONE IS AFTER HIM

The city chuckled over the Bible-quoting *Sunday Advertiser*'s headline and rocked with the news of Croker's alleged flight. Croker had not intended to leave New York, but public reaction changed his mind. Croker's henchmen slipped him the word it might not be healthy to return to his old haunts. The Tammany chief's ship slid from the dock as the cops waved a warrant for his arrest at their elusive prey. Croker found it convenient to take a lazy holiday in Ireland.

The public steamed with indignation. Under pressure of Cockerill's editorial pleas and with the support of other newspapers, the Lexow Committee of Investigation went to work. Out of its disclosures a fusion of political parties elected as mayor William L. Strong, a Republican wholesale merchant. The new mayor lived up to his name. He kicked off the police board Republicans and Democrats alike. His appointees elected as president of the board a brash young politician by the name of Theodore Roosevelt. Roosevelt proceeded to incur Joseph Pulitzer's ire. He started a drive to curb the sale of liquor beyond prescribed hours. Cockerill supported the move; Pulitzer opposed it as a waste of time. The *World* thought of Roosevelt as a child of fortune in need of a strong curb. New York sided with Roosevelt; letters from readers indicated strong support of the police board reform.

Brilliance in the news and editorial departments, however, was no substitute for receipts in the counting-house. The years 1891, 1892, and 1893 kept Cockerill's hopes alive, but Collis P. Huntington buried them in 1894. The Huntington checkbook became as elusive as a racketeer's tax return. The counting house was saying the wrong things. The *Fourth Estate*, a "newspaper for the makers of newspapers," on October 4, 1894, observed:

> The announcement that Colonel John A. Cockerill, editor of the New York *Commercial Advertiser* and *Morning Advertiser*, had resigned was not a surprise to the newspaper world.
> It had been known for some time that Colonel Cockerill was not entirely satisfied with his position in the Advertiser office. . . .
> When he was invited to assume charge of the *Commercial Advertiser*, it is said that he was promised absolute control of the property and that abundant funds would be provided to develop the business and put it on a paying basis. Friends of Colonel Cockerill say that these promises have not been kept.[22]

Cockerill withdrew in good grace. He resigned at the time a new general manager was appointed and thus avoided a situation that could have been as distasteful to the Colonel as harmful to the papers. A contemporary editor wrote that "Cockerill, despite some differences with his associates, had converted the deficit-plagued *Advertisers* into successful newspapers."[23] Success hinges on definition. A not impossible anomaly in newspaper journalism is an editorial success and a business failure. It is not likely that Cockerill would have dropped out if the enterprise had been making substantial financial gains. He had failed to shake the *World*'s domination. That accomplishment was destined instead for the flamboyant William Randolph Hearst, who was not disturbed by such prosaic woes as a puny bank account.

Louis Thorn Golding, who moved into the managing editor's slot of the *Commercial Advertiser* when Coates succeeded Cockerill as editor-in-chief, was not among the Colonel's admirers, but his reaction touches on the departing editor's dilemma. "When I went to the paper," Golding recalled, "Cockerill was there but I saw him only once, as his office was on another floor. He left soon after and I must say that the staff was not much impressed by him. The general opinion was that he had been much overrated. . . . But the Colonel had a great reputation in connection with the success of the World."[24]

The Colonel's problem was two-edged. As any active editor who is horrified by business office worries can attest, few newspaper executives have either the inclination or talent for both roles. On the *World* Cockerill had no worries over circulation or advertising revenues. At the *Advertisers*, he kept an eye on spending and earning while supervising the editorial staffs. Cockerill was not long in realizing that the reputation he brought from the *World* was more of a liability than an asset. His colleagues on the *Advertisers* seemed to regard Cockerill's reputation as a piece of magic that would transform their properties into a profitable enterprise. By 1894 New York newspaper competition was furious and its mortality rate high. Equipment was improving but it cost more. Other would-be Pulitzers were trying their hands on Park Row. Readers were demanding more for their money— more pages, more features, more pictures, more comics. For the *Advertisers* to keep pace there must be money, plenty of it, more than Collis P. Huntington was willing to invest— money for top reporters, artists and editors, for syndicated material, for competent executives. Cockerill and the gentlemen with the money bags could not reconcile their differences.

The *Morning Advertiser* died quietly, with few mourners. The *Commercial Advertiser* survived until 1905, when it was merged with the New York *Globe*. The amalgamation lasted until 1923, when Frank A. Munsey combined it with the New York *Sun*.

It was during the Colonel's tenure as editor of the *Commercial Advertiser* that Cockerill endeared himself to the Benevolent and Protective Order of Elks. While Cockerill was in St. Louis the Elks acquired a circular burial plot near the center of Bellefontaine Cemetery. There, at "Elks' Rest," a twelve-foot pedestal of Missouri granite was erected. Brother Elks waited hopefully for someone to provide an appropriate monument. Their hopes were fulfilled October 11, 1891, when a nine-foot, 1,350-pound likeness of Landseer's "Monarch of the Glen" was unveiled in dedication ceremonies. An audience that included Elk dignitaries from a dozen states attended. The statue was a gift of Colonel Cockerill. Although he did not reveal the price, the bronze figure of an elk cost a substantial sum.

In his presentation speech, one of several to which the audience of 250 listened, the magnanimous New York editor warmed the cockles of every Elk heart with his eloquence and urbanity. In the confidence that even non-Elks will find something of interest in the Colonel's remarks, a few sentences are excerpted:

An organization based upon charity, justice, brotherly love, and fidelity must endure. Such an organization is the B. P. O. E. . . .

It has been claimed by those who are opposed to secret societies that they belong to the era of barbarism and are not part of our civilization. Brotherhood is a necessity in that it brings men of kindred purposes into closer communion, broadens them, makes them helpful, and, better still, smooths the asperities engendered in the selfish struggle for existence. Our order maintains a code of morals as rigid as the golden rules of Pythagoras grafted upon the noble teachings of the New Testament. As one who has felt the sympathetic touch of St. Louis Lodge No. 9, it is my great pleasure to present a statue symbolic of our order. . . .

In choosing the elk as an emblem our founders were inspired with poesy. In all natural history there is no animal more beautiful . . . majestic of mien, swift of foot, timid and shy, an eye as soft as a child, the elk is, nevertheless, resolute in defense of its rights. The prey of many, it brings no grief to any child of the forest. It is neither rapacious nor vengeful. Its home is sylvan, and its ways are ways of pleasantness. Its existence is idyllic and, in a measure, pathetic. . . .[25]

It was a solemn occasion in pronounced contrast to the gaiety that pervaded the festive board the evening of the next day. The banquet, at the Elks club rooms, was a homecoming affair in honor of the Colonel. St. Louis Mayor Noonan welcomed Cockerill, and the Colonel, responding, according to one account, "showed that distance has not lessened his regard for his old city." The president of the Elks, F. M. Estes, seemed to have only one end in view—the comfort and pleasure of every guest and seeing that every cup was kept filled. The evening was long, the toasts were many, indicating that both conviviality and libations were in abundant supply.

It was John Cockerill's last visit, alive, to St. Louis.

Prior to Colonel Cockerill's exit from the *Advertisers*, he had established himself in still another field of journalism—syndicated material. The Colonel was given prominent mention by the *Journalist* in its December 26, 1891, issue. New York, said the *Journalist*, was responsible for nearly all the syndicated letters published all over the country. "We have Bill Nye, John A. Cockerill, M. Quad, Marshall P. Wilder, Foster Coates, Joe Howard, Clara Belle, Bab, and Helen Watterson," the *Journalist* reported. "These are the writers most widely read."[26] Of the serious writers the *Journalist* found Colonel Cockerill's letters (the word "column" was not generally used to earmark such material) most interesting, explaining: "He treats of what is happening, and of his personal experiences with famous men and women. He is a keen observer and tells things as they are, not as the imagination of an enthusiast paints them. There are no frills in a Cockerill letter. No persiflage. Straight-forward common sense—like the man. But just how the Colonel finds time to edit two metropolitan dailies, see things, and write weekly letters is one of the things no fellow can find out."[27]

In the *Commercial Advertiser* the feature, which appeared in several other newspapers, ran under the caption "Folks

You Have Heard Of" on the Saturday editorial page. In its preparation the Colonel capitalized on his contacts and his travels. When Serge Julich Vitte was named Russia's finance minister, Cockerill did a three-paragraph profile under "The Czar's Right-Hand Man," drawing upon his first-hand knowledge of the Russo-Turkish War to relate Vitte's rise to power. The Colonel, never one to neglect women readers, might do a tongue-in-cheek item on Mrs. John A. Logan's warning that working women are less likely to snare husbands; or he might recapitulate Senator Peffer's creed for the Populist party.[28] And so it went. Cockerill illustrated his personality pieces with half-column sketches by the newspaper artist. The appeal of the Colonel's syndicated feature lay in newspaper readers' deep interest in the people who make the news. Its treatment was dignified and accurate. The brevity and good taste of each sketch would have been appropriate for introducing the subject to an audience. Through his weekly letter Colonel Cockerill introduced leading figures of the world to millions of American readers.

XXII. Cockerill, Critic and Prophet

As a practitioner and observer of the newspaper profession, Colonel Cockerill was a mixture of apologist, critic, prophet, and cynic. Less the idealist than Joseph Pulitzer, he was always the realist and pragmatist. Revealed in his well articulated views are a disillusionment in the extremes of sensationalism to which the *World* reached and, conversely, a glowing faith in the potential of "responsible" newspapers (the Colonel was careful to include the qualifying adjective).

He saw a growing influence for the press in local and municipal affairs as the cities of the United States burgeoned in all directions. "The newspaper," wrote Cockerill, must grow in proportion and inevitably lead the procession. Our civilization will develop in many directions. Our standard of public intelligence, which is now greater than that of any other country, will reach a higher level. . . . The newspaper is the only trustworthy medium of communication between the people and their official servants. When a newspaper ceases to speak for the public its importance and influence will disappear.[1]

It had become "impossible for any openly wicked, dishonest or base man to be elected or appointed to any office of consequence anywhere in the United States; no other power than that of the press ever would or ever could have produced this result. The good is incalculable."[2] In his view the newspaper's most compelling obligation is to inform. "How else is it possible under a scheme of government so simple as ours seems to be, relatively, and yet so complex in reality," the Colonel asked, "for the public to keep track of the doings of its public agents, now numbered in the hundreds of thousands?"[3] As to the "tremendous leverage of the press on national affairs," the New York *Times*'s aggressive interest in the Tilden-Hayes presidential election campaign of 1876 was cited as a case in point. The Colonel asserted that had the *Times* not made a bold claim that Rutherford B. Hayes was the real victor, Tilden might have won. The *Times* contended that Hayes had earned the office by garnering the electoral votes of three Southern states. Otherwise those votes might have been counted for Tilden. Cockerill attributes this alertness with having changed the course of history.[4]

Unlike Pulitzer, who was constantly defensive of the press, Cockerill did not hesitate to point out its imperfections. Because of his pre-eminence in the sensational and sensationally successful New York *World*, his views were seized upon by critics as those of a disillusioned editor. He lashed out at some practices known to have been part of the *World*'s stock in trade. Yet Cockerill was not a vindictive man; there is not a word in what he wrote suggesting resentment specifically of any circumstance attending his break with Pulitzer. His quarrels were with principles, not personalities.

Pulitzer defended the publication of sensational material as a means of attracting a mass audience to whom the *World* could address itself on important public issues. Cockerill, with a less lofty view, saw in the American stage an analogy that made his point:

If there was eliminated from American plays what the critics call trash and what they denounce as unworthy, there would not be today a successful drama on the boards. It remains equally true that if we take away from the daily newspaper, as we find it at the beginning of the last decade of the 19th Century, what all must condemn as its faults, the public would probably decline to buy the remainder.

It would be difficult to dissociate the *World* and its elegant million-dollar gold-domed Park Row edifice from Cockerill's reflections when he observed:

The constant effort to gather at any cost and to present in the most meretricious form occurrences which will catch the curious eye and hold the morbid fancy, has found its best reward in the accumulation of newspaper millions and the erection of costly newspaper buildings. But there seems a certain desecration in applying the superlative of good to such a result; there is nothing good in it, and cannot be.

. . . . This collection of crime and outrage on the news pages of a leading morning newspaper [the *World* was a morning news-sheet] was a spectacle that should make good men shudder and angels weep. . . . The crying and pressing need is for sensation, scandal, crime—something to sell papers. . . . It is a mighty maelstrom, whose vortex centers over the counter of the business office. It is successful as the papers sell and the advertisements pour in their gold . . . it is unsuccessful if sales are not made and advertisements are few. This being the case with the owner present, how much more painfully apparent is it with the owner absent across the seas? . . . .

The editor-in-chief, the editor-in-charge, the managing editor, the news editor, or the night editor—the man upon whose shoulders falls the brunt of procuring, at all hazards, news which will sell the paper and gratify his employer with the clink of new dollars—stands on a dull day with a great despair in his heart, like the farmer on his sunburnt plains. Reproach, humiliation, perhaps revolt or suspension, he feels assured must follow if he fails to make the newspaper in his charge as interesting as those of his rivals, or as his predecessors have succeeded in making it.

What is the great phenomenon which can bring him relief, and appease the news drought? Nothing short of a terrible crime, an awful domestic tragedy, a revolting scandal in high life, a heartrending sorrow, agony by land or sea, some new development on the trail of an old crime, or some new outburst of human frailty.[5]

Cockerill, the cynic, coined his own definition of news as a previously unprinted occurrence which involves the fracture of any one of the following Ten Commandments—the fifth (Honor thy father and thy mother), sixth (Thou shalt not kill), seventh (Thou shalt not commit adultery), eighth (Thou shalt not steal), or ninth (Thou shalt not bear false witness against thy neighbor); if it involves the names of persons whose names the readers have heard of, from their official or social positions, then it is great news. "The Daily Crimes" would be the best name for almost any sensational newspaper today.[6]

Cockerill professed to be shocked at newspapers' lack of respect for and their invasion of privacy in digging up lurid or scandalous news.

Was it significant of the accuracy of the Colonel's charges that no rumble of protest was heard from newspaper publishers?

Elsewhere there was response. Standing loftily outside the newspaper fold, the *Review of Reviews* observed that as a lifelong newspaperman and the former managing editor of the *World*, Cockerill had "eminently every right to be heard; but his unmitigated arraignment of the lurid faults in our journalistic methods is so sweeping and incisive that one has to rub his eyes to awake to the fact that the writer is talking about his own life-work—that it is, as it were, a confession." The magazine hastened to point out that Cockerill was "the editor and absolute dictator of New York's oldest newspaper, the *Commercial Advertiser*, whose tone is wholesome and bright. It is a different class of newspaper he discusses. Colonel Cockerill does not allow himself even the comfort of holding that the shortcomings of the 'great daily' are accidents of prosperity or of merely human management, with a nobler essence of success underlying them."[7]

In an unsigned commentary *Harper*'s conceded that Cockerill spoke with authority, that his record in making newspapers was conspicuous, and that he was conversant with "all the horrors of the subject." As to the invasion of privacy, the publication wondered "why the district attorney does not bestir himself to see that private life is not needlessly sacrificed to the public greed for gossip. If the statutes are not adequate, there should be some that are.... It would be a peculiarly fit task for Cockerill, knowing what he knows, to secure the enactment and enforcement of statutes which should restrain the indecencies of which he complains and protect both the press and the public from the demoralization which attends them."[8]

Cockerill, as far as the magazine files show, did not accept the suggestion. When the Colonel was asked whether "it must be inferred that the reading masses prefer offal to clean food," he admitted it might seem so but expressed hope "that time and education may enable the American public to correct this and other evils; and when I say the American public I have in mind the wealth, intellectual influence, material resources and achievements which such great English journals as the London *Telegraph* and *Standard* have been able to realize without self-abasement."[9]

Colonel Cockerill did not relish the decline of personal journalism and the emergence of the newspaper as an impersonal institution. This could account for his not wholly consistent appraisals of the editorial page. Thus in one "diagnosis" of the ailing press Cockerill found that the editorial page had passed the peak of its influence;[10] but in a more optimistic mood he asserted that "a dozen responsible editorial pages across the country, each standing conspicuously for its own city and area, could keep Washington under tighter control than any political party.... As long as public officials read the editorial pages of responsible newspapers, eagerly and fearfully, our republic will endure."[11] The injection of the manner of reading them—"eagerly and fearfully"—implied, of course, that the merit of such pages should command this kind of readership.

The daily press was feeling the pains of transition. Fading into limbo were the days when the names of editors like Horace Greeley of the New York *Tribune*, Joseph Medill of the Chicago *Tribune*, and Charles A. Dana of the New York *Sun* were better known than the names of their newspapers. Succeeding them was the "institutional" era when editorial pages no longer presented the views of individuals. Of the half dozen editors whose personalities Cockerill felt were identified with their editorial pages, the Colonel rated the *Sun*'s Charles A. Dana, before the pathetic waning of his influence, as one of the most skilled and interesting. Dana ran his editorial page on the basis of his definition of a newspaper as a creature for a day. To borrow Cockerill's phrasing: "In that day and for that day it is born and dies, and there is no iron chain of consistency necessarily reaching from one to another." Dana for so many years had identified the *Sun* with himself, Cockerill recalled, that its readers went to its editorial page

reasonably sure that he would surprise and interest them. The *Sun*'s cherished tradition was that no citizen in town could go to bed at night with the certainty that he could foretell the *Sun*'s editorial course the next morning on any subject. Mr. Dana had the faculty of saying vicious things in a smart way. He tickled the intellects of his readers until they forgot about their morals.[12]

Cockerill conceded that the very nature of contemporary newspaper effort seemed to necessitate the impersonal approach, observing, cynically, that "it is no longer character which counts but success—deserved, it may be, but achieved at any hazard."[13] The Colonel, who had known the frustrations of communicating with the roving publisher of the *World*, felt that absentee ownership hastened the advent of the impersonalized press. There were other celebrated absentee proprietors, of whom James Gordon Bennett, Jr. was a conspicuous example. Cockerill probably was remembering ruefully the hash of overlapping functions that occurred in Pulitzer's absence when he wrote:

What the *Tribune*, the *Herald*, or the *World* says is an impersonal utterance, carrying the stamp of nobody's individuality, the sanction of nobody's power. The readers are ignorant of what Whitelaw Reid, James Gordon Bennett or Joseph Pulitzer thinks or says. It is the newspaper that announces its opinions . . . lamentably weak ones often enough and constructed of necessity on the principle that it is safer to wheedle than to threaten, when no power to execute the threat exists. The fashion of editing by cablegram has destroyed what little virility was left in the editorial pages.[14]

Colonel Cockerill left no doubt of his abhorrence of absentee ownership and its obsession with reports from the counting-room. He felt the newspaper's integrity suffered under remote control. Unlike most grumblers in editorial rooms, Cockerill unleashed his indignation publicly thus:

The owner receives from his newspaper property, at stated intervals, returns in money. He is beyond the reach of proofs and often inaccessible to direct questions in regard to newspaper policy.

But the address of his bank is always known. Thither, on the first of every month, large sums of money must be forwarded, and if they are not forthcoming, sharp criticism of the policy and management which have led to their diminution is sure to follow.

The tendency of non-resident ownership must be to measure everything by a pecuniary test. The morals of the paper, its course on public measures, and its treatment of the interests of the people whose trustee it professes to be are considered only from the point of view of the counting-room.

When the receipts fall off, there must have been something wrong; when the receipts increase, the management of the paper has been excellent. But it is to be observed that one never sees the business manager of a newspaper going to Europe or leaving his charge 3,000 miles behind him. He keeps his eye on the cash box every day, as his master does every month.

They both look at journalism from precisely the same point of view, and their moral vision is in the same way obscured to the duties and responsibilities of newspaper management by the dollars which might cover either eye.[15]

Cockerill was not alone on the firing line. The *Bookman*, ten years after the Colonel's published excoriation of 1892, found the *World* was run "by a business man pure and simple. . . . With Mr. Pulitzer the counting-room begins to play a more important part in journalism than ever before."[16] But just as he disclaimed any taint of sensationalism, Pulitzer insisted that newspaper revenue was not his primary interest. A little more than a decade after Cockerill had assailed his former chief, Pulitzer, in explaining his proposal to endow a College of Journalism at Columbia University, explained that the college was to "set up ideals, to keep the counting-house in its proper place and to make the soul of the editor the soul of the newspaper."[17]

On the formulation of editorial policy Cockerill was prolific in counsel. He contended that if he could scan the news displayed most prominently in a newspaper, he could read the character of the editorial page without looking at it.[18] Whether a journal should be partisan or neutral, particularly a newly born paper, he opined, may be a problem of majorities; some cities may be intolerant of a newspaper that does not take sides in politics and tries to please everybody by not attacking the opinions of anybody. The answer, said the Colonel, must be decided upon the basis of a specific situation. If expediency is to be the determining factor, Cockerill advised that newspaper policy follow the prevalent opinions of the best informed people of the community, rather than to try leading the people in other directions:

In this advice I am sustained not only by reason and reality but also by the example of certain great journals which have become famous as exponents of national opinion and in fact have never dictated an opinion of their own. Conspicuous among such is the London *Times*, which is one of the most influential journals on the planet, perhaps the most so, and yet its manner of progression is like that of a ship: it is moved by the wind of popular opinion behind its sails, and, like a ship, it never travels faster than the wind. Human nature is constant in its habits: such a course as we have indicated will always insure popularity, and there is no more useful ally to the newspaper proprietor than the good will of his community.... Indeed one element of positively useful popularity is the systematic cultivation of civic pride.

Cockerill warned against pointless involvements in local squabbles. Newspapers cannot avoid reporting transient quarrels when they produce overt acts, he said, but they would do well to refrain from publishing editorials about them.

If Mr. A. and Mr. B. come to blows on the street, the incident must be narrated, else the paper is wanting in its duty; but ... if the editor justifies A., he makes an enemy of B., and when the parties become reconciled, the editor will find that he has not gained a friend, and has certainly made a foe ... and several other enemies among partisans of Mr. A.... Religious controversies should be avoided ... [yet] there is almost no limit to local church news ... and not to chronicle them would be inexcusable neglect.

On the subject of local news, whatever its category, Cockerill had strong convictions. "The editor of a local paper must always bear in mind," he wrote,

that his journal is not and cannot be a substitute for the great city newspapers, which carry the world's news.... The local newspaper's function is to supply the demand for local information. A farmer may not care to know that the Dreibund in Europe is overslaughed by the French and Russian alliance, but he is sure to want to know whether the break in the dam on the other side of the township is going to be repaired during the present season.... This demand for home news is constant and the supply is constant.[19]

Terse and timely letters from readers were an editorial page delight to Cockerill as they are today to another generation of editors. The editor enlarged thus upon a favorite type of newspaper copy:

In no way are the people of the press kept in more immediate touch than by letters from its readers.... In no more immediate way may the public pulse be touched; for these letters are the spontaneous testimonials of the readers to the forcefulness of the journal which they read, whether they approve or condemn its course.[20]

To Pulitzer the dedicated editor was the soul of the newspaper; to Cockerill the indefatigable reporter was the real hero. Of all newspapermen it is the reporters, he insisted, who could make or break a newspaper.[21] The reporter's role was more Spartan than romantic. His job required a constitution of iron, a bottomless well of energy, and inexhaustible patience merely to cope with working conditions. On a morning newspaper he toiled from one o'clock in the afternoon to three o'clock the next morning, without relaxation, year after year, Sundays and weekdays, rain or shine, snow or parching heat. His was a life of gaslight and night air. When better presses came along, the period of labor was extended until four in the morning, so that in summer months the reporter was lucky to be home in bed by sunrise. In times of elections newsmen not infrequently worked thirty-six hours without sleep.

Cockerill was annoyed by the popular concept of the reporter as a long-haired, frequently inebriated, unkempt, wild-eyed specimen. He felt such a portrayal degraded his fellow workers in whom he found growing self-respect and "a heartening aspiration to improve their lot." Newsmen were professional people who should command the respect of doctors, lawyers, and clergymen.[22]

Although the Colonel was handsomely paid, earning up to $20,000 a year, he must be recorded as one of the earliest protesting voices from the top editorial echelons against what he held to be inadequate salaries for all newsmen except star reporters and executives. "How insufficient and often grudgingly given are the rewards of journalism," he complained.

No greater reproach attaches to an honorable vocation than that originality of thought, skill and courage of execution in which a half dozen other pursuits would have made their possessor rich and famous, have in journalism redounded altogether to the name and coffers of the capitalist, leaving the rightful reaper of the reward barefooted and hungry on the threshing floor.[23]

Yet no one knew better than Cockerill that journalism was not a series of glorious adventures. New York publishers must have winced as they read the Colonel's unflattering impressions of internal conflicts attributed to news and editorial personnel. Although not identifying his subjects, Cockerill left the clear implication that he was remembering the dissensions and tale-bearing at the New York *World* when he wrote:

The assistant city editor strives and schemes to replace his chief, or to get his own salary raised. The city editor, with his little clique, loses no opportunity to discredit in the eyes of their mutual owner the managing editor, or the news editor who is above him. The managing editor in the same way is tempted to plan the overthrow of the editor-in-chief, who is his superior; each one is encouraged to be a secret tale-bearer against all of the others. This is the moral influence of the organization: each rejoices in the misfortunes of the others, and all gloat over the defeat of the common enemy.[24]

This revelation so shocked the sedate *Review of Reviews* that it expressed the hope that Colonel Cockerill "has been led by his subject into a rut of pessimism which may account for his severe characterization of . . . writers on the same journal."[25]

What of the demands upon the body and soul of a managing editor in the merciless pace of competition among New York journals? Cockerill, having directed the news staffs of five metropolitan newspapers, could speak from intimate experience. He recalled James Gordon Bennett's estimate of five years as the average tenure for New York managing editors and agreed that no ordinary man, week in and week out in that capacity, could exceed that allotment. The Colonel exceeded the quota by three years at the *World*, but then Cockerill was no ordinary man and no ordinary editor. Colonel Cockerill left his own impression of the managing editor's ordeal:

The concentration of mind and energy of body which are now required for the daily conduct of a first class newspaper; the fourteen or fifteen hours of anxiety spent in functioning at high pressure, followed by the nervous exhaustion which seems to suggest, if it does not require, an artificial stimulant; sleep lost from worry and daylight hours wasted in the vain effort to woo back that sleep—all these leave little worth having in the day of twenty-four hours. Many such days leave little of value in the year; a very few such years are enough.[26]

When Cockerill joined the *World* in 1883 he was a rugged specimen of good health. In at least one letter to Pulitzer he affirmed his physical well being. His own description of the rigors and vicissitudes of a managing editor is the nearest he came to a complaint about his health. Were the brutal requisites of an editor beginning to take their toll? The Colonel had less than six years to live.

Cockerill's concept of the future newspaper was remarkably accurate. In the following thumbnail sketch Cockerill might have been blueprinting a modern American newspaper:

The editor must become more and more an anonymous entity. He will simply be the engineer who has charge of the locomotive for one "run" or for one day. His personality will change perhaps from morning to evening and from week to week; but while on duty, whoever he may be, he must keep an intelligent hand on the lever. The fireman, conductor, brakeman may all change, too; but, whatever comes, the train must sweep on down the rails of progress.[27]

Using the London *Times* as a guidepost to the future, Cockerill noted that it discarded the concept of a newspaper as the reflection of one man. "The *Times* moved from one administration in one decade to another administration in another decade, from one editorial tenure to another," he said, "with no palpable diminution or variation in the weight and consequence of its thunderous voice."[28] John Thaddeus Delane, the London *Times*'s distinguished editor for thirty-five years, left a deep impression on Cockerill, as may be sensed in Cockerill's sensitive tribute: "Never writing a line himself,

Delane contributed in his own inimitable way to publishing a newspaper which for its own public and its chosen scope was the greatest. . . . Delane's impersonal technique in newspaper production was to equip himself with a staff of half a dozen or so specialists with whom he talked on current issues. It was a lively editorial conference in which ideas were set up, tested and if vulnerable knocked down. The great editor himself could wake up their intuitions, inspire their imaginations, refresh their memories and so produce the best result. He was a great suggester himself."[29]

Today America's great newspapers are heavily weighted with specialists whose forte is interpreting and backgrounding news in an electronic age in which television and radio have pre-empted "spot news" reporting. Despite generous use of bylines, modern newspapers conform to the impersonal posture foreseen by the Colonel. They have confirmed his prediction that large newspapers would be compelled to employ hundreds of workers. Such newspapers as the New York *Times*, New York *Daily News* and the Chicago *Tribune* employ thousands.

Cockerill conceded "changes there must be, in time, in all respects, methods and instruments but mechanical progress attained by the higher exponents of the newspaper art is such as to preclude any significant and startling changes in the near future."[30] One cannot be sure what Cockerill meant by the "near future." If he was thinking of the next fifteen to twenty years his prediction was accurate. In that period there was no change on the mechanical side of newspaper production that could be described as "significant or startling." Before the Colonel's death in 1896 important steps in the improvement of printing had already been made. Ottmar Mergenthaler's linotype, perfected in 1886 and introduced in 1890, could turn out type three times faster than it could be set by hand. Use of solid stereotyped plates, produced from curved type forms to fit the cylinders of rotary presses, permitted a speed-up in printing. High-speed presses were not new: as early as 1890 the *World*'s combined presses could print up to 312,000 eight-page papers per hour. Color printing on newspaper presses was a nineteenth-century accomplishment. Development of practical newspaper use of the halftone photo-engraving process was well on its way to practical use during Cockerill's career.

It is understandable how these and other developments persuaded the Colonel to expect no great advances in the near future. He was substantially correct in his prediction, and he could have safely projected it over the next half-century. For until World War II there was painful acknowledgment in the newspaper world that no really "significant and startling" changes had occurred. The operations of setting type (in scores of newspaper composing rooms linotypes made early in the century were still in use after 1960), the assembling of types in chases, stereotyping (except for development of the dry mat), and printing the newspaper remained basically unchanged. If Cockerill could have stepped into newspaper plants in that period, it is doubtful that he would have been much surprised by anything he saw.

But what of a visit to an ultramodern newspaper plant today? The normally imperturbable Colonel would be dazzled by the technical wonders to behold, no doubt of it. Since 1950 newspaper production techniques have spurted ahead phenomenally under the impetus of increasing costs and fierce competition with other communication media. Today Cockerill would see the linotype looking little different from the very first models with which he was familiar in the *World* plant. But upon some he would notice attachments (and no human operators) through which teletypesetter tape "feeds," enabling the machines each to set twelve lines rather than the six or seven lines of type per minute when operated manually. At the Los Angeles *Times* Cockerill could watch the magic of automatic typesetting built around a computer in such a way that news copy is processed electronically from the reporter's typewriter to hot type. He would see that the system even incorporates editing changes and corrections, divides the copy into lines of column width and decides where split words are to be hyphenated. In modernized stereotyping departments he would find that page plates can be cast, conveyed to the press room, returned, and remelted—all automatically. The Colonel could not fail to be intrigued by the highly refined giant presses that print, fold, and count newspapers of up to 128 pages at the rate of 70,000 an hour, or by an automated mail room operation that conveys, stacks, bales, and conveys its product to waiting delivery trucks, all under control of an electric console.

The Colonel would be properly impressed by such a tour. In 1893 it took far less to prompt him to make this rhapsodic report of a visit to the Chicago *Herald* plant:

What would the ante-bellum journalist say to a business office with 3,600 square feet of floor space flanked by 16 columns of genuine Sienna marble? Of a composing room with walls of white enamel, its typestands with cases for 180 men, its electric calls connecting each case with the copy-box, its aerial railway conveying advertising matter up to the business office? Of its separate clothes closets, filtered ice-water coolers with solid silver, gold-lined drinking cups? Of its 348 incandescent electric lights and marble-topped lunch counters and tables? Of a great central library for the editors and reporters, around which are arranged a score of handsome editorial rooms, each connected by copy and speaking tubes with all others? What would the old-time journalist, with his long hair lingering affectionately on his greasy coat collar, say to a publisher's apartment in which all metal fixtures are oxidized silver and all woodwork of solid mahogany? What would the old-time handpress foreman think of ten Scott-Potter presses in a straight-line operation on a single-line shaft 124 feet in length? Of marble clothes closets and bathrooms for all employes and a constant flow of cold, clean water, day and night, in every room from an unfailing artesian well?

But the future, said the Colonel, will surpass the product of his own era "as the Chicago *Herald* operation today surpasses the cheap and dingy buildings of twenty years ago. . . .

What vast strides remain to be made," he wrote, "before the goddess of Journalism plumes her pinions for new flights!"[31]

Cockerill's attitude toward the daily press was both rhapsodic and disapproving. In a remarkable passage the Colonel wedded its wonders and its horrors thus:

It is exactly by reason of its glaring obliquities and moral shortcomings, sad as it may seem, that the great metropolitan newspaper is now apparently enabled to:

Address an audience of millions each day;

Send out expeditions to remote corners of the world;

Explore unknown seas and climb inaccessible mountains;

Dictate to presidents and bully statesmen;

Foretell the news so accurately as almost to compel the vindication of its predictions;

Delve into the inmost heart of man or woman and pluck from it a secret dearer than life itself;

Desecrate the sanctity of the fireside and violate all that the family and the individual hold dear;

Pursue malefactors beyond the slow processes and instruments of the law;

Annihilate space and make all the difference of time in the world as nothing;

In short, to be the greatest marvel of the intellectual and material powers of man at the period of their highest development.[32]

As a final, reproachful note Cockerill observed:

After a good many years of experience in newspaper work, I am convinced that a newspaper cannot afford, any more than an individual, to be without character. If a man's character is summed up from his life, from the good he has done, the homes he has brightened and the hearts he has gladdened, just so will the inexorable judgment of posterity, and of the greater public, measure out merciless justice to the journal whose sole object and aim it has been to grind the woes of the human race into grist for its owner.[33]

XXIII. Cockerill as Wit and Stylist

John Cockerill's wit ranged from the bluntness of a rhetorical bludgeon to the sting of a verbal dart. He could, by turn, be cynical and gracious, facetious and benevolent, whimsical and eloquent. A rough skill in sarcasm could make adversaries squirm and subordinates quail. He was merciless in turning ridicule upon a political foe, but he was equally adept in phrasing a compliment. He could man the heaviest verbal guns without losing the lighter touch. Drawing upon his newspaper experience, an abundant supply of quips and anecdotes, and a flair for a timely phrase, Cockerill excelled as an after-dinner speaker. When sponsors of the mammoth New York City banquet honoring Henry Morton Stanley, African explorer, sought a toastmaster, Cockerill's wit and urbanity won him the job.[1] As time and mood dictated, the Colonel could enjoy or contrive a clever prank. He was a conversationalist who felt equally at home with pauper or potentate.

George Cary Eggleston, a contemporary of Cockerill who served the *World* as editorial writer for eleven years, found the Colonel to be "one of the kindliest, gentlest of men, and at the same time one of the most irascible. His irascibility was like the froth that rises to the top of the glass and quickly disappears . . . not at all like the 'head' on a glass of champagne which goes on threateningly rising long after the first effervescence is gone."

"When anything irritated him the impulse to break out into intemperate speech seemed wholly irresistible," wrote Eggleston, "but in the very midst of such utterance the irritation would pass away as suddenly as it had come and he would become again the kindly comrade he had meant to be all the while. This was due to the saving grace of his sense of humor. I think I never knew a man so capable as he of intense serious-

ness, who was at the same time so alertly and irresistibly
impelled to see the humorous aspects of things. He would
rail violently at an interfering circumstance, but in the midst
of his vituperation he would suddenly see something ridicu-
lous about it or in his own ill-temper concerning it. He would
laugh at the suggestion in his mind, laugh at himself, and
tell some brief anecdote—of which his quiver was always
full—by way of turning his own irritation and indignation
into fun and thus making an end of them."[2]

There were reservations about the Cockerill charm. Walt
McDougall, a contemporary, found it marred by one defect
that hampered his associations with men of his own mental
endowments:

This was an unfortunate proclivity to be caustically witty at
the expense of one who had just left the festive board. . . . The
joyous cohesiveness of liberal drinkers is not materially improved
by free or even pointed criticism; this has been demonstrated by
the long and successful careers of many famous drinking clubs
for ages, for few there be who do not quiver at the thought of
poisoned arrows winging behind their backs. Many a man's departure was delayed by the thought that he would be Cockerill's
next victim, and it also prevented the return on the morrow of
sensitive wassailers. It was a trait commented upon by the Colonel's most genial companions and its memory persisted as though
it were his main characteristic. But it was his only blemish and
was unknown to those he encountered in business hours.[3]

Cockerill has rightly been described as the best exponent
of the "new journalism" introduced in New York by the *World*
and in Cincinnati by the *Enquirer*. Style was a major com-
ponent of the "new journalism." When the *World* celebrated
the attainment of 100,000 in circulation, Cockerill found
"that the eastern public appreciated a style of journalism that
is just a bit breezy while at times honest, earnest and sincere,
and a journalism that represents every day a laborious effort
to meet the popular demand seasoned by just convictions."[4]
Dr. Julian Rammelkamp, who made an extensive study of the
St. Louis *Post-Dispatch*, wrote: "As for Cockerill's style, there

is no doubt in my mind that he 'made' the editorial page of
the newspaper. His editorials are clearly distinguishable from
Pulitzer's and far more readable. What a bubbly, spontaneous
humor he had! The paper became well known throughout
St. Louis and Missouri for the humor Cockerill injected into
the editorial page. In fact, I don't think I've ever run across
an editorial page like that of the *Post-Dispatch* when Cockerill
ran it; it had a humorous but sledge-hammer quality that was
terrifically effective."

Had Cockerill chosen to restrict his career to writing, he
might have achieved distinction as a novelist or biographer.
A flaw evident to a discerning reader of his by-lined material
is the mark of habitual haste in which it was written. The
Colonel's writing occasionally does not stand up to critical
analysis in matters of sequence and unity.

In his work as a young assistant on the West Union, Ohio,
Scion, one may detect early signs of a tongue-in-cheek approach that would serve the Colonel so well later on. In the
following excerpt from "Maxims for Married Women" the
teen-ager brashly offered this counsel:

> Avoid contradicting your husband. Occupy yourself only with
> household affairs; wait till your husband confides to you those of
> higher importance and do not give advice until he asks for it.
> Never censor your husband's morals, and do not read lectures to
> him. Command attention by being always kind to him. A wife
> may have more sense than her husband but she should never seem
> to know it. . . .[5]

Apparently West Union wives accepted the "advice" in good
grace; at least no letter of feminine indignation appeared in
rebuttal.

The young editor was not long in making his biting humor
felt at the avidly Democratic Dayton *Daily Ledger*. Describing
the product of a new enterprise opened under the "euphonious
appellation of Grant Bakery," Cockerill commented: "The
only article manufactured is a pretzel, and the specimen we

saw was as devoid of sustenance as the Republican party is
of principle. . . ."[6]

Then as today there were national debt worriers. Of the
nation's fiscal health (under a Republican administration, of
course) the *Ledger* observed that "There is one great objection
against leaving posterity to pay the public debt—the debt is
growing faster than posterity."[7] Modern newspapers are fond
of computing the average citizen's tax burden in terms of his
work hours. Cockerill was doing so in 1868. On September 21
he wrote for the Dayton *Ledger*:

> What now lengthens the time of toil for the workingman? If
> we were free from any form of taxation, six hours of work would
> earn as much as ten do now. One hour of work ought to meet a
> laborer's share of the cost of government; another should pay his
> share of the national debt. He now works two hours more each
> day than he ought to pay for the policies of Congress and its cor-
> rupt schemes; and while the Radicals remain in power the burden
> will daily become heavier.[8]

To readers perturbed over their lots in life, whether high
or low, Cockerill offered a consoling note: "Let us remember
that in death our lots lie side by side, encompassed by the
boundaries of the graveyard."[9]

The *Ledger* solemnly proclaimed the Moscow *Gazette* as
the most influential journal in Russia, then facetiously added:
"The editor escapes all trouble because no one can pronounce
his name or write an order for his arrest."[10]

An anecdote in Cockerill's Cincinnati *Enquirer* should
comfort those who see each crop of young people as worse
than the preceding one:

> A very old man went to the King of Sparta and lamented over
> the degeneracy of the times. The king replied, "What you say is
> undoubtedly true. I remember that, as a boy, I heard my father
> say that when he was a boy, he heard my grandfather say the same
> thing."[11]

The Colonel could not resist a pun. Assailing New York
Republican papers for their displeasure in George H. Pendle-

ton's defeat for the Democratic nomination for president, the *Ledger* observed, "We guess they had better SEE MORE [Horatio Seymour] about it."[12] The *Ledger* referred to a Republican campaign speaker as "the South American who created such a disgusting creation by his canoodlements with lewd women while minister to Chile," then sourly predicted that "the distinguished foreigner will no doubt receive a CHILLY reception."[13] Finally, Cockerill once wrote that "Several young ladies wish to know if good and bad bills have anything to do with Sweet Williams."[14]

The tough and untiring editor could be idyllic when the mood dictated:

We yesterday had a ride to the country. Men may talk and poets may sing of "May, sweet May." Give us brown Autumn, the melancholy days. There is a sedate loveliness in all nature in this season . . . when the gold and yellow leaf is visible, and russet tinges deck the woods and meads in variegated loveliness, veiling the face of nature on all sides with the "grey livery of the autumn." There is a grandeur, a sublimity about this season of decay that is truly admirable. Reader, if you are an ardent admirer of the beautiful in nature, do not fail to take a trip into the country at this season of the year.[15]

All but vanished from the American scene today are the ferocious newspaper clashes of Cockerill's era. Few editors were plopped into more major rivalries than he. Rival publishers used every weapon at their command, from strong arms to mercurial prose. A running duel between the *Ledger* and the Republican *Journal* enlivened Cockerill's brief tenure as a Dayton, Ohio, editor. The feuding was not without its lighter moments. In the political campaign of 1868 the *Journal's* publisher, William D. Bickham, found Cockerill, his young adversary on the *Ledger*, ready to thrust at any opening.

For example, Cockerill's competitor, after polling a number of Montgomery County voters, published the results which purportedly forecast a Republican victory. "The Journal continues to publish 'straws,' " retorted the *Ledger*. "These are

what drowning people are supposed to clutch at." The *Journal*
observed that Theodore Bentley, the Republican nominee for
sheriff, "has peculiar claims upon the people." Cockerill's
paper asserted "the Journal has peculiar claims upon Theodore
Bentley—if he is elected it obtains another lease upon official
plunder."[16] The hassle was not limited to soft jabs. More
often the principals engaged in bare-knuckle, name-calling
tactics such as when the *Journal* outraged the *Ledger* by
reprinting portions of a speech made by Clement L. Vallandigham, Cockerill's associate, eighteen months before the war,
but dating it as a Vallandigham utterance of 1861. There
followed this verbal blast from the *Ledger*:

If William D. Bickham, the carpet-bagger and loafer who
controls the Journal, and the man behind him who does most of
the writing, think they can draw attention of people from debt,
taxation, tariff, greenbacks, Republican corruption and other issues,
they will find themselves mistaken. . . . The Journal now superadds
to everything else in the way of abuse and calumny, a deliberate
and willful forgery helped out by falsehood. . . . They show themselves no better than criminals.

The *Ledger* demanded that Publisher Bickham make a correction in the next morning's *Journal,* vowing that "if they do
not, we will publish the record of a certain suit now pending
in the U. S. Court at Cincinnati. . . ."[17] The threat worked.
The *Journal* admitted that the speech was indeed made in
1859, not in 1861, as it had charged.

The *Ledger* won the skirmish but lost the election. The
Republicans won, carrying Montgomery County, "not through
any actual gain or increase of their own vote," as Cockerill's
paper explained it, "but simply because Democrats refused to
go to the polls. Let Brother Bickham crow. We've seen sicker
roosters get well." Cockerill's editorial was generous. Para-
phrasing a famous victory remark, he wrote: "We have met
the enemy and we are his."[18] And Vallandigham, in a spate
of agonizing self-appraisal, admitted: "We are a desperate,

discouraged, demoralized Democrat . . . the situation, as we gaze upon it now, presents no very flattering prospect. . . ."[19]

As in Dayton, Cockerill, when managing editor of the Cincinnati *Enquirer*, found himself embroiled in fierce competition with another paper, this time the Cincinnati *Commercial*. A favorite device of the day was to lift a passage from the rival's newspaper, sometimes out of context, and demolish it. A couple of samples show how the technique worked:

"The *Enquirer* thinks it has discovered one honest man."—Cincinnati *Commercial*.

No. We've only discovered a fellow who thinks he is an honest man, and who is trying to convince the public of his honesty by bawling about it every day . . . females who stand on the street corner and proclaim their virtue are subjected to severe suspicion.[20]

In this exchange Cockerill applied his skill in satire:

The Cincinnati *Commercial* has discovered that the *Enquirer* supported the Greeley movement in 1872. The editor of the *Commercial*, who is in his dotage, may be depended on to publish an account of the Crucifixion in his news columns some of these days. His appetite for news is marvelous.[21]

In the 1876 election campaign Cockerill's *Enquirer* missed few opportunities to identify itself as the poor man's crusader against the rich and the holders of political patronage:

The postmasters are just like the business men. They view with alarm any proposition looking to the turning of the Republican party out to grass. . . . The business men and great capitalists of New York City are always brought to the front when the Republican party is in a fair way to receive their death-blow. The spectacle of a lot of rich Republicans protesting against the removal of their favorite party from power will hardly create a panic this year. . . .[22]

But the time came when the Colonel was as militantly Republican as he had been vigorously Democratic. The switchover is apparent in 1892 when Cockerill provided this observation on the three-way scramble for the mayoralty of Long Island City:

The race furnishes much food for gossip among the political wiseacres of that abused municipality. Gleason, the incumbent, has bet on himself to win. Judge Manley, the Republican nominee, feels the race . . . is a walkover for him, and has staked several hundred dollars on the result. Horatio S. Sanford, practically a stranger in the city, has not wagered any money. . . . There is a merry twinkle in the Republican candidate's eye . . . and that is significant.[23]

Nineteenth-century editors, unlike their mid-twentieth-century counterparts, showed no hesitancy in writing pleasantly or otherwise about rival editors and their families. Such a rival in the early 1890's was Whitelaw Reid, editor of the New York *Tribune*, about whose family Cockerill's column "Good Afternoon" contained an enlightening passage. In light of Cockerill's marital difficulties, a note of wistfulness may be read into his comment:

The home life of Whitelaw Reid is as lovely a study of domestic happiness as can be found anywhere in this country. It is plain and good. He is admired and loved by his wife and children and he in return thinks that Mrs. Reid, who is his intellectual peer in every way, is a queen among women. It was she who made the American Legation at Paris, where she presided so creditably, a Mecca for diplomats and litterateurs. She did not cultivate the swell set . . . but for the brainy men and women of the period she was delighted to act the part of hostess.[24]

Was that "who is his intellectual peer" a sly little dig to which the *Tribune* editor obviously could not reply?

Cockerill's off-beat approach might even include gentlemen of the cloth, such as when he told of the "great hold the Rev. Walpole Warren, rector of Holy Trinity Church, has on his congregation. He looks like . . . a well fed, well groomed, dapper clergyman of the English type. His air, too, is so imperious and haughty that it commands the respect of the extremely fashionable and Anglican congregation. . . . Mr. Warren takes no pains to conceal his disgust at everything American except the princely American salary he draws."[25]

Because Cockerill so often softened his punches with flat-

tery, his targets were usually defenseless, as the last two passages attest. Yet through the Colonel's nature there coursed
a streak of cruelty. Inside his velvet gloves the fingernails were
sharp.

XXIV. John Cockerill, Foreign Correspondent

John Cockerill relaxed on deck as the ship carrying him
to a new assignment plied its course toward Japan. The Colonel was full of speculation on what his new duties would be
like; and he would not have been the curious journalist he
was if he had not allowed himself a few guesses on what his
fickle and tigerish new employer might have in store for him
along non-journalistic lines.

When the news that Cockerill had resigned from the *Advertisers* reached James Gordon Bennett, Jr., the irrepressible
owner of the New York *Herald* sought the Colonel as an addition to his foreign staff. A legend exists that Bennett, as a
precaution, ordered a preliminary investigation of the Colonel's qualifications.

Shortly after his departure in October, 1894, from the
Advertisers the Colonel accepted an invitation to be the guest
of J. C. Oswald of the Colorado Coal and Iron Company on
a Western tour.[1] Although the Colonel was then unaware of
it, the "investigation"—so the story goes—began in the lobby
of the Astor House as the Colonel awaited a cab that would
take him to his westbound train. A *Herald* man whom the
Colonel barely knew engaged him in what seemed to be a
desultory exchange of amenities, except for one question. The
interrogator adroitly led the conversation to the subject of
dogs. Did the Colonel like dogs? Cockerill had time to respond
only briefly when his cab arrived. Within an hour Cockerill,

eager for an opportunity to "unwind," was rolling westward on a leisurely trip that included visits to several western states. The curious little chat was all but forgotten.

Weeks later a cable from James Gordon Bennett, Jr., datelined Paris, where the *Herald* publisher spent most of his time, caught up with the touring Colonel. Cockerill, said Bennett, should make a good *Herald* man. Would he be interested in joining the *Herald*'s foreign news service? Bennett had been impressed, the Colonel learned later, by Cockerill's colorful and authoritative dispatches on the Turkish-Russian war published in the *Herald* and the Cincinnati *Enquirer* and by his Park Row editorial achievements with the *World* and the *Advertisers*. The Colonel presumably needed time to think over the offer. This was understandable. Working for Bennett would be no ordinary experience because Bennett was no ordinary publisher. Cockerill had met Bennett a few times at public functions. The reports he had heard of the *Herald*'s proprietor would have bewildered, if not frightened, an ordinary newspaperman.

Bennett, like Pulitzer, has been described as a tyrant. The strapping, aggressive, unpredictable New York publisher was one of the rudest, most eccentric, and yet one of the most extraordinary men who ever lived. His behavior under the impetus of a few drinks, to state the case charitably, was colorful. Even in his day Colonel Cockerill could not be sure which of the tales he had heard were fact and which were fancy. Since then, legend has garnished Bennett's escapades with a few tasty flourishes, but none of those retold here was beyond the Commodore's bizarre capabilities, and each is reported as fact in Bennett's biographies.

The Commodore was the son of a pioneering editor but he lived to overshadow the achievements of the elder Bennett. In 1871, when he took over the *Herald* upon his father's death, he was one of the richest young men in the world. When a nephew, Isaac Bell, Jr., was born, Bennett casually laid a check for $100,000 in the infant's cradle. He is reputed to have spent $30,000,000 on personal pleasures. Under the Commodore the New York *Herald*, until the fierce competition of the Hearst-Pulitzer era began to stifle it, was a fabulous money-maker. But profits seemed of little interest to Bennett. He was disturbed only when they slumped. For many years he cheerfully lost $100,000 annually on the Paris edition of the *Herald*, which had to be nursed along on New York *Herald* profits.

Bennett had twice been Commodore of the New York Yacht Club; the title stuck. A master pilot, he charted his own courses on the luxury yacht *Lysistrata*. His stateroom was equipped with a telltale gadget that betrayed the slightest undue shifting of the helm. Because of the Commodore's interest in and close touch with maritime affairs, the *Herald* was considered New York's bible of the yachting and shipping world. On seafaring news Bennett's passion for accuracy took severe forms. Woe to the reporter who blundered in use of nautical terms. It was not unusual for the Commodore to blast an offender by cable from Paris. ("Doesn't that idiot know the wind and tide in that area never perform as he states it? See that he never touches a sea story again.")[2]

Cockerill had been amused by the tale of Bennett's juiciest escapade. Eighteen years earlier Bennett had sowed wild oats at a furious pace. He belonged to the swanky Union Club, where the normal exuberance of youth could be smothered in respectability. There were limits, of course. It was in observance of a Union Club tradition that young Bennett managed to crack the limit. On New Year's Day members at early morning hours serenaded as many homes as their endurance and sobriety would permit. Hostesses kept the festivities "flowing" with heavily-spiked liquid refreshments. Young Bennett had been courting Caroline, beautiful daughter of a distinguished physician, Dr. William May of 44 West Nineteenth Street, not far from the Union Club. Caroline had a strong and protective brother, Frederick. Bennett was among those who, in the spirit of the holiday, progressed from house to house, enhancing a reckless gaiety at every stop. By the time he arrived at the Mays' festive board, he was beyond accountability for his acts. To the horror of his host and the guests Bennett calmly urinated in the fireplace.

The repercussions were awful to behold. The next day Frederick May, in front of the august Union Club, sought to punish Bennett with a bull whip. Bennett, defending himself, tussled with May and the two rolled in the snow. Except the *Herald*, which was discreetly silent, the New York newspapers enjoyed a field day reporting the scandal. The pair subsequently "fought" a duel. Armed with pistols at twelve paces, the principals missed their targets. Some suspected neither tried too hard. The scandal is said to have driven Bennett from America. Thereafter he spent most of his time in Paris or cruising on his yacht. But neither the duel nor the flight to Paris ended the affair. One version is that the *Herald* proprietor, warned that Frederick May was in Paris intent upon gunning down the publisher, donned a coat of mail. Finally under the weight of this protection, Bennett sent a messenger to learn May's intentions. May responded with assurances that he had no homicidal plans. Relieved, Bennett shed his cuirass.[3]

Sometimes Bennett summoned men to Paris and then forgot why he had sent for them. Two key executives, responding to a cable, arrived in a dither, assuming some new and exotic assignments awaited them. Confronted by the pair, Bennett rasped: "What in hell are you doing here?"

"You cabled for us," they reminded him.

"Go back to New York," Bennett replied, curtly.[4]

Such a summons once took a drastic turn. Bennett ordered a New York staff member to Paris. The editor in charge made the mistake of objecting on the basis that the man was "indispensable." There quickly came a second cable requesting a list of indispensable men. Upon receipt of the list, Bennett fired them all.[5]

There was no way to predict where the Commodore's vagaries would take him. One of his favorite diversions in

Paris was to enter a restaurant, walk along the tables pulling the tablecloths out from under the dishes and laughing at the dismay of the diners. No proprietor minded; he knew a check the next day would more than compensate for the annoyance.

There were other sides to the blustery Bennett. He could be unexpectedly generous. In the Paris *Herald* office some of the beer-drinking staffers as a prank stacked their empty bottles on the desk of a teetotaling colleague. Bennett showed up without warning. Noticing the stack, he asked the startled reporter: "You seem to have quite a liking for beer. How can you afford to drink so much on your salary?" The newsman babbled something unintelligible in reply.[6] In his next pay envelope the teetotaler found a substantial increase, and immediately his thirsty deskmates started piling bottles on their own desks, to no avail!

Bennett expended huge sums on charities. His $100,000 gift to relieve economic distress in Ireland was widely hailed; the *Herald*'s free ice supplied hundreds of tenement families; the historic site of Fort Washington on upper Manhattan was graced by a Bennett-financed memorial.

The *Herald* spent lavishly on its own newsmaking enterprises. With those historic words "Go find Livingstone," the *Herald* sent Henry M. Stanley to search for David Livingstone, the Scotch-Presbyterian missionary who had dropped from sight in Africa. When the missionary was found, the *Herald* recorded a memorable scoop. The *Herald*'s news enterprise occasionally misfired. Bennett parted with $25,000 on the basis of a phony claim by Dr. Frederick A. Cook that he had found the North Pole.

Although the trait seldom showed, Bennett was capable of humility. Emma Eames, an American singer, found this to be true when Bennett called on her in Paris. The *Herald* had been duped by a jealous rival, who made a malicious accusation against Miss Eames. As a result the *Herald*'s reviews of Miss Eames's concerts slighted the artist. When Bennett learned the truth, he wanted to rectify the wrong. Miss Eames gave this impression of the publisher:

> He was hard, austere. . . . He possessed a keen sense of justice . . . a very tender heart. He adored animals, and he perpetuated his affection for them in a motley array of china and painted iron figures of every size which took up a large part of his lawn at Beaulieu. . . . he added to his collection by purchasing new specimens from a poor old woman who sold such wares. . . .[7]

The Commodore was plagued, irrationally, by a number of aversions. While an astonished guest watched, the Commodore, irritated by a bulge in his back pocket, once pulled out a roll of banknotes and nonchalantly tossed them toward the fireplace. His visitor, aghast, quickly rescued the bundle from the flames and returned them, expecting a word of gratitude. "Perhaps that's where I wanted that roll," Bennett replied and, improving his aim, hurled the bills into the fire, then chuckled as the caller watched in despair.

Bennett had a phobia against mustaches and unusual haircuts, although he sported a handle-bar mustache himself. He once cabled New York: "Tell Meltzer to cut his hair."[8] The order was handed to Charles Henry Meltzer, music critic, whose bushy thatch seemed to be in keeping with his title. Meltzer had some unmusical words of contempt for such a suggestion. When a second Bennett inquiry elicited a second negative grunt, the publisher ordered the nonconformist to St. Petersburg. Meltzer went to Russia unshorn. He finally lost his job but sued and collected damages. Most *Herald* men found it wise to co-operate.

Bennett's fondness for dogs carried him to curious extremes. Pomeranians, Pekingese, and cocker spaniels were favorites in the Bennett household. He was not averse to sending anywhere in the world at any cost for a dog that met his fancy. Bennett had a theory that dogs were shrewd judges of human character. If his canine pals did not take to a *Herald* reporter, dire things could happen to that worthy. An Irish attaché of the London office, wise to this quirk in the Commodore, was summoned to Paris. Fearing the worst, he went prepared—not by summarizing his achievements for an eloquent presentation but by pinning a slice of raw liver in his topper and scenting a pocket handkerchief with anise. Hailed into the official presence, the visitor was enthusiastically received; the dogs swarmed all over him. The Commodore was so impressed that the visitor left with high praise, his prestige substantially improved and the real reason for the errand apparently forgotten.[9]

It may well be that John Cockerill knew from the first hour of weighing the *Herald*'s offer that he could not turn down the opportunity. There is cause to suspect also that the Colonel may have wryly sensed in himself a growing propensity for associating with eccentric characters. There had been Clement L. Vallandigham, the former Copperhead; Lafcadio Hearn, the myopic and queer little reporter in Cincinnati; the playboy publisher John McLean of the Cincinnati *Enquirer*; and Joseph Pulitzer, the taut-nerved "impresario" of the New York *World*. And now the inimitable James Gordon Bennett, Jr.?

Puzzling as it may seem, good, even brilliant men were drawn to the *Herald* despite its hell-raising proprietor. In his biography of the Bennetts Don Seitz wrote:

... despite ill-usage men withstood a service as desperate ... as that of the French Foreign Legion ... some who were dismissed were never themselves again. They missed their shirts of hair and the excitement of accomplishment ... always plentiful in the *Herald* office. ... Women are said to be fascinated by such characters. Certainly, newspapermen were. Besides, the *Herald* was a conquering force and they liked to be associated with victory and achievement. ... No one with real sense or any hope of the hereafter would work for a metropolitan daily, even of the best sort. Journalists are, however, seldom sensible persons. They prefer irregularity to routine, excitement to ease. Money is secondary. ... This trait kept the *Herald* staff full of capable men.[10]

Consequently, the *Herald* was a highly respected journal in the extent of its exclusive news. Its foreign news service rated as unexcelled. The Bennett-owned cable company gave the *Herald* a decided competitive advantage besides earning additional revenue from commercial clients.

It was several weeks before Cockerill decided he would join the *Herald* staff. Since leaving the *Advertisers* he had had ample time to refresh himself during his Western trip and to contemplate the possibilities of his new situation. The *Herald* files show he started working for Bennett in February, 1895.

No written record is available of Cockerill's impressions of his interview with Bennett. But the circumstances suggest that it took place in Paris. According to the story handed down to relatives, Cockerill vowed that he would stand up to the Commodore, if necessary, for the preservation of his mustache. But—to continue the account as pieced together from their version—Cockerill, upon being ushered into the great man's presence, quickly sensed that Bennett's mind was not upon mustaches. Nor was it upon such professional matters as Cockerill's new duties with the *Herald*. The publisher is said to have disposed of Cockerill's assignment as if it were a boresome detail: "You'll go to the Far East—Tokyo." Cockerill was eager for details but there was no time for his questions. The Commodore broke into a broad smile. "I've had a wonderful report on you, Colonel," said the publisher. "You really love dogs, don't you?"

The Colonel ransacked his mind before remembering that seemingly innocuous chat with the *Herald* man in the Astor House. The Colonel at the time had told of his boyish affection for the family dog, a friendly collie at the Cockerill home in Locust Grove, unaware he had been "tested." The Commodore directed a stream of questions at Cockerill, none about his journalistic qualifications, all about dogs. The Colonel tried hard to supply answers in the same eager spirit. The Commodore was so obsessed with this new friend of the canine world that when his new correspondent tried once more to ask about the job, the publisher brushed him off.

"Ed Townsend, my assistant at the Paris *Herald* office, will fill you in," he explained. The interview was ended.[11]

There was no mention of mustaches. Now, musing aboard the Tokyo-bound steamship, the Colonel, one may surmise, attributed to the Commodore the probable reasoning that a man so fond of dogs as Cockerill was supposed to be had earned the right to wear a mustache. There is even a stronger probability that the Commodore elected not to discuss the assignment because he already knew enough about the Colonel's record to persuade himself that he had added an outstanding journalist to his overseas staff.

XXV. Accolade from an Emperor

John Cockerill, newly assigned to the Far East as the New York *Herald* correspondent, and Lafcadio Hearn, the Cincinnati *Enquirer*'s star reporter whom he hired and fired, were joyously reunited in Tokyo. Hearn, by now married to a Japanese girl, an established author and a professor of English at the Imperial University in Tokyo, bore his onetime boss no grudge. In a letter to a friend, Hearn recalled the occasion: "I met Cockerill here today and talked over old times. He has become much gentler, and more pleasant, and seems to be very kindly. He is also a little grey. . . . he is no very common person. The man who can make three or four fortunes for other men, without doing the same thing for himself, seldom is."[1]

As a tutor for Cockerill in the politics, history, and culture of Japan, Hearn was excellently prepared. *Harper's Magazine* had sent him to Japan to write a series of articles. En route from the United States, Hearn learned that the artist accompanying him was to be paid twice his own fee. Furious, he broke his contract and was stranded in Japan without funds.

He eventually obtained a teaching post in Matsue, and later transferred to the Imperial University in Tokyo. Hearn demonstrated a deep understanding of the Japanese. Twelve books about Japanese manners and morals bear his name. Cockerill, since the two were often together, apparently took full advantage of his mentor's knowledge of Japan. It may be surmised that he learned much of the language. Soon Cockerill's dispatches on various phases of life in Nippon were educating Americans on the Far East.

Of Japanese journalism, for instance, the Colonel in an August, 1895, dispatch wrote that

it is still in an inchoate condition. Remember that only thirty-one years ago the *Kaigai Shimbun*, the first newspaper ever printed in the Japanese language, was started in Yokohama. We have no end of Japanese newspapers now. A free press is guaranteed, but it is held to a very rigid accountability by the government. To print matter which the government disapproves is to "disturb the peace," and suspension follows. Suspension by order of the censor can last up to ten days but a newspaper constantly suspended does not survive.[2]

Japanese censors later were to bring down the wrath of the Colonel in a censorship crisis of his own.

Unlike New York City, Cockerill found in Tokyo no boys hawking newspapers. Instead Japanese newspapers were delivered to regular subscribers by carriers equipped with little bells which they rang to notify customers the news was on its way.

The vernacular Osaka *Asahi Shumbun*, noted the Colonel, was proud to be known as the "New York *Herald* of Japan."

On Japanese news gathering Cockerill contributed this paragraph:

The Japanese reporter is a very industrious fellow. He loves minutiae, and he can be depended on always for details. Accuracy, owing to his lively imagination, is not his forte. He is fond of interviewing people. One of the Japanese reporters, notebook in hand, interviewed me. Of eight statements which he printed, four were incorrect, and three had no foundation whatever. . . .

John Cockerill found "considerable recklessness on the part of some political organs" but "the general character of the press of Japan is steadily improving." He named as journals of excellent character and marked influence the *Nichi-Nichi Shumbun* and the *Fiji Shimpo*, both of Tokyo.

Local news, he reported, consisted mostly of translations from the vernacular press and general news clipped from Hong-Kong, Shanghai, and San Francisco newspapers. The Japan *Mail*, in the Colonel's view, was the best newspaper printed in the English language in Japan, at 20 sen (10 cents) per copy. Its editor was Captain F. Brinkley, who had gone to Japan thirty years earlier as an officer of the Royal Artillery when Britain occupied Yokohama. Cockerill found the only American-operated newspaper in Japan to be a Yokohama weekly called *The Box of Cures*, published by E. V. Thorne, once of California. "Tourists send copies home," he reported, "as specimens of American journalism abroad."

The Colonel registered disgust in his February 8, 1896, dispatch in a description of the newspaper circumnavigator, the carpetbagger of the nineties. "Most of them are grievous nuisances," he wrote. "The catch basin for this genius is Yokohama, and whether going or coming, he is inferentially, at least, an object of charity."[3] The Colonel cited the case of a Chicago bicyclist and his wife who were stranded in Tokyo. Out of funds, the pair was forced to live on charity until money from home could be sent. "The globe trotter is no longer a novelty," wrote the Colonel. "Travelers limited as to cash but inspired with a desire to break some sort of a record are ranked as ordinary tramps. They have had their day, and my advice to newspapers anxious to be represented in foreign countries by skilled pedestrians and wheelers is to provide their agents with liberal letters of credit."

The Colonel's pen had not lost its bite. Its point was felt when a rumor spread that the United States would be flooded by twelve-dollar Japanese bicycles. A California

Senator had expressed alarm. From Tokyo came Cockerill's retort:

Notwithstanding the existence of this wonderfully cheap and airy Japanese bicycle, every ship that comes to the Port of Yokohama from San Francisco and Tacoma brings a consignment of American-built bicycles. They are sold to foreigners of intelligence for $100 in gold—sometimes $125. Now, if Japan can produce a bicycle which can be sold in the United States for $12, why is it that common sense people living and riding here will persist in paying such high prices for foreign wheels? This tells the story. Our distinguished American legislator is unnecessarily alarmed. One man in San Francisco talking through his ill-adjusted headgear should not be permitted to disturb the commercial adjustments of a whole continent!

The Senator was squelched . . . and all over America, bicycle makers, with a sigh of relief, peddled their products, apparently comforted that it was a two-way "flood."

The Colonel's published correspondence had a chatty, personal flavor that endeared him to *Herald* readers. Note his reaction to a Russian journalist freshly arrived from Moscow en route to Vladisvostok:

His name is Gerfeld [the press of the 1890's persistently omitted first names] and he is accredited to the Moscow Gazette. He is making a profound study of Korea, if I may judge by the number of questions he put to me touching that sweet-scented country. He tells me that everybody in Moscow and St. Petersburg is expecting Russia to assert herself in the Orient when the vernal birds begin to sing. He also confirms my well settled belief that the Vladisvostok correspondent is the most stupendous fabricator in the high altitudes. . . .

And this tongue-in-cheek treatment of a projected cruise:

Two young Americans—Dr. W. H. Furness and Dr. H. M. Hiller of Philadelphia—have bought a schooner in Yokohama and fitted her up for a voyage in the southern seas. Their destination is Borneo. . . . The boys have money to enjoy life to the limit. They have a cannon and an abundance of modern arms on their schooner. It is thought that they may capture the Wild Man of Borneo and take him to America as a rare ethnological exhibit.

They are pretty certain to pick up some unsolicited ophidian specimens on their trip.

Of the Japanese puppet regime in Korea the Colonel had a low opinion, as evidenced in this excerpt from a Tokyo dispatch:

Mr. So Kwong Pom, the newly accredited Korean Minister to the United States, is on his way to Washington. He is accompanied by a measly-looking creature named Pak. They have credentials from a government made by bloody conspiracy, and which should never be recognized. These men should have no more status in Washington than a delegation of stump-tailed baboons from the King of Dahomey [a West African state, annexed by France in 1894, known for its barbarities and cannibalism]. . . .

Colonel Cockerill did not hesitate to promote his newspaper when the occasion arose:

Ovide Musin, New York violinist, and Louise Musin, soprano, are making a tour of Japan with a small concert company. On their arrival in Yokohama they had the pleasure of hearing a Japanese band at the Grand Hotel play the "New York Herald March."[4]

Demonstrating a competence to write on a wide range of subjects, Colonel Cockerill offered an eye-opening report on Japanese medical achievements. Under the catchy title of "Wondrous Cures in New Japan," he told of three medical triumphs scored in the past year: Dr. Kitasato's announcement of the curative properties of a new cholera serum; Dr. Kurimoto's success in stamping out rabies in southern Japan; and Dr. Yoshimatsu's treatment of vomiting in pregnancy. Excerpts of Cockerill's report indicate an obvious admiration of Dr. Bunji Yoshimatsu, both as medical expert and as a person:

This man, a country physician, is now daily performing marvelous cures. . . . Yet nothing could be more above-board than the methods pursued. He has obtained a pinnacle of celebrity reached by few in Japan or elsewhere. He made no effort at concealing his curative method and refused to reap any profits. All the great hospitals of Tokyo have now adopted his methods. Dr. Yoshimatsu, now forty-four years old, little, wiry, energetic, nervous, with keen, friendly eyes and a pleasing smile, is, in accordance with Eastern custom, a doctor in a direct line of more than a dozen generations of physicians . . . going back three centuries. . . . He elects to remain in Oiso, a seaside resort, twenty-five miles from Yokohama, at the foot of the Hakone Mountains. His little hospital and clinic are attended by constantly increasing numbers. . . .

In Dr. Yoshimatsu's essay, widely published and now in pamphlet form, he narrates how his first experiments had been instituted to obviate the necessity of artificial abortion, which is sometimes compulsory when vomiting yields to no other treatment. During the last fifteen years, Dr. Yoshimatsu states, he has treated over fifty such cases, in all classes of society from court circles downward, and his treatment has been invariably successful. He holds this kind of illness is nervous in origin and has nothing to do with the stomach primarily, so that all treatment in that direction is worse than useless. So he prescribes and makes hypodermic injection of a strong solution of carbolic acid with glycerine as a solvent and base. Generally one, never more than two injections, is rapidly successful. . . .[5]

Cockerill's enthusiasm moved him to hail Dr. Yoshimatsu's achievement as the beginning of a new era in medical science—"the best testimony being found in the gratitude of people who are daily mending their way from this little provincial town restored to health and with a new lease on life."[6]

High echelon government officials were elated by glowing reports to New York, from which the following are quoted:

Japan has proved the truth of "ex-Oriente lux," and if this is true, a new sun has risen "with healing in its wings." At all events, no people—the Germans not excepted—are doing more experimental microscopic and general scientific work than the Japanese. They can certainly not be characterized as imitators in the field of medicine. Neither can it be said that they are copyists in surgery. It was settled during the Sino-Japanese War that no European ambulance was ever better conducted than that of the Japanese, and in Tokyo one can buy today as beautiful a set of surgical instruments as can be found in Paris or Berlin. . . .[7]

From Colonel Cockerill's pen there flowed a steady stream of material interpreting Japan to the West. One day *Herald* readers might read an interview with Admiral Ito, Japan's great naval commander, and the next a light-handed portrait of Kawakami Otojiro, Japan's leading actor. The variety seemed endless. Cockerill's reports were described by a critic as among the finest examples of English composition. Members of his profession said no correspondent had more accurately or vividly portrayed the character, the civilization, the genius of their institutions and the government of the Japanese. The influential *Fourth Estate* asserted, "Cockerill's distinguished work has opened the eyes of America to the achievements and possibilities of Japan."[8] On October 24, 1895, the *Herald* published, unknown to the Colonel at the time, a touching tribute to its Far Eastern correspondent. It was written by a friend, M. Ganesco, a French correspondent, who had been sent to cover the Sino-Japanese War:

I think it would be difficult to conceive of a more distinguished journalist, a more charming writer, or a more fascinating story teller. I am not surprised if Colonel Cockerill is the most popular foreigner in Japan. He has the gift, as none other has, of attaching himself to those who come in contact with him. He is a personal friend of all the Japanese ministers and the confidant of many of their secret thoughts. He is always at the right spot at the right moment. . . . The Japanese are not the only ones to love him. Numerous Americans who make Yokohama their favorite winter station always seek his society. This brilliant correspondent is never taken at a loss. He always has a good story for a friend. Mr. Eppinger, manager of the Grand Hotel at Yokohama, declares he has never known a more precious client.[9]

When Cockerill was a clerk in the Ohio legislature, he was known as a prankster. During one session the legislators were startled one morning to behold in the rotunda of the capitol a weird transformation. Someone had redone in color the figure in a statue in such a comical way that it touched off gales of laughter. Cockerill had yielded to an "artistic" impulse and applied the crayons in the dead of night. He confided this later to a "few friends," who soon included every member of the legislature. Now in Yokohama, the Colonel had not lost his appetite for a prank. On July 4 he saw a way to flavor his fun with patriotism. The story is told by M. Ganesco of the Paris *Figaro*:

In spite of all the good which I am happy to be able to say of the correspondent of the Herald, it is impossible for me to pass over in silence the farce of which he was the hero and which cost me a sleepless night. On July 4 all Yokohama was alert to celebrate the "glorious Fourth." The American colony had things done in grand style. I never was present at a more imposing fete. Even the Japanese had taken an active part in the demonstration—too active for my taste.

On the eve of the great day, Colonel Cockerill, accompanied by a friend, had gone through a populous quarter of Yokohama distributing enormous bags of squibs and crackers to all the boys. Every family had its own. Then he posted the youngsters under the windows of the hotel and himself gave the order to fire on the stroke of three A.M. . . . The cannonade lasted until morning. I must admit that on that day I thought my confrere's patriotism too noisy.[10]

When an official messenger notified the Colonel he was to come to the Palace at once, he was only mildly surprised. He assumed some important news was in the making, or else he was to be reprimanded for the prank. At the Palace, the Colonel noticed meaningful glances in his direction. Count Ito, a high Japanese official, greeted him. "You are requested to appear before the Emperor," said the Count. The Colonel was ushered into a room filled with high government officials and diplomats from other countries. There the Emperor conferred upon the astonished *Herald* correspondent one of Japan's most cherished citations, the Third Order of the Sacred Treasure. The American ambassador gave an address of tribute to the Colonel's high standards as a newspaper correspondent. Count Ito handed the award to the Colonel. It consisted of the traditional mirror, collar and sword. It was first ascribed to Emperor Jimmu, the first Mikado. Back of the ceremony lay 2,500 years of tradition. Indicative of the veneration in which the citation was held was its conferral upon each new Mikado. It was the Colonel's finest hour abroad. "As a faithful historian and journalist, Colonel Cockerill is singled out for this honor," said the Emperor, "in recognition of his service to Japan and out of the high esteem he has gained among the Japanese people."[11] Only two men other than Japanese had ever received the honor; Cockerill was the first newspaperman. News of the citation was prominently displayed by the *Herald* and by its competitors. It was a distinction that could not be ignored.

Had Japanese officials been able to foresee the Colonel's critical reports of their government's fumbling and ineptitude in handling that little kingdom of trouble, Korea, they might have exercised more restraint in praise of the *Herald* correspondent.

In one sense it is remarkable that Cockerill performed so notably. He was constantly distracted by trivial commissions from Bennett. Cockerill often found it impossible to do any real work because the *Herald*'s owner kept him busy answering cablegrams. It was not unusual to have a daily message in which Bennett reported weather conditions in Paris and demanded a similar resumé on the weather in Yokohama. Bennett fired a stream of requests for accounts of his correspondent's personal experiences. He sent Cockerill looking for and occasionally buying strange breeds of dogs. There came a steady flow of requests having nothing to do with the newspaper business.[12] Nevertheless, as a result of the Colonel's letters and dispatches to the United States, the veil of ignorance and misinformation was at least partially raised as Western communication and trade with the Far East increased. But it took a World War four and a half decades later to demonstrate how tragically the West had underestimated Japan's industrial and military might.

XXVI. Murder of Queen Min

During his visit to Kyoto, the former Japanese capital, in 1895 to report on the Japanese National Exhibition, Colonel Cockerill was confronted by a grotesque and horrifying landmark. It was the famous Ear and Nose Tomb, a reminder of a massive blood bath.[1] Buried in a mound, by some accounts, were the severed ears and noses of 185,738 Koreans and 29,014 Chinese, although historians do not explain how they arrived at such a precise count.[2] When Japanese forces led by Hideyoshi invaded the hermit Kingdom of Korea in 1592, a standing Korean army of about 50,000 resisted. Some sources say nearly three million men, women, and children, of whom only 10 per cent were combatants, were slaughtered by the invaders. Two centuries passed before Korea recovered from one of the most needless, unprovoked, cruel, and desolating wars that ever cursed the hermit kingdom.[3] The severed nasal and auditory appendages were trophies of war. The ghastly custom was to decapitate victims, collect and count the heads. The ears and noses were sheared off and, along with the commander's head, were packed with salt and quicklime in casks and sent to Kyoto to form the great nose and ear tomb, "a horrible monument to an unrighteous war."[4]

This grisly chapter of Japanese-Korean history fascinated the Colonel. Soon he would be in Seoul to observe and report developments in Korea. He was beginning to appreciate that Korea was indeed "history's stepchild." Twice only had Korea ever been able to fight off an aggressor. It had been harassed for two thousand years by robber raids and extortions. Finally in 1390 a Korean general inflicted so much punishment upon the corsairs that the Japanese called off the forays for a time. But Hideyoshi, dissatisfied with peace terms after his first victory, again invaded Korea. This time the Chinese joined the Koreans, and in a seven-year effort drove out the Japanese invaders. The victory put a stop to Japanese aggression for 250 years.[5] As a buffer area between China and Japan, Korea, it was clear to Cockerill, had limited the expansion of both Asian powers.

The Sino-Japanese War had ended with the signing in April, 1895, of the Treaty of Shimonoseki. The Japanese victory removed China at the time as a threat to Nipponese designs in Korea. Cockerill's dispatches reported the treaty terms, which, like so many previous pacts, were supposed to reassure Korea. Both China and Japan, the treaty stipulated, "recognize definitely the full and complete independence and autonomy, and guarantee the complete neutrality of Korea."[6] With Cockerill the growing image of Korea was that of an economic and political pawn at the never-ceasing mercy of powerful countries hovering over her. Yet the Koreans yearned deeply for the independence and freedom that constantly eluded them.

American-Korean ties dated from 1882, when Korea broke with tradition and signed pacts inaugurating diplomatic relations and trade agreements with Western powers. Cockerill was impressed by Korea's record of respecting treaties. American missionaries found Korea, "the Switzerland of Asia," the most receptive of all Oriental countries to their messages, although missionaries suffered heavily from Japanese persecution in Korea. Koreans welcomed United States assistance in building railroads, water works, and ships. A contemporary found "the potential genius of Korea awakening under the guiding influence of Western culture."[7]

For the period that Colonel Cockerill spent in the Far East the story of Korean turbulence can be told in the *Herald* correspondent's cables and letters. The Colonel set the stage in June, 1895, when he interviewed, "over tea and cigarettes," Count Inouye, minister plenipotentiary to Korea. Japan insisted it wanted an independent Korea, but suspicions arose that what it meant was a Korea independent of any foreign intrusion or interference except its own. There loomed now the ominous shadow of Russian interest in the hermit kingdom. Tokyo had delegated to the Count the task of instituting "reforms" to keep Korea in line with Japanese policies. The Colonel's interview of the fifty-nine-year-old diplomat occurred in Tokyo while the latter was on leave from Seoul. No interview better illustrated the *Herald*'s tribute to Cockerill, upon his death, when it wrote: "He was quick to seize upon the salient points of a situation.... This, combined with his natural diplomacy and tact, made him a good interviewer. He knew what questions to ask, how to ask them, and how to give the proper perspective to the facts elicited."

As a first "reform" measure Japan had placed the King and Queen and other members of the Court under "protective custody," virtually making them prisoners in their own palace. The Colonel opened the interview by asking the Count the ground upon which Japan had assumed its protectorate over Korea, "seeing that its independence had been guaranteed by the Treaty of Shimonoseki." Excerpts of the interview follow:

"For the reason," said the Count, "that Korea needs our help, and without it she would fall at once into anarchy. We are commercially interested in her. We have more of our people settled upon her soil than any other country. She is filled with distractions and we cannot afford to see her go to pieces. The war was undertaken for the reformation and welfare of Korea, and we must go on with the work."

"But," said I [Cockerill, quoting himself], "suppose that Russia should assert that she had interests in Korea, and, being a closer neighbor, should even seek a moderate occupancy of the peninsula with her troops."

The Count shrugged his shoulders.

"How many troops has Japan in Korea?" I asked.

"Only about three thousand," he replied, "and they are scattered about doing simple police duty."

"Are the insurrectionary Tonghaks [anti-Japanese nationalists in Korea] opposing the government and resisting the present order of things?"

"No," said the Count. "The Tonghaks have at no time been hostile to the King. Their warfare is upon the oppressive, corrupt and wicked local authorities."

The Count admitted that he had felt the effect of Russian intrigue in Korea. He expressed great respect for the political sagacity of the Queen. She has many enemies in Korea, but she is a woman of unusual force, albeit given to superstitious practices. She fears for her son, the Crown Prince, who is a remarkably bright and promising lad, and she is constantly praying to Buddhist gods for his safety.

The Count then for half an hour gave me a most interesting history of the prolonged war between the Tai-Won-Kun family and the Min family of the Queen, which had done so much to degrade Korea. It was a story of conspiracy, plot, assassinations, poisonings, infernal machines, cold blooded treachery, fratricide and common murder unequaled in the world's annals. In the recital of this the Count displayed wonderful familiarity with the facts and a tenacity of memory that was phenomenal. No one hearing the Count's narrative could possibly hope for internal reform in Korea. Korea, he said, was the sick man resenting the "good treatment" offered and turning to quacks and charlatans for aid.

The Count, at the Colonel's request, defined what he believed should be Japanese policy in Korea. Japan should keep "a kindly control over Korea," he said, "because we cannot afford to withdraw." And with a prophetic note, he added, "It is a sore spot and eventually complications will rise to vex Japan."[8]

The "complications" created for Cockerill the year's most dramatic, the bloodiest news beat of his Far Eastern assignment.

Cockerill was not long in Seoul before realizing that the most remarkable character in this crucial chapter of Korean history was Queen Min. She was a pale-cheeked, thin-faced woman of small stature. Her frailty was deceptive. She was more powerful than even the old regent, Tai-Won-Kun, her father-in-law, who hated her. She was not without personal shortcomings. She was intolerant of opposition; she was overstocked with vanity; she loved intrigue; she did not hesitate to plot with the Japanese if it served her. She was an aggressive executive who made the weak-willed King look anemic.

The astute Queen could decide in ten minutes an issue over which the Cabinet had haggled for months.

The Queen found herself in a complicated, precarious plight. She had to reckon with Tai-Won-Kun and his notorious accomplices, the *soshi* (political bullies from Tokyo who professed to believe the Queen was plotting with the Russians against the Japanese) and Count Inouye, minister to Korea. None of these hazards weakened the Queen's determination to resist the Japanese "reforms" and Japan's efforts to exploit Korea commercially and politically. Her first success in frustrating them was to achieve the overthrow of Pak-Yong-Hio, son-in-law of the former King, the Japanese-picked premier and home minister. Tokyo regarded him as an easy tool, but the twenty-three-year-old premier confounded Tokyo by trying hard to build a new Korea. He, too, resisted the Japanese, who shortly started mistrusting him. The Koreans, knowing the Japanese had sponsored him, likewise mistrusted him. Under these circumstances the Queen engineered his ouster.

If Count Inouye had retained his post, history might have taken a less violent turn. He assured Queen Min that the Mikado's government would not fail to protect the royal house of Korea. He had purged thousands of useless persons from government payrolls, including hundreds of the Queen's palace attendants. This infuriated the Queen. When the Count left his Seoul post in September, 1895, the parasites returned at her invitation. Once more the palace was crowded with her clansfolk, servants, eunuchs, underlings of all descriptions.

With the arrival of General Viscount Miura, a military officer sent to succeed Count Inouye, the atmosphere of intrigue seemed to thicken. The new envoy brought the methods of the soldier to a task that required patience, leadership, and diplomacy. Being a soldier, Miura was attracted to direct methods. The new envoy and the Tai-Won-Kun, presumably brought together by Sugimura, Miura's secretary, found they had a mutual enemy. Each wanted to be rid of the Queen, but for different reasons. The Tai-Won-Kun wanted to return to power and he was not averse to the use of such direct means as fire, poison, dynamite, or the sword if it would remove his daughter-in-law, who stood in the way. Miura found his "reforms" blocked by the Queen's defiance.

Early in October an agreement between Miura and the former Regent was reached. The Tai-Won-Kun would not interfere in the actual administration of the country and would give the Japanese the commercial and political privileges they sought. In return the Tai-Won-Kun would take over the palace, name a cabinet, and be the nominal head of government. Standing resolutely in their way was Queen Min. Their plan, involving other Japanese conspirators, called for drastic measures.

Before dawn on Tuesday, October 8, 1895, the militant voice of Queen Min was silenced forever. Colonel Cockerill broke the news to the rest of the world. He took the precaution of making copies of his cabled report, which follows:

The palace was broken into by a body of Korean troops and a band of Japanese soshi in civilian dress.

The colonel in command of the troops, on refusing to enter the palace, was killed, and a number of palace guards were slain.

The Japanese entered the Queen's room and killed the Queen, the minister of the household and three women. The bodies were taken outside and burned. The Japanese troops were at the palace, but took no part in the proceedings.

Tai-Won-Kun, the King's father, reached the palace soon after the assault and assumed the chief authority. He is now dictator and is known to have been in the plot.

The pro-Japanese party is in control. Many of the Queen's party have been arrested, many more have fled.

It is believed that the King will be forced to abdicate.

Guards from the United States warship Yorktown and a Russian cruiser at Chemulpo have been ordered up.

Great excitement prevails. It is thought the butchery will hasten action on the part of Russia.[9]

Colonel Cockerill dispatched his cabled report—or so he thought. A few hours later he was handed a message that the cable had been interdicted at Tokyo. The Colonel's reaction was swift and frightening. A stream of profanity smote the innocent Japanese messenger boy, who understood not a word.

This act of temporary suppression was to prove costly to the Japanese. The *Herald* correspondent was not to be frustrated. Although delayed, the Colonel's news beat appeared in the New York *Herald* October 14. How did he bypass the Japanese censor? A plausible explanation is that a British diplomatic friend of Cockerill who was leaving Seoul relayed the Colonel's cable from Shanghai to the *Herald*. In the meantime the Japanese officials apologized, a fact that Cockerill was careful to report.[10] Although the Japanese thereafter permitted his cables to go through uncensored, the Colonel's suspicions were thoroughly aroused.

Cockerill's first report linked the Tai-Won-Kun to the assassination plot. Lacking evidence he could only say there was nothing to show, up to October 13, that the Japanese minister, General Miura, was implicated. The Colonel at that time charged that the plot had been engineered by the Korean friends of Tai-Won-Kun and irresponsible *soshi*. The King and Crown Prince were prisoners in their own palace. The Tai-Won-Kun, now in the saddle, bargained with the Japanese for political power.

Three days later the Crown Prince, who had inherited a generous share of his mother's spunk and shrewdness, smuggled out of the palace the most damaging evidence against the plotters. The Crown Prince's information included an eyewitness account of the murders and a description of the assassins. Cockerill bolstered this evidence with a statement from the commandant of the palace body guards, who had seen the Japanese assassins enter the Queen's apartment and burn her body. Cabling these developments, the Colonel revealed, for the first time, existence of proof connecting Miura to the plot. It was now clear why his cable had been intercepted.

"Procurator Kamura and a commission have arrived from Japan to investigate the outbreak," the Colonel wrote. "There have been more arrests of soshi. The usurper, Tai-Won-Kun, has appointed a Cabinet but it is not recognized and is falling to pieces."[11]

From the Crown Prince's story and other accounts the Colonel pieced together the lurid details of the assassination. The royal apartment in the palace was approached by stone steps. The quarters were the one-storied type with thin wooden doors and oil-paper windows. The intruders easily broke down the doors and barged inside. The Queen was not in sight. They tried in vain to force the King to lead them to the Queen. The minister of household was killed on the spot. The *soshi* terrified the palace females by dragging them around by their hair as they searched for the Queen. None of the Queen's attendants would tell where she was. Finally she was spotted. She broke away once but there was no escape. Three members of her staff were forced to "recognize" the Queen and were promptly put to death by the sword. The Queen's body was wrapped in bedclothes and taken to a nearby grove where faggots were piled upon it and set afire. Neither the King nor the Crown Prince was harmed. Before the embers were cold the Tai-Won-Kun was borne to the palace under Japanese military escort and placed in power.

The story was received in foreign capitals with incredulity and horror. The Korean people were enraged. Like Cockerill, they held Japan accountable. In the wake of John Cockerill's cables and letters that followed the assassination, Japan's influence and prestige were shaken. In death Queen Min continued to plague the Japanese.

In handling the situation Tokyo went from simple mistakes to sorry stupidities. For a while the Japanese authorities tried to give the impression the Queen had escaped. They forced the issuance of a royal decree denouncing Min as a prostitute and otherwise degrading her memory. The talebearers overstepped themselves; few believed them.

Miura publicly disclaimed responsibility; he blamed disgruntled Koreans. The Japanese government disavowed any knowledge of the death plot. Illustrative of the absurd attempts to divert attention from the guilty Tai-Won-Kun was the execution of three innocent Koreans. The Colonel made a few sarcastic observations in his *Herald* report:

Although there has been no public investigation of the palace revolution of October 8, the actual butcherers of the Queen, we are told, have been discovered. Strange to say they were Koreans. Although the Japanese swordsmen who killed the Queen escaped to Chemulpo on the day after the crime and were subsequently arrested and held in Hiroshima, the Japanese find it possible now to fasten the killing upon three miserable Koreans.

I have given in former letters the proofs now in the possession of the Russian and American ministers, establishing very clearly the guilt of the Japanese. . . .

It was not until my dispatches were filed, containing the facts, that the Japanese would admit the Queen had met with misfortune. Then, after much silence, the "terrible Korean" who slew his Queen was discovered, convicted upon the testimony of one witness, and promptly taken out and hanged the same evening. Two other Korean miscreants were hanged along with him, because it had to be shown that he had some assistance in his gigantic performance. The court which convicted and executed these alleged assassins is composed of persons named by the usurping Tai-Won-Kun. . . . The civilized world will look upon this barbaric farce with loathing and disgust.[12]

When a few of the old palace guards loyal to the King tried a counter revolution, the Japanese leaped upon the incident as a useful distraction. They played it up, hinting that Russian and American representatives were involved. The Japanese correspondents in Korea circulated the story abroad and brought down a tongue-lashing from Cockerill:

I decline to believe anything in the shape of news sent out of Korea by the correspondents of the Japanese newspapers. A more flagitious and unconscionable lot of liars I have never known. As the Japanese government exercises a strong censorship over its home press, it might be well for it to try its repressional hand upon the Japanese sheet published in Seoul, the *Kanjoshimpo*, which is laboring zealously, it would seem, to bring about the massacre of foreign representatives in Korea.[13]

Tokyo's strategy at the outset was to pretend surprise at the palace butchery. But as Colonel Cockerill built his case against the Japanese minister and Tai-Won-Kun in the New York and Paris editions of the *Herald*, Tokyo modified its line. When it became obvious that General Miura could not continue under the shadow of such accusations, he was recalled. Count Inouye was appointed Envoy Extraordinary to mollify the Koreans. Prime Minister Ito declared that the usurpation of power by Tai-Won-Kun must be repudiated. In January, 1896, Miura's ranks and honors were withdrawn. Upon his return to Japan Miura, six military officers, and forty-seven civilian members of his staff were arrested and accused of conspiring to murder the Queen.

In a conciliatory gesture Count Inouye issued a decree upgrading the late Queen from prostitute, as branded by Tai-Won-Kun, to her royal rank, all in one stroke of the pen. The Count used such adjectives as "guileless" and "revered" in alluding to Queen Min. A temple was dedicated to her memory and twenty-two officials of high rank were commissioned to write her biography.

While the praise of the late Queen Min was sung, the King and the Crown Prince remained prisoners in the palace. Two days after the Queen was stabbed to death, Colonel Cockerill was granted an audience with the King. Cockerill had insisted on the meeting. He put no credence in the Tai-Won-Kun communiqués. He found the King in a state of near prostration. Palace attendants, officials, and servants had cleared out of the palace like rats from a blazing barn. As may be sensed in the following excerpts, the Colonel saw small hope for Korean salvation in this pitiful little man who had seemed to be overshadowed by his aggressive wife:

Mounting a few steps and crossing a verandah, we entered a small room and turned to the left. There in the doorway we saw a still smaller apartment, decorated in simple Korean style. The poor King was standing, pigeon-toed and pallid, beside his son . . . the Crown Prince. The King is small in stature, thin, and blood-less-looking; the events of the past few days have added to his waxiness. His nervousness was painful to behold.

Turning to the interpreter, he inquired if he might shake hands with us. He shook our hand with considerable fervor, and then placed the hand of each visitor in that of his grinning son. . . .

At this point the Russian minister passed to the King a tin box which contained, as he explained, some fruits and food from his own table. The King lives in hourly fear of poison. . . .

His whole body twitched as though he was afflicted with St. Vitus' dance, and his eyes were pleading sorrowfully.[14]

A subsequent coup proved, however, that the King and Crown Prince were capable of ingenuity that would surprise the Colonel.

Now that the more obvious suspects were in custody in Hiroshima awaiting trial, would justice be served? John Cockerill was skeptical, predicting in the New York *Herald* of January 14, 1896: "The real criminals . . . will be one by one released."

The verdict and reasoning of the Japanese Court of Military Inquiries were described as unprecedented. The court found that Miura, prior to the murder, had entered into conspiracy with Tai-Won-Kun. The evidence showed, beyond doubt, the court conceded, that the Japanese minister at Seoul was the principal leader in the plot. The nature of the plot was detailed and the conspirators identified. "The whole party," the court pointed out, "entered the palace through the Kwangwha Gate and at once proceeded to the inner chambers." The court concluded with this astonishing observation: "Notwithstanding these facts, there is no sufficient evidence to prove that any of the accused actually committed the crime originally meditated by them."[15] The defense attorney had contended that "whatever may be thought by weaker minds, the result of the *émeute* has been most happy for the peace and progress of the world. Had the Queen been successful in her conspiracy, all the efforts made by Japan for the resuscitation of Korea would have been fruitless."[16] General Miura and his fifty-three co-defendants were acquitted. All of Miura's ranks and honors were returned to him. Miura's exoneration, a diplomat friend of the Colonel explained, illustrates a principle deeply ingrained in the Japanese concept of justice—that killing is not murder when it is done to secure political supremacy. The verdict made Miura a hero. While crowds in Hiroshima cheered the verdict, the Colonel was filing an angry report to the *Herald*:

I wonder if Tokyo has some idea that this sort of thing will raise Japan in the estimation of the world at large.

Does not Marquis Ito, the Prime Minister, know that in the diplomacy of civilized nations the empire of Japan, which was advancing so proudly and rapidly, has dropped a quarter of a century? If he does not, then he is not the statesman I took him to be.

The semi-barbaric condition of Korea has given to her benevolent neighbor an opportunity to teach bloody instructions which will not soon be forgotten, I fear, and as a sincere well-wisher of Japan, I grieve to record facts which not only proclaim her cruelty, but her injustice and indifference where her interests are involved.

It is to be hoped that Viscount Miura will not be advanced in rank by his government nor rewarded with a medal commemorative of his great diplomatic sagacity. . . .

I learn that at Hiroshima he is now the idol of the hour. He is called upon by distinguished officials and upon the evening of his release, he gave a grand banquet. His friend, the Tai-Won-Kun, has probably sent him a letter of congratulation. . . .[17]

Early in February, 1896, Colonel Cockerill, who visited the ministries of Seoul in quest of news, sensed an air of excitement at the Russian Legation. In contrast to the usual small squad of guards on duty, two hundred sailors and marines surrounded the grounds. The answer was soon forthcoming. By a clever ruse the King and Crown Prince had escaped, disguised and carried in closed chairs, from the palace under the noses of the Tai-Won-Kun's guards. The two took refuge in the Russian Legation.

Coincident with their escape Korean rebels overpowered a small party of Japanese soldiers, and a force of one hundred Russians landed at Chemulpo. As if by magic the King de-

serted his meek role as prisoner and asserted himself, violently. Within an hour he had appointed a new cabinet. A
proclamation ordered the Korean soldiers to protect their King
and to cut off the heads of the traitors and deliver the spoils
to his majesty. Two of the Tai-Won-Kun cabinet members
were dragged through the streets and slaughtered. A third
was killed later. Foreign ministers called to pay their respects
to the King. The Japanese minister dutifully brought up the
rear. The carnage had one hopeful aspect. The Koreans had
been at the point of open rebellion against the Japanese. Now
that their vindictive King was back in power, they had at
least an uneasy peace.

For eleven months the King conducted his business from
the Russian Legation. For use of a part of the building the
Russians charged the Korean monarch a rental fee that set
some kind of historical record. The Russians obtained a
signed permit to cut all the timber they pleased in the Yalu
Valley, an arrangement liberally construed to let the Russians
virtually take over an area half as large as Korea. The privilege was estimated to be worth fifty million dollars.

Russia would loom larger in the Korean picture of the
next decade. The New York *Herald* saw great significance in
Russia's landing of a hundred-man force at the seaport of
Chemulpo (Inchon), near Seoul. It suggested that Russia,
with a hungry eye on Korea, may have fomented antagonism
against Japan and made possible the King's coup.

"The ill feeling between Japan and Russia," said the
Herald, "has often been indicated in Colonel Cockerill's letters
and in the special dispatches from the Far East. It may very
well have been brought on by Japan's decision to assert her
hegemony over the western half of the Pacific and to retain
Korea within her sphere of influence. Such a decision could
mean only a conflict with Russia and would of itself account
for the fact referred to in one of Colonel Cockerill's recent
letters, that 'everyone in Moscow and St. Petersburg is ex-

pecting Russia to assert herself on the Orient when the vernal birds begin to sing.' "[18]

The war that Colonel Cockerill predicted came nine years after his death. Japan and Korea formed an alliance against Russia in 1904, the Japanese, as their treaty of mutual assistance phrased it, once more hypocritically "guaranteeing Korea's independence and territorial integrity." Japan won. In the treaty of 1905 Korea, to appease Nipponese militarists, was ceded to Japan's "protection." The United States probably could have precluded this opportunity for Japanese imperialism. It chose not to do so: the United States helped to negotiate the treaty that virtually handed over Korea to the Japanese. It gave Japan a bastion for her aggressive designs on the Asiatic mainland. Events of the twentieth century gave historical substance to John Cockerill's misgivings over the imperialistic motives of the nation which had decorated him.

XXVII. Night Falls in Cairo

On Friday afternoon, April 10, 1896, John Cockerill's carriage moved leisurely through the teeming streets of Cairo. The correspondent was feeling as relaxed as it was possible for any *Herald* man abroad. The Colonel had been ordered from the Far East to London by way of Egypt.[1] Because of his disclosures of Japanese ineptitude and blundering in its Korean policies, the atmosphere toward the *Herald* correspondent in Tokyo and Yokohama had grown noticeably cooler. Besides, *Herald* owner James Gordon Bennett, Jr., had in mind other plans for Cockerill. From Cairo Cockerill had been reporting developments of the Anglo-Egyptian expedition up the Nile. The Colonel arrived in Egypt just as war on the dervishes, a fanatical tribe of upper Egypt, was decided upon. "In accordance with his loyalty to his newspaper," reported the *Herald*, "the Colonel at once went to Cairo and busied himself in learning all about the details of the Nile expedition."[2]

Like his colleagues in scattered points on the globe, Cockerill continued to run errands of a trivial nature in Egypt for Bennett. Except to complain of distractions imposed on him by the *Herald* owner,[3] Cockerill left no record of these digressions from professional duties. Don Seitz, however, wrote that "Bennett presented an Egyptian princess with a prize pup. For days after its arrival the Paris *Herald* carried bulletins concerning the state of its health."[4] Cockerill presumably delivered the pet and flashed reports on its health to Paris.

Although correspondent Cockerill would not live to report it, Egypt and Britain were determined to re-assert their domination over the Sudan. Their first objective was Dongola, a province in the region of Nubia. In the Mahdist revolt the province fell into the hands of the dervishes when the latter drove the Egyptians from the Sudan. After interviewing Egypt's Khedive Abbas at the palace, Cockerill cabled his newspaper that

The demand for war news here is so great that every evening we hear fresh rumors of attacks and reverses somewhere up the Nile.

The movement of troops at this point has about ceased, though recruiting and forced enlistment go on vigorously. The officers of the Connaught Rangers have been given a farewell dinner, in expectation of an early forward move.

At the palace the Khedive took great interest in the Upper Nile campaign, although he was sorry that it was so suddenly forced upon Egypt that due preparations could not be made. He regretted that his military education had not been concluded when he was called to succeed his father.

His Highness thought that there were now over ten thousand Egyptian and English troops between Assouand and Akasheb. He asked about the Japanese army and navy and showed deep interest in all that I told him. When something was said about his Sudanese troops being officered by English, he expressed great confidence in them. . . .[5]

On the attitude of Lord Cromer, the British representative in Egypt, toward the Dongola expedition, Cockerill told his readers that question could easily be answered from Cairo, adding:

From the outset the British representative has disapproved of the movement. He did not advise it, and his opinion was not sought. He believes that the revenues of Egypt should be used for relieving and improving the country and not in reconquering territory not needed at present. He fears that all his past financial labors will be lost. He is, however, giving the expedition his hearty support now that it has been entered upon. British military men here express contempt for the hostile face of France toward the policy up the Nile. The dervishes, members of Moslem orders taking vows of poverty and austerity, living in monasteries and wandering as friars, are gathering in strength for offensive action, and at the War Office this afternoon the opinion was freely expressed that the situation at the front is growing serious. There is a feeling that the advancing column is entirely inadequate.[6]

There was good reason for the Colonel's misgivings. Anglo-Egyptian forces, under Lord Kitchener, in their immediate objective, took over Dongola. But it was not until 1899 that the Sudan was reoccupied and a "condominium" established by London and Cairo. Sixteen years later Egypt became a British protectorate.

The Colonel's carriage threaded its way through the city. This was Cairo, welding point of two continents, moulded in the Nile Valley, built upon the remnants of former civilizations. Since the accession of Mohammed Ali the city had grown phenomenally. The medieval city of Fostat retained its picturesqueness. In the quarter between Bab-en-Nasr and the Citadel the Colonel beheld its Oriental charm. The modern sections reflected the French influence. Around the Place Ezbedieh, the center of Cairo, were grouped the principal hotels, theaters and consulates. The Colonel could see in the crowded sidewalks and throngs of Egyptians along the Nile and the canals early evidences of the population explosion that would create colossal economic and sociological prob-

lems for President Gamal Abdel Nasser six decades later.
This was Cairo, a many-splendored city, ranking high as an
educational center, famed for its art and medical advances,
magnificent with its mosques denoting the finest in Arabic
architecture. The other side of Egypt did not escape the
Colonel's perceptive eye—its thousands of dirty, diseased
children, its overturned dustbins, its poverty-stricken fellaheen
struggling for a subsistence on pathetically small plots of land
in the narrow finger of the Nile Valley.

Colonel Cockerill's vehicle at length rolled to a stop at
Shepheard's Hotel. Opened in 1841, Sam Shepheard's establishment was more than a hotel. It was a center of life in the
Middle East, the romantic setting for fabulous stories of truth
and fancy and a symbol of the colonial era. Sam Shepheard,
a stocky man who wore ballooning Turkish trousers, an
oriental jacket, and a confident smile, foresaw the opportunities that would come with the opening of the Suez Canal in
1869. His establishment was superbly situated to serve travelers arriving by land or by sea. Whether they came via camel
caravan through the desert dust or by ship from the Mediterranean, they found a welcome at Shepheard's door. The
375 creaky-floored, high-ceiling rooms flanking wind-tunnel
hallways on four floors were usually filled. Cockerill was
lucky—the *Herald*'s ample expense allowance assured one
of the few rooms equipped with a gigantic iron-framed bed
and a bathtub long enough to permit a man to stretch out
at full length.

Visitors, lured by the elegance, the air of quality, the
echoes of a gracious age, flocked to the terrace where, Colonel
Cockerill could agree, "If you wait long enough, you will
meet the world." If scandal ever touched Shepheard's, it was
discreetly hushed. An ambassador was found dead in bed but,
the management hastened to explain, "death was due to natural causes." The quiet and decorum were felt even in the world-
famous bar, Sinners' Haven. Here was concocted the hotel's
specialty, a cocktail known as "Suffering Bar Steward," which

light-hearted celebrators mischievously mispronounced. The Colonel, who indulged freely without losing his composure, was told the ingredients of the specialty were brandy, gin, bitters, lime juice, lemon, and ginger ale but the proportions were never disclosed.

Many of the campaigns that spread British power through the Eastern world were charted at Shepheard's. Cockerill was on hand when Lord Kitchener and his staff mapped their drive against the Mahdi, the desert foe. Victories that followed were celebrated in Shepheard's banquet halls. Shepheard's had a priceless testimonial to the procession of kings, queens, tyrants, tycoons, Eastern potentates, writers, statesmen, charlatans, and explorers who had accepted its hospitality at one time or another. It was known as the "Gold Book." There in company with the signatures of the mighty was that of "Colonel John A. Cockerill, New York Herald, 1896."

Shepheard's was destroyed by fire in a wild anti-British demonstration in 1952. All that remained as this was written were the charred foundation, a scorched sycamore tree standing forlornly nearby—and memories. Today in modern splendor a multi-storied Egyptian-owned hotel proudly displaying the name of Shepheard's stands near the original site.[7]

Rested and refreshed, Colonel Cockerill climbed from his carriage and walked slowly into the lobby. The clerk handed him several letters. The Colonel probably wondered whether they would include word on his petition for a divorce, or—as unlikely as he knew it to be—whether Leonora might have written him, having resolved to make their marriage work. It hadn't worked, but the Colonel told himself it could have. There was no letter. Colonel Cockerill felt the pleasant pangs of hunger. Before repairing to the terrace for dinner, the *Herald* correspondent, always an immaculate dresser, headed for the hotel barber shop.

At 7:20 o'clock he settled easily into the barber's chair. No one paid any attention except the British barber, who recognized him. The two chatted amiably for a few moments as the barber wielded his shears. The Colonel lapsed into silence. Minutes passed. Suddenly, without warning, he toppled out of the barber's chair. Startled, the frightened barber called for help. Dr. George Murison was summoned and the Colonel was carried to his room. There he lay, partially undressed, his face flushed, his breathing noisy and stertorous. Dr. Murison diagnosed the Colonel's illness as cerebral apoplexy from hemorrhage. One of the small cranial arteries had ruptured with resulting destruction to an area of the brain. The most frequent cause is high blood pressure. A contributing factor may be hardening of the arteries or some inborn defect. The Colonel did not regain consciousness. He was pronounced dead at 10:06 o'clock, approximately two and a half hours after the attack. The end came while John Cockerill was on duty as he would have wished. The correspondent, in his final moment, lived up to the Shepheard's finest tradition. He had died quietly and decorously.

Colonel Cockerill's death was unexpected, even though his health had deteriorated. "It is true," reported the *Herald*, "that he had suffered from the grippe, with a touch of pneumonia; on his journey to Egypt. . . . he was obliged to stop at Hong Kong in order to recruit his strength. He subsequently experienced poor health and complained of liver trouble. Had it not been for his failing health he would have accompanied the Anglo-Egyptian expedition to Dongola. But all this had nothing to do with the cerebral hemorrhage."[8]

Nothing in the Colonel's news-gathering proclivities indicated any serious health problem up to his last few weeks of life. The *Herald* said the Colonel was in the prime of life and that "everything pointed to a long and brilliant career when he was so suddenly and unfortunately taken away."[9] While on the *World* the Colonel's letters to Joseph Pulitzer contained such reassuring passages as "My health continues tip-top," "I am 'on deck' thirteen hours a day," and "My health continues excellent despite the fact that I am working harder than usual."[10] Nevertheless, Colonel Cockerill may have paid in death at fifty-one the heavy toll exacted by a succession of tense and strenuous editorships.

Notified of the Colonel's stroke, a member of the United States diplomatic corps identified as "Mr. Penfield" and Barney Washington, the U. S. vice consul-general, hurried to the newspaperman's hotel room. They were there when death came. The body was conveyed to a Cairo mortuary, embalmed Egyptian-style, and shipped to New York City by way of Liverpool via the SS *Campania* of the Cunard line.

Colonel Cockerill's last letter was datelined Djibouti, the then new French port on the East Coast of Africa. It concluded with a prophetic note of more conflict, in these words:

> The red sun is drooping behind the far-off hills, which shut Djibouti from the desert sand storms. I hear the steam winch lugging at the anchor chain. The black diving boys are crying loudly for the last sou. The much be-champagned Russians and their jolly French comrades are singing in the smoking-room in loud rejoicing over the Italian repulse in Abyssinia, and in ten minutes we shall be ploughing peaceful blue waters which one day may be troubled by thunders such as were heard at Trafalgar. Who knows?"[11]

It seemed a pity that the Colonel's sun should have gone down while it was yet day. The New York *Herald*'s obituary notice and tributes on April 11 and 12, 1896, ran to more than four columns.

Colonel Cockerill had stopped off in Cairo on his way to London, where he was to have taken charge of the London correspondence of the *Herald*'s New York and Paris editions. This was the post in which the newspaper trade journal, the *Fourth Estate*, predicted "Colonel Cockerill undoubtedly would have achieved the same success that marked all of his other endeavors of journalism."[12]

XXVIII. "Gathered to the Quiet West"

In the May 17, 1896, issue of the New York *Times,* the late John A. Cockerill shared attention with old Tuck. Under a notice of the arrival of the Cockerill remains on the steamship *Campania* was the obituary of Cape May County's senior horse.[1] As a newspaperman the Colonel would not have begrudged the paragraph given to a distinguished horse, or its nearness to the *Times*'s notice of three funeral services arranged for the editor. "Why shouldn't our notices appear together?" the Colonel might have quipped. "We were both workhorses."

The Colonel's body was taken to a mortuary at 27 Great Jones Street in preparation for burial. The coffin was transported later to the New York Press Club, 34 West Twenty-sixth Street, where the body lay in state. At the Scottish Rite Hall on Twenty-ninth Street Joseph Howard, Jr., president of the Press Club, delivered an address and the Elks paid their respects. A procession followed the hearse to the Calvary Baptist Church on West Fifty-seventh Street, where the Reverend Robert S. MacArthur gave the funeral sermon. At a third service Republic Lodge, Free and Accepted Masons, conducted their obsequies.

Both the Scottish Rite Hall and the church were jammed by friends and acquaintances, and about three hundred persons followed the hearse to the church. Dr. MacArthur was confident that the Colonel, so averse to other kinds of formality, would have approved the elaborate ceremonies marking his demise. Before Cockerill left for the Far East, the clergyman recalled, he had attended similar rites for a brother Elk. "That's the kind of a funeral I want," said the Colonel.[2]

The Colonel might have been awed by the range and prominence of those who paid their respects. Heading the list of pallbearers was Chauncey M. Depew, the Colonel's close friend, who had delivered the oration when the cornerstone

of the *World* building was laid; others were General Horace
Porter of the Army of Missouri; Gardner G. Howland and
Joseph I. C. Clarke, representing the New York *Herald*;
Joseph Howard, Jr., president of the Press Club; Congress-
man William Sulzer of the Masons; Frank Mordaunt and John
G. Hart of the Elks, and Charles W. Price of the Quaint
Club. The Emperor of Japan was represented at the New
York rites by Miyagawa Kyufiro, consul in New York. The
Loyal Legion, national organization of Civil War veterans,
sent a delegation including General Horatio C. King, Colonel
T. B. Rand, and Captain Francis Gerraty.

The chief mourner was Leonora Cockerill. There she was,
apparently not divorced, "watching sorrowfully," as one report
phrased it. In the Calvary Baptist Church rites Mrs. Cockerill
was led to a seat at the foot of the bier by Mr. and Mrs. Robert
W. Criswell. She was accompanied also by Mrs. William
Connor, wife of the man who had introduced her to her late
husband. The other principal mourners were the Colonel's
sister, Esther Elizabeth, and her husband, Dr. John Campbell.
In the choice of a clergyman to officiate and the burial place,
the Colonel's wishes were carried out. Leonora relayed his
preference for the Reverend Dr. MacArthur and his hope
that he would be interred in the Elks' Rest at St. Louis, where
the Colonel had presented the elk in bronze. Leonora and
her friends, the Campbells, and committees of the Masonic
Lodge, the Press Club, the Loyal Legion, and the Elks
accompanied the body by train to St. Louis for the final rites.

The St. Louis *Republic*'s prose of May 22, 1896, was
equal to the occasion:

Within a few feet of the last earthly resting place of his friend,
John W. Norton, the mortal remains of John A. Cockerill were
laid away yesterday afternoon in Elks' Rest, Bellefontaine Cemetery. In cadence with the sad burial chant of the Elks' funeral
service subdued rolls of thunder rattled sympathetic salvos from
a black cloud overhead. But when the members of the lodge
deposited in the grave their tributes of amaranth and ivy the cloud
rolled away, and a bath of golden sunlight tinted brightly the

foliage and the big bronze elk, the silent guardian of the beautiful resting place of the dead. The services at the grave were simple and impressive. The carriages conveying the Elks to the cemetery discharged their burdens close to the lot, and the members formed a long line, through which the coffin was carried. At the grave the casket was placed in a cedar case and lowered to the bottom. . . .[3]

Mrs. Cockerill, supported by her friends the Criswells of New York and P. C. Boyle, editor of the Oil City, Pennsylvania, *Derrick*, was a perfect image of the grief-stricken widow. "Not since Colonel Cockerill, in all the enjoyment of health and vigor left New York for his foreign mission, has Mrs. Cockerill looked upon his face," reported the *Republic*. "When the body arrived from Egypt it was not deemed advisable to open the casket, for the embalming was done according to Egyptian methods. Mrs. Cockerill preferred to remember her handsome husband as he was in life."[4]

Earlier in the day the body had been taken from the undertaking rooms of Harrigan and Sheehan to the Church of the Messiah, Garrison Avenue and Locust Street. There, "in the midst of a perfect flood of floral offerings," the Reverend John Snyder conducted the rites, concluding with comforting words for the widow and friends. A platoon of mounted police escorted the procession to the cemetery.[5]

In his graveside eulogy Congressman Charles F. Joy said "death occurred just as Colonel Cockerill's progress toward success and renown were reaching for fruition. His genius added much to the total of life's intellectual storehouse, which will help to aid and elevate humanity. . . ." The speaker called attention to the Colonel's career in the nation's largest metropolis, where "he stepped at once to the first place and maintained a rank equal to the foremost." Of Cockerill's assignment to interpret to America the "growing enlightenment and military prowess of the Japanese Empire," Congressman Joy added:

With a journalistic experience, commencing at the desk of the typesetter, and ranging upward to the highest place in metropolitan journalism, endowed with the noblest and highest American sentiment from boyhood by reason of a complete military and political experience in all its phases, no one better equipped could have been chosen to interpret American ideas and institutions to the people of this great empire just emerging into the fight of modern civilization.

It is not too much to say that Colonel Cockerill . . . did more than any other person toward familiarizing 70,000,000 Americans with Japanese advancement from feudalism to constitutional monarchy; from semi-barbarism to an enviable rank among the enlightened nations of the earth.

At the breakfast of every reading American, for months, his reports upon events transpiring in the Antipodes were read and accepted and became part of American knowledge and belief. His honesty of thought and accuracy of judgment in this way have added immeasurably to the permanent sum of human knowledge.

The legislator concluded with these favorite lines of the Colonel:

> So be my passing:
> My task accomplished and the long day done,
> My wages taken, and in my heart some
> late lark singing,
> Let me be gathered to the quiet west
> That sundown splendid and serene death.[6]

Active pallbearers at St. Louis were H. C. Townsend, Charles E. Ware, James J. Kerns, and Alexander Carpenter Howard of the St. Louis Lodge of Elks; James A. Armstrong and J. J. Shannon of the New York Elks. The names of those who sent floral tributes read like a Who's Who in American journalism. Beside them was a conspicuous wreath bearing the words "John's wife." On a huge spread of carnations was the name of Colonel William F. (Buffalo Bill) Cody, a close friend. One name was conspicuously missing—Joseph Pulitzer.

There was no dearth of eulogies to the Colonel—from members of the New York Press Club, in the five rites conducted in New York and St. Louis, and on the editorial pages of the nation's newspapers. Foster Coates, who followed Cockerill's editorial footsteps on the *Advertisers* and the

World, characterized the Colonel as a "brilliant reporter, an able correspondent, a skillful editor and a talented manager with a manner as winsome as a woman's." Joseph Pulitzer's *World*, in whose climb to fame and riches the Colonel had figured so prominently, declared his death removed one of the best-known and most popular newspaper workers of the country, adding:

> Colonel Cockerill was for some years the managing editor of the *World*. He brought to the discharge of his responsible duties trained ability as a journalist, unsurpassed fidelity and industry, great personal loyalty, and qualities of mind and heart that endeared him to all his associates. No "newspaper man," as he preferred to call himself, ever had more friends or better deserved them. At the time of his death he was in the service of the New York *Herald* as special correspondent, and his letters from Japan to that journal have been exceptionally interesting and valuable.[7]

For a newspaper which in the view of some observers Colonel Cockerill had made, the *World* was restrained in its tribute. No such inhibition hampered the Buffalo *News*. On April 11, the day after the Colonel's death, the *News* coupled a summary of the journalist's career with this comment:

> The news [of his death] came with a startling suddenness and seemed hardly credible at first, for Colonel Cockerill has always been a young man for his age and had lived but fifty-one years. He was, perhaps, the best type of the progressive generation of American newspapermen, and in the art of imparting nervous force to editorial expression he had scarcely a peer. As a paragrapher he was unequaled among the metropolitan writers. He rarely gave more than two or three sentences to a subject, but it always epitomized the vital features of the situation.
>
> His sarcasm was something terrific as some of the most prominent men in public life learned to their cost. He was versatile, incisive and epigrammatic. His censure bore a barb. In the broad field of general newspaper enterprise Colonel Cockerill was in the front rank. He made the New York World a great newspaper. . . . To his editorial management are due the immense strides in power made by the World. . . . His generosity to younger or poorer men of his profession was unbounded. He was brusque in his exterior but had a big heart and a pocket always open.

The New York *Herald* found that "few journalists have had such a brilliant career as Colonel John A. Cockerill." Excerpted from the *Herald*'s extensive coverage of the Colonel's death and funeral services are the following observations:

He was essentially a self-made man, working steadily upward, until, by his own unaided efforts, he attained the highest rank in his profession. There is no aristocracy in journalism, no royal road to favor, no short cut to success. . . .

Colonel Cockerill's achievements were the measure of his personal worth. . . .

His true vocation was that of correspondent, an occupation which combined love for stirring scenes with literary tastes. The signal services which he rendered the Herald during the war between China and Japan gave him a world-wide reputation. . . .[8]

He was always proud that he had done everything about a newspaper office, from setting type and making rollers to editing and directing the whole concern. He had filled every chair except that of financial reporter. . . .

Colonel Cockerill was bothered for several years by gentlemen of the South, who regarded him as a backslider and a renegade. He was a War Democrat and had always been a modest reformer, but was unalterably opposed to free trade, and in the 1880s became a Republican.

He was a member of the Loyal Legion, the Ohio Society, the Republican Club and the Quaint Club. . . .

Colonel Cockerill was a handsome man, above middle height and compactly built. He was one of the most popular men in New York during his long residence here . . . His judgment of news was quick and invariably correct. He never gave contradictory orders, as his first impression of the value of news matter proved to be the best. The loyalty of his staff was one of the best recognitions of his journalistic genius.[9]

The Colonel's reputation abroad was noted in a dispatch from Rome, published by the *Herald* of April 12, 1896, reporting that "the journals here published obituary notices of Colonel Cockerill and recalled his brilliant services as correspondent of the Herald."[10]

In his home state of Ohio every important newspaper editorialized on the Colonel's career. The Ohio State *Journal* extolled the Colonel as one of the most talented newspaper men Ohio had ever produced, backing up its appraisal thus:

His first experience in the newspaper field where he had an opportunity to make a name for himself was as managing editor of the Cincinnati *Enquirer*. He afterward had charge of the New York *World* and made that paper a power in New York. All the big news enterprises in which the *World* engaged were directly due to the fertile brain of John A. Cockerill. . . . It was he who engineered the Nellie Bly trip around the world . . . and many a news sensation that set the country by the ear was his creation. . . .[11]

Eulogized the Columbus, Ohio, Democratic *Call*: "Thus passes away one of the brightest journalistic minds of the age, and one of whom every Ohioan was justly proud."[12]

As pictured by the press, the image of Leonora Cockerill was that of a young and beautiful widow entering a protracted period of grief. Interviewed in New York shortly after the Colonel's funeral, Leonora gave this account: "I first heard of my husband's death through the newspapers. You can imagine what a shock it was. I thought I should have died. I nearly went wild with grief."[13] The widow was reported ill for several days. At the various services her apparent anguish excited expressions of deepest sympathy.

Leonora made an astonishingly swift recovery. Three weeks after the Colonel was buried in St. Louis, Leonora was a bride again. The Colonel's widow was proposed to in a cab. Less than twenty minutes later, she was the wife of Walter Louis Lineau, once the Colonel's rival. The ceremony was performed by Justice of the Peace Louis R. McCullough of nearby Hoboken, New Jersey, shortly before midnight of June 10, 1896. "It all came about suddenly," Leonora told a newsman at her 150 West Eighty-fourth Street flat. "I am sorry it has become known so quickly. The wedding was really as unexpected to both of us as the news will be to our friends."[14]

Leonora told how it happened. Mr. Lineau had dined

with Leonora in her apartment. To help the young widow overcome her grief Mr. Lineau drove her to Hoboken to see a friend. Suddenly, on the way back, Lineau turned to her and asked: "What's the matter with us getting married?"

"I could think of nothing the matter with the idea," Leonora said she replied, "and I consented on the impulse of the moment."[15]

Could it be that the comfort of Walter's financial resources softened the blow of Leonora's grief? Walter was the son of the late Rudolph Lineau, onetime president of the Germania Bank of Brooklyn, and as such was a member of one of Brooklyn's oldest, most exclusive families. Furthermore Walter's future prospects were excellent; he was rising fast in the importing house of Frederick Victor & Achelis. Interviewed by a persistent Hearst reporter, Leonora was defensive about the sudden nuptials: "Mr. Lineau wanted me to marry him very much. Because he is so young, though, I presume my consent to it will subject me to all sorts of criticism. I suppose the marriage will be severely condemned by my husband's family. I understand that some of them wanted him to marry a Brooklyn girl who is to inherit $2,000,000. Our marriage is purely one of love." The bridegroom confirmed it was "purely a love match." He said the couple had sought to keep their marriage a secret until November "because," as he put it, "we thought it would not look well to marry so soon after the Colonel's death."[16]

Leonora was sensitive about her age. Walter was twenty-six. Leonora hesitated about answering when the justice asked. She finally gave it as thirty. On other points Leonora, who was clearly the spokesman for the couple, was less reticent. When Justice of the Peace McCullough intoned the word "obey" in the marriage vow, Leonora quickly broke in, "No, no, I will not promise that." And turning, she reminded her betrothed, "You know we agreed to omit that word." Apparently Lineau was not going to intervene if the word slipped in. The ceremony had to be started again. Later Leonora explained herself: "I had the word 'obey' omitted because it is now customary to delete it in the Episcopal Church."[17]

The Colonel's will leaving his estate to Leonora was admitted to probate. As beneficiary of the Colonel's life insurance policies, the widow received $20,000. The estate bequeathed to her thus totaled about $30,000, considered a small fortune by contemporary standards.

On March 1, 1897, nine months after the will was probated, the Colonel's sister, Mrs. John Campbell, belatedly sought to contest it. Her attorney, Charles M. Beattle, filed an affidavit in which Hettie declared the Colonel had signed over his insurance policies to her and made her his sole heir. The Colonel, she contended, did so in an exchange of correspondence. The Surrogate was requested to order Mrs. Lineau to allow Mrs. Campbell to examine Colonel Cockerill's personal effects, which by several months followed in transit the correspondent's body from Egypt. Included in this shipment, Mrs. Campbell swore, was a second will leaving everything to her. Shortly after the Colonel's death, Mrs. Campbell continued, she had asked Leonora to hand over certain of her brother's effects and to let her look at others. "Leonora shook her fist in my face and refused," Hettie ruefully reported.[18] She urged that the court act promptly on her petition, lest the shipment fall into the hands of Mrs. Lineau before other interested parties could examine its contents.

On March 21 the Surrogate, to no one's surprise, denied Mrs. Campbell's petition. "The will of the decedent," ruled the court, "has been admitted to probate, and that proceeding closed by the entry of a decree thereon. The petitioner was duly cited to the probate proceedings at the time, but made no opposition thereto. There is no authority under which the order asked for can be granted."[19] Even if the court had granted the petition, Mrs. Campbell's attorney admitted later, it probably would have been useless. The box containing the Colonel's effects, it was learned, was in the firm custody of Leonora Lineau. It was never established that a second will existed, nor was any legal proof offered that the insurance policies had been assigned to the Colonel's sister, a fact which would have come to the attention of the insurance companies. Since Mrs. Campbell could produce neither the policies nor a newer will, she had no case.

In the Colonel's probated will one paragraph offered a final testimony to the tie that bound in spirit two stormy figures of American journalism, so much alike and yet so different: "I name as my executor Joseph Pulitzer, who has been a faithful and sincere friend to me, and to whom I am indebted for much that I enjoy."[20]

Notes

Introduction

1. *National Cyclopaedia of American Biography*, I, 153.
2. Valerian Gribayédoff, "Pictorial Journalism," *Cosmopolitan*, XI (Aug., 1891), 474.
3. O. H. Rothacker, "Joe and John," *The Journalist*, III, May 8, 1886, p. 3.
4. Don C. Seitz, *Joseph Pulitzer, His Life and Letters*, p. 106.
5. *Ibid.*, p. 26.
6. *Ibid.*
7. *Ibid.*
8. Letter from Samuel Hopkins Adams to author, May 8, 1958.
9. Seitz, *Joseph Pulitzer*, p. 186.
10. Edwin Emery, *The Press and America*, pp. 345, 516.

I. Distinguished Sire

1. Nelson W. Evans and Emmons B. Stivers, *History of Adams County*, p. 313. Much of the background for this chapter is drawn from the voluminous Evans-Stivers work. Among many local histories examined in the preparation of this biography, this one stands out as an exceptionally well written and generally well documented record. It presented the "feel" and the "flavor" of Colonel Cockerill's early environment that would have been unavailable from any other source. Tom W. Eylar, editor and manager of the *People's Defender*, West Union, Ohio, newspaper, supplemented information on the Cockerill and Eylar families.
2. From unidentified newspaper clipping provided by Mrs. Margaret McClure-Stitt of Cincinnati.
3. *Biographical Directory of the American Congress, 1774-1949*, p. 261.
4. *Congressional Globe*, XXXV, Part II, Debates and Procedures of the 35th Congress, 2032.
5. *Ibid.*, p. 2146.
6. Mrs. McClure-Stitt to author.
7. Evans and Stivers, *History of Adams County*, p. 311.
8. *Ibid.*, p. 313.

II. Cockerills at War

1. *Biographical Cyclopaedia and Portrait Gallery*, p. 1519.
2. Evans and Stivers, *History of Adams County*, p. 714.
3. Corydon Edward Foote, *With Sherman to the Sea*, p. 13.
4. Evans and Stivers, *History of Adams County*, p. 715.
5. *Ibid.*, p. 312.
6. *Ibid.*, p. 312.
7. Military Order of the Loyal Legion of the U. S., Ohio Commandery, Circular No. 20, Sept. 15, 1897, p. 1.

8. Evans and Stivers, *History of Adams County*, p. 419. Who was the "real" Drummer Boy of Shiloh? Was it John Cockerill or someone else? The *Saturday Evening Post*, April 30, 1960, pp. 22-23, published "The Drummer Boy of Shiloh," a short story in which the author, Ray Bradbury, drew his inspiration from the death notice of Olin Howlin, actor, identified in the Los Angeles *Times* as the son of the "famed drummer boy of Shiloh, Joby A. Howland."

9. *Great Battles of the Civil War*, by Editors of *Life*, p. 10.

10. Military Order of the Loyal Legion of the U. S., Ohio Commandery, Circular No. 20, Sept. 15, 1897, p. 1.

11. New York *Herald*, April 11, 1896, p. 9.

12. *Biographical Cyclopaedia and Portrait Gallery*, p. 1519.

13. *Biographical Directory of American Congress*, p. 997; Evans and Stivers, *History of Adams County*, p. 312.

14. Evans and Stivers, *History of Adams County*, p. 714.

15. Seitz, *Joseph Pulitzer*, p. 105.

16. John S. Still, "A Fortnight of Fear: Morgan's Raid," *Museum Echoes*, XXXIV (Sept., 1961), 67-70.

17. Evans and Stivers, *History of Adams County*, p. 362.

18. *Ibid.*, pp. 394-395.

19. No precise date is available for John Cockerill's discharge as a bugler from the Ohio Artillery. But his name first appears as a co-publisher of the West Union *Democratic Union* on December 18, 1862, indicating he was mustered out shortly prior to associating with the weekly newspaper.

20. New York *World*, April 11, 1896, p. 5.

III. Sam and the "Scion"

1. Osman Castle Hooper, *History of Ohio Journalism*, p. iii.

2. *Ibid.*, p. 14.

3. Data on Adams County newspapers is drawn chiefly from Evans and Stivers, *History of Adams County*, pp. 415-420.

4. *Ibid.*, p. 693.

5. *Ibid.*

6. Tom W. Eylar, editor and manager, *People's Defender*, West Union, Ohio, to author.

7. Evans and Stivers, *History of Adams County*, pp. 694-695.

8. *Ibid.*, p. 444; West Union *Scion*, Nov. 28, 1856.

9. Military Order of Loyal Legion of U. S., Ohio State Commandery, Circular No. 20, Sept. 15, 1897, p. 1.

10. *Ibid.*, p. 2.

11. New York *Herald*, April 11, 1896, p. 9.

12. Evans and Stivers, *History of Adams County*, p. 695.

13. New York *Herald*, April 11, 1896, p. 9.

14. *Ibid.*

15. Evans and Stivers, *History of Adams County*, p. 694.

16. New York *Herald*, April 11, 1896, p. 9.

17. West Union *Scion*, Feb. 24, 1860.

18. *Ibid.*

19. *Ibid.*

20. *Ibid.*

21. "Was It Just the Same 100 Years Ago?—A Look at 1858 and 1958," *U. S. News & World Report*, XLV (Dec. 26, 1958), 42.

22. Evans and Stivers, *History of Adams County*, p. 695.

IV. Hamilton, Dayton, and a Copperhead

1. Evans and Stivers, *History of Adams County*, pp. 417 ff.
2. *Democratic Union*, West Union, Dec. 18, 1862.
3. *Ibid.*, April 3, 1863.
4. *Ibid.*, April 10, 1863.
5. *Ibid.*
6. *Ibid.*, May 15, 1863.
7. *Ibid.*, June 19, 1863.
8. *Ibid.*
9. *Ibid.*, April 3, 1863.
10. *Ibid.*, April 10, 1863.
11. *Ibid.*, April 17, 1863.
12. *Ibid.*, May 15, 1863.
13. *Ibid.*, April 10, 1863.
14. *Ibid.*, May 29, 1863.
15. *Ibid.*, April 24, 1863.
16. *History and Biographical Cyclopaedia of Butler County, Ohio*, p. 116, is the source for the transfers in ownership and editorship of the Hamilton *True Telegraph*.
17. *True Telegraph*, Oct. 20, 1864.
18. From obituary of Colonel Cockerill, "Dead in the Harness," *Ohio State Journal*, April 11, 1896.
19. *Biographical Cyclopaedia and Portrait Gallery*, p. 1519.
20. Seitz, *Joseph Pulitzer*, p. 105.
21. Russel B. Nye, *A Baker's Dozen—Thirteen Unusual Americans*, p. 193.
22. *History and Biographical Cyclopaedia of Butler County*, p. 116.
23. James Laird Vallandigham, *Life of Clement L. Vallandigham*, p. 36. This is a brother's understandably sympathetic version of Vallandigham's career.
24. Nye, *A Baker's Dozen*, p. 196.
25. *Ibid.*, p. 201.
26. *Ibid.*, p. 203.
27. *Ibid.*, p. 205.
28. Richard Hofstadter, William Miller, Daniel Aaron, *The United States: History of a Republic*, p. 379.
29. Hooper, *History of Ohio Journalism*, pp. 114-115.
30. *History and Biographical Cyclopaedia of Butler County, Ohio*, p. 117.
31. Dayton *Daily Ledger*, Aug. 8, 1868, p. 2.
32. See chap. xxiii, pp. 254, 255.
33. *Dayton Daily Ledger*, Aug. 8, 1868.
34. *Ibid.*, Aug. 13, 1868.
35. New York *Herald*, April 11, 1896, p. 9. The *Herald* writer found that Vallandigham "was a good deal broken in fortune at the time and between his political work and his labors as a lawyer he gave but little attention to his paper."
36. Dayton *Daily Ledger*, Sept. 5, 1868.
37. New York *Herald*, April 11, 1896, p. 9.
38. Quoted in Vallandigham, *Life of Clement L. Vallandigham*, pp. 562-563. Cockerill is not quoted by name but the quoted editorial, appearing in the Cincinnati *Enquirer*, leaves little doubt that the Colonel was the writer.
39. *Ibid.*, p. 563.

V. City of Serenity and Sin

Two works provided the background for much of this chapter and were drawn on for other chapters on Cockerill's Cincinnati tenure:

Alvin F. Harlow, *The Serene Cincinnatians*, one of the Society in America Series devoted to important cities and sections of the country. This volume portrays the individual characteristics, underscores the idiosyncrasies, and traces the growth of Cincinnati, with emphasis on local traditions and the personalities who embodied them. Its research is unimpeachable and it catches the atmosphere of the city as well as any other work.

The Cincinnati Guide, compiled by the Writers' Program of the Works Project Administration of Ohio. This volume was the last of the American Guide Series. A series of essays giving historical background is followed by a tour section that describes the community in infinite detail. Because of its elaborate documentation and the highly professional standing of its many writers, the *Guide* proved to be an excellent source.

1. Harlow, *The Serene Cincinnatians*, p. 57.
2. Elizabeth Bisland, *Life and Letters of Lafcadio Hearn*, pp. 51-52.
3. Both versions by unidentified writers appear in Cockerill obituary comments, New York *Herald*, April 11, 1896, p. 9.
4. Ibid.
5. Cincinnati Guide, p. 38.
6. Ibid., p. 61.
7. Ibid., p. 111.
8. Ibid., p. 75.
9. As quoted in Harlow, *The Serene Cincinnatians*, p. 242.

VI. Murder a Profitable Commodity

1. Bisland, *Life and Letters of Lafcadio Hearn*, I, 51.
2. Lee Allen, "Lafcadio Hearn" (an unpublished manuscript by Lee Allen, former member of the Cincinnati *Enquirer* staff, now historian of the Baseball Hall of Fame and author of several books), p. 7; Vera McWilliams, *Lafcadio Hearn*, p. 64.
3. Cincinnati *Enquirer*, Nov. 9, 1874, p. 1.
4. Ibid., p. 4.
5. Ibid., Nov. 11, 1874, p. 4.
6. Ibid., Nov. 10, 1874, p. 8.
7. According to the *National Cyclopaedia of American Biography*, I, p. 444, during John R. McLean's management of the *Enquirer* its circulation grew from 16,000 to 90,000. Since Cockerill was with the Enquirer until 1877 it is probable the circulation figure approached the 90,000 level during the managing editor's stay. Hearn (Bisland, *Life and Letters of Lafcadio Hearn*, p. 54) wrote that "in a few years Cockerill forced up the circulation of the Enquirer to a very large figure and made a fortune for the publisher."
8. Cincinnati *Enquirer*, Nov. 9, 1874, p. 1.
9. McWilliams, *Lafcadio Hearn*, p. 65.
10. John A. Cockerill, "Lafcadio Hearn: Author of Kokoro," *Current Literature*, XIX (June, 1896), p. 476.
11. Ibid.
12. Ibid.
13. Ibid.
14. Ibid.
15. Edward Larocque Tinker, *Lafcadio Hearn's American Days*, p. 15.
16. Cockerill, "Lafcadio Hearn," p. 476.
17. McWilliams, *Lafcadio Hearn*, p. 66; Tinker, *Hearn's American Days*, p. 23.

18. O. W. Frost, *Young Hearn*, pp. 125-126.
19. McWilliams, *Lafcadio Hearn*, pp. 69-70.
20. Ibid., p. 70.

VII. Fortune Made—Exit Editor

1. Rothacker, *The Journalist*, p. 3.
2. Charles Theodore Greve, *Centennial History of Cincinnati and Representative Citizens* (1904), I, 1037.
3. Harlow, *The Serene Cincinnatians*, p. 270.
4. Ibid., p. 271.
5. George Sibley Johns, "Joseph Pulitzer," *Missouri Historical Review*, XXV (1931), 246.
6. Cincinnati *Enquirer*, Sunday Magazine, May 23, 1923, p. 6.
7. Cincinnati *Enquirer*, Nov. 2, 1876, p. 4.
8. Ibid., Oct. 1, 1876, p. 4.
9. Ibid.
10. Ibid., Nov. 2, 1876, p. 4.
11. Ibid., Nov. 2, 1876, p. 2.
12. Ibid., Oct. 1, 1876, p. 4.
13. Ibid.
14. Ibid.
15. This and preceding two passages, *ibid.*, Oct. 1, 1876, p. 4.
16. Ibid.
17. Ibid.
18. Ibid., Dec. 5, 1876, p. 4.
19. Ibid., Nov. 2, 1876, p. 4.
20. Ibid., Oct. 1, 1876, p. 4.
21. Ibid.
22. Ibid.
23. Ibid.
24. Circumstances of McLean's pre-empting Cockerill's editorial chair are sketched in the New York *Herald*, April 11, 1896, p. 9.
25. From an editorial, "The Atlantic Cable—Its Effect Upon the Press," New York *Herald*, Aug. 11, 1866, p. 4.
26. Passages from Cincinnati *Enquirer*, July 10, 17, and 20, 1877.
27. New York *World*, April 11, 1896, p. 5

VIII. Summons from St. Louis

1. Data on the hiring of Calista Halsey and basic facts on the founding and history of the Washington *Post* are drawn from "Orientation," a pamphlet for new employees, undated, issued by that newspaper. *The Biographical Cyclopaedia and Portrait Gallery*, p. 1519: "He [Cockerill] spent the winter of 1877-78 in Washington, D. C. [where] he assisted in establishing the Washington *Post*."
2. In 1933 McLean suffered a breakdown. The *Post*, which Lord Northcliffe said he would rather have than any American paper because it reached the breakfast tables of congressmen, all but died on its feet. The *Post* fought United States membership in the League of Nations and championed the candidacy of Warren G. Harding. It coined the slogan for another Republican's campaign—"Coolidge or Chaos."

Months after McLean's breakdown, with the circulation down to a pathetic 54,000, the once proud *Post* was sold at public auction for $825,000. The buyer was Eugene Meyer, banker, financier and frequent federal appointee. Under Meyer the *Post*, whose staffers won several Pulitzer Prizes, was often rated among the top ten American newspapers. Mr. Meyer was succeeded as publisher by his son-in-law, Philip L. Graham, who committed suicide on August 3, 1963. In 1954 the *Post* purchased the *Times Herald*, a morning newspaper.

3. *Baltimore Gazette*, Oct. 8, 1878, p. 1.
4. *Ibid.*
5. *Ibid.*
6. James Wyman Barrett, *Joseph Pulitzer and his World*, p. 52.
7. *The Journalist*, May 8, 1886, p. 3.
8. Orrick Johns, *Time of Our Lives*, p. 61. This volume can be described as a dual autobiography, although the authorship is credited to Orrick Johns. He described his father, George Sibley Johns, as the last of Joseph Pulitzer's fighting editors. It is not a wholly accurate work on details, yet it served as a useful source on the St. Louis Cockerill found in 1869. From a contemporary of Cockerill, the impressions of George S. Johns are significant and probably as reliable as any other recorded recollections. Orrick Johns was also a journalist, but his proclivities for radicalism were a disappointment to his father.
9. *Ibid.*, pp. 64-65.
10. *Ibid.*, p. 66.
11. As quoted in Johns, *Time of Our Lives*, p. 67.
12. *Ibid.*
13. George Mills, "On History of St. Louis Newspapers," *American Journalist*, I (Sept. 15, 1883), p. 4. *The American Journalist*, as distinguished from the *Journalist*, nationally circulated journal for newspapermen, was published in St. Louis from September, 1883, to June, 1885.

IX. Homicide with Honor

1. Biographical data on Colonel Broadhead are drawn from the *Encyclopedia of the History of St. Louis*, I, 239-243.
2. Seitz, *Joseph Pulitzer*, p. 109.
3. George Sibley Johns, "Joseph Pulitzer," *Missouri Historical Review*, XXVI (April, 1932), 277.
4. Seitz, *Joseph Pulitzer*, pp. 109-110.
5. Walt McDougall, *This Is the Life!*, p. 207.
6. George Sibley Johns, "Joseph Pulitzer," *Missouri Historical Review*, XXVI (April, 1932), 274; Seitz, *Joseph Pulitzer*, p. 110.
7. St. Louis *Post-Dispatch*, Dec. 18, 1882.
8. Seitz, *Joseph Pulitzer*, p. 110.
9. St. Louis *Post-Dispatch*, Oct. 13, 1882.
10. Although other accounts of the Slayback shooting were consulted, that of George Sibley Johns, "Joseph Pulitzer," *Missouri Historical Review*, XXVI (April, 1932), 273-278, is, in the author's judgment, the most authentic. For that reason it is relied on heavily but not exclusively in this reconstruction of the tragedy that played an important role in shaping the careers of both Cockerill and Pulitzer. It is possible that had it not occurred the New York chapters in the lives of these men would never have been written.

X. Ordeal and Exoneration

1. Seitz, *Joseph Pulitzer*, p. 111; George Sibley Johns, "Joseph Pulitzer," *Missouri Historical Review*, XXVI (April, 1932), 276.
2. *Ibid.*, p. 276.
3. Seitz, *Joseph Pulitzer*, p. 111.
4. St. Louis *Globe-Democrat*, Dec. 6, 1882.
5. Letter to author from Alexander Cockerill Howard of St. Louis, April 16, 1958. "My father, Alexander Carpenter Howard, and John A. Cockerill," wrote Mr. Howard, "were bosom friends and were among the organizers and original members of the St. Louis Lodge of the Benevolent Protective Order of Elks.... After the Slayback affair, Cockerill was depressed and felt his usefulness and future in St. Louis had been impaired and he was anxious to seek a new environment....
   "All during his life John Cockerill always remembered me on the 13th day of each December. It was a gold watch on my ninth birthday anniversary. I still have it."
6. St. Louis *Post-Dispatch*, Dec. 7, 1882, p. 2.
7. For a detailed account of the Pulitzer shooting incident, see the George Sibley Johns, "Joseph Pulitzer," *Missouri Historical Review*, XXV (April, 1931), 405-408.
8. St. Louis *Post-Dispatch*, Dec. 18, 1882. Those who wish to read further on the Cockerill-Broadhead-Slayback affair should consult: St. Louis *Globe-Democrat*, Oct. 14, 1882 (favorable to Cockerill); St. Louis *Republican*, Oct. 14, 1882 (unfavorable, by writer who later admitted he had been unfair); St. Louis *Chronicle*, Oct. 14, 1882 (unfavorable to Cockerill); *Spectator*, Oct. 21, 1882, *Criterion*, Oct. 21, 1882 (both impartially done).
9. From lecture by Benjamin H. Reese, American Press Institute.
10. Johns, *Time of Our Lives*, p. 60.

XI. The Colonel Bows Out

1. Johns, *Time of Our Lives*. Young Johns's interview with Colonel Cockerill, the incidents pertaining to their association and impressions of Cockerill are based on this source, pp. 60-80.
2. Mills, "On History of St. Louis Newspapers," p. 5.
3. George Sibley Johns, "Joseph Pulitzer," *Missouri Historical Review*, XXVI (Jan., 1932), 166.
4. The supposition of this exchange is plausible enough. McGuffin as the business manager was the logical one to carry the sad news of slumping circulation and revenue to Pulitzer and Cockerill.
5. Barrett, *Joseph Pulitzer*, p. 53; Seitz, *Joseph Pulitzer*, p. 112.
6. A letter dated December 2, 1880, and written on *Post-Dispatch* stationery to Stillson Hutchins suggests that the Colonel had considered leaving the newspaper long before the shooting. In it Cockerill, the writer, credited Hutchins with having "effectually poisoned me against St. L." Apparently referring to a proposal to buy another newspaper, the Colonel told Hutchins that if he "can effect the Boston scheme, I hope you will do so." "Let me know what the prospect is and I will see what I can do in the way of raising a small amount of money," he continued. "The new deal should take place on the first of January, if possible. Another month here I think will do me completely." This letter, incidentally, minimizes the possibility that a quarrel with

Hutchins, as suggested in Chapter VIII, prompted the Colonel to pull out of the Washington *Post.* This letter indicates they remained on good terms. It is unclear how Hutchins "poisoned" the Colonel against St. Louis or just what was meant by the term.

XII. Park Row Invasion

1. Barrett, *Joseph Pulitzer,* p. 63.
2. Ibid.
3. Seitz, *Joseph Pulitzer,* p. 130.
4. John Heaton, *The Story of a Page,* p. 4. This is an excellent analysis of the *World* editorial crusades over a thirty-year period.
5. Ibid., p. 136.
6. Willard Grosvenor Bleyer, *Main Currents in the History of American Journalism,* p. 325.
7. McDougall, *This Is the Life!,* p. 207.
8. Barrett, *Joseph Pulitzer,* pp. 75, 76.
9. New York *World,* March 16, 1885.
10. Letter from Cockerill to Pulitzer, June 23, 1885. (All Cockerill letters quoted in this chapter from Pulitzer Papers, Columbia University.)
11. Cockerill letter of June 17, 1885.
12. Cockerill letter of June 23, 1885.
13. Barrett, *Joseph Pulitzer,* p. 84.
14. Ibid., p. 87.
15. Ibid., p. 89.
16. Ibid., p. 88.
17. Ibid., p. 92 (In *This Is the Life!,* p. 133, Walt McDougall quotes Blaine as supporting the *World*'s claim that "Belshazzar's Feast" influenced the election sufficiently to account for the 1,100 odd votes that lost him the state of New York.)
18. This account of the hiring of the *World* cartoonist is based on his own version as told in Walt McDougall, *This Is the Life!,* pp. 95-98.
19. McDougall, *This Is the Life!,* pp. 138-39.
20. Ibid., pp. 101-102.
21. Ibid., p. 101.
22. Ibid., pp. 95, 96.
23. Heaton, *Story of a Page,* p. 35.
24. Barrett, *Joseph Pulitzer,* p. 132.
25. New York *World,* Nov. 6, 1888, p. 1.
26. Ibid., p. 2.
27. Statement of Jack W. Germond, Gannett News Service, New York City.
28. Seitz, *Joseph Pulitzer,* p. 148.
29. Ibid., p. 141.
30. Bleyer, *History of American Journalism,* pp. 329, 342.
31. Barrett, *Joseph Pulitzer,* p. 107.
32. New York *Sun,* Oct. 18, 1887.
33. New York *World,* Oct. 19, 1887.
34. Barrett, *Joseph Pulitzer,* p. 109.

Three of the above sources require special mention:

James Wyman Barrett's *Joseph Pulitzer and His World* (1941) is an opinionated, anecdotal volume that includes both office legend and information available only to an insider such as the author, last city editor of the *World.* It is a friendly accounting of the Pulitzer career but it reflects a working newspaperman's respect for truth. It contains many references to Cockerill.

Walt McDougall's *This Is the Life!* (1941) is a portrayal of the period by the *World*'s cartoonist. It is a popularized version told with a hearty relish in which the author obviously depends chiefly upon his memory. Yet because Cockerill, with Pulitzer's approval, hired McDougall, his recollections cannot be ignored. One aspect is refreshing: Nobody—Cockerill, Pulitzer, go down the list of distinguished journalists—is "sacred" in McDougall's book. In several mentions of Cockerill, McDougall makes it clear he had both respect and affection for the editor.

Don C. Seitz's *Joseph Pulitzer, His Life & Letters* (1924) is the nearest thing to an "approved" biography. It completes a biography started by Dr. George W. Hosmer, Pulitzer's physician, to whom the publisher gave an intimacy denied all others. Seitz had eighteen years of association with Pulitzer as business manager and in other roles at the New York *World*. Cockerill, in this "official" biography, is mentioned twenty-two times and is the second among the "Men of the World" to whom Seitz inscribes his book. Seitz and Cockerill were not contemporaries on the *World*, and so Seitz's account of the Colonel's role was necessarily drawn from the recollections of others, some of whom, one suspects, may not have been wholly reliable. Yet the most lavish tribute to the Colonel—that he was never really replaced at the *World*—was Seitz's own estimate.

XIII. Gal Reporter

1. Iris Noble, *Nellie Bly, First Woman Reporter*, p. 45.
2. *Ibid.*, p. 50. There is no unanimity among sources on the circumstances of Elizabeth Cochrane's first meeting with Cockerill. Nina Brown Baker in *Nellie Bly*, pp. 51-60, writes that the Colonel nearly tripped over Nellie's feet as she sat waiting to see Joseph Pulitzer. Assured by Nellie that she intended to stay until she could see the publisher, Cockerill, after an initial interview with the applicant, took her to Pulitzer's adjoining office, where she wheedled the pair into giving her a job. In *The Amazing Nellie Bly*, pp. 55-60, Mignon Rittenhouse's version is that after three hours of waiting Nellie persuaded the city editor to take her to Pulitzer's office, where she found the publisher in conference with Cockerill. After the preliminaries Cockerill instructed her at length on her Blackwell's Island assignment. According to Iris Noble, p. 45, Nellie asked to see Cockerill, not Pulitzer, which seems logical since she had written the Colonel in advance of her application (p. 50). Ishbel Ross in *Ladies of the Press*, p. 50, writes: "Nellie badgered the custodian of the gate for three hours until she got to John A. Cockerill and finally to Mr. Pulitzer himself." The account in this book is drawn from what seem to be the most likely details of the above versions.
3. Rittenhouse, *The Amazing Nellie Bly*, p. 13.
4. *Ibid.*, p. 61.
5. Elizabeth Cochrane, *Ten Days in a Mad-House* (a compilation in book form of Miss Cochrane's stories appearing in the *World*), p. 5. Nellie Bly was not the first reporter to impersonate a patient in an insane asylum in order to expose abuses. Julius Chambers used the ruse in 1872 (see his *News Hunting on Three Continents*).
6. Could Julius Chambers' "Descent Into a Mad World" have inspired Cockerill to have Nellie Bly impersonate a mental patient? In a chapter so titled Chambers, in his *News Hunting on Three Continents*, pp. 50-75, tells of his experience in 1872 in being committed to Bloomingdale Asylum while in the employ of the New York *Tribune*. His exposé led to a new code of laws for protecting insane persons.

Cockerill, of course, knew of Chambers' adventure. At Pulitzer's behest the Colonel in 1889 hired Chambers at $250 a week as a member of the *World*'s editorial staff.
7. *Orientation*. Washington *Post*, p. 4. Fannie Aymar Mathews, writing on "The Woman's Press Club of New York," *Cosmopolitan*, XI (Aug., 1891), 454, named Mrs. J. C. Croly as the first woman to be employed on the staff of a daily newspaper in New York. Her pen name was "Jennie June."
8. Cochrane, *Ten Days in a Mad-House*, p. 6.
9. Noble, *Nellie Bly*, p. 78.
10. Cochrane, *Ten Days in a Mad-House*, p. 86.
11. *Ibid.*, p. 91.
12. *Ibid.*, pp. 91, 98.
13. *Ibid.*, p. 3.
14. Rittenhouse, *The Amazing Nellie Bly*, pp. 108-109.

XIV. Outfoxing a "Fox"

1. Baker, *Nellie Bly*, p. 76.
2. Noble, *Nellie Bly*, p. 97.
3. New York *World*, December 18, 1887.
4. Noble, *Nellie Bly*, pp. 91-93.
5. *Ibid.*, p. 83.
6. The story of the Albion restaurant incident is based on the account by Noble in *Nellie Bly*, pp. 84-86.
7. *Ibid.*, p. 97.
8. *Ibid.*
9. Elizabeth Cochrane, in her story in the New York *World*, April 1, 1888, records her conversation with Phelps.
10. *Ibid.*
11. Noble, *Nellie Bly*, p. 112.
12. This conversation is based on Iris Noble's version of Nellie Bly's relationships with Colonel Cockerill, the most complete and plausible account published. There is ample evidence in the files of the *World* that Cockerill fulfilled his promise of assigning Nellie Bly more exposés of social and economic injustice.
13. Noble, *Nellie Bly*, p. 225.
14. Baker, *Nellie Bly*, p. 115.
15. *Ohio State Journal*, April 11, 1896, p. 2.
16. Baker, *Nellie Bly*, pp. 90, 91.
17. *Ibid.*, p. 124.

XV. Conflict: Cockerill vs. Smith

1. Seitz, *Joseph Pulitzer*, p. 160.
2. Julius Chambers, in his *News Hunting on Three Continents,* p. 312, contributes an illuminating comment on this brand of scrambled authority: "I learned ... that organization and discipline were not favored by the proprietor (Pulitzer), who thought the best results were attained by playing man against man."
3. Elizabeth Jordan, *Three Rousing Cheers*, p. 20.
4. *Ibid.*, p. 18.
5. *Ibid.*, p. 20. (Dr. Helen Ross, a London psychiatrist, in research on swearing, found it to be a healthy habit that relieves high blood pres-

sure caused by daily tensions. Her studies indicated that the professional and well-to-do cussers are more prone to blasphemy than the working class, which sticks mostly to obscenity. Dr. Ross's explanation is that the upper class is rebelling against early religious training, the working class is renouncing sex taboos. Colonel Cockerill's preference ran to blasphemy.)

6. *Ibid.*, p. 20.
7. McDougall, *This Is the Life!*, p. 102.
8. Jordan, *Three Rousing Cheers*, pp. 20-22.
9. *Ibid.*
10. *Ibid.*, p. 22.
11. *Ibid.*
12. Barrett, *Joseph Pulitzer*, p. 98; Seitz, *Joseph Pulitzer*, p. 161.
13. Jordan, *Three Rousing Cheers*, pp. 26, 27.
14. *Ibid.*, p. 32.
15. *Ibid.*, p. 35.

XVI. For the Good of the World, Mostly

1. Edgar Wilson Nye, *Bill Nye, His Own Life Story*, p. 177.
2. *Ibid.*
3. *Ibid.*, pp. 177-178.
4. The seven Nye passages are from James Whitcomb Riley and Bill Nye, *Wit and Humor* (a volume containing many of Nye's pieces published in the New York *World*), pp. 114, 17, 53, 230, 207-208, 231, 117, respectively.
5. McDougall, *This Is the Life!*, p. 150.
6. By now this story, told by McDougall in *This Is the Life!*, pp. 169-170, undoubtedly has taken on some legendary aspects. McDougall places the responsibility of the blizzard assignment upon E. A. Grozier, city editor. But Cockerill as managing editor presumably knew what was going on and cannot escape responsibility. (Interestingly enough it was Grozier who, we are told, had Pulitzer and others excited with his plan to signal Mars by means of enormous letters of fire on the Western plains until someone irreverently asked in what language the message would be sent.)
7. Johns, *Time of Our Lives*, p. 63.
8. Valerian Gribayédoff, "Pictorial Journalism," *Cosmopolitan*, II (Aug., 1891) pp. 471-481.
9. New York *World*, Feb. 3, 1884, p. 1.
10. Gribayédoff, "Pictorial Journalism," p. 477.
11. Bleyer, *History of American Journalism*, p. 329.
12. From William C. Whitney Papers, Library of Congress.
13. *Ibid.*
14. From Daniel S. Lamont Papers, Library of Congress.

XVII. Leonora Barner

1. New York *Journal*, June 14, 1896, p. 9.
2. Arthur Hobson Quinn, *History of the American Drama*, p. 328, refers to Bartley Campbell as the author of *The White Slave*. The New York *Journal*, June 14, 1896, p. 9, says Leonora Barner was a member of Bartley Campbell's *White Star* company. This evidently was a typographical error; Campbell wrote no such play.

3. Letter from Mrs. Margaret McClure Stitt (June 15, 1959) quotes an unidentified clipping as follows: "While editor of the *World* Colonel Cockerill's salary was $20,000, the largest salary up to that time ever paid a newspaper editor. He has been pronounced by competent critics as one of the five great editors of the world." "The *World* paid Cockerill $15,000 a year," said the Buffalo *News*, April 11, 1896, "and he was worth it."

4. Information on the Cockerill relatives' attitude toward Mrs. Cockerill was provided by Mrs. Flo Wickersham Giffin of Peebles, Ohio.

5. New York Daily *Tribune*, March 21, 1897, p. 5.

6. These highly personal incidents are reconstructed on the basis of scattered references to the separation of the Colonel and his wife, subsequent divorce petitions, and the report of an unsuccessful attempt to contest Cockerill's will, New York *Daily Tribune*, March 21, 1897, p. 5.

7. Affidavit filed in Surrogate, New York City, by Mrs. John Campbell, March 1, 1897.

8. New York *Daily Tribune*, March 21, 1897, p. 5.

XVIII. Press Club Prestige

1. *Journalism Illustrated*, I, 1.
2. *Ibid.*, p. 2.
3. *Ibid.*, p. 8.
4. *Ibid.*, pp. 10-11.
5. *Ibid.*, p. 5.
6. It fell by tradition to Greene to pick his successor; hence this exchange.
7. *Journalism*, p. 17.
8. Seitz, *Joseph Pulitzer*, pp. 166-167.
9. Samuel Hopkins Adams to author, April 11 and May 8, 1958.
10. *Journalism*, p. 15.

XIX. Walkout on the "World"

1. Alleyne Ireland, *An Adventure with a Genius*, p. 221. First published in 1914 under the title *Joseph Pulitzer: Reminiscences of a Secretary*, this volume, published six years later, narrates Ireland's personal association with Pulitzer. Cockerill is not mentioned.

2. Cockerill to Pulitzer, June 30, 1885, from Pulitzer Papers, Columbia University.

3. Seitz, *Joseph Pulitzer*, p. 142.
4. *Ibid.*, p. 143.
5. *Biographical Cyclopaedia and Portrait Gallery*, p. 1519.
6. New York *World*, April 11, 1896, p. 5.
7. Cockerill to Pulitzer, Pulitzer Papers, June 23, 1885.
8. Cockerill to Pulitzer, Pulitzer Papers, June 27, 1885.
9. Cockerill to Pulitzer, Pulitzer Papers, June 23, 1885.
10. Cockerill to Pulitzer, Pulitzer Papers, June 30, 1885.
11. Cockerill to Pulitzer, Pulitzer Papers, June 27, 1885.
12. Cockerill to Pulitzer, Pulitzer Papers, June 12, 1885.
13. Cockerill to Pulitzer, Pulitzer Papers, June 30, 1885.
14. Barrett, *Joseph Pulitzer*, pp. 114-120.
15. Pulitzer to New York Press Club, Feb. 16, 1888.
16. Seitz, *Joseph Pulitzer*, pp. 177-178.

17. *Ibid.*, p. 183.
18. Cockerill to Pulitzer, June 23, 1885.
19. Barrett, *Joseph Pulitzer*, p. 140.
20. Seitz, *Joseph Pulitzer*, p. 135.
21. *Ibid.*, p. 174.
22. *Ibid.*, p. 183.
23. *Ibid.*, p. 184.
24. Unfortunately neither the Pulitzer Papers nor the Cockerill letters contain any correspondence on the termination of Cockerill-Pulitzer relations. Nor are there details available from any other source. It seems inconceivable that the Colonel should have ended his service to Pulitzer without a reminder of his own considerable part in reinvigorating the *World*.
25. McDougall, *This Is the Life!*, p. 206.
26. Cockerill to Professor Thomas Davidson, June 7, 1888, from Thomas Davidson Papers, Yale University Library.
27. Seitz, *Joseph Pulitzer*, p. 183.
28. Cockerill to Professor Thomas Davidson, Sept. 17, 1888.
29. Seitz, *Joseph Pulitzer*, p. 186.
30. *Ibid.*, pp. 22-23.
31. Frank Luther Mott, *American Journalism: A History, 1690-1960*, p. 440.

XX. Pulitzer's Portrait

1. Don C. Seitz, "Portrait of an Editor," *Atlantic Monthly*, CXXXIV (Sept., 1924), 294-295.
2. Seitz, *Joseph Pulitzer*, p. xiv.
3. McDougall, *This Is the Life!*, pp. 102-104.
4. Arthur Brisbane, "Joseph Pulitzer," *Cosmopolitan*, XXXIII (May, 1902), 51.
5. Seitz, *Joseph Pulitzer*, pp. 1, 2.
6. Seitz, "Portrait of An Editor," p. 289.
7. Irvin S. Cobb, *Exit Laughing*, pp. 130-131.
8. *Ibid.*, p. 131.
9. Ireland, *An Adventure with a Genius*, pp. 143-144.
10. James Creelman, "The Dramatic Intensity of Joseph Pulitzer," *Current Literature*, XLVI (April, 1909), p. 382.
11. Brisbane, "*Joseph Pulitzer*," p. 54.
12. McDougall, *This Is the Life!*, p. 166.
13. Seitz, "Portrait of An Editor," p. 295.
14. McDougall, *This Is the Life!*, pp. 102-104.
15. *Ibid.*, p. 106.
16. Letter to author from Samuel Hopkins Adams, April 29, 1958.
17. McDougall, *This Is the Life!*, p. 196.
18. Seitz, *Joseph Pulitzer*, p. 18.
19. *Ibid.*
20. Ireland, *An Adventure with a Genius*, pp. 115-116.
21. Cobb, *Exit Laughing*, p. 154.
22. McDougall, *This Is the Life!*, p. 107.
23. Oswald Garrison Villard, *Some Newspapers and Newspapermen*, p. 45.
24. Harry Thurston Peck, "Twenty Years of the Republic," *Bookman*, XXIII (June, 1906), 410.
25. *Ibid.*
26. Ireland, *An Adventure with a Genius*, pp. 113-115.
27. Johns, *Time of Our Lives*, p. 109.
28. Emery, *The Press of America*, pp. 369-370.

29. *Ibid.*, p. 457.
30. Dr. Julian Rammelkamp to author, March 19, 1962.
31. James Wyman Barrett, *The World, the Flesh and Messrs. Pulitzer,* pp. 40-41.

XXI. Cockerill and the "Advertisers"

1. *Fourth Estate,* II, No. 5 (Oct. 4, 1894), p. 1.
2. Rochester *Post-Express,* June 11, 1891; Buffalo *Evening News,* April 11, 1896.
3. *Ibid.*
4. *Ibid.*
5. *The Journalist,* Dec. 26, 1891, p. 5. It is seriously to be doubted whether the *Journalist* writer, in referring to a capacity of 96,000 an hour, meant one press. It is probable this capacity referred to that of several units. No single press had reached such phenomenal speed at that time.
6. *Commercial Advertiser,* Dec. 9, 1893, p. 6.
7. *Ibid.*, Oct. 24, 1892, p. 4.
8. *Ibid.*, Dec. 9, 1893, p. 6.
9. *Ibid.*
10. *Ibid.*
11. *Ibid.*
12. *Ibid.*
13. *Ibid.*
14. *Ibid.*, Oct. 24, 1892, p. 4.
15. *Ibid.*
16. *Ibid.*, Dec. 9, 1893, p. 6.
17. *Ibid.*
18. *Ibid.*, Oct. 24, 1892, p. 4.
19. *Ibid.*, Dec. 9, 1893, p. 6.
20. *Ibid.*
21. *Ibid.*, Oct. 24, 1892, p. 4.
22. *Fourth Estate,* II, No. 5 (Oct. 4, 1894), 1.
23. Rochester *Post-Express,* April 11, 1896 (editorial).
24. Louis Thorn Golding, Brookline, Mass., to author, Jan. 8, 1959.
25. This incident based on report of St. Louis *Globe-Democrat,* Oct. 12, 1891, p. 9.
26. *The Journalist,* Dec. 26, 1891, p. 4.
27. *Ibid.*
28. *Commercial Advertiser,* Dec. 9, 1893.

XXII. Cockerill, Critic and Prophet

1. John A. Cockerill, "The Newspaper of the Future," *Lippincott's Monthly Magazine,* L (Aug., 1892), 221.
2. *Ibid.*, pp. 220-221.
3. *Ibid.*, p. 221.
4. *Ibid.*, p. 222.
5. John A. Cockerill, "Some Phases of Contemporary Journalism," *Cosmopolitan,* XIII (Oct., 1892), 696-700.
6. *Ibid.*, p. 696.
7. John A. Cockerill, "The Trend of the Great Daily," *Review of Reviews,* VI (Nov., 1893), 449-451.

8. "An Indictment and a Remedy," *Harper's Weekly*, XXXVI (Nov. 5, 1892), 1062.
9. Cockerill, "Some Phases of Contemporary Journalism," p. 697-698.
10. *Ibid.*, p. 698.
11. Cockerill, "The Newspaper of the Future," p. 222.
12. Cockerill, "Some Phases of Contemporary Journalism," p. 699.
13. *Ibid.*, p. 698.
14. *Ibid.*, p. 699.
15. *Ibid.*, p. 700.
16. Hutchins Hapgood and Arthur Bartlett Maurice, "Great Newspapers of the United States," *The Bookman*, XV (March, 1902), 43.
17. Joseph Pulitzer, "The College of Journalism, *North American Review*, CLXXVIII (May, 1904), 641-680 (Pulitzer elaborates on his hopes and plans for a college of journalism.)
18. Cockerill, "Some Phases of Contemporary Journalism," p. 696.
19. John A. Cockerill, "How to Conduct a Local Newspaper," *Lippincott's Magazine*, LVIII (Sept., 1896), 395-399. This article, which was published after Cockerill's death, remains remarkably timely and practical. Millville, a fictional farm-community, "has no newspaper and needs one," he wrote. "It may not know that it needs one, but it is the business of the newspaper aspirant to convince it that it does. This is the first step." Cockerill discussed the various problems attending the founding of a newspaper: obtaining a site and equipment, establishing credit, lining up correspondents, getting acquainted with the leading townsmen, establishing editorial policy, soliciting advertising, and keeping abreast of the news.

Cockerill made personal integrity a prior requisite of the publisher. "He should be a resident who intends to continue so," he counseled. "He must have a good reputation for veracity and for paying his debts. There is no better ally in the affairs of life than common honesty—since the paradox is true that common honesty is apt to be somewhat uncommon."

The Colonel would bar advertisements calculated to offend good taste and good morals. This rule, he conceded, cuts off a source of profit but "unlike saving at the spigot and wasting at the bung-hole, it reverses the proceeding. You lose a trifle and gain enormously. When you have published a clean newspaper for a term of years, you have established a reputation that is worth in money vastly more than the petty sums you have allowed to pass by because you would not soil your pages with falsehoods. . . ."

As to civic pride engendered by the local newspaper, "let the outside world smile if it chooses. . . . Millville may not be the garden of Eden . . . but there is no reason why its inhabitants should not entertain that opinion, and no reason why the *Millville Journal* should not support such an opinion. . . . It is familiar wisdom that 'he will make a poor day's work as a fish-salesman who cries down the freshness of his own mackerel.' "

Mechanical execution has much to do with a paper's popularity, in Cockerill's view. He urged that when the new publisher has adopted a certain page size and method of placing its contents—"literary columns here, news columns there, correspondence here, foreign summary there, markets here, deaths and marriages there—stick to it if your readers like it. Newspaper reading is a matter of habit. Let the reader find what he is accustomed to find in its usual place."

Finally, Cockerill, like editors before and after him, was sensitive to typographical errors. In this trouble area Cockerill demanded letter-perfect proofreading, no less. "Without good proof-reading," he wrote, "not even an advertisement of gold bullion at a penny a

pound can satisfy the eye of the reader. Printers' mistakes are fatal; and the compositors who make them, the proof-readers who pass them over, and the editors who permit them to appear unpunished, all alike ought to abandon callings for which they are unfitted...."
20. Cockerill, "The Newspapers of the Future," p. 221.
21. *Ibid.*, p. 223.
22. *Ibid.*, pp. 223-224.
23. *Ibid.*, pp. 223-224. (The demands upon a reporter prompted an unidentified pundit to observe that he "had to have the manners of a gentleman, the acuteness of a diplomat, the patience of a Job and the stomach of an ostrich.")
24. Cockerill, "Some Phases of Contemporary Journalism," p. 703.
25. *Review of Reviews*, VI (Nov., 1893), 450.
26. Cockerill, "Some Phases of Contemporary Journalism," p. 696.
27. *Lippincott's Magazine*, L, 225.
28. *Ibid.*, p. 224.
29. *Ibid.*, p. 225.
30. *Ibid.*, p. 223.
31. *Ibid.*, pp. 225-226.
32. Cockerill, "Some Phases of Contemporary Journalism," pp. 695-696.
33. *Ibid.*, p. 702.

XXIII. Cockerill as Wit and Stylist

1. McDougall, *This Is the Life!*, p. 183.
2. George Cary Eggleston, *Recollections of a Varied Life*, pp. 308-309. In this loosely organized autobiography referring to dozens of press personalities, Eggleston acknowledged that Cockerill was in control of the *World* when Pulitzer engaged Eggleston as editorial writer. Eggleston wrote that Colonel Cockerill "had so much robust manhood in his nature, so much courage and generous good will that we soon learned to find pleasure in each other's company, to like each other and, above all, to trust each other." He found in Cockerill a man incapable of lying, deceit or treachery. Eggleston's estimate of Cockerill as an executive was a high one but, unlike other contemporaries, he contended the Colonel had no great creative imagination. Curiously, other critics made the same observation of Pulitzer (see page 210). Eggleston conceded Pulitzer was fortunate to have a man like Cockerill to carry out his plans. He credits to Cockerill's readiness in grasping an idea and translating it into achievement genius in its own way. "His industry in translating the ideas of his chief into action was ceaseless, tireless, sleepless," wrote Eggleston. "He would hit upon scores of ways in which a campaign projected by another mind could be carried out effectively."
3. McDougall, *This Is the Life!*, p. 207.
4. Edith M. Bartow, *News and These United States*, p. 234.
5. West Union *Scion*, March 30, 1860.
6. Dayton *Daily Ledger*, Sept. 5, 1868, p. 3.
7. *Ibid.*, Oct. 3, 1868, p. 3.
8. *Ibid.*, Sept. 21, 1868, p. 2.
9. *Ibid.*, Oct. 3, 1868, p. 3.
10. *Ibid.*, Sept. 23, 1868, p. 3.
11. Cincinnati *Enquirer*, Dec. 26, 1875.
12. Dayton *Daily Ledger*, July 13, 1868, p. 3.
13. *Ibid.*, Oct. 3, 1868, p. 1.
14. *Ibid.*, Oct. 22, 1868, p. 3.

15. Ibid., Oct. 5, 1868, p. 1.
16. Ibid., Oct. 3, 1868, p. 3.
17. Ibid., Aug. 19, 1868, p. 3.
18. Ibid., Nov. 4, 1868, p. 2.
19. Ibid.
20. Cincinnati *Enquirer*, Nov. 27, 1874, p. 4.
21. Ibid., Nov. 30, 1874, p. 4.
22. Ibid., Nov. 2, 1876, p. 4.
23. New York *Commercial Advertiser*, Oct. 24, 1892, p. 4.
24. Ibid.
25. Ibid.

XXIV. John Cockerill, Foreign Correspondent

1. *Fourth Estate*, II, No. 5 (Oct. 4, 1894), 1. (It was during this tour that Cockerill gathered material for an article for *Cosmopolitan*, XIX (Sept., 1895), 501-512, entitled "Brigham Young and the Modern Utah." The article was a touching tribute to a devout and sturdy people. With all his surface irreverence, the Colonel was capable of deep emotion and sentiment, both of which showed through in this report. Cockerill's visit to the territory of Utah came at a politically propitious moment. Statehood prospects were bright, yet there remained widespread resentment of the Mormons. Cockerill's published impressions of the Mormons were credited with softening opposition to Utah's statehood bid. The public image of the Mormon improved. Cockerill's contention that Utah was ready for its new responsibilities was confirmed January 4, 1896, three months after the Colonel's article appeared. On that day a forty-fifth star appeared in the United States flag.)
2. Don C. Seitz, *The James Gordon Bennetts*, p. 264.
3. *Ibid.*, pp. 269-270.
4. *Ibid.*, p. 241.
5. *Ibid.*, pp. 242-243.
6. *Ibid.*, p. 243.
7. Emma Eames, *Some Memories and Reflections*, pp. 216-217.
8. Seitz, *The James Gordon Bennetts*, p. 236.
9. *Ibid.*, pp. 226-227.
10. *Ibid.*, p. 224.
11. Vague impressions of Cockerill's relatives that the Colonel was interviewed by Bennett and other evidence which points strongly in that direction suggest that the Cockerill-Bennett meeting occurred substantially as related. It is assumed that the interview took place in Paris since the *Herald* publisher rarely came to New York in this period. It is unlikely that Bennett would have entrusted the hiring of a journalist of Cockerill's stature to subordinates in New York. Some aspects of this version of the interview are speculative but those conversant with James Gordon Bennett, Jr., will agree that it might have taken an even more bizarre turn. It is not conjecture that Bennett was concerned with Cockerill's appreciation of dogs; he was concerned with everybody's attitude toward dogs. Seitz in the Bennetts' biographies, pp. 262-263, portrays Bennett's eroticism with dogs.

XXV. Accolade from an Emperor

1. Bisland, *Life and Letters of Lafcadio Hearn*, p. 54.

2. "Japanese Papers: Colonel Cockerill's Letter to the *Fourth Estate*," *The Fourth Estate*, III, No. 77, Aug. 15, 1895, pp. 1, 2. Cockerill's observations on the Japanese press are drawn from this article.
3. New York *Herald*, Feb. 8, 1896, p. 9.
4. This and the preceding five passages are from the New York *Herald*, Feb. 8, 1896, p. 10.
5. *Ibid.*, Feb. 2, 1896, sec. 4, p. 6.
6. *Ibid.*
7. *Ibid.*
8. *Fourth Estate*, V, No. 112, p. 1.
9. New York *Herald*, April 11, 1896, p. 9 (reprinted in Cockerill obituary).
10. *Ibid.*
11. Corroboration of Japan's citation, New York *Herald*, April 11, 1896, p. 9; New York *Times*, Feb. 13, 1896, p. 1; New York *Tribune*, Feb. 13, 1896, p. 1 and April 1, 1896, p. 7; and in a number of biographical sketches in standard reference works.
12. Johns, *Time of Our Lives*, p. 62. Johns's account indicates Cockerill gave up his job, out of disgust, and went to another New York newspaper. This is erroneous. He was with the *Herald* at his death.

XXVI. Murder of Queen Min

1. Cockerill first heard of the Ear and Nose Tomb from Lafcadio Hearn.
2. William Eliot Griffis, *Corea, the Hermit Nation*, p. 144.
3. *Ibid.*
4. *Ibid.*, p. 133.
5. Henry Chung, *The Case of Korea*, p. 41.
6. *Ibid.*, p. 43.
7. *Ibid.*, p. 37.
8. New York *Herald*, Oct. 7, 1895, p. 9.
9. *Ibid.*, Oct. 14, 1895, p. 7.
10. *Ibid.*
11. *Ibid.*, Oct. 17, 1895, p. 7.
12. *Ibid.*, Feb. 14, 1896, p. 9. After reading this chapter Kyonshill "Connie" Kang, M.S.J., of Seoul, a graduate of Medill School of Journalism and at this writing a reporter for the Rochester, N. Y., *Democrat and Chronicle*, gave this reaction: "Queen Min is no longer hated by the Koreans. Her sins—a tight grip of the court and an inflexible ambition to orient the Hermit Kingdom to China and Russia—seem to have been fully forgiven. The Koreans today give her a kind, sympathetic, and highly favorable review."
13. F. A. McKenzie, *The Tragedy of Korea*, p. 77.
14. New York *Herald*, Oct. 12, 1895, p. 7.
15. McKenzie, *Tragedy of Korea*, p. 267. From text of findings of Japanese Court of Preliminary Inquiries, Local Court of Hiroshima.
16. Chung, *The Case of Korea*, pp. 46, 73.
17. McKenzie, *Tragedy of Korea*, pp. 74-75.
18. New York *Herald*, Feb. 14, 1896, p. 9.

XXVII. Night Falls in Cairo

1. New York *Herald*, April 12, 1896, p. 9.
2. *Ibid.*
3. Johns, *Time of Our Lives*, p. 62.
4. Seitz, *The James Gordon Bennetts*, p. 227.

5. New York *Herald*, April 3, 1896, p. 9.
6. *Ibid.*
7. Background of Shepheard's Hotel is drawn from an Associated Press dispatch of September 20, 1958, by Relman Morin, published in Rochester *Democrat and Chronicle*, p. 1H, and from my own impressions on a visit to Cairo in July, 1958.
8. New York *Herald*, April 12, 1896, p. 9.
9. *Ibid.*
10. Letter from Cockerill to Joseph Pulitzer, June 23, 1885, Department of Special Collections, Butler Library, Columbia University.
11. New York *Herald*, April 5, 1896, p. 9.
12. *Fourth Estate*, V, No. 112, April, 1896, p. 2.

XXVIII. "Gathered to the Quiet West"

1. New York *Times*, May 17, 1896, p. 9.
2. New York *Times*, May 19, 1896, p. 9.
3. St. Louis *Republic*, May 22, 1896, p. 6.
4. *Ibid.*
5. *Ibid.*
6. *Ibid.*
7. New York *World*, April 11, 1896.
8. New York *Herald*, April 12, 1896, p. 9.
9. New York *Herald*, April 11, 1896, p. 9.
10. *Ibid.*
11. *Ohio State Journal*, April 11, 1896.
12. Columbus, Ohio, *Democratic Call*, April 16, 1896.
13. New York *Journal*, June 14, 1896, p. 9.
14. *Ibid.*
15. *Ibid.*
16. *Ibid.*
17. *Ibid.*
18. New York *Daily Tribune*, March 21, 1897, p. 5.
19. *Ibid.*
20. Seitz, *Joseph Pulitzer*, p. 185.

Bibliography

General Works

ADAMS, SAMUEL HOPKINS. *Tenderloin*. New York: Random House, 1959.

BAKER, NINA BROWN. *Nellie Bly*. New York: Henry Holt and Company, 1956.

BARLOW, ALVIN F. *The Serene Cincinnatians*. New York: E. P. Dutton and Company, 1950.

BARRETT, JAMES WYMAN. *Joseph Pulitzer and His World*. New York: Vanguard Press, 1941.

————. *The World, the Flesh and Messrs. Pulitzer*. New York: Vanguard Press, 1931.

BARTOW, EDITH M. *News and These United States*. New York: Funk & Wagnalls Company, 1952.

BISLAND, ELIZABETH. *Life and Letters of Lafcadio Hearn*. Boston: Houghton Mifflin and Company, 1906.

BLEYER, WILLARD GROSVENOR. *Main Currents in the History of American Journalism*. New York: Houghton Mifflin Company, 1927.

BORTON, HUGH. *Japan's Modern Century*. New York: Ronald Press Company, 1955.

CHAMBERS, JULIUS. *News Hunting on Three Continents*. New York: Mitchell Kennerley, 1921.

CHUNG, HENRY. *The Case of Korea*. Chicago: Fleming H. Revell Company, 1921.

Cincinnati Guide. Ohio Writers Project. Cincinnati: Wiesen-Hart Press, 1943.

COBB, IRVIN S. *Exit Laughing*. Garden City, N. Y.: Garden City Publishing Co., Inc., 1942.

COCHRANE, ELIZABETH. *Ten Days in a Madhouse*. New York: Norman L. Munro Publishing House, 1887.

CROCKETT, ALBERT STEVENS. *When James Gordon Bennett Was Caliph of Bagdad*. New York: Funk & Wagnalls Company, 1926.

EAMES, EMMA. *Some Memories and Reflections*. New York: D. Appleton and Company, 1927.

EGGLESTON, GEORGE CARY. *Recollections of a Varied Life*. New York: Henry Holt and Company, 1910.

EMERY, EDWIN. *The Press and America.* Englewood Cliffs, N. J.: Prentice-Hall, Inc., 1962.

EVANS, NELSON W., and EMMONS B. STIVERS. *History of Adams County (Ohio).* West Union, Ohio: E. B. Stivers, 1900.

FOOTE, CORYDON EDWARD (as told to OLIVE DEANE HORMEL). *With Sherman to the Sea.* New York: John Day Company, 1960.

FROST, O. W. *Young Hearn.* Tokyo: Hokuseido Press, 1959.

GOLDING, LOUIS THORN. *Memories of Old Park Row (1887-1897).* New York: Privately printed, 1946.

Great Battles of the Civil War, produced by editors of *Life* Magazine. New York: Time, Inc., 1961.

GREVE, CHARLES THEODORE. *Centennial History of Cincinnati and Representative Citizens.* 2 Vols. Chicago: Biographical Publishing Company, 1904.

GRIFFIS, WILLIAM ELIOT. *Corea, the Hermit Nation.* New York: Charles Scribner's Sons, 1911.

HARLOW, ALVIN F. *The Serene Cincinnatians.* New York: E. P. Dutton and Company, Inc., 1950.

HARTSHORNE, ANNA C. *Japan and Her People.* Philadelphia: Henry T. Coates & Co., 1902.

HEATON, JOHN L. *The Story of a Page.* New York: Harper & Brothers, 1913.

History and Biographical Cyclopaedia of Butler County, Ohio. Cincinnati: Western Biographical Publishing Co., 1882.

History of Montgomery County, Ohio. Chicago: W. H. Beers & Co., 1882.

HOFSTADTER, RICHARD, WILLIAM MILLER, and DANIEL AARON. *The United States—History of a Republic.* Englewood Cliffs, N. J.: Prentice-Hall, Inc., 1959.

HOOPER, OSMAN CASTLE. *History of Ohio Journalism.* Columbus, Ohio: Spahr & Glenn Company, 1933.

IRELAND, ALLEYNE. *Joseph Pulitzer: Reminiscences of a Secretary.* New York: Mitchell Kennerley, 1914.

JOHNS, ORRICK. *Time of Our Lives.* New York: Stackpole Sons, 1937.

JORDAN, ELIZABETH. *Three Rousing Cheers.* New York: D. Appleton-Century Company, Inc., 1938.

Journalism Illustrated, Vol. I. New York: New York Press Club, 1905.

LEE, JAMES MELVIN. *History of American Journalism.* Boston: Garden City Publishing Co., 1917.

McDougall, Walt. *This Is the Life!* New York: Alfred A. Knopf, 1926.

McKenzie, F. A. *The Tragedy of Korea.* London: Hodder and Stoughton, 1908.

McWilliams, Vera. *Lafcadio Hearn.* Boston: Houghton Mifflin Co., 1946.

Merrill, Horace Samuel. *Bourbon Leader: Grover Cleveland and the Democratic Party.* Boston: Little, Brown & Company, 1957.

Morris, Lloyd. *Postscript to Yesterday.* New York: Random House, 1947.

Mott, Frank Luther. *American Journalism: A History, 1690-1960.* New York: The Macmillan Company, 1962.

Noble, Iris. *Nellie Bly, First Woman Reporter.* New York: Julian Messner, Inc., 1957.

Nye, Edgar Wilson. *Bill Nye, His Own Life Story.* New York: The Century Co., 1926.

——. *Nye and Riley's Wit and Humor* (Poems and yarns by James Whitcomb Riley and Bill Nye). Chicago: Thompson and Thomas, 1900.

Nye, Russel B. *A Baker's Dozen: Thirteen Unusual Americans.* East Lansing, Michigan: Michigan State University Press, 1956.

Oliver, Robert T. *Korea, Forgotten Nation.* Washington, D. C.: Public Affairs Press, 1944.

Quinn, Arthur Hobson. *History of the American Drama,* Vol. I. New York: F. S. Crofts & Co., 1945.

Rittenhouse, Mignon. *The Amazing Nellie Bly.* New York: E. P. Dutton and Company, Inc., 1956.

Roe, George Mortimer, ed. *Cincinnati, the Queen City of the West.* Cincinnati: Cincinnati Times-Star Co. by press of C. J. Krehbiel and Co., 1895.

Ross, Ishbel. *Ladies of the Press.* New York: Harper & Brothers, 1936.

Seitz, Don C. *The James Gordon Bennetts.* Indianapolis: Bobbs-Merrill Company, 1928.

——. *Joseph Pulitzer, His Life and Letters.* New York: Simon and Schuster, 1924.

Tebbel, John. *The Life and Good Times of William Randolph Hearst.* New York: E. P. Dutton and Company, 1952.

Tinker, Edward Larocque. *Lafcadio Hearn's American Days.* New York: Dodd, Mead & Company, 1925.

VALLANDIGHAM, JAMES L. *Life of Clement L. Vallandigham.* Baltimore: Turnbull Brothers, 1872.
VILLARD, OSWALD GARRISON. *Some Newspapers and Newspapermen.* New York: A. A. Knopf, 1923.

Reference Works

Biographical Cyclopaedia and Portrait Gallery. Cincinnati: Western Biographical Publishing Co., 1895.
Biographical Dictionary of the American Congress. Washington: U.S. Government Printing Office, 1928.
BOATNER, MARK MAYO, III. *The Civil War Dictionary.* New York: David McKay Company, Inc., 1959.
Congressional Globe. Vol. XXXV, Part 2. Debates and Procedures of 35th Congress, 1857-58. Washington, D. C.: John C. Rives, Publisher, 1858.
Dictionary of American Biography. Edited by Allen Johnson and Dumas Malone. New York: Charles Scribner's Sons, 1933.
Encyclopedia of the History of St. Louis, Vol. I. Edited by William Hyde and Howard L. Conard. New York: Southern History Co., 1899.
The National Cyclopaedia of American Biography. New York: James T. White & Company, 1898.

Periodicals

BRISBANE, ARTHUR. "Joseph Pulitzer," *Cosmopolitan,* XXXIII (May, 1902), 51-54.
Buffalo *News* quoted on death of Colonel John A. Cockerill, *Current Literature,* XIX (June, 1896), 484-485.
COCKERILL, JOHN A. "Brigham Young and the Modern Utah," *Cosmopolitan,* XIX (Sept., 1895), 501-512.
———. "How to Conduct a Local Newspaper," *Lippincott's Magazine,* LVIII (Sept., 1896), 395-399.
———. "Lafcadio Hearn: The Author of Kokoro," *Current Literature,* XIX (June, 1896), 476.
———. "The Newspaper of the Future," *Lippincott's Monthly Magazine,* L (Aug., 1892), 220-226.
———. "Some Phases of Contemporary Journalism," *Cosmopolitan,* XIII (Oct., 1892), 695-703.

————. "The Trend of the Great Daily," *Review of Reviews*, VI (Nov., 1893), 449-451.

CREELMAN, JAMES. "The Dramatic Intensity of Joseph Pulitzer," *Current Literature*, XLVI (April, 1909), 382-385.

The Fourth Estate (a newspaper for the makers of newspapers). (New York). Numerous references.

GRIBAYÉDOFF, VALERIAN. "Pictorial Journalism," *Cosmopolitan*, XI (Aug., 1891), 471-481.

HAPGOOD, HUTCHINS, and ARTHUR BARTLETT MAURICE. "The Great Newspapers of the United States," *The Bookman*, XV (March, 1902), 26-44.

"An Indictment and a Remedy" (unsigned comment on Cockerill's views on contemporary journalism), *Harper's Weekly,* XXXVI (Nov. 5, 1892), 1062.

JOHNS, GEORGE SIBLEY. "Joseph Pulitzer," *Missouri Historical Review,* XXV (Jan., 1931), 201-218, 246 (April, 1931), 404-420 (July, 1931), 563-575; XXVI (Oct., 1931), 54-67 (Jan., 1932), 163-178 (April, 1932), 267-280.

The Journalist ("A magazine for all who read and write"). New York. Scattered references.

MATHEWS, FANNIE AYMAR. "The Woman's Press Club of New York," *Cosmopolitan*, XI (Aug., 1891), 455.

MILLS, GEORGE. "On History of St. Louis Newspapers," *American Journalist*, I (Sept. 15, 1883), 1-6.

PECK, HARRY THURSTON. "Twenty Years of the Republic," *Bookman*, XXIII (June, 1906), 410.

PULITZER, JOSEPH. "The College of Journalism," *North American Review*, CLXXVIII (May, 1904), 641-680.

"Pulitzer's Men Come to Celebrate Keeping of a Faith," unsigned, *Newsweek*, XXV (March 26, 1945), 82-83.

"The Prudent Publishers," unsigned, *Outlook*, XCIX (Nov. 11, 1911), 608-609.

SEITZ, DON C. "Portrait of an Editor," *Atlantic Monthly*, CXXXIV (Sept., 1924), 289-300.

STILL, JOHN S. "A Fortnight of Fear: Morgan's Raid," *Museum Echoes*, Ohio Historical Society (Columbus, Ohio), XXXIV, (Sept., 1961), 67-70.

"Was It Just the Same 100 Years Ago?—A Look at 1858 and 1958," *U.S. News & World Report*, XLV (Dec. 26, 1958), 40-45.

COCKERILL, JOHN A. *Custer Battlefield, Burlington Route.* Chicago: Poole Brothers, 1898.

Pamphlets

MILITARY ORDER OF THE LOYAL LEGION OF THE U.S. OHIO COMMANDERY. Circular No. 20. Cincinnati, September 15, 1897. *In Memoriam. Companion John Albert Cockerill.*

"Orientation." Washington *Post.* A brochure for new employees. 22 pages.

Newspapers

Baltimore
  Gazette
Buffalo
  News
Cincinnati
  Commercial
  Enquirer
  Gazette
Columbus, Ohio
  Democratic Call
  Ohio State Journal
Dayton
  Democratic Call
  Empire
  Ledger
Hamilton, Ohio
  True Telegraph

New York
  Commercial Advertiser
  Morning Advertiser
  Herald
  Journal
  Star
  Times
  Tribune
  World
Rochester, New York
  Democrat and Chronicle
  Post-Express
St. Louis
  Post-Dispatch
  Republic
Washington
  Post
West Union, Ohio
  Democratic Union
  Scion of Temperance, later
    the *Scion*

And others of the era.

Index

Abbas, Khedive of Egypt, 289
Adams, Samuel Hopkins, 127, 192, 212
Aeschylus, 84
American Israelite, 83
American Journalist, 123
American Press Association, 178
American Protestant Association, 228
Anthony, Susan B., 147
Argosy, 220
Asahi Shumbun, Osaka (Japanese newspaper), 267
Associated Press, 222
Astor, John Jacob, 193
Atlantic Cable, 31-32
Aug's Clubhouse, Cincinnati, 79

Bab, 233
Barleycorn, John, 22
Barner, Leonora, wife of John A. Cockerill, 182-187, 296, 297, 298, 301-303
Barner, Mr. and Mrs. W. T., parents of Leonora Barner, 182
Barrett, James W., 124, 131, 218, 219
Bartholdi, Auguste, 135
Beecher, Henry Ward, 122, 189, 190
Belle, Clara, 233
Bellefontaine Cemetery, Cockerill's burial place, 232, 296
"Belshazzar's Feast" (cartoon), 179
Bennett, James Gordon, Sr., 188, 189, 214, 216
Bennett, James Gordon, Jr., 86, 126, 164, 216, 240, 258-266, 274, 288
Bickham, William D., 254, 255
Billings, John K., 33
Blaine, James G., 136, 179
Bly, Nellie, nee Elizabeth Cochrane, 148-163
Bollmeyer, J. F., slain over states' rights, 44
Bookman, The, 241
Boyle, P. C., of Oil City *Derrick*, 297
Breckinridge, John C., 11
Brisbane, Arthur, 207, 209
Broadhead, Colonel James O., 100 ff.
Brough, Charles, 51

Brough, John, candidate for governor of Ohio, 43, 51
Brown, B. Gratz, 77, 78
Brown, Henry, 44
Bryan, William Jennings, 12, 193
Bryant, William Cullen, 221
Buchanan, James, 10
Buell, General Don Carlos, 15
Buffalo Bill. *See* Cody, William F.
Burnside, General Ambrose E., 38, 42
Burwell, Samuel, editor of West Union *Scion*, 10, 22, 23, 32, 35
Butler, Benjamin F., 142

Caesar, 213
Call, Columbus, 301
Campbell, Bartley, 182, 183
Campbell, Dr. John, 6, 181, 184
Campbell, Esther Elizabeth, 6, 181, 184, 186, 303, 304
Campbell, Joseph Randolph, 181
Campbell, Thomas C., 73, 187
Carnegie, Andrew, 193
Carroll, Howard, 188, 193
Carvalho, S. S., 205
Chambers, Julius, 163
Chevalier, Michel, on impression of Cincinnati, 51
Childs, George W., 170
Clark, James, 223
Clarke, Joseph I. C., 296
Cleveland, Grover, 136 ff., 223, 224, 226, 227
Clopton, William H., 107-09
Coates, Foster, 233, 298
Cobb, Frank I., 204, 217
Cobb, Irvin S., 208, 213
Cochrane, Elizabeth. *See* Bly, Nellie [pseud.]
Cockerill, Armstead Thompson Mason, 6, 12, 13, 14, 24, 30, 31, 39, 40
Cockerill, Daniel, 3, 7
Cockerill, Captain Daniel T., 15
Cockerill, Captain Giles Jackson, 15
Cockerill, John (ancestor), 3
Cockerill, John A.: antecedents, 3-5; boyhood, family life, 5-12; as soldier, 12-19; as a "colonel," 19; his newspaper career begins at West

Cockerill, John A. (*cont.*)
Union *Scion*, 24-33; his first story, 26; sensitivity to news values, 30; first newspaper proprietorship, 33-39; partnership with brother, editorship of Hamilton, Ohio, *True Telegraph*, 39-45; hired as correspondent of Cincinnati, *Enquirer*, 40, 41; joins Clement G. Vallandigham, ex-Copperhead, on Dayton *Daily Ledger*, 45; editorship of *Ledger* beset by financial problems, 45-50; as reporter, editor on Cincinnati *Enquirer*, 51-85; personal portrait, 69-71; meets Joseph Pulitzer, 77; assignment to cover Russo-Turkish War, 85-86; his Cincinnati editorship preempted by John McLean, 89; he pairs with Stilson Hutchins in founding Washington *Post*, 89; the *Post* under Cockerill, 90-91; hires Calista Halsey, one of first girl reporters in U. S., 91; edits Baltimore *Gazette*, 91, 92; Pulitzer invites him to be managing editor of St. Louis *Post-Dispatch*, 93; the *Post* under Pulitzer and Cockerill, 93-125; fatal encounter with Alonzo W. Slayback, 107-109; called to New York *World*, 130; his trials and tribulations with the *World*, 131-182, 194-206; Cockerill, Pulitzer engage Nellie Bly, 147-153; Cockerill's courtship, marriage, separation from his wife, 182-187; his role in enhancing New York Press Club prestige, 188-194; Pulitzer-Cockerill as a team, 217, 218; "war" in the *World*, 201-204; Cockerill's walkout on the *World*, 203-204; editorship of the New York *Advertisers*, 219-232; his gift to St. Louis Elks, 232-233; as syndicated columnist, 233-234; analysis of Cockerill as critic and prophet of his profession, 234-249; probable salary, 243; wit and style, 250-258; named Far Eastern correspondent of New York *World*, 258-266; reunion with Lafcadio Hearn, 266, 267; his impressions of Japan, 268-272; as prankster, 272, 273; decorated by Japan, 273, 274; James Gordon Bennett's eccentric requests keep him busy, 274; assignment to Korea, his exposé of Japa-

Cockerill, John A. (*cont.*)
nese bungling, his report of a queen's assassination, 275-288; ordered to London by way of Egypt, 288; coverage of Anglo-Egyptian expedition on Nile, 288-291; death by apoplexy, 293; his body shipped home via SS *Campania*, 294; his last dispatch from Djibouti, 294; funerals, eulogies, burial, 295-301; his widow remarries, 301; dissension over Cockerill's will, 303-304; his tribute to Joseph Pulitzer, 304
Cockerill, General Joseph R. (father), 3-12; as officer in Civil War, 14-17, 24, 30, 31, 37, 40
Cockerill, Oliver Oscar, 6
Cockerill, Ruth (mother), 5, 6, 26, 36
Cockerill, Sanford, 3
Cockerill, Sarah Mary, 6
Cockerill, Thomas, 3
Cody, William F., 298
Cole, Victor C., 107, 109
College of Journalism, Columbia University, 241
Colton, George, 91
Columbian Exposition, 223
Columns, newspaper, 122, 123, 223, 224, 233, 234, 257
Commercial, Cincinnati, 81
Commercial Advertiser, New York, 126, 220-224, 227, 229-233, 237
Connor, Billy, 182, 296
Connor, Mrs. William, 296
Continent, New York, 219-222
Cook, Dr. Frederick A., 262
Cook, Dr. Vincent, 169
Cosmopolitan Magazine, 163
Courier and Enquirer, New York, 128
Courier, West Union, 21
Cox, George Barnsdale, 74
Crapsey, Jacob, 21
Creelman, James, 209
Croker, Boss Richard, 229
Cromer, Lord, 290

Daily Ledger, Dayton, 45-50, 252, 253, 254, 255
Daily News, Chicago, 172
Daily News, New York, 126, 246
Dana, Charles A., 126; his feud with Joseph Pulitzer, 142-147, 189, 212, 227, 239
Davidson, Professor Thomas, 203
Davis, William L., 200, 201
Delane, John Thaddeus, 245

Delmonico's (New York restaurant), 179, 185
Democrat, Adams County, 22, 33
Democratic Union, Adams County, 33-40
Depew, Chauncey M., 190, 193, 226, 295
Derrick, Oil City, 297
Dewey, John, 172
Dickens, Charles, 53
Dillon, John, 92, 204
Dillon, Sidney, 177
Dispatch, Pittsburgh, 149
Donelly, Joseph, 223
Douglas, Stephen A., 10, 11
Dred Scott Decision, 10
"Drummer Boy of Shiloh," 13, 15, 33
Dudley, Colonel W. W., 140

Eames, Emma, 262, 263
Editor and Publisher, 216
Edson, Mayor Franklin, 143
Eggleston, George Cary, 250
Egner, Andreas, 59 ff.
Egner, Fred, 59 ff.
Elks, Benevolent and Protective Order of, 232, 233
Elks' Rest, 232, 296
Emery, Edwin, 134, 216, 217
Emrie, Jonas R., Joseph Cockerill's opponent for Congress, 8
Enquirer, Cincinnati, 40, 41, 51-89, 132, 176, 183, 251, 253, 256, 264, 301
Eulalie, aunt of King of Spain, 223
Evans, Edward Patton, 10, 11
Evans, Nelson W., 22, 26, 32
Evening World, New York, 175
Eylar, Elizabeth Fenton, 5
Eylar, Judge Joseph, 5, 22
Eylar, Captain Oliver H., 15
Eylar, Ruth, 5
Eylar, Thomas, 22

Faran, James A., purchaser of Cincinnati *Enquirer*, 51-53
Farrelly, Richard, 174, 175
Fellows, John T., 144 ff.
Field, Cyrus W., 177
Field, Eugene: poem by, Cockerill mentioned, 76-77
Figaro, Paris (French newspaper), 273
Fiji Shimpo, Tokyo (Japanese newspaper), 268
Finely, James, 21
Fogg, Phineas, 163

Foley, Althea, 67-68
Foster, Stephen, 150
Fourth Estate, 230, 272, 294
Franklin, Benjamin, 27
Free Press, Adams County, 22
Free Press, Detroit, 204
Frederick Victor & Achelis, 186, 302
Freiberg's Tannery, 57 ff.
Fremont, General John, 10
Fremont, General John C., 76

Ganesco, M., 272, 273
Gazette, Baltimore, 91 f.
Gazette, Cincinnati, 81
Gazette, Moscow, 253
Globe-Democrat, St. Louis, 40, 92, 94 ff.
Globe, New York, 231
Glover, John, 104, 106, 107
Goddard, Morrill, 163, 176
Godwin, Harold, 221
Golding, Louis Thorn, 230, 231
Gould, Benjamin A., Sanitary Commission actuary, 13
Gould, Jay, 126, 128, 129, 137, 143, 167, 177, 179
Grand Opera House, Cincinnati, 84
Grant, General Ulysses, 16, 17, 47, 77, 78, 82, 90, 181
Grant, Mrs. Ulysses, 162
Greeley, Horace, 10, 77, 78, 126, 216, 234
Greene, John A., 191
Gribayédoff, Valerian, 177, 178

Halsey, Calista, 91, 152
Halstead, Murat, 69
Hamilton, Alexander, 21, 221
Hancock, E. C., 129, 130
Harper's Bazaar, 171
Harper's Magazine, 238, 266
Harrison, General Benjamin, 170
Harrison, Mrs. Benjamin, 170
Harvey, Colonel George B. McLellan, 204
Hasbrook, Charles E., 222
Hatch, Rufus, 177
Haverley's Fourteenth Street Theater, 182
Hayes, Rutherford B., 79, 80, 90, 235
Herald, Chicago, 248
Herald, New York, 86, 126, 132, 135, 142, 143, 164, 172, 180, 188, 214, 258-267, 269, 272-274, 276, 277, 281, 283, 284-288, 289-294, 296, 300
Hearn, Lafcadio, 58 ff., 266

Hearst, William Randolph, 75, 206, 209, 214, 230
Hilton, Judge Henry, 193
Hobson, General Edward H., 18, 19
Home Journal, 28
Hooper, Osman Castle, quoted on Ohio journalism, 20
Hopkins, Mark, 219
Hosmer, Dr. George W., 206
Howard, Alexander Carpenter, 113, 298
Howard, Joseph, Jr., 191, 220, 233, 295, 296
Huntington, C. P., 177, 219, 220, 222, 230, 231
Hurlbert, William Henry, 129
Hutchins, Stilson, 89, 90, 91
Hyde, Colonel W. B., 105

Ingersoll, Robert G., 80, 190
Inouye, Count, 276, 277, 278
Ireland, Alleyne, 208

Jackson, Andrew, 21
Japanese National Exhibition, Kyoto, Japan, 275
Jefferson, Thomas, 21
Johns, George Sibley, 119-123, 216
Johns, Orrick, 123
Johnson, President Andrew, 76
Johnston, Mayor G. W. C., Cincinnati, 56, 73
Jones, Charles H., 205
Jordan, Elizabeth, 165-171
Journal, Atlanta, 226
Journal, Columbus, 82, 83, 255
Journal, Dayton, 37, 254
Journal, Missouri, 119
Journal, Ohio State, 300
Journalist, The, 233
Joy, Congressman Charles F., 113, 114, 297

Kaigai Shimbun, Yokohama (Japanese newspaper), 267
Kellogg, Daniel, 192
Kelly, John, 220
Key, Alice, 78
Key, Francis Scott, 78
King, General Horatio C., 296
King, Rufus, 221
King, William, 213
Kitchener, Lord, 290, 292

Lamont, Daniel S., 181
Landseer's "Monarch of the Glen," 232

Lexow Committee of Investigation, 229
Lincoln, Abraham, 11, 13, 43, 128
Lineau, Walter Louis, Leonora Barner's second husband, 185, 301, 302
"Little Mack" (poem), 76-77
Livingstone, David, 262
Lockwood, Belva, 147, 162
Logan, Mrs. John A., 234
Logan, William T., 44
Long, Jacob H., 46
Lysistrata (luxury yacht), 260

MacArthur, Rev. Robert S., 295
McCoy-Corbett prize fight, 212
McCullagh, Joseph Burbridge, 40, 52, 75-77, 94
McCullough, John, 182
McDougall, Walt, 102, 137, 138, 167, 174, 205, 206, 210, 211, 214, 250
McGehan, Thomas, 50
McGuffin, John B., 107 ff., 123, 124, 133, 195, 196
McGuinness, Bridget, 154
MacKay, John W., 177
McLean, Edward, 92
McLean, John R., 52, 72-75, 85, 89, 264
McLean, Washington, 40, 78; called "Warwick of Democracy," 52
Madden, George A., 149, 150
Mail, Japan, 268
Mail and Express, New York, 126
Masons, Order of Free and Accepted, 295, 296
May, Caroline, 260
May, Frederick, 260, 261
May, Dr. William, 260
Mayo, John, 42
Medill, Joseph, 239
Meltzer, Charles Henry, 263
Menary, George, 22
Menary, Samuel, 22
Mergenthaler, Ottmar, 246
Merrill, William H., 141, 217
Minerva, New York, 221
Miura, General Viscount, 279 ff.
Mohammed Ali, 290
Moore, Henry, 105
Moore, Robert, 73
Morgan, Colonel Ralph, 18
Morgan, General John Hunt, 17, 18, 31
Morning Advertiser, New York, 221, 223, 230, 231

Morning Journal, New York, 126, 128, 206, 214
Morris, Mrs. Albert, 23
Morrison, Dr. George, physician in attendance at death of Cockerill, 293
Morse, Samuel F. V., 120
Morton, Levi P., 193
Mott, Dr. Frank Luther, 214
Mullen, T. J., 33
Munsey, Frank A., 220, 231

Nessler, Mike, 19
New Testament, 232
New York Newspaper Club, merged with Press Club, 193
New York Press Club, 185, 188-194, 198
News, Buffalo, 299
News, Hillsboro, 22
Newspaper Row, 130, 143
Nichi-Nichi Shumbun, Tokyo (Japanese newspaper), 268
Nicoll, De Lancey, 144 ff.
Noonan, St. Louis Mayor, 233
Nye, Bill (Edgar Wilson Nye), 148, 171-174, 194, 233

Oswald, J. C., 258

Pagenstecher, Dr. Herman, 198
Pallen, Dr. Montrose, 180
Park Row, 126, 128, 130, 150, 169, 190, 192, 199, 222, 223, 231, 236
Parkhurst, Rev. Charles, 228, 229
Patterson, John P., partner to Cockerill, 34
Pearson, S. E., partner to Cockerill, 34
Peck, George W., 165
Peck, Harry Thurston, 214
Peck, John P., 41, 42
Pendleton, "Gentleman George" H., 78, 253, 254
People's Defender, West Union, 22
Phelps, Edward R. "Foxy," 155-163
Pictures, Cockerill's use of, 58, 59, 71, 177, 180
Pike's Opera House, Cincinnati, 57
Poe, Edgar Allen, 63
Pooton, James, 188
"Porkopolis" (Cincinnati), 54
Post, Boston, 81
Post, Washington, 89 ff.
Post, George B., architect of *World* building, 199
Post-Dispatch, St. Louis, 92 ff., 130,

Post-Dispatch (cont.)
146, 149, 195, 204, 216, 218, 219, 251, 252
Post-Express, Rochester, 222
Pretorius, Dr. Emil, 209
Prohibitionist, 82
Puck Magazine, 172
Pulitzer, Albert, 128
Pulitzer, Joseph: meets John Cockerill, 77; campaigns for Horace Greeley, 78; buys, merges St. Louis *Dispatch* with St. Louis *Post,* 92; impressed by Cockerill, 93; Pulitzer-Cockerill team "clicks," 94; lays groundwork for newspaper, 95; nears exhaustion, 98; learns much from Cockerill, prepares for vacation, 99; "kills" Glover card, 104; assaulted by W. B. Hyde, 105; defends Cockerill in Slayback shooting, 115 ff.; candid portrayal by Cockerill, 123; Cockerill's release by Pulitzer, 124; lingering resentment of Pulitzer in St. Louis, 125; "invasion" of New York, 125 ff.; part owner of New York *Morning Journal,* 128; purchases New York *World* his credo, 129; brings Cockerill to New York, 130; his genius as publisher, 131; Pulitzer, Cockerill plot course of *World,* 133 ff.; report from Cockerill on Statue of Liberty, 135; as "king-maker" and supporter of Cleveland, 136 ff.; Dana-Pulitzer feud, 142 ff.; meets, approves hiring of Nellie Bly, 151, 152; names Ballard Smith as managing editor, 165, 166; agrees to hiring of Nye, 172; little disposed to listen to picture suggestions, 177; his order to get rid of wood-cuts reversed, 180; tribute to Cockerill, 191; reclaims Press Club property, 192; his relationship to Cockerill on *World,* 194 ff.; settles strike, 195, 196; Cockerill finds him unable to read, 198; buys site for new *World* building, 199; his three-man regency, 200; his break with Cockerill, 201 ff.; allocation of *World* stock to Cockerill disputed, 203; hires parade of successors to Cockerill, 204 f.; "find a man who gets drunk and hire him," 205; his split with Cockerill termed "serious mistake," 206; his character portrayed in depth, 206-

Pulitzer, Joseph (*cont.*)
219; definitive biography needed,
206, 207; impressions by Irvin S.
Cobb, 208; loses in cards to Arthur Brisbane, 209; "no stage manager like him"—James Creelman,
209; timid in adopting new ideas,
a "highly commercial gentleman,"
210; as Congressman, 211-212;
assessment by Samuel Hopkins
Adams, 212; on gratuities, 212,
213; his "no friends" policy, 213;
on handling personnel, 213, 214;
on sensationalism and news, 214-
216; theories on success of *World*,
216, 217; "jealous of Cockerill,"
218; writing style, 218; business
capacity, 218; retirement statement
in St. Louis *Post-Dispatch*, 219;
opposes curb of liquor sales in
New York, 229, 230; no resentment expressed by Cockerill on
their split-up, 235; as absentee
newspaper owner, 240; his attitude
toward profits, 241; on dedicated
editors, 243; named as executor
of Cockerill's will, 304
Pulitzer, Joseph, Jr., grandson of
Joseph Pulitzer, his role as publisher, St. Louis *Post-Dispatch*,
219
Pulitzer, Kate, wife of Joseph Pulitzer, Sr., 98, 125, 128, 198
Pulitzer, Ralph, 125
Pythagoras, 232

Quad, M., 233
Queen Min, of Korea, 278 ff.

Ramage Press, 26
Rammelkamp, Dr. Julian, 218, 251
Reavis, John R., 134
Recorder, New York, 204
Red Stockings (baseball club), Cin-
cinnati, 55
Register, West Union, 21
Reid, Whitelaw, 240, 257
Republic, St. Louis, 296, 297
Republican, St. Louis, 98
Republican, Washington, 91
Review of Reviews, 237, 244
Reynolds, General Joseph J., 15
Roche, Jeremiah, 188
Roebling Suspension Bridge, Cincin-
nati, 55
Roosevelt, Theodore, 193, 229, 230
Rose, Squire Jacob, 15
Rosemiller, Mary Ann, 5

Rosencrans, General William S., 15
Ross, Ishbel, 151
Rufer, George, 59 ff.
Russell, Charles Edward, 212
Russo-Turkish War, 87
Ryan, Thomas Fortune, 143

Sacred Treasure, Third Order of,
Japanese decoration conferred up-
on Cockerill, 273
Sage, Russell, 137, 177
Sargent, John S., 206
Schilling, Herman, Tanyard murder
victim, 60 ff.
Schurz, Carl, 77, 209
Scion [*of Temperance*], West Union,
10, 22-33, 252
Scott, Thomas A., 128
Seitz, Don, 95, 98, 124, 129, 130,
194, 201, 204, 207, 264, 289
Sensationalism 132, 214, 215, 234,
236, 241
Sentinel, Ohio, 21
Seymour, Horatio, 254
Sharp, Jacob, 143
Shepheard, Sam, 291
Shepheard's Hotel (Egypt), 291
Sherman, General William T., 16,
17, 102, 121, 122
Simpson, Bishop, 127
Slayback, Alonzo W., 101 ff., 119,
130, 144
Smith, Ballard, 164, 165, 167, 169,
170, 171, 204, 213
Smith, J. McLain, 45
Smith, Joseph P., 25
Snelbaker, Tom, 55
Speed, Gilmer, 129
Staats-Zeitung, New York, 126, 189
Stanley, Henry M., 193, 194, 250,
262
Stanton, Elizabeth Cady, 147
Star, New York, 126, 220
Statue of Liberty, 134 ff.
Stewart, Lieutenant W. R., 6
Stevens, Thaddeus, 10
Stivers, Emmons B., 6, 12
Stone, Melville E., 172
Strauss, Mrs. Beatrice, 32
Strong, George Templeton, 31
Strong, William L., 229
"Stuffed Prophet," 227
Style, news-writing, 35, 38, 58, 71,
72, 86, 87, 92, 94, 99, 123, 218,
223, 225, 227, 250, 252, 256, 257
Sun, Milwaukee, 165
Sun, New York, 126, 132, 135, 142-
147, 153, 192, 212, 227, 231, 239

Sunday Advertiser, New York, 221, 229

Tai-Won-Kun, 278 ff.
Tammany Hall, 211
Tanyard Murder, Cincinnati, 60 ff., 176
Telegraph and Standard, London, 238
Ten Commandments, 237
Terry, William, lynching of, 23, 24
Thaw, Harry K., 212
Tilden, Samuel J., 79, 235
Times, London, 241, 245
Times, Los Angeles, 247
Times, New York, 126, 132, 180, 191, 199, 235, 246, 295
Times, St. Louis, 89
Tod, David, Governor of Ohio, 1861, 14
Townsend, Ed, 266
Tribune, Chicago, 84, 165, 239, 246
Tribune, New York, 10, 126, 132, 142, 239, 257
True Telegraph, Hamilton, 39-44, 46
Trumble, Alfred, 190
Turner, George W., business manager of *World*, 199, 200, 202, 204
Twain, Mark, 172, 194
Tweed, Boss, 220
Typographical Union, 195, 196

Vallandigham, Clement L., Copper-
head leader, 36, 41-50, 52, 255, 264
Vanderbilt, William H., 177
Victoria, Queen, 133
Village Censor, Adams County, 21
Villard, Oswald Garrison, 214

Waldorf, William, 193
Wallack's Theater, 190
Warren, Rev. Walpole, 257
Watterson, Helen, 233
Watterson, Henry, 194
Webster, Noah, 126
Weed, Thurlow, 189, 194
White Slave, The (melodrama), 182, 183
Whitman, Walt, 189
Whitney, William C., 143, 180, 181
Wilder, Marshall P., 233
Williams, George F., 193
Williams, Sam, 101
World, New York, 89, 126, 128 ff., 221, 231, 235, 236, 237, 239, 240, 244, 245, 247, 250, 251, 293, 299, 301
World, New York Sunday, 175 f.
World-Telegram and Sun, New York, 147, 219

Yeats, William Butler, 194
Yellow Book, 214
Yellow journalism, one theory of how term was coined, 214, 215
Yellow Kids, 215